NIGHT OF THE LIVING CAT.

Story by HAWKMAN   Art by MECHA-ROOTS

1

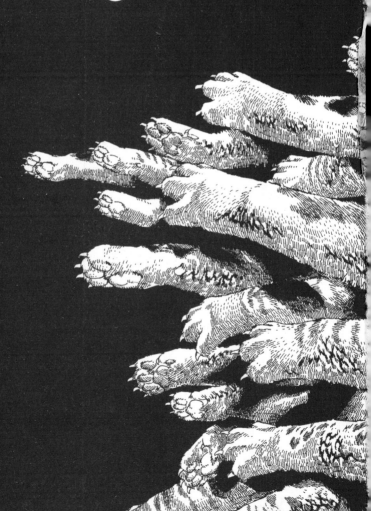

CONTENTS

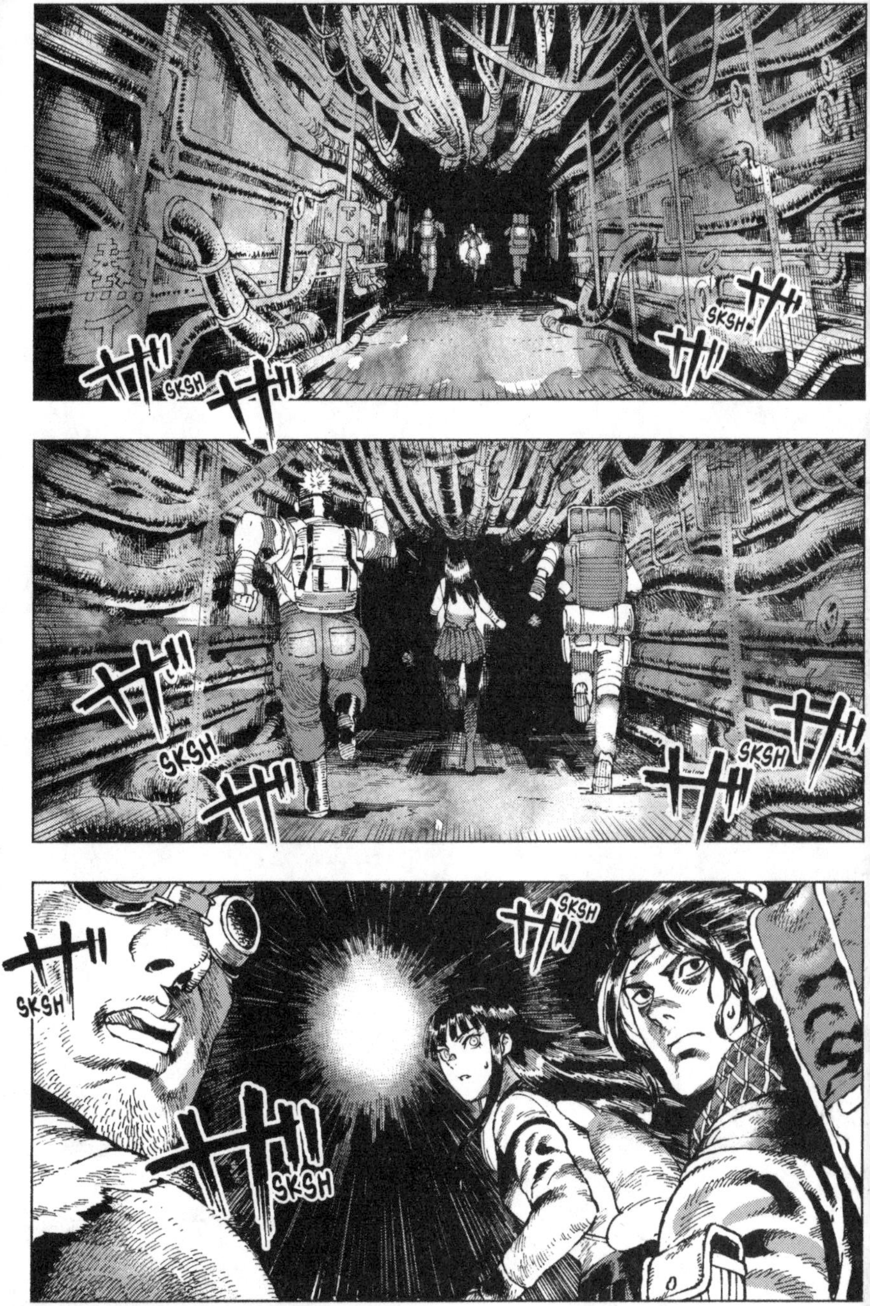
SKSH
SKSH
SKSH
SKSH
SKSH
SKSH
SKSH

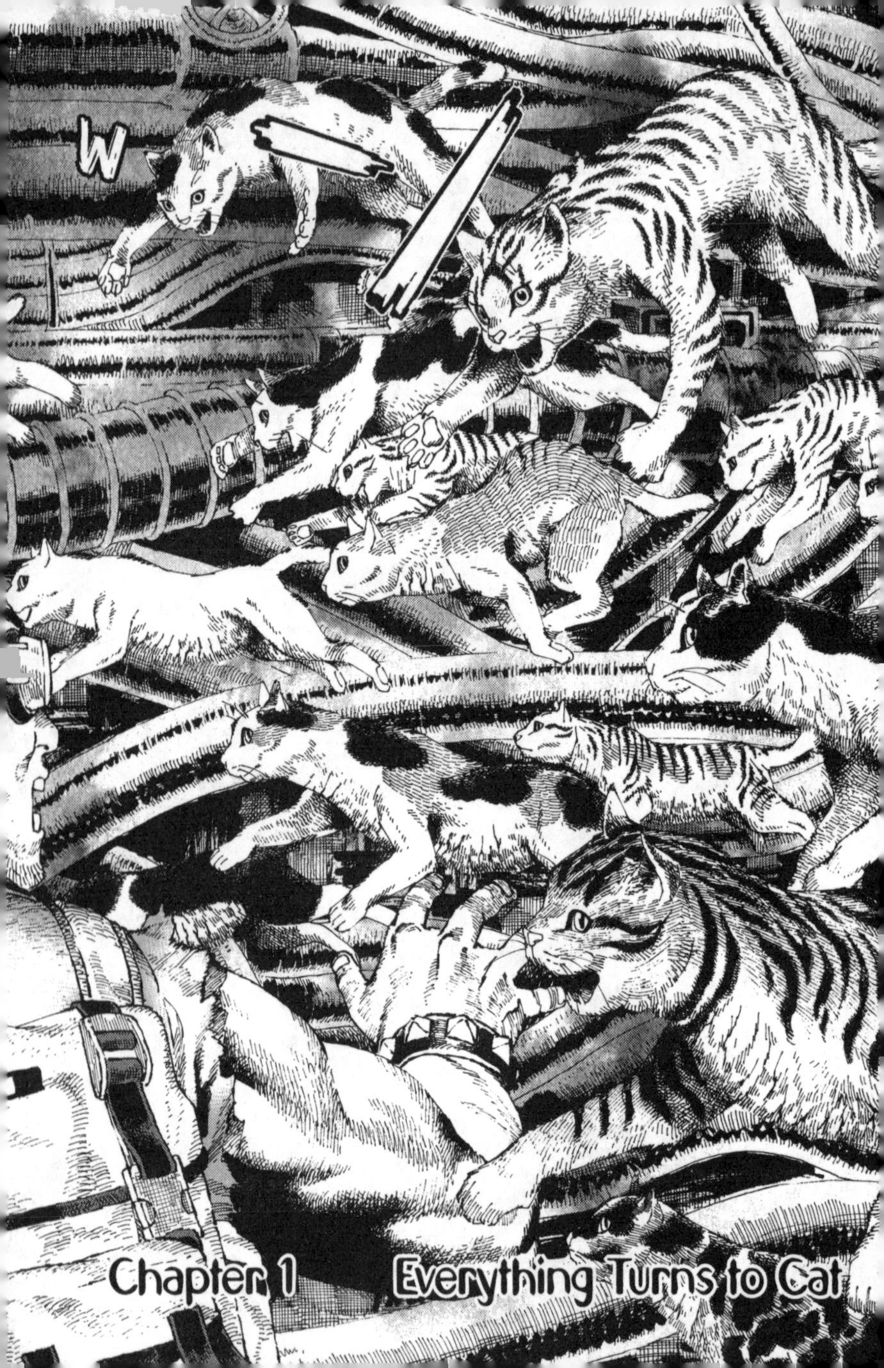
W

Chapter 1 Everything Turns to Cat

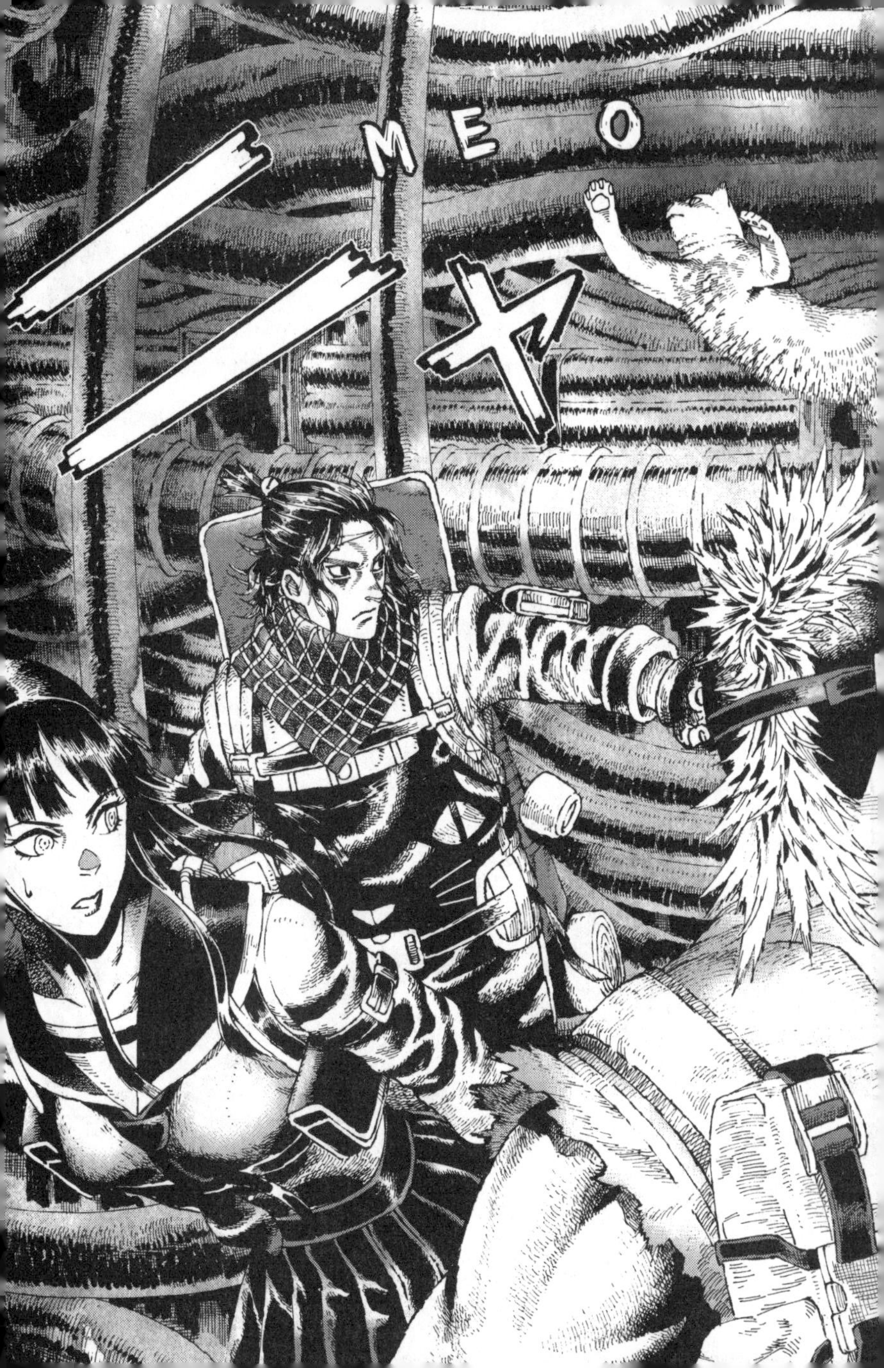
MEO

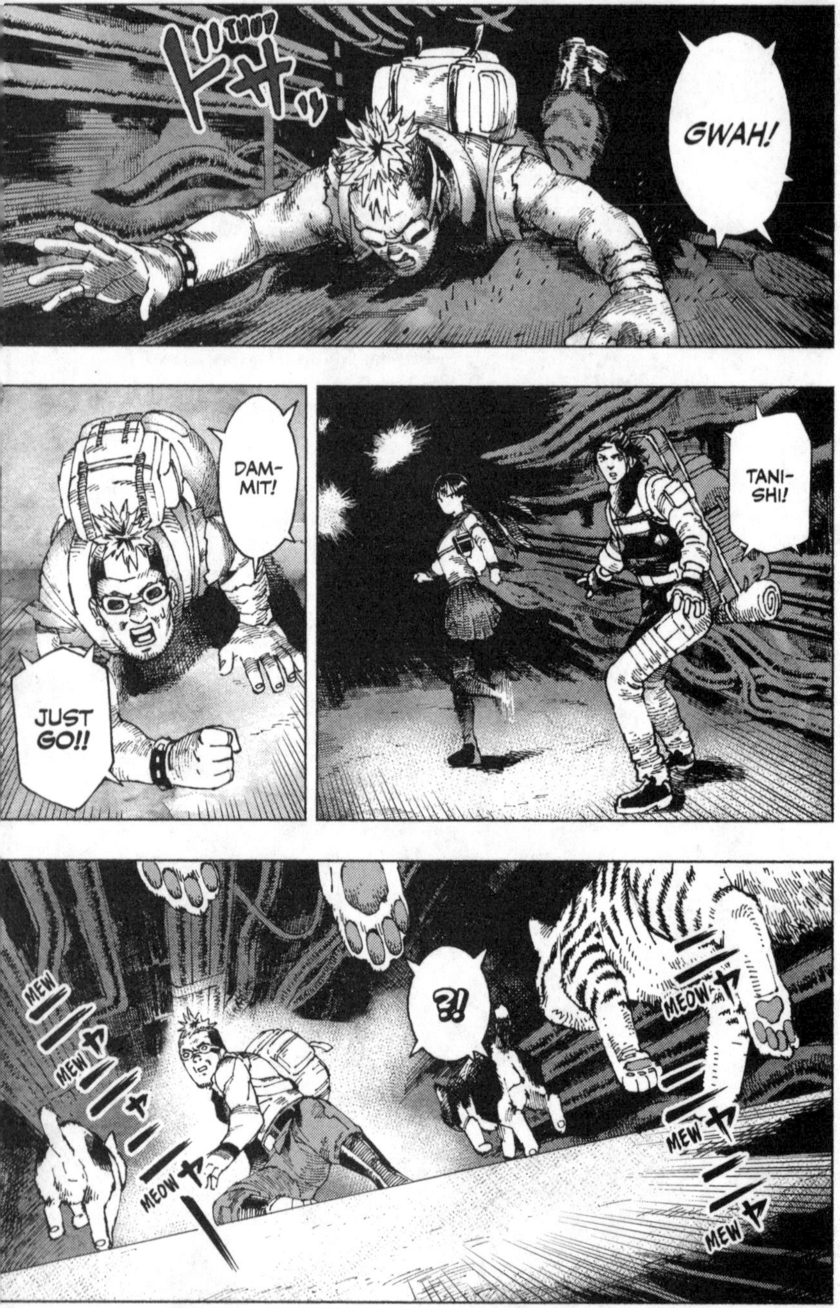
GWAH!
THUD
ドサッ
TANI-SHI!
DAM-MIT!
JUST GO!!
MEOW ヤ
?!
MEW ヤ
MEW ヤ
MEW
MEW ヤ
MEOW ヤ

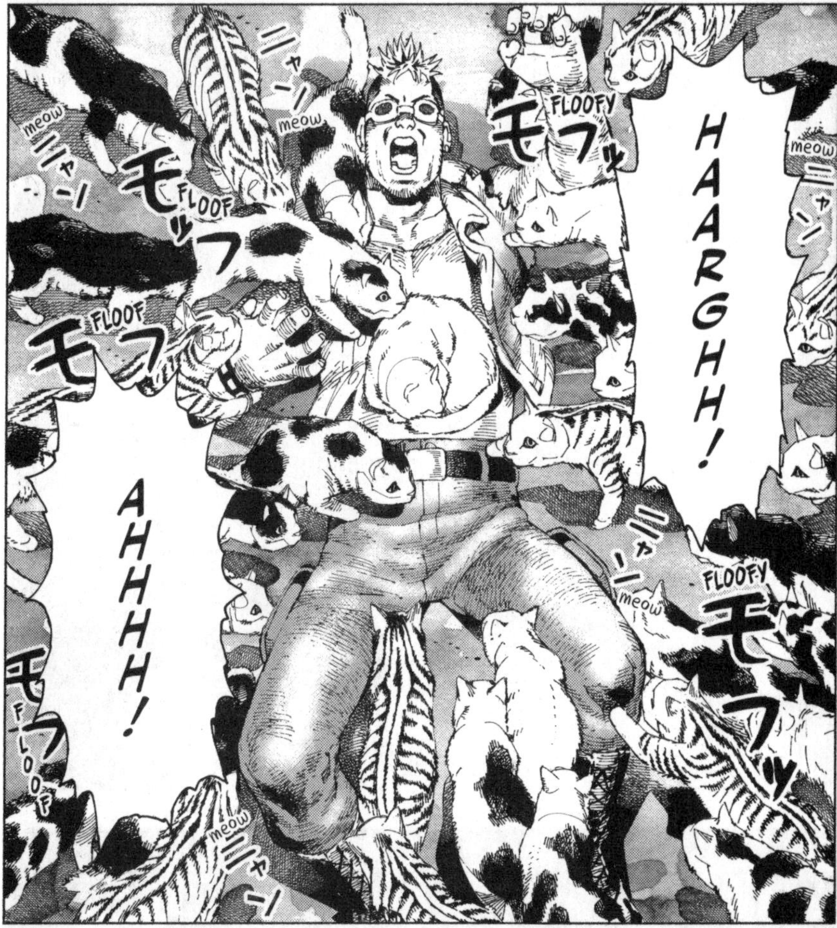
meow ニャーン
HAARGHH!
FLOOFY モフッ
ニャーン meow
meow ニャーン
モッフ FLOOF
FLOOF モフ
ニャーン meow
FLOOFY モフッ
AHHHHH!
モフ FLOOF
meow ニャーン

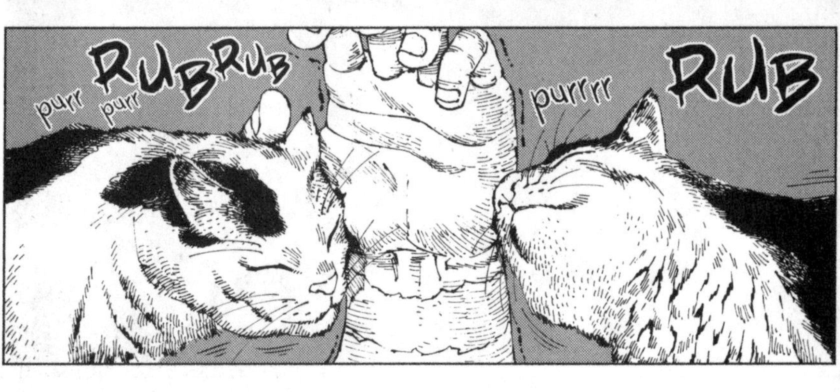
RUB
purrrr
RUBRUB
purr purr

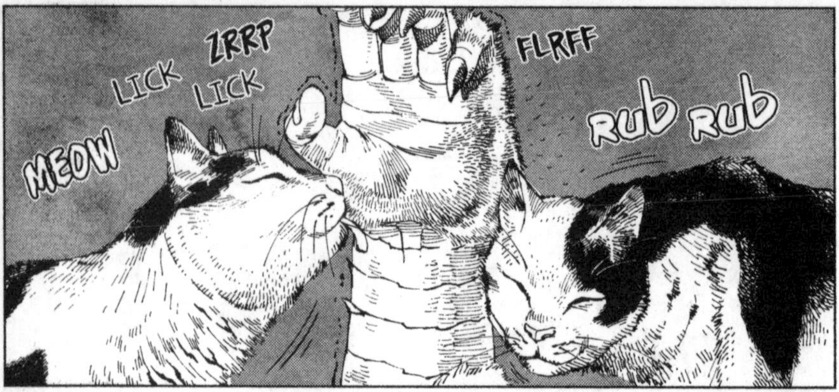
FLRFF
Rub Rub
ZRRP
LICK
LICK
MEOW
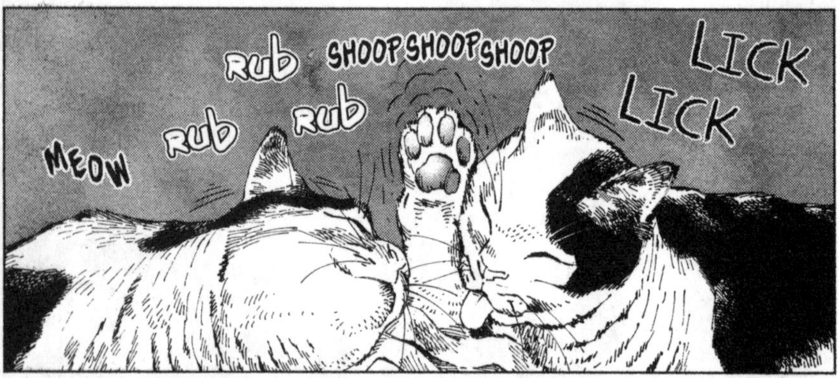
LICK
LICK
SHOOP SHOOP SHOOP
Rub
Rub
Rub
MEOW
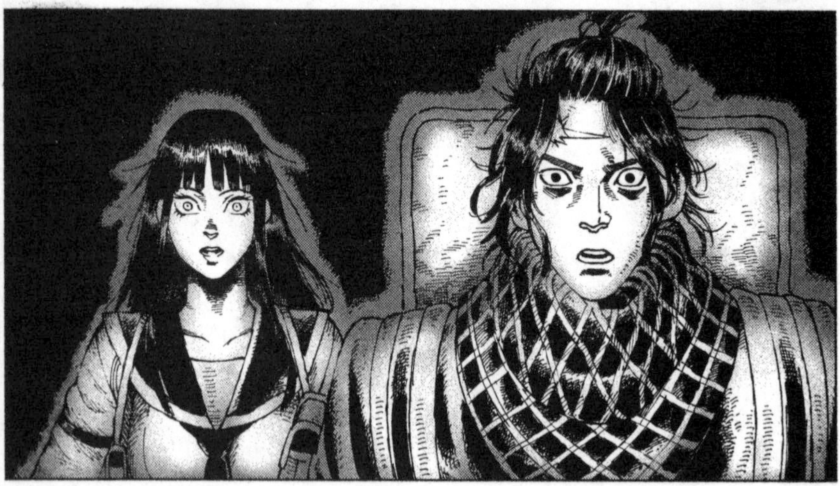

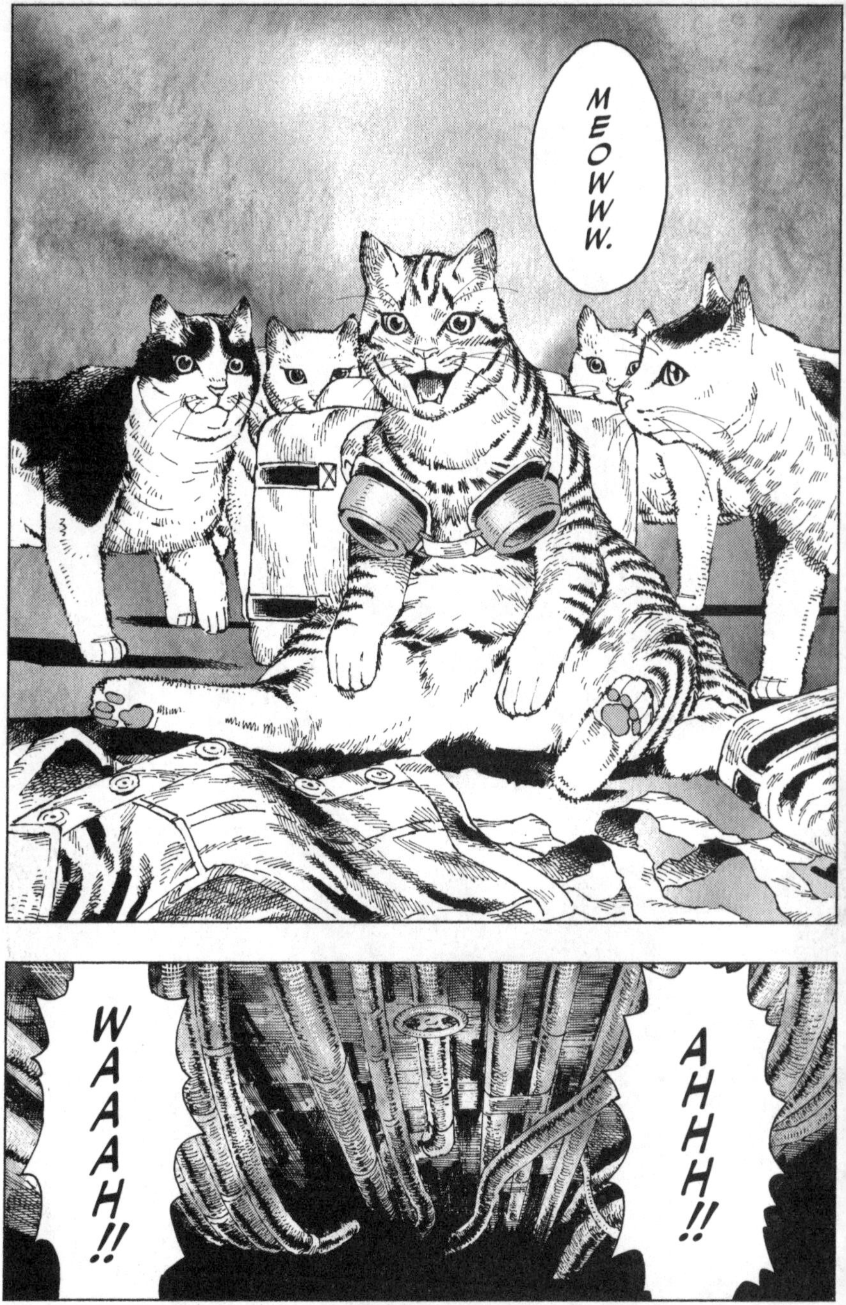
MEOWWW.
AHHHH!!
WAAAAH!!

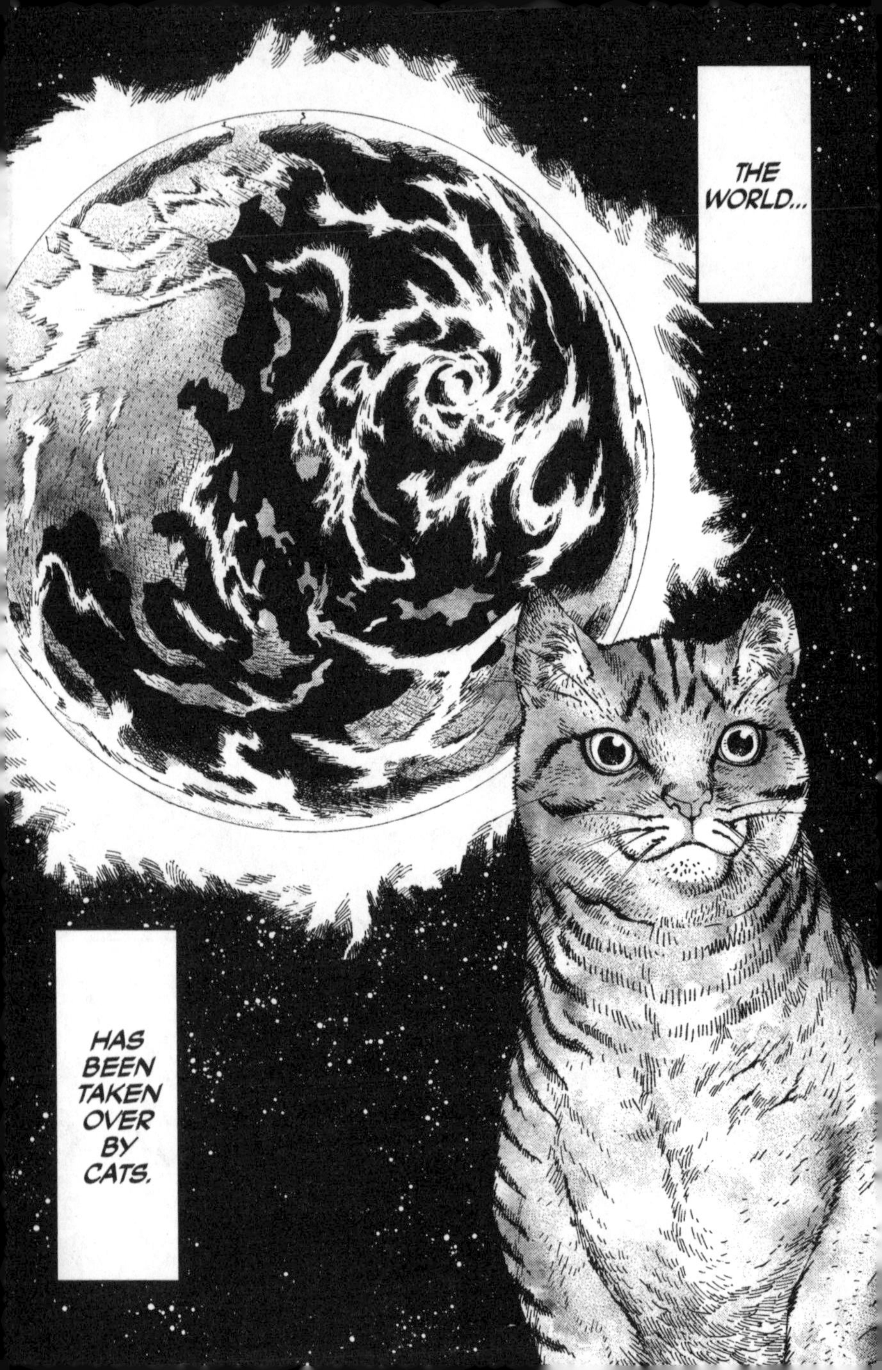
THE WORLD...
HAS BEEN TAKEN OVER BY CATS.

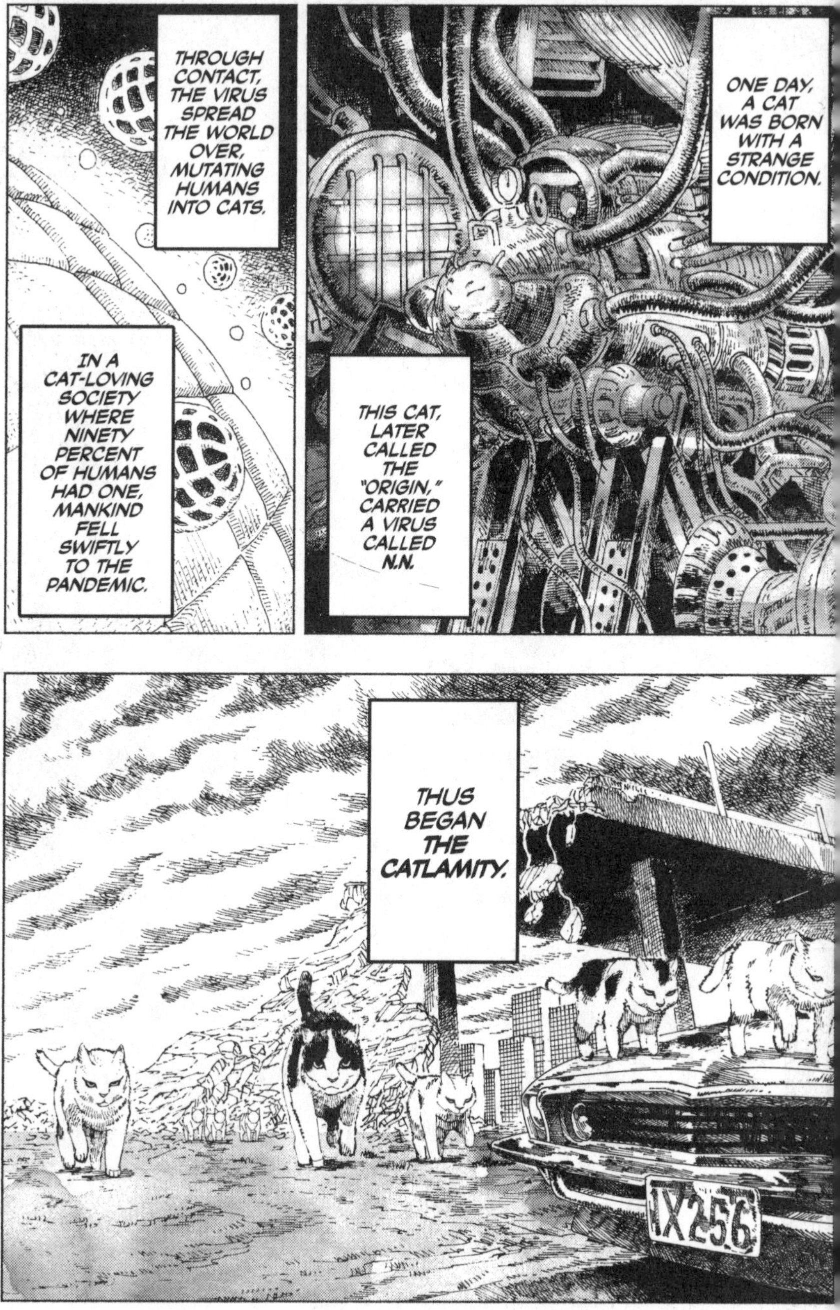
ONE DAY, A CAT WAS BORN WITH A STRANGE CONDITION.
THIS CAT, LATER CALLED THE "ORIGIN," CARRIED A VIRUS CALLED N.N.
THROUGH CONTACT, THE VIRUS SPREAD THE WORLD OVER, MUTATING HUMANS INTO CATS.
IN A CAT-LOVING SOCIETY WHERE NINETY PERCENT OF HUMANS HAD ONE, MANKIND FELL SWIFTLY TO THE PANDEMIC.
THUS BEGAN THE CATLAMITY.
IX256

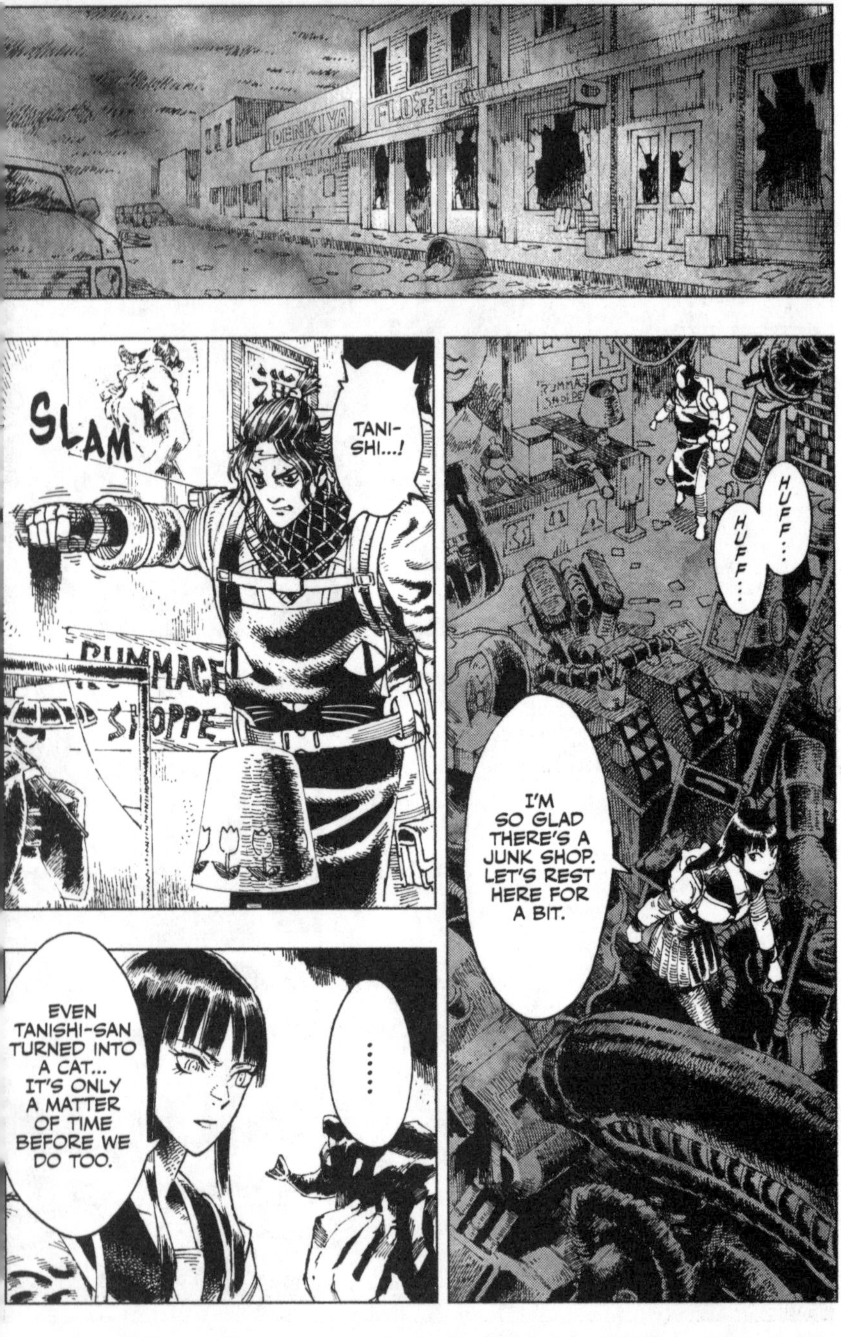
DENKIYA
HUFF... HUFF...
I'M SO GLAD THERE'S A JUNK SHOP. LET'S REST HERE FOR A BIT.
TANI-SHI...!
SLAM
RUMMAGE SHOPPE
......
EVEN TANISHI-SAN TURNED INTO A CAT... IT'S ONLY A MATTER OF TIME BEFORE WE DO TOO.

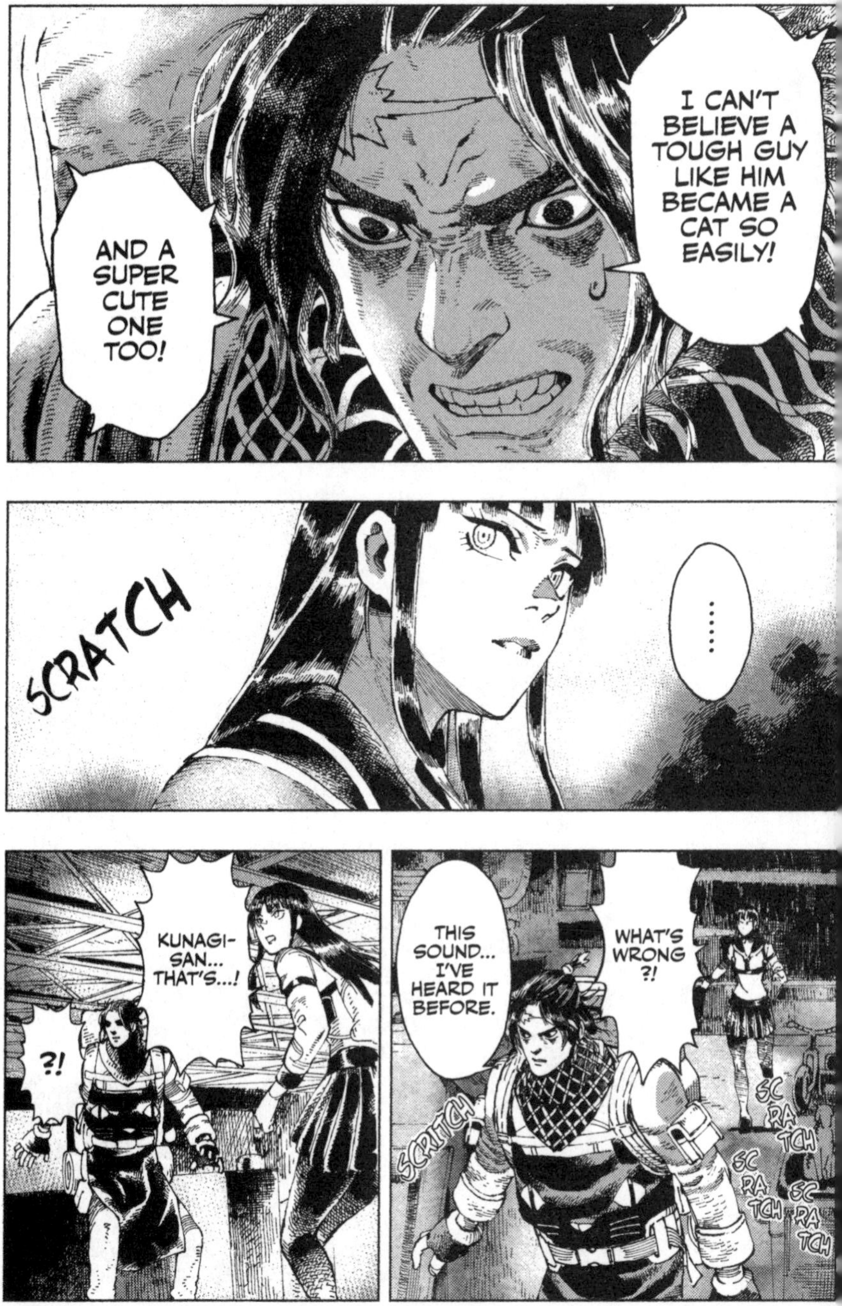
I CAN'T BELIEVE A TOUGH GUY LIKE HIM BECAME A CAT SO EASILY!
AND A SUPER CUTE ONE TOO!
……
SCRATCH
WHAT'S WRONG ?!
THIS SOUND... I'VE HEARD IT BEFORE.
SCRATCH
SCRATCH
SCRATCH
SCRATCH
KUNAGI-SAN... THAT'S...!
?!

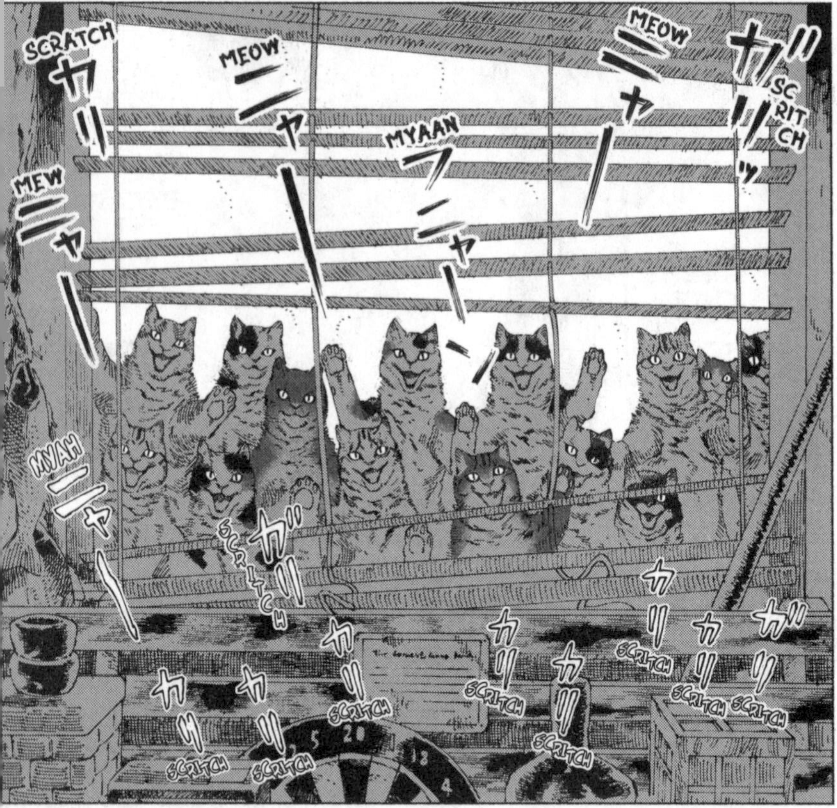
ガリッ
SCRITCH
ニャー
MEOW
フニャー
MYAAN
ニャー
MEOW
ガリ
SCRATCH
ニャー
MEW
ガリ
SCRITCH
ガリ
SCRITCH
カリ
SCRITCH
カリ
SCRITCH
カリ
SCRITCH
カリ
SCRITCH
カリ
SCRITCH
カリ
SCRITCH
ガリ
SCRITCH
ニャー
MYAH

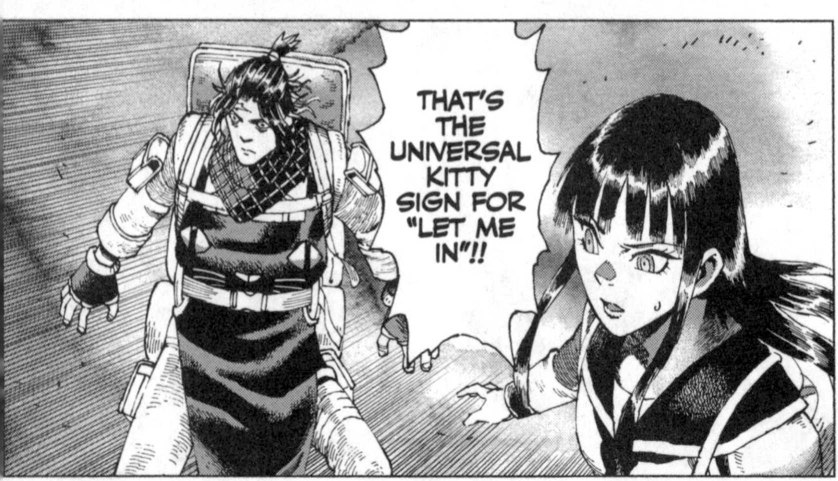
THAT'S THE UNIVERSAL KITTY SIGN FOR "LET ME IN"!!

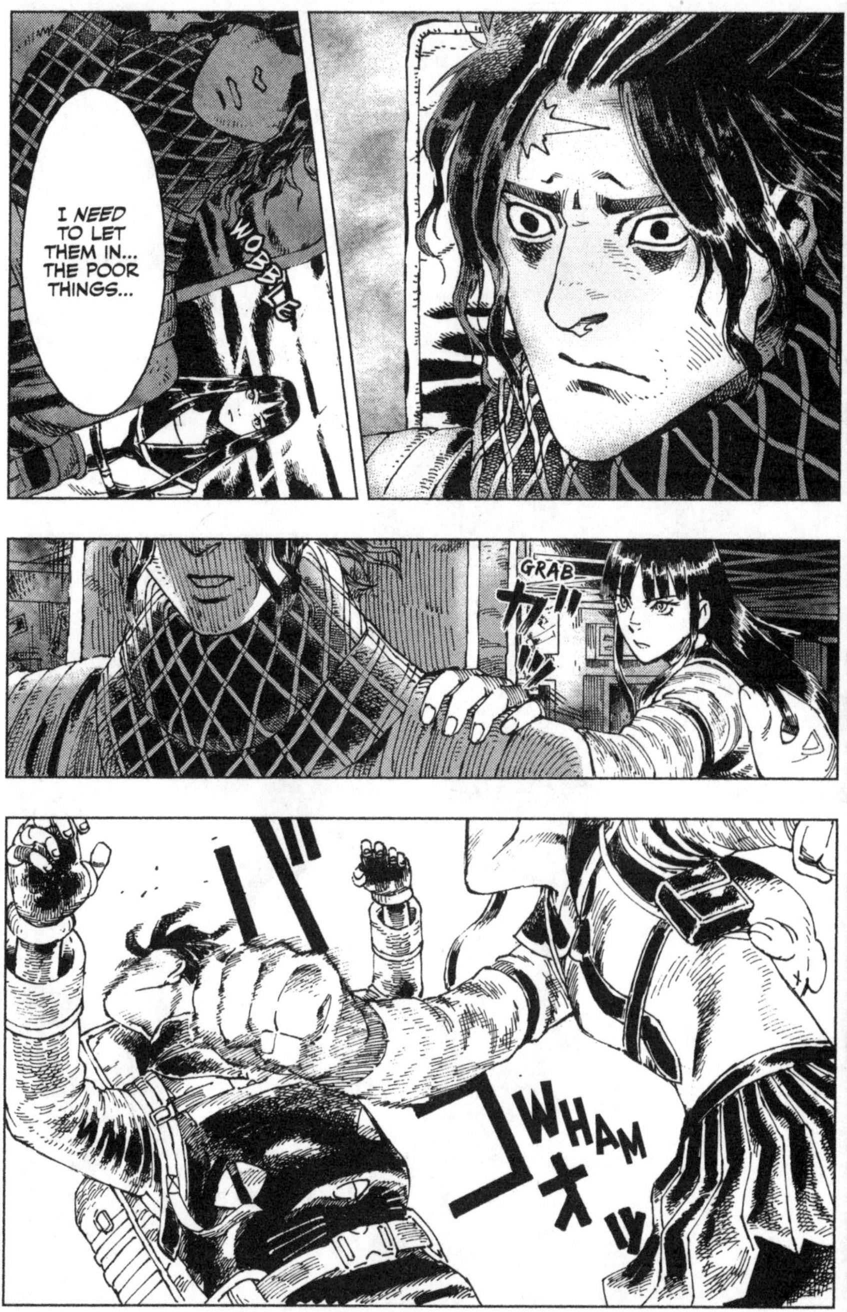
I *NEED* TO LET THEM IN... THE POOR THINGS...
WOBBLE
GRAB
WHAM

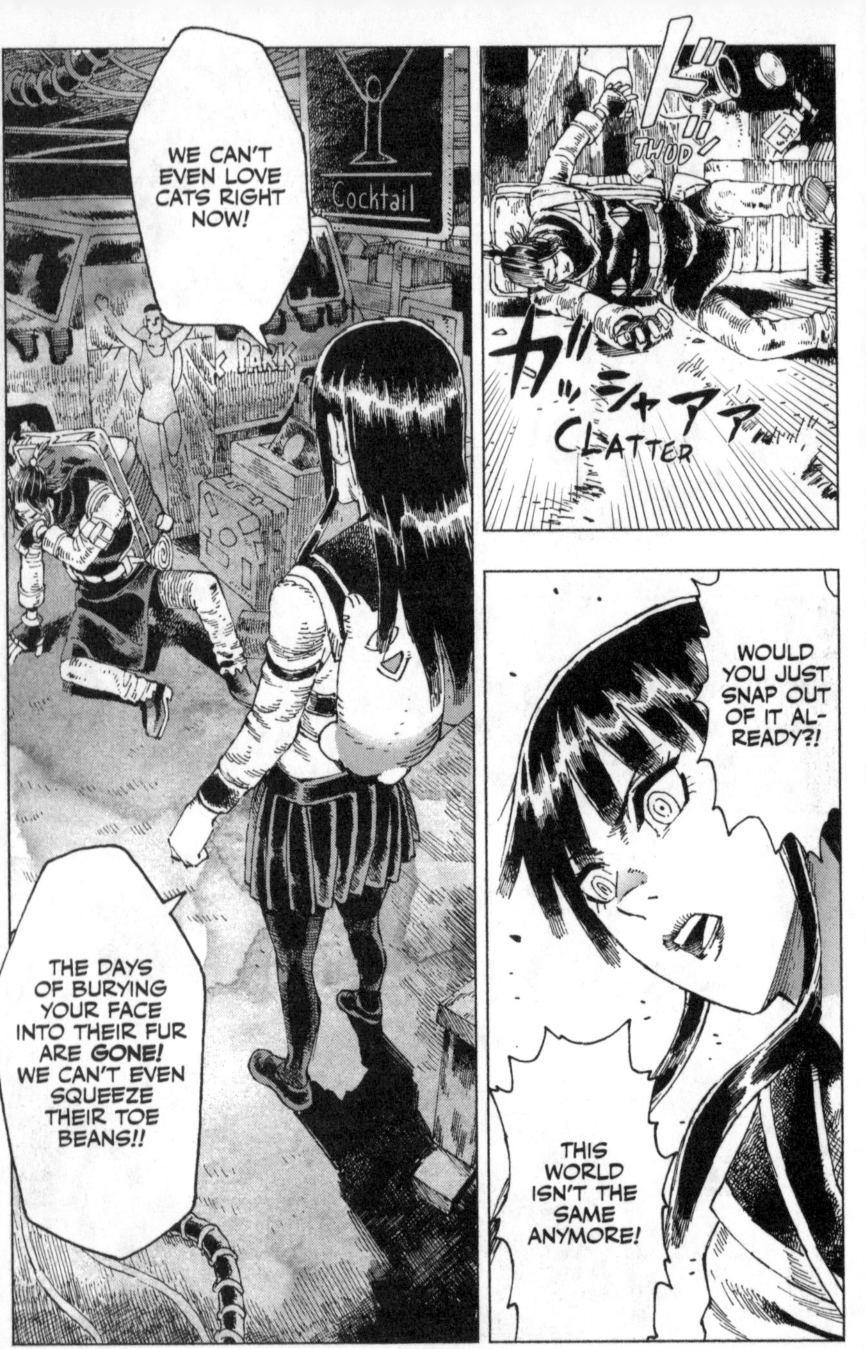
ドド
THUD
ガシャアア
CLATTER
WOULD YOU JUST SNAP OUT OF IT AL-READY?!
THIS WORLD ISN'T THE SAME ANYMORE!
Cocktail
WE CAN'T EVEN LOVE CATS RIGHT NOW!
PARK
THE DAYS OF BURYING YOUR FACE INTO THEIR FUR ARE GONE! WE CAN'T EVEN SQUEEZE THEIR TOE BEANS!!

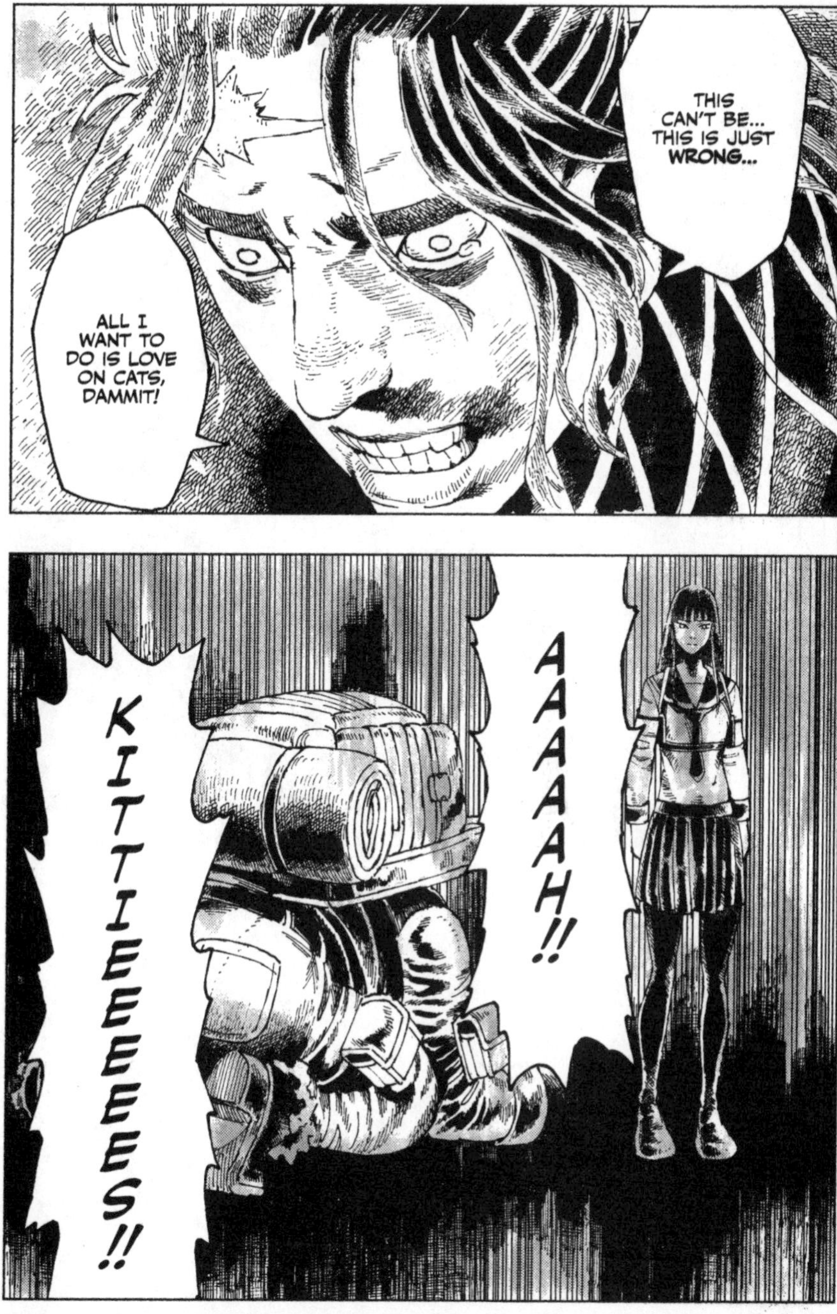
THIS CAN'T BE... THIS IS JUST **WRONG...**
ALL I WANT TO DO IS LOVE ON CATS, DAMMIT!
AAAAAH!!
KITTIEEEEES!!

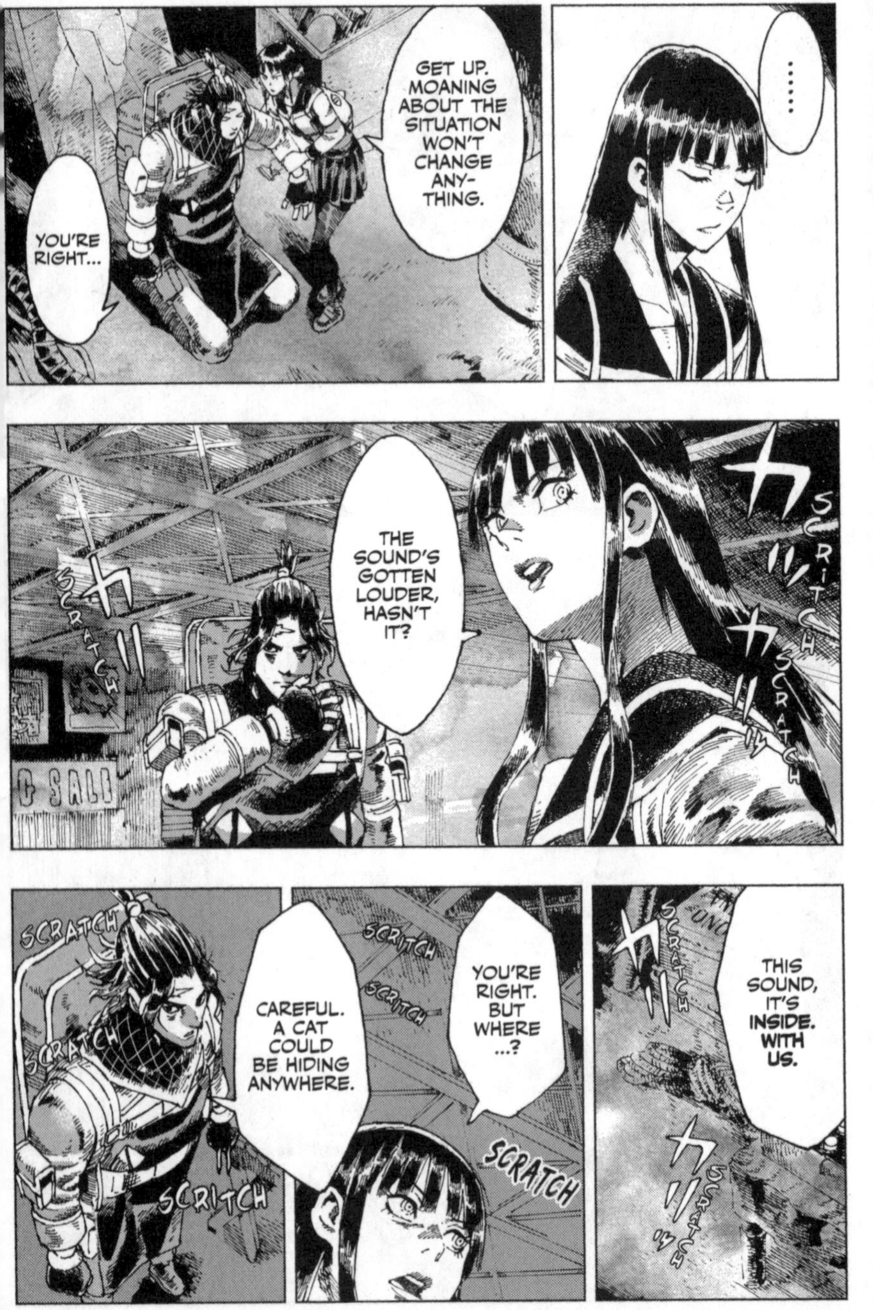
......
GET UP. MOANING ABOUT THE SITUATION WON'T CHANGE ANYTHING.
YOU'RE RIGHT...
SCRITCH
SCRATCH
THE SOUND'S GOTTEN LOUDER, HASN'T IT?
SCRATCH
C SALE
SCRATCH
THIS SOUND, IT'S **INSIDE. WITH US.**
SCRATCH
SCRITCH
SCRITCH
YOU'RE RIGHT. BUT WHERE ...?
SCRATCH
SCRATCH
SCRATCH
CAREFUL. A CAT COULD BE HIDING ANYWHERE.
SCRITCH

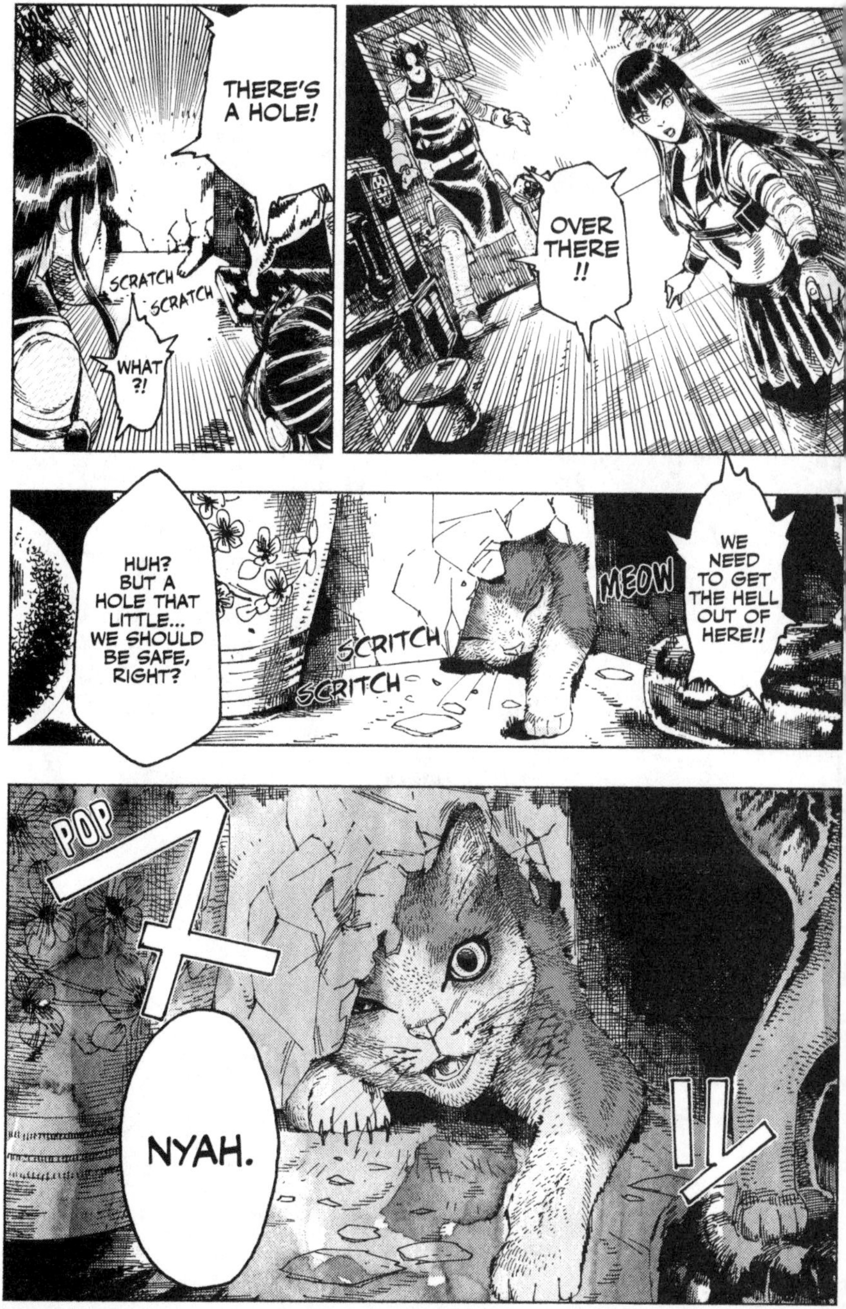
OVER THERE!!
THERE'S A HOLE!
SCRATCH
SCRATCH
WHAT?!
WE NEED TO GET THE HELL OUT OF HERE!!
MEOW
SCRITCH
SCRITCH
HUH? BUT A HOLE THAT LITTLE... WE SHOULD BE SAFE, RIGHT?
POP
NYAH.

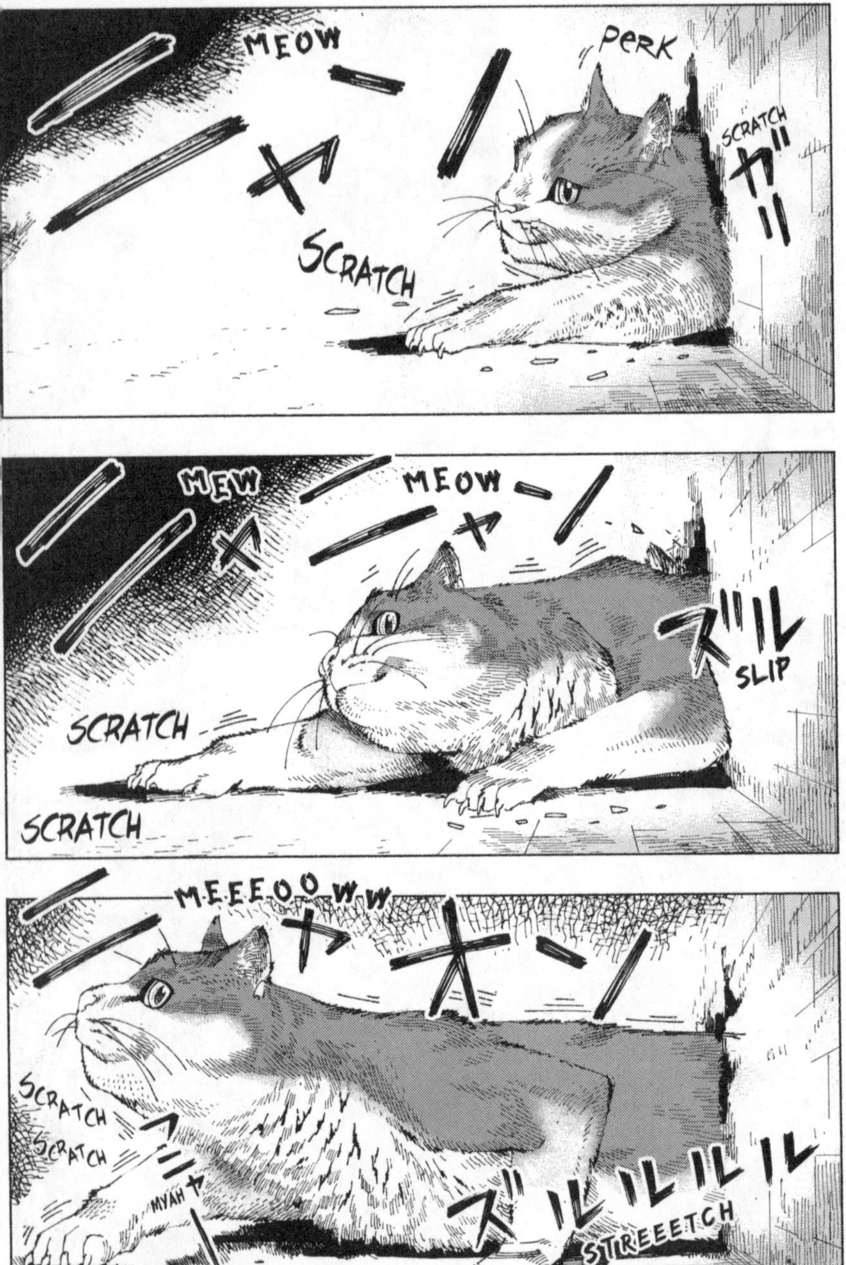
PERK
SCRATCH
MEOW
SCRATCH
ズル
SLIP
MEOW
MEW
SCRATCH
SCRATCH
ズルルルル
STREEETCH
MEEEOOWW
MYAH
SCRATCH
SCRATCH

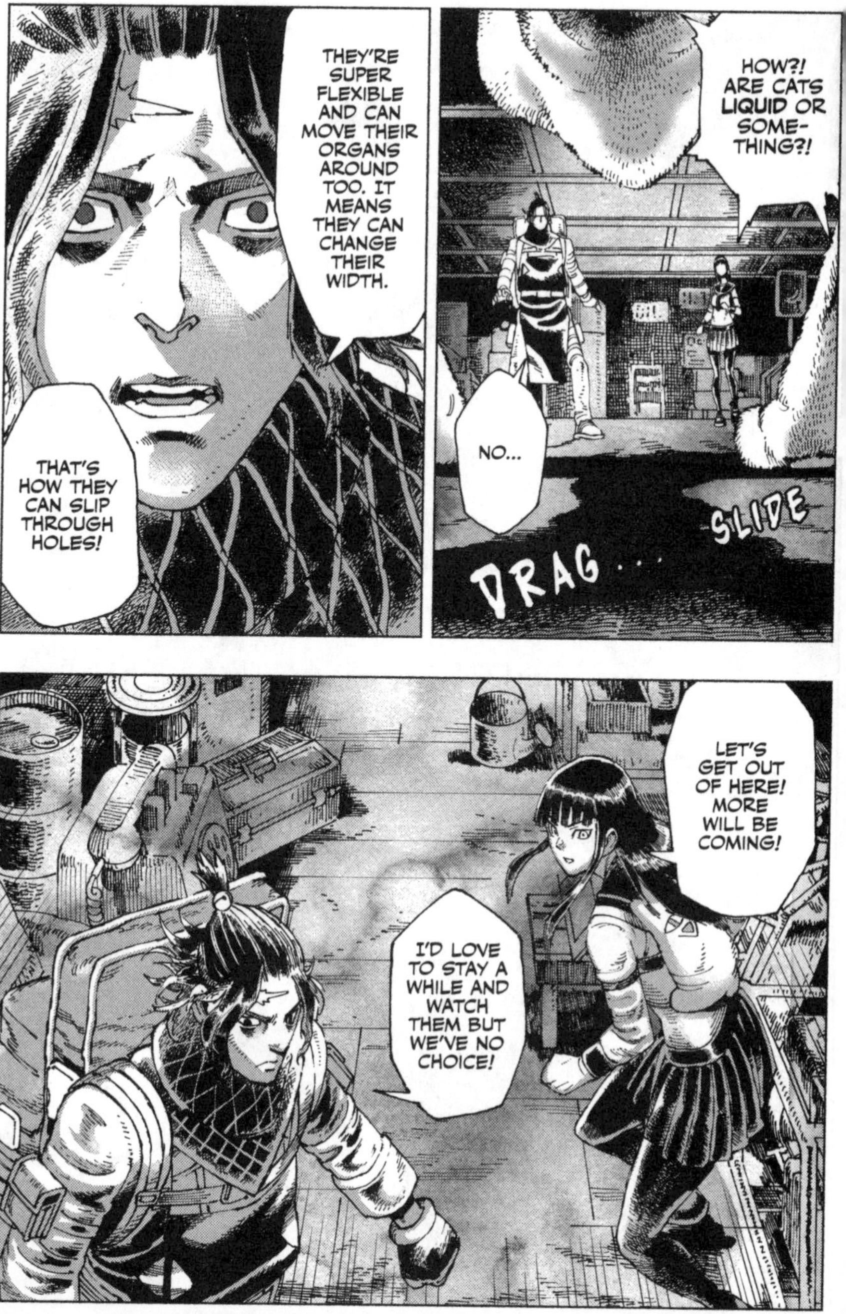
HOW?! ARE CATS **LIQUID** OR SOME-THING?!
NO...
SLIDE
DRAG...
THEY'RE SUPER FLEXIBLE AND CAN MOVE THEIR ORGANS AROUND TOO. IT MEANS THEY CAN CHANGE THEIR WIDTH.
THAT'S HOW THEY CAN SLIP THROUGH HOLES!
LET'S GET OUT OF HERE! MORE WILL BE COMING!
I'D LOVE TO STAY A WHILE AND WATCH THEM BUT WE'VE NO CHOICE!

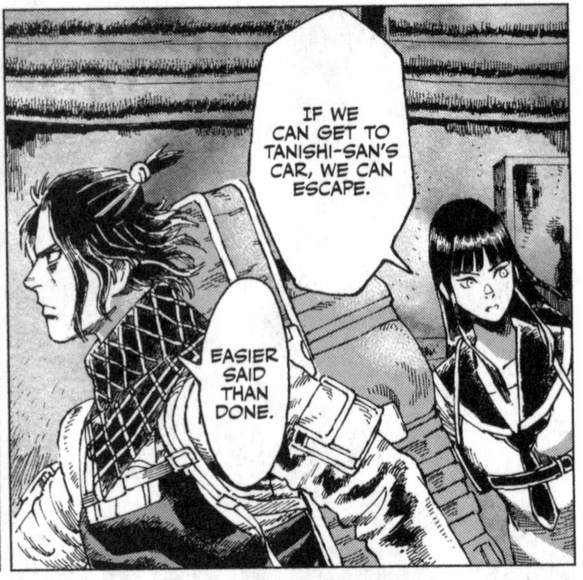
IF WE CAN GET TO TANISHI-SAN'S CAR, WE CAN ESCAPE.
EASIER SAID THAN DONE.

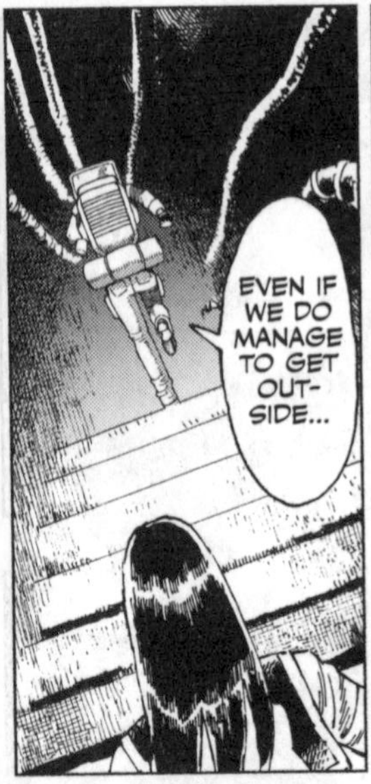
EVEN IF WE DO MANAGE TO GET OUT-SIDE...

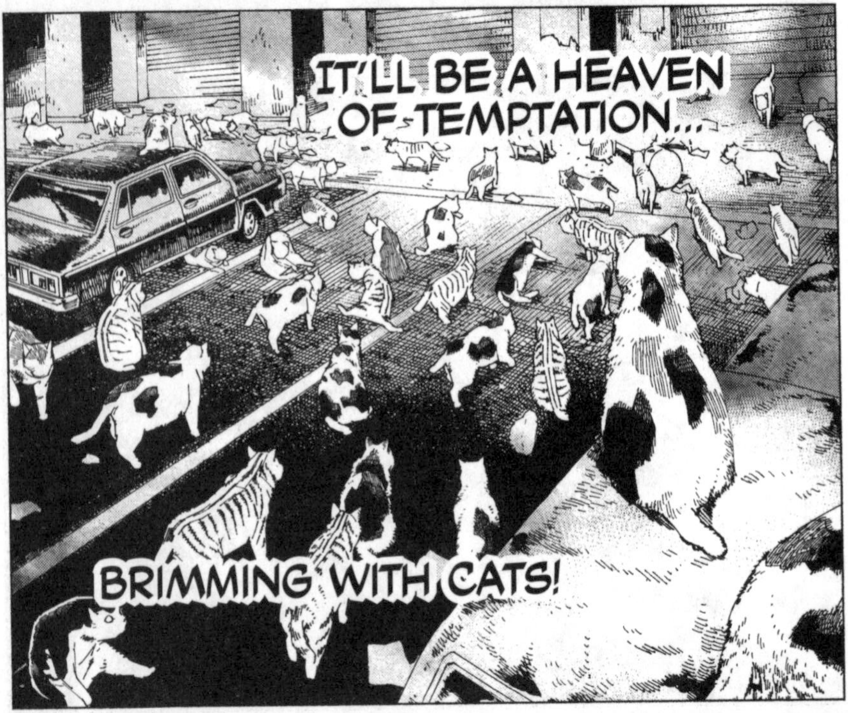
IT'LL BE A HEAVEN OF TEMPTATION...
BRIMMING WITH CATS!

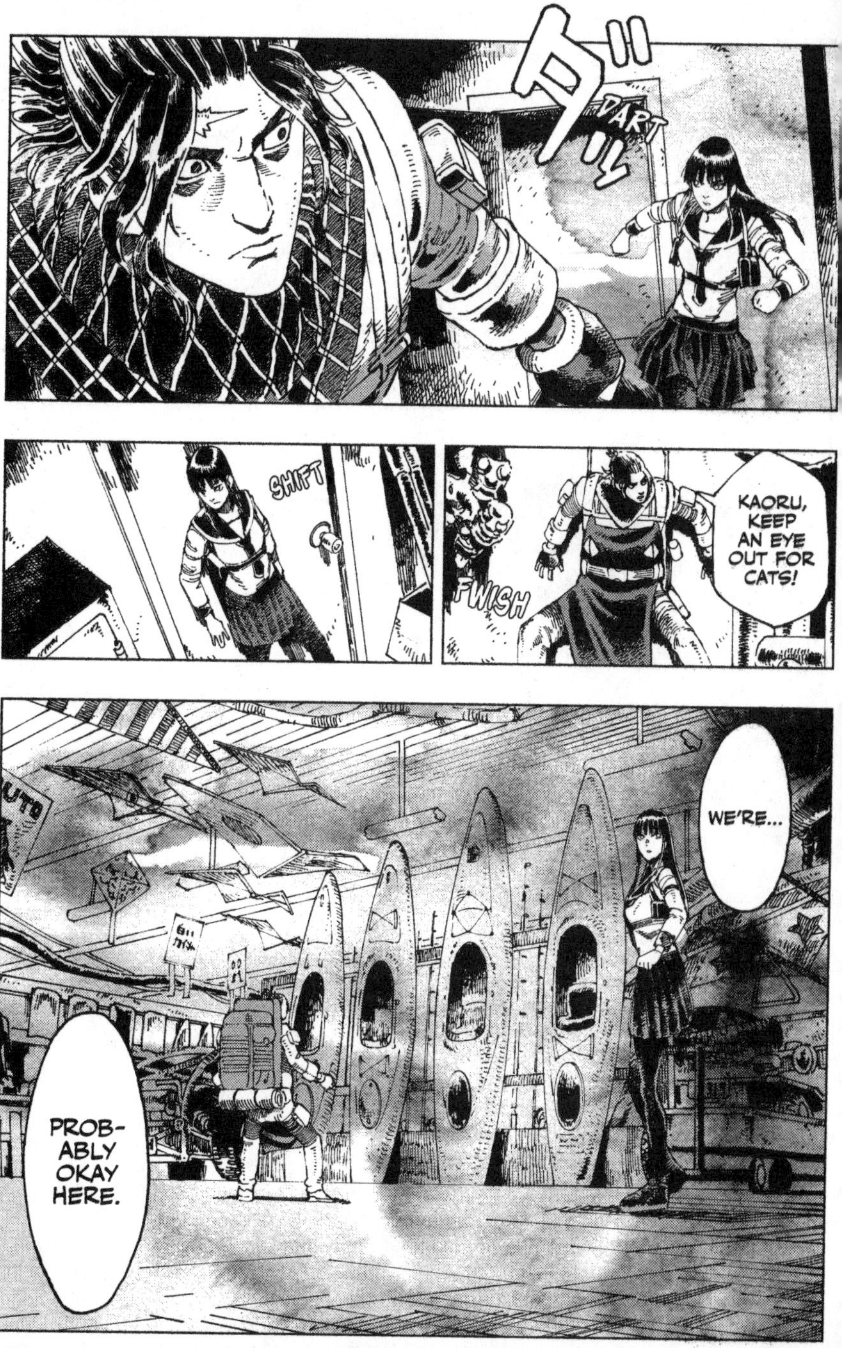
ダッ
DART
FWISH
KAORU, KEEP AN EYE OUT FOR CATS!
SHIFT
WE'RE...
PROB-ABLY OKAY HERE.

PULL TO OPEN

BUT CATS SURE ARE FAST, AREN'T THEY?

WHEW...

CLICK

IF WE STAY HERE, WE'LL JUST BE CORNERED RATS.

WHAT DO WE DO?

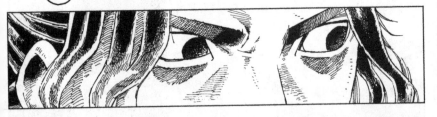

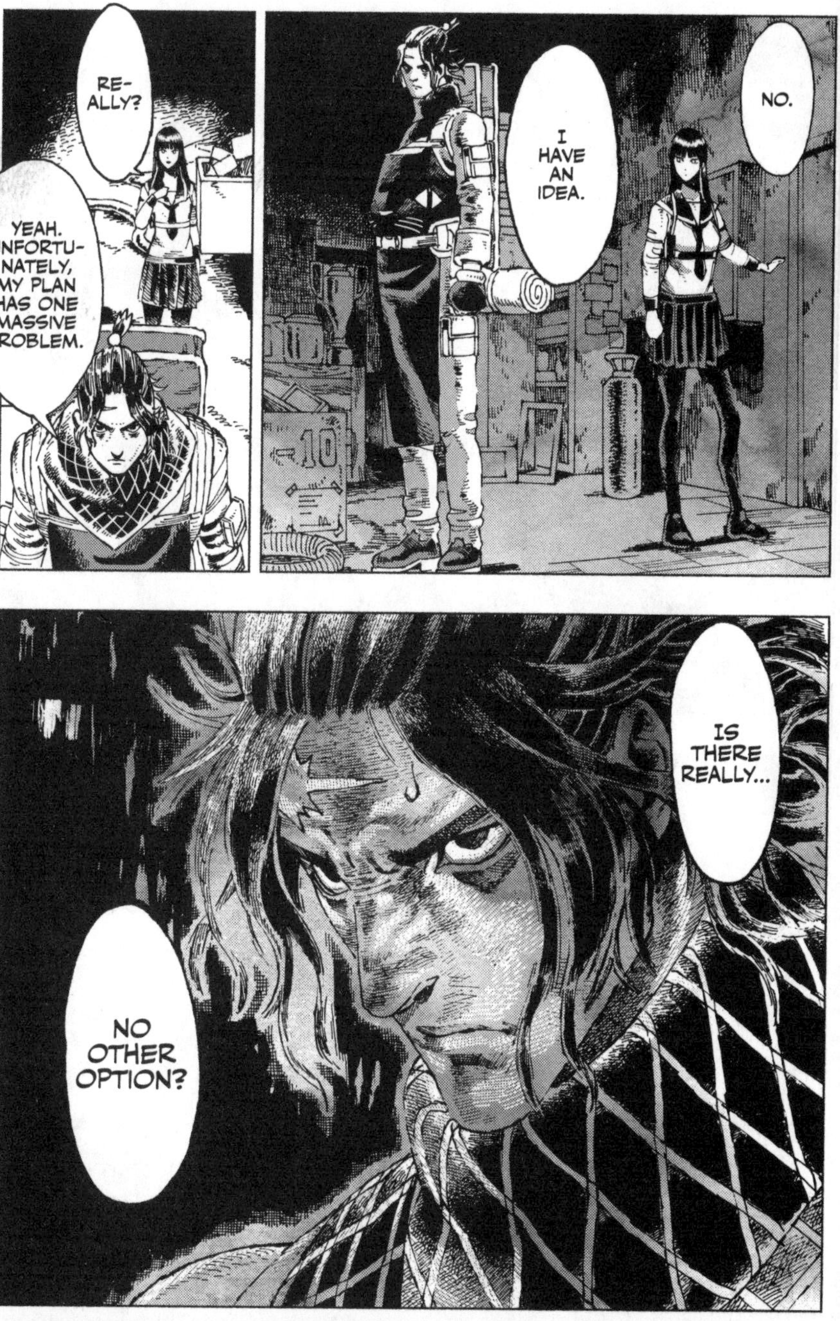
NO.
I HAVE AN IDEA.
RE-ALLY?
YEAH. UNFORTU-NATELY, MY PLAN HAS ONE MASSIVE PROBLEM.
IS THERE REALLY...
NO OTHER OPTION?

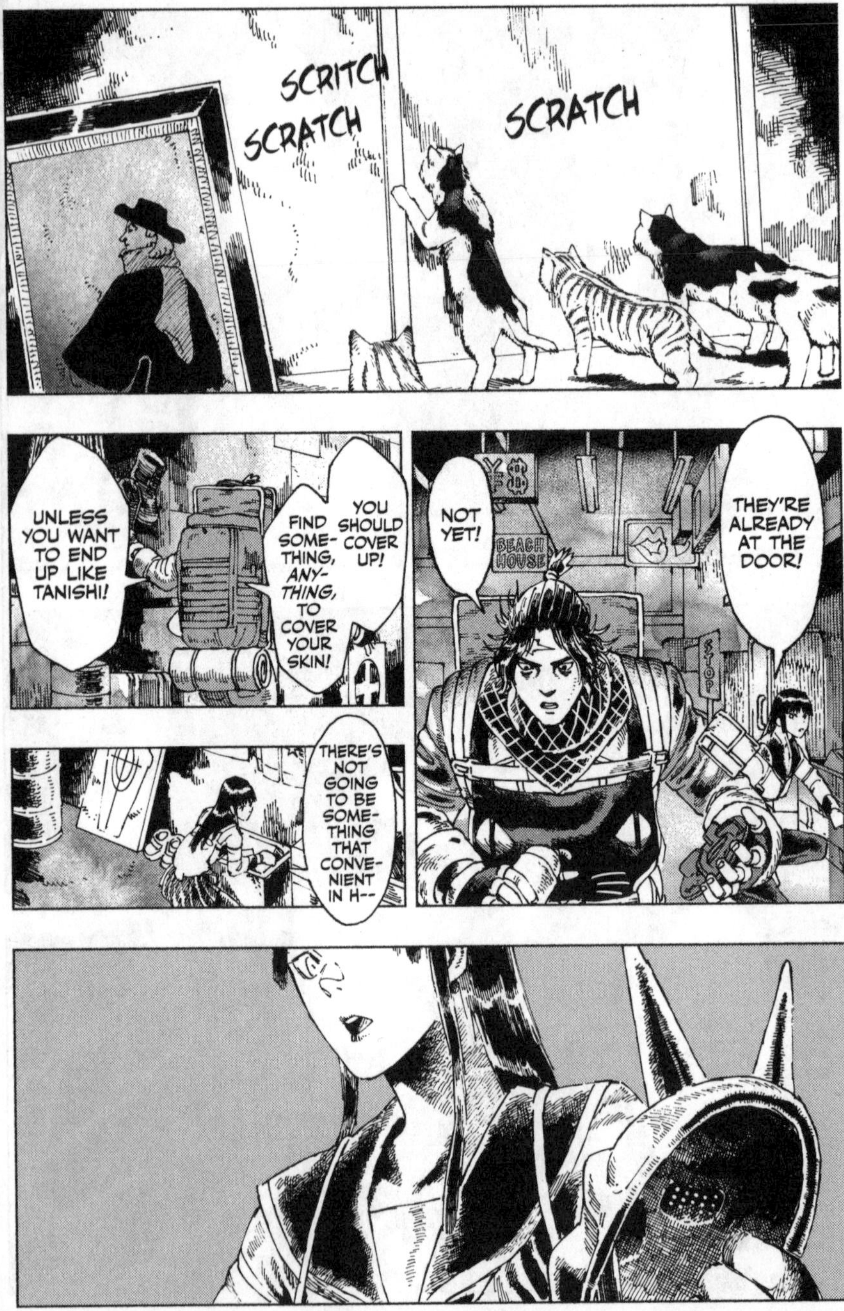
SCRATCH
SCRITCH
SCRATCH
THEY'RE ALREADY AT THE DOOR!
NOT YET!
BEACH HOUSE
STOP
YOU SHOULD COVER UP!
FIND SOMETHING, ANYTHING, TO COVER YOUR SKIN!
UNLESS YOU WANT TO END UP LIKE TANISHI!
THERE'S NOT GOING TO BE SOMETHING THAT CONVENIENT IN H--

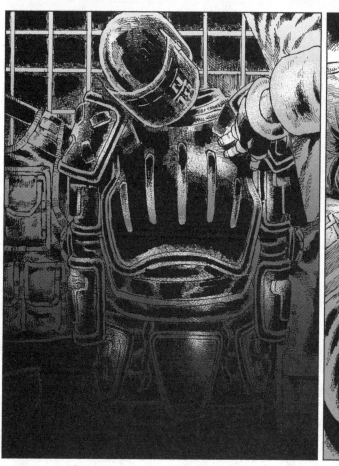

KER-CHAK

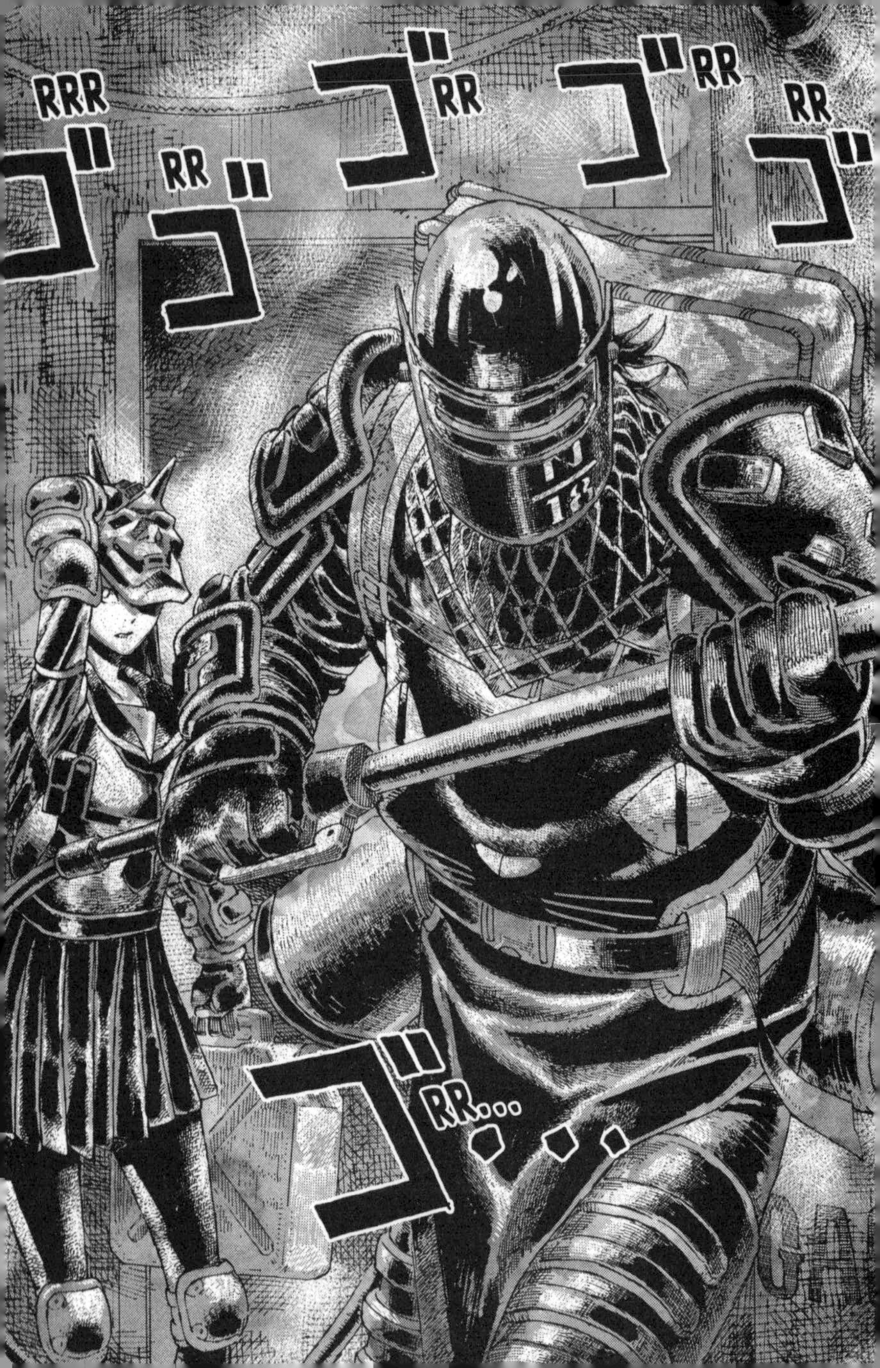
ゴRR
ゴRR
ゴRR
ゴRR
ゴRRR
ゴRR...

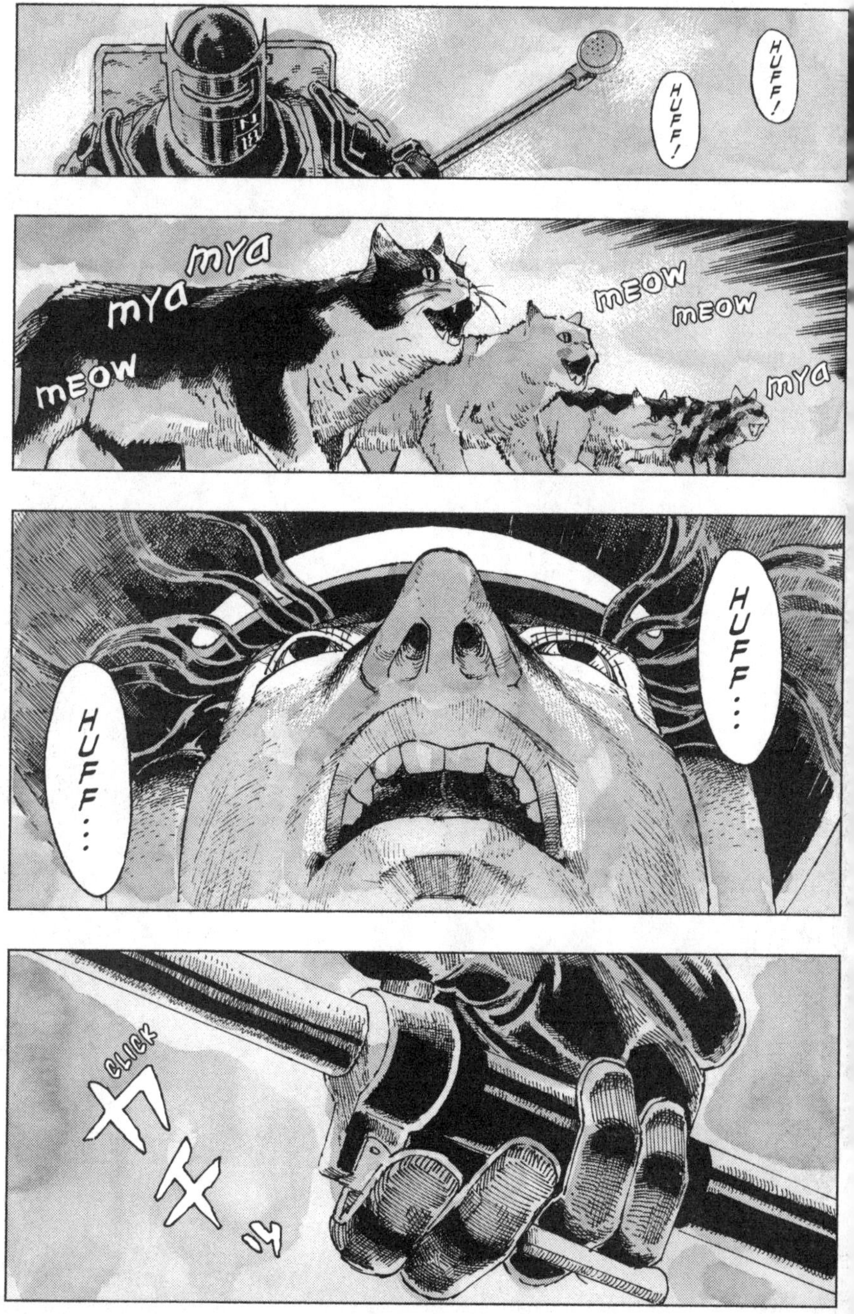
HUFF!
HUFF!
meow
meow
mya
mya
mya
meow
HUFF...
HUFF...
CLICK

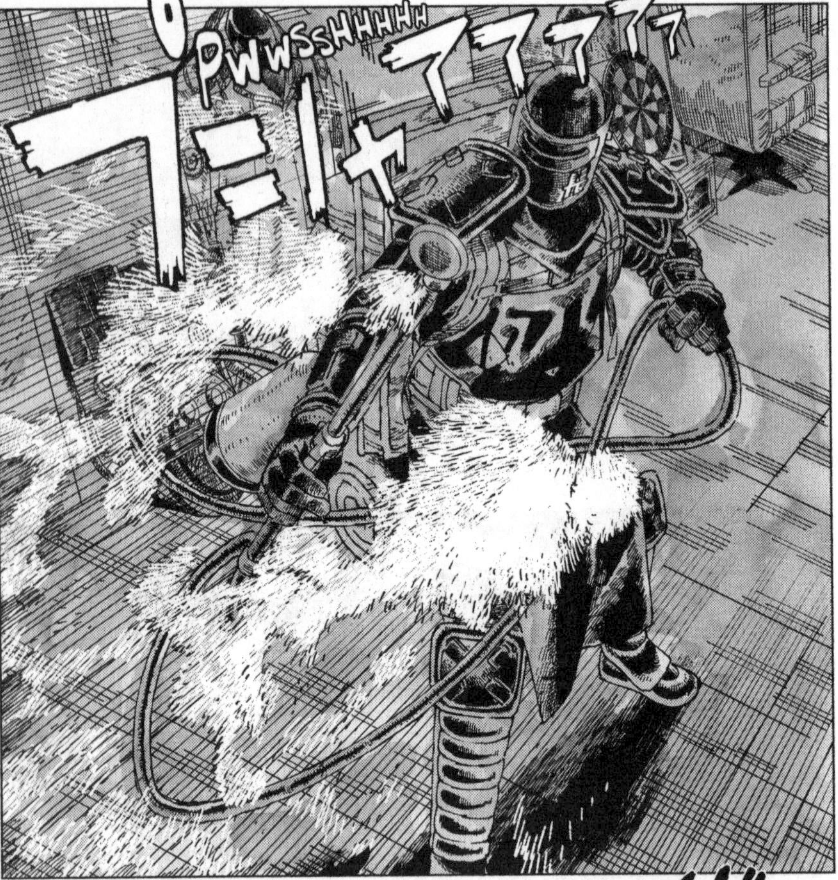
PWWSSHHHHH
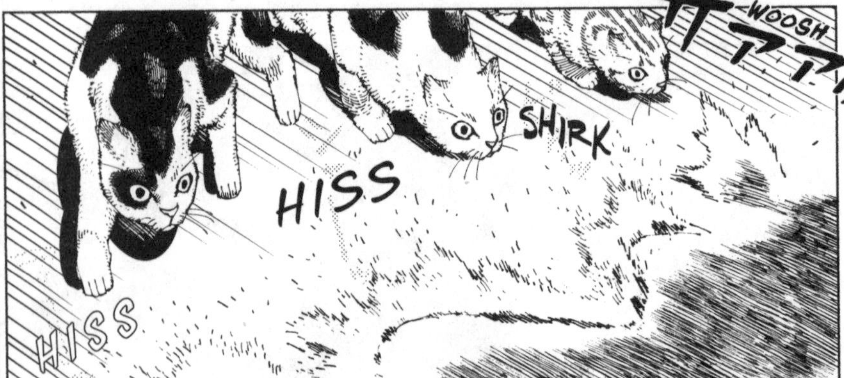
WOOSH
SHIRK
HISS
HISS

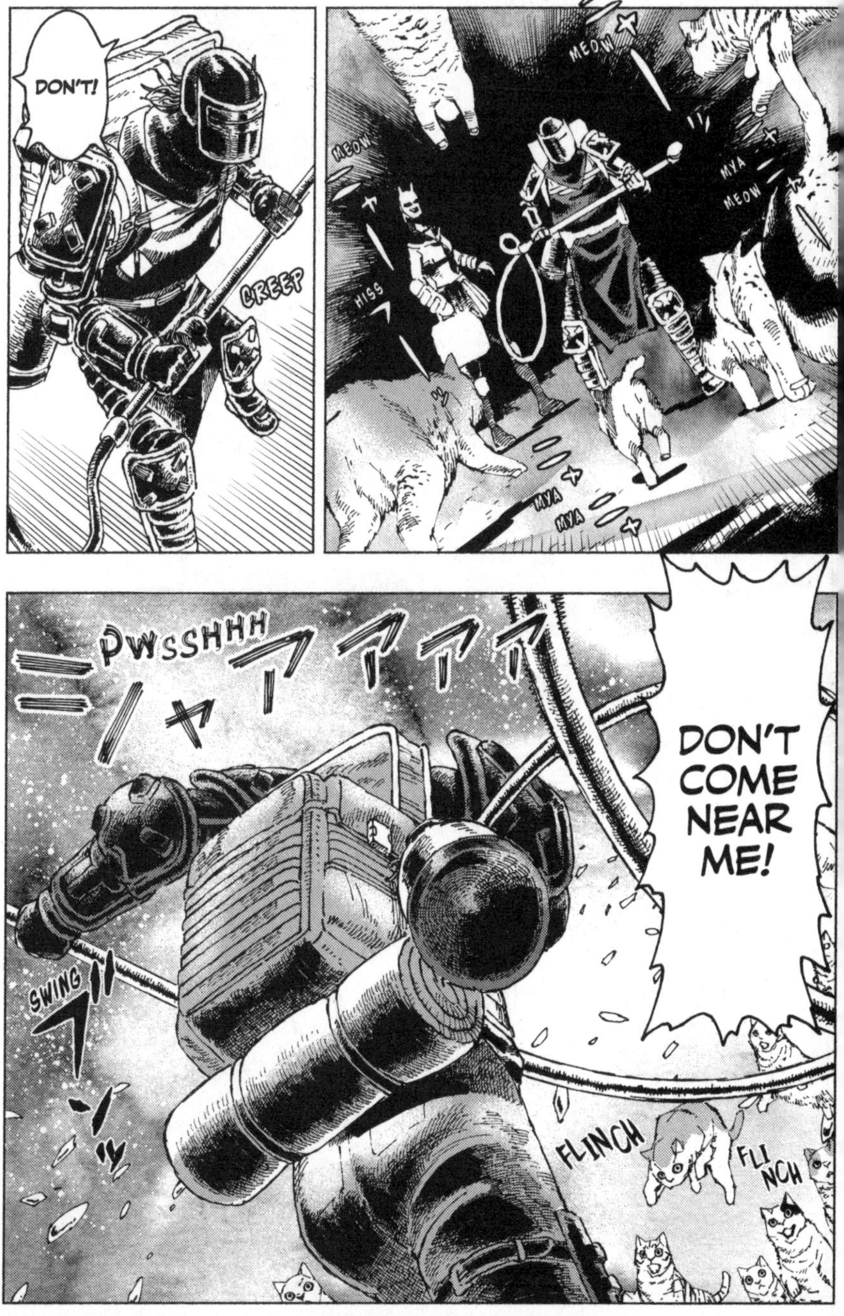
MEOW
MYA
MEOW
MEOW
HISS
MYA
MYA
DON'T!
CREEP
DON'T COME NEAR ME!
PWSSHHH
ニャアアア
FLINCH
FLINCH
SWING

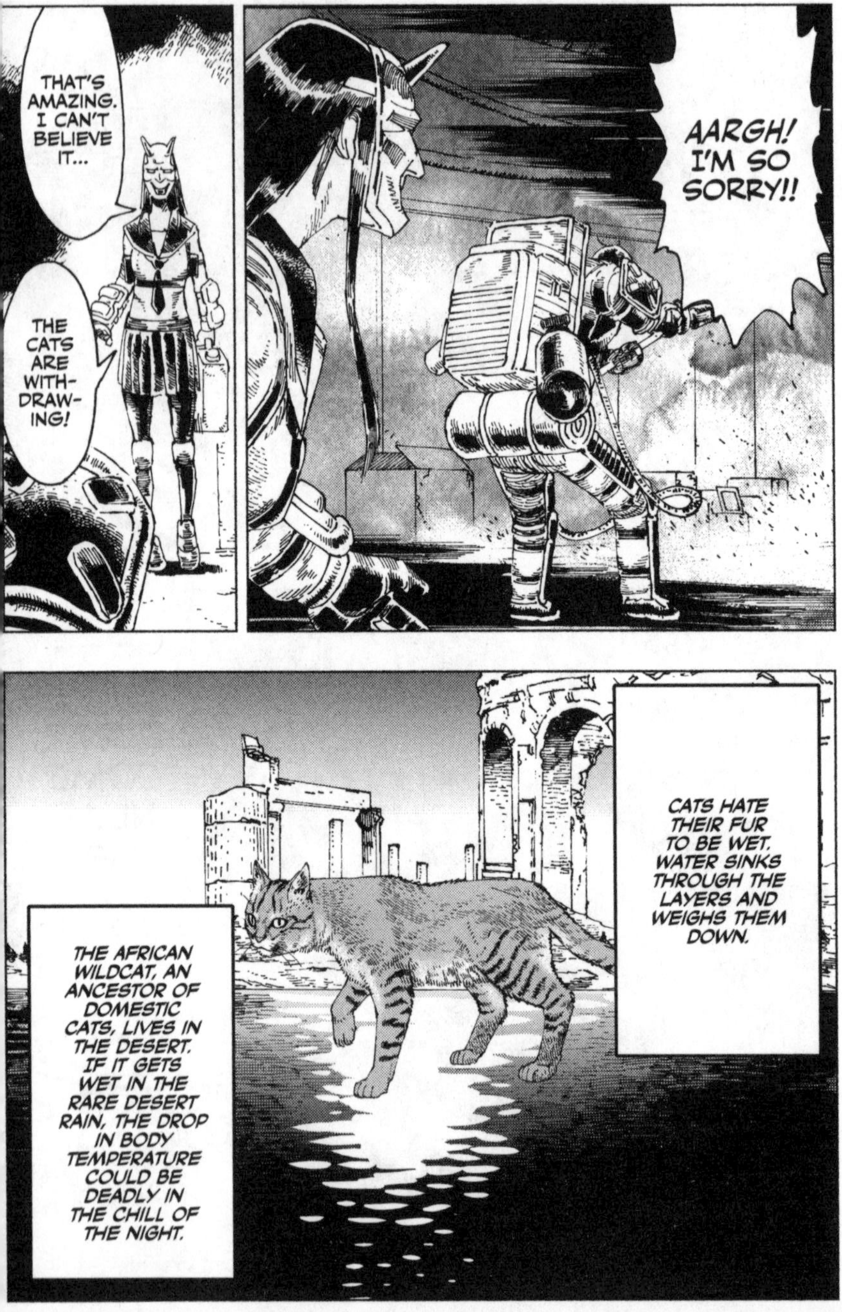
AARGH! I'M SO SORRY!!
THAT'S AMAZING. I CAN'T BELIEVE IT...
THE CATS ARE WITH-DRAWING!
CATS HATE THEIR FUR TO BE WET. WATER SINKS THROUGH THE LAYERS AND WEIGHS THEM DOWN.
THE AFRICAN WILDCAT, AN ANCESTOR OF DOMESTIC CATS, LIVES IN THE DESERT. IF IT GETS WET IN THE RARE DESERT RAIN, THE DROP IN BODY TEMPERATURE COULD BE DEADLY IN THE CHILL OF THE NIGHT.

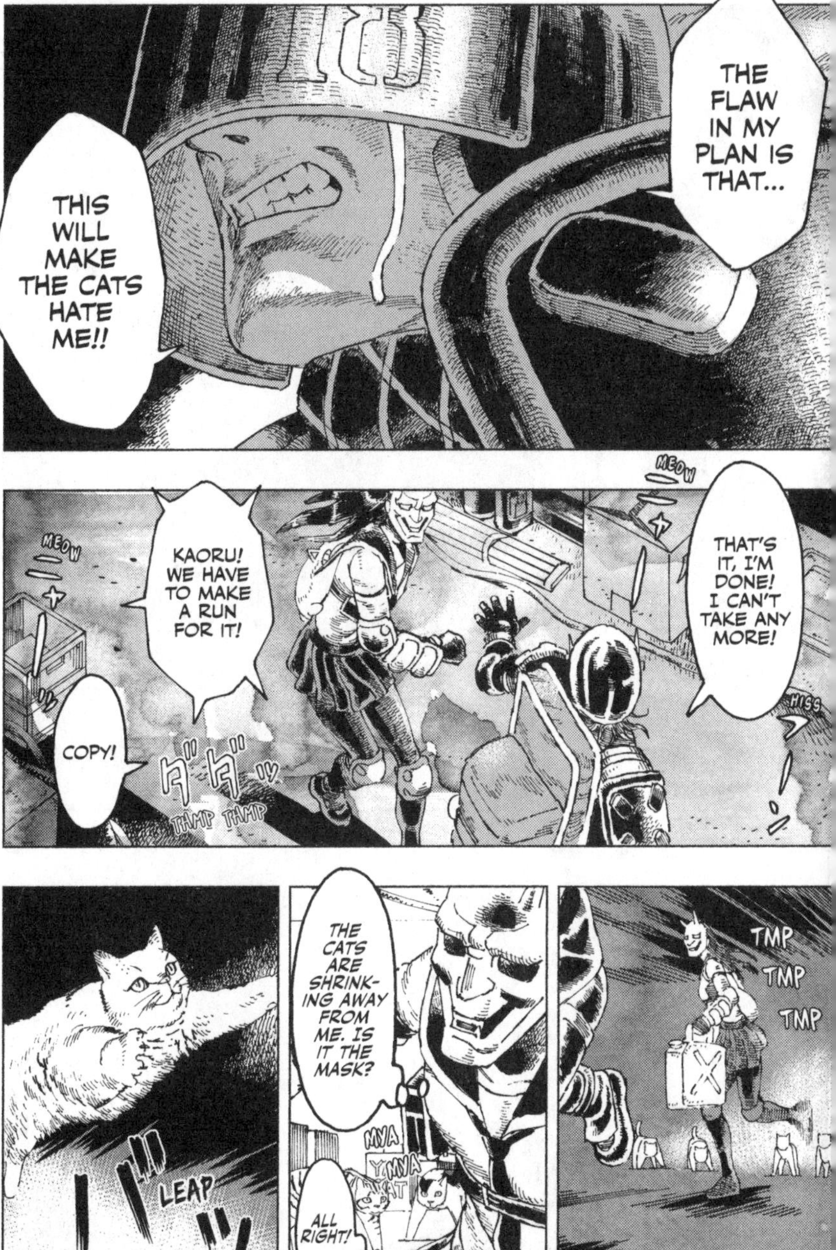
THE FLAW IN MY PLAN IS THAT...
THIS WILL MAKE THE CATS HATE ME!!
MEOW
THAT'S IT, I'M DONE! I CAN'T TAKE ANY MORE!
HISS
KAORU! WE HAVE TO MAKE A RUN FOR IT!
MEOW
COPY!
ダダッ
THMP THMP
TMP
TMP
TMP
THE CATS ARE SHRINK-ING AWAY FROM ME. IS IT THE MASK?
MYA
MYA
ALL RIGHT!
LEAP

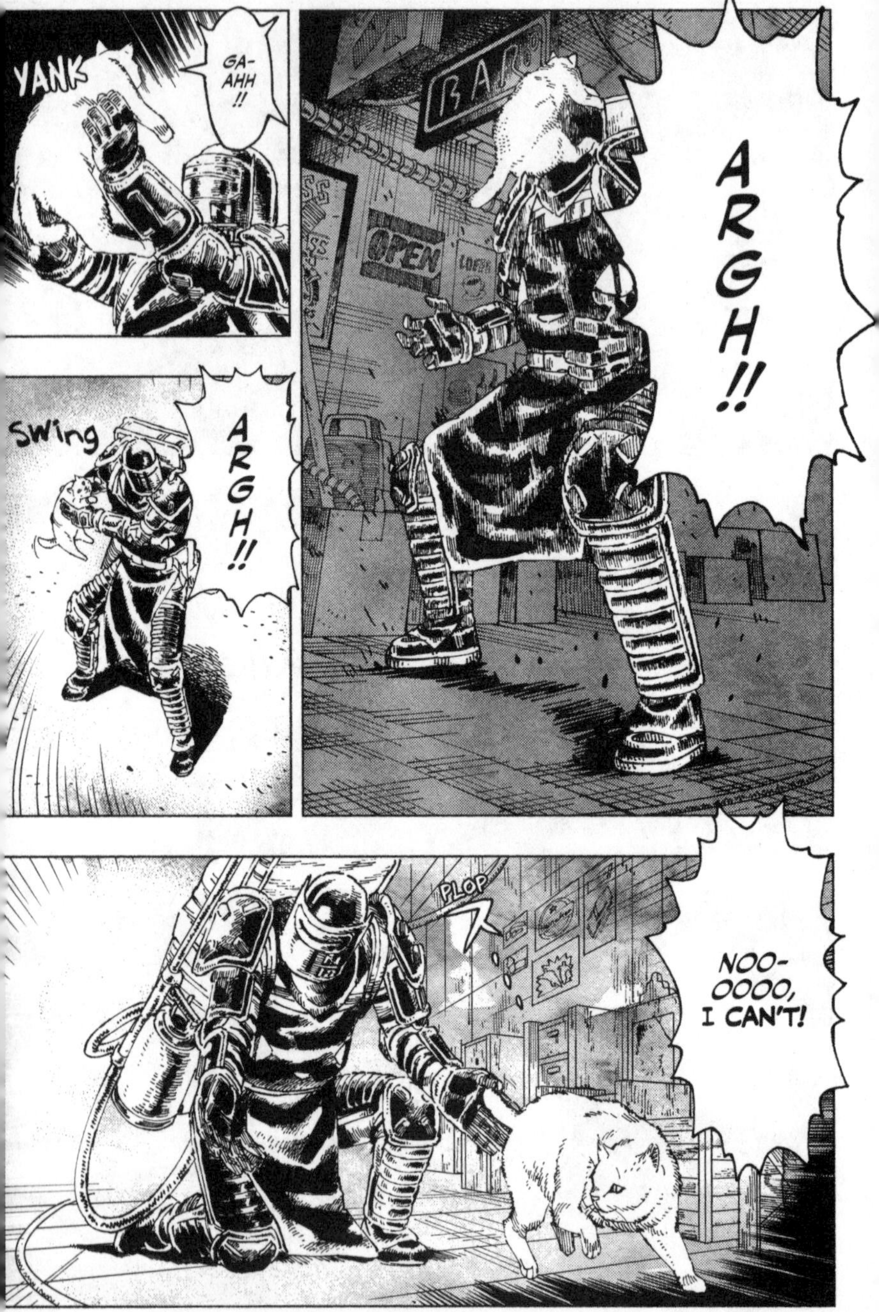
ARGH!!
BAR
OPEN
YANK
GA-AHH!!
Swing
ARGH!!
NOO-OOOO, I CAN'T!
PLOP

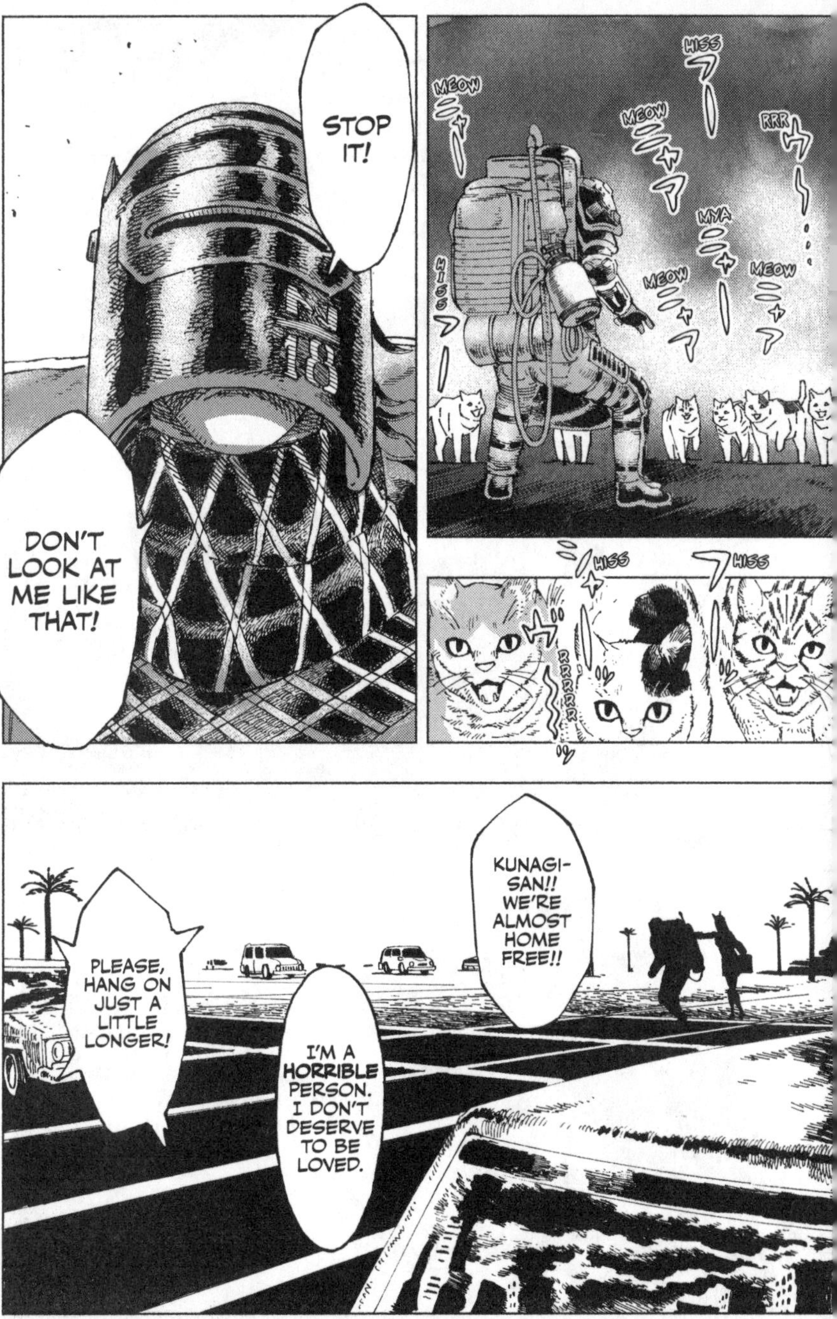
HISS
RRR
MEOW
MEOW
MYA
MEOW
MEOW
HISS
HISS
HISS
RRRRR
STOP IT!
DON'T LOOK AT ME LIKE THAT!
KUNAGI-SAN!! WE'RE ALMOST HOME FREE!!
I'M A **HORRIBLE** PERSON. I DON'T DESERVE TO BE LOVED.
PLEASE, HANG ON JUST A LITTLE LONGER!

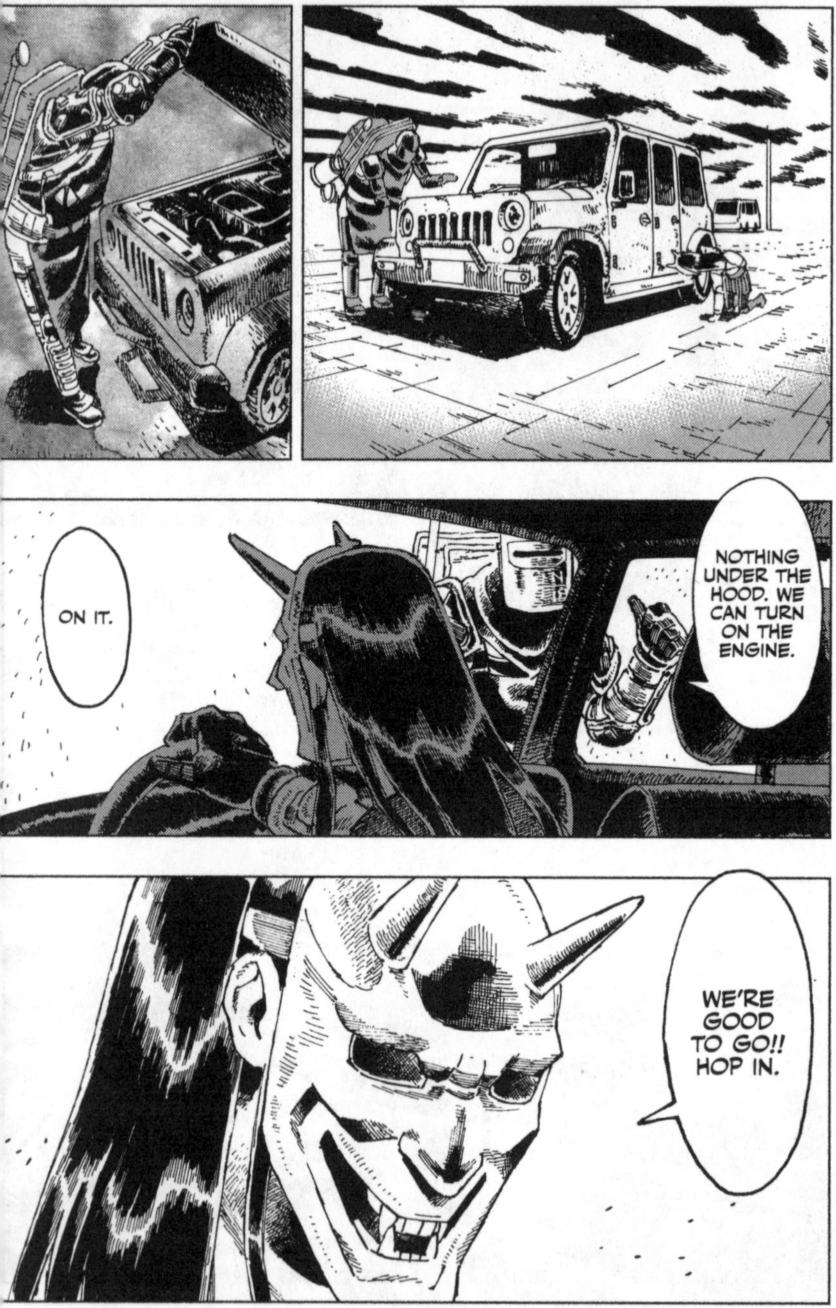
NOTHING UNDER THE HOOD. WE CAN TURN ON THE ENGINE.
ON IT.
WE'RE GOOD TO GO!! HOP IN.

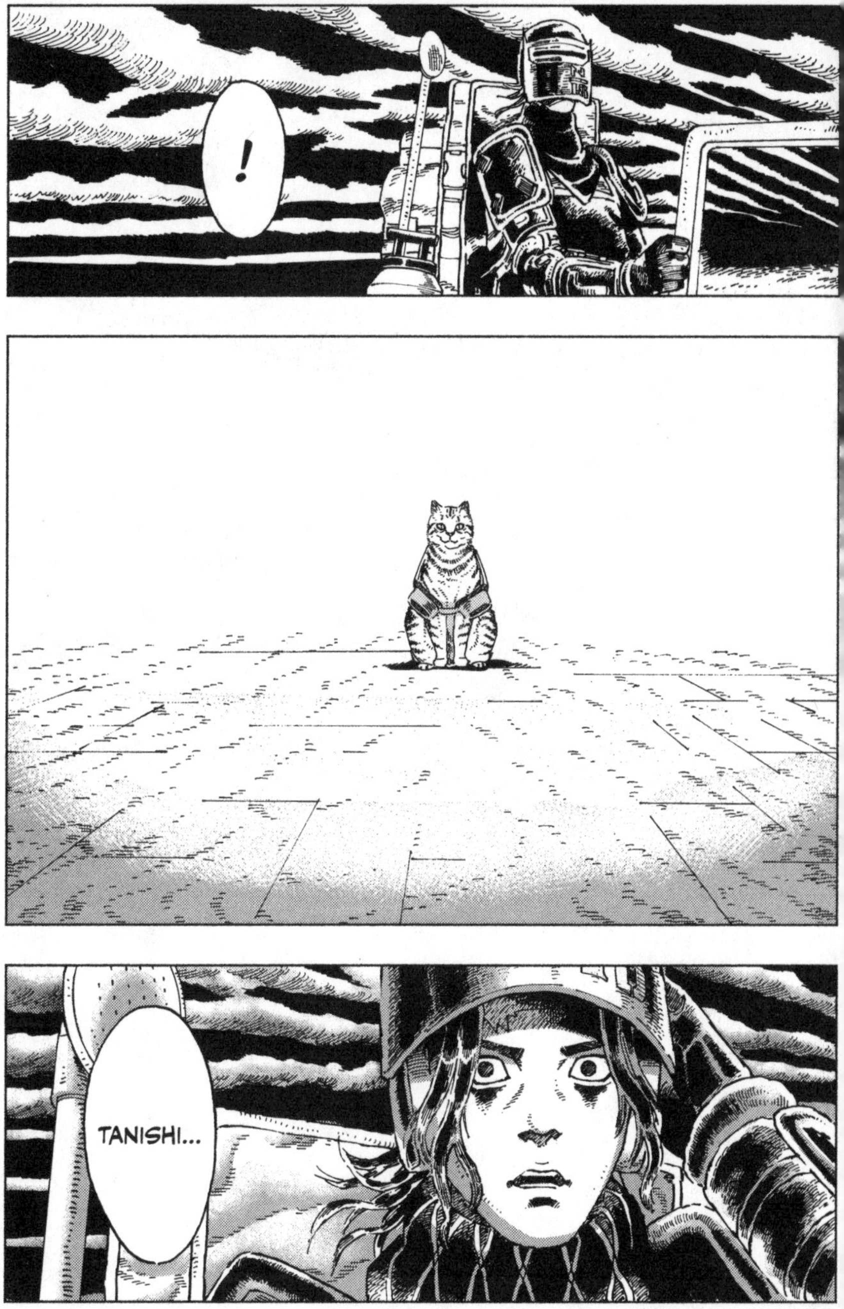
!
TANISHI...

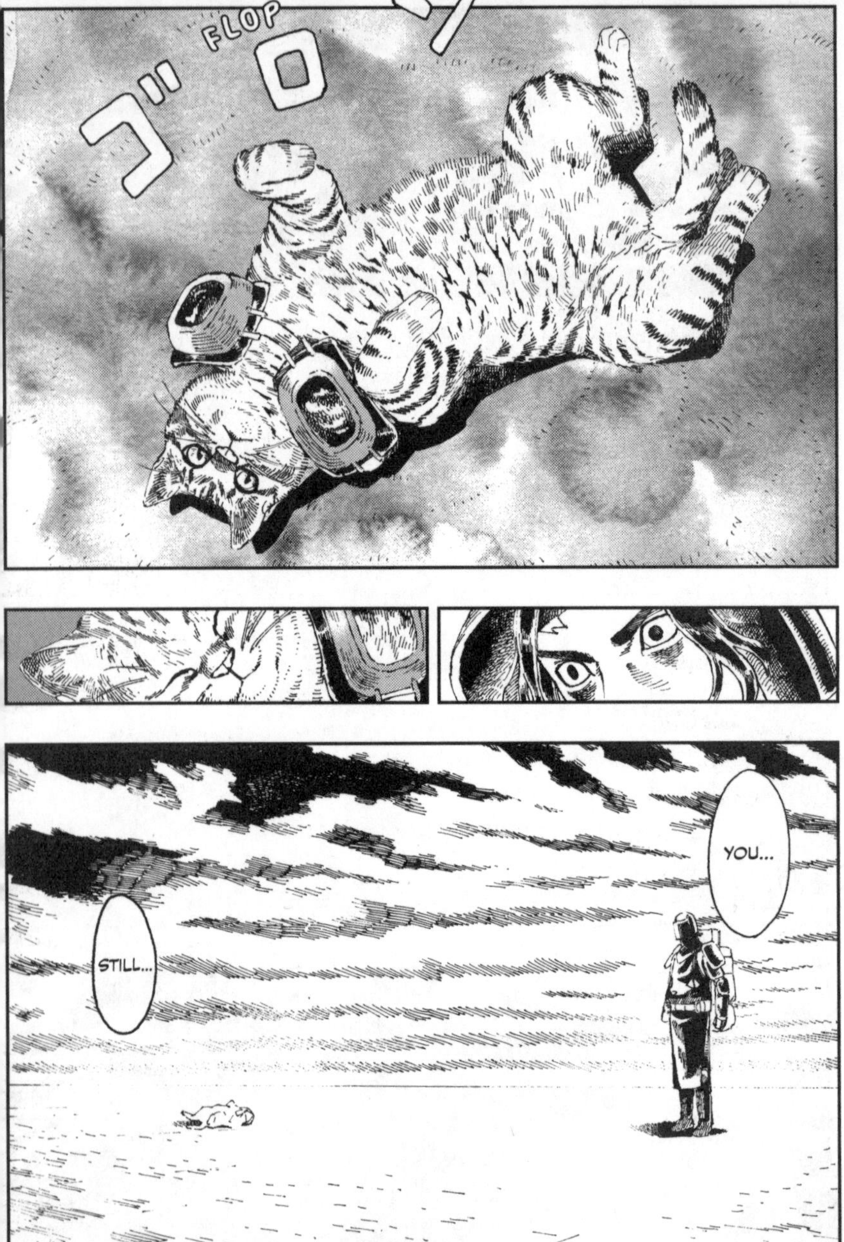
ゴロン
FLOP
YOU...
STILL...

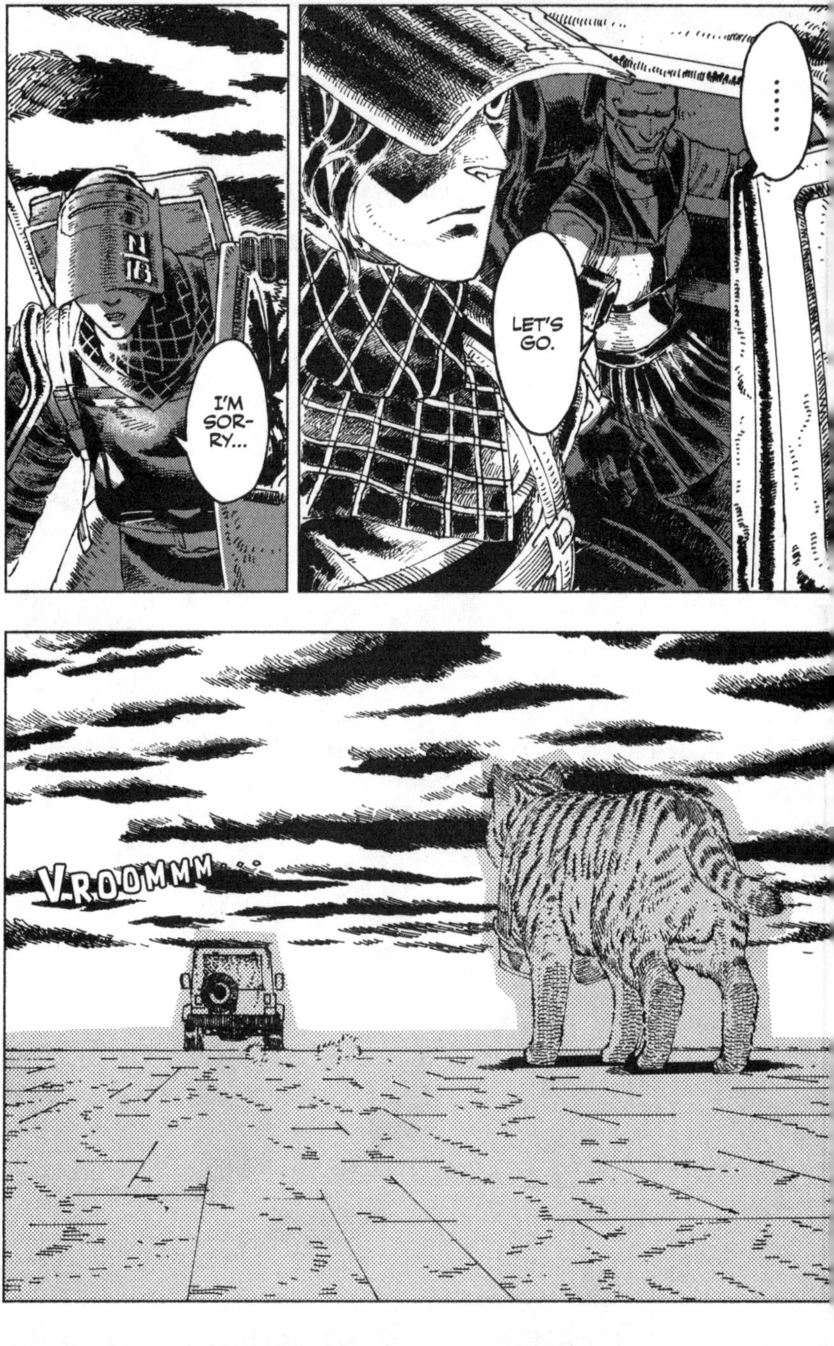
......
LET'S GO.
I'M SOR-RY...
VROOMMM

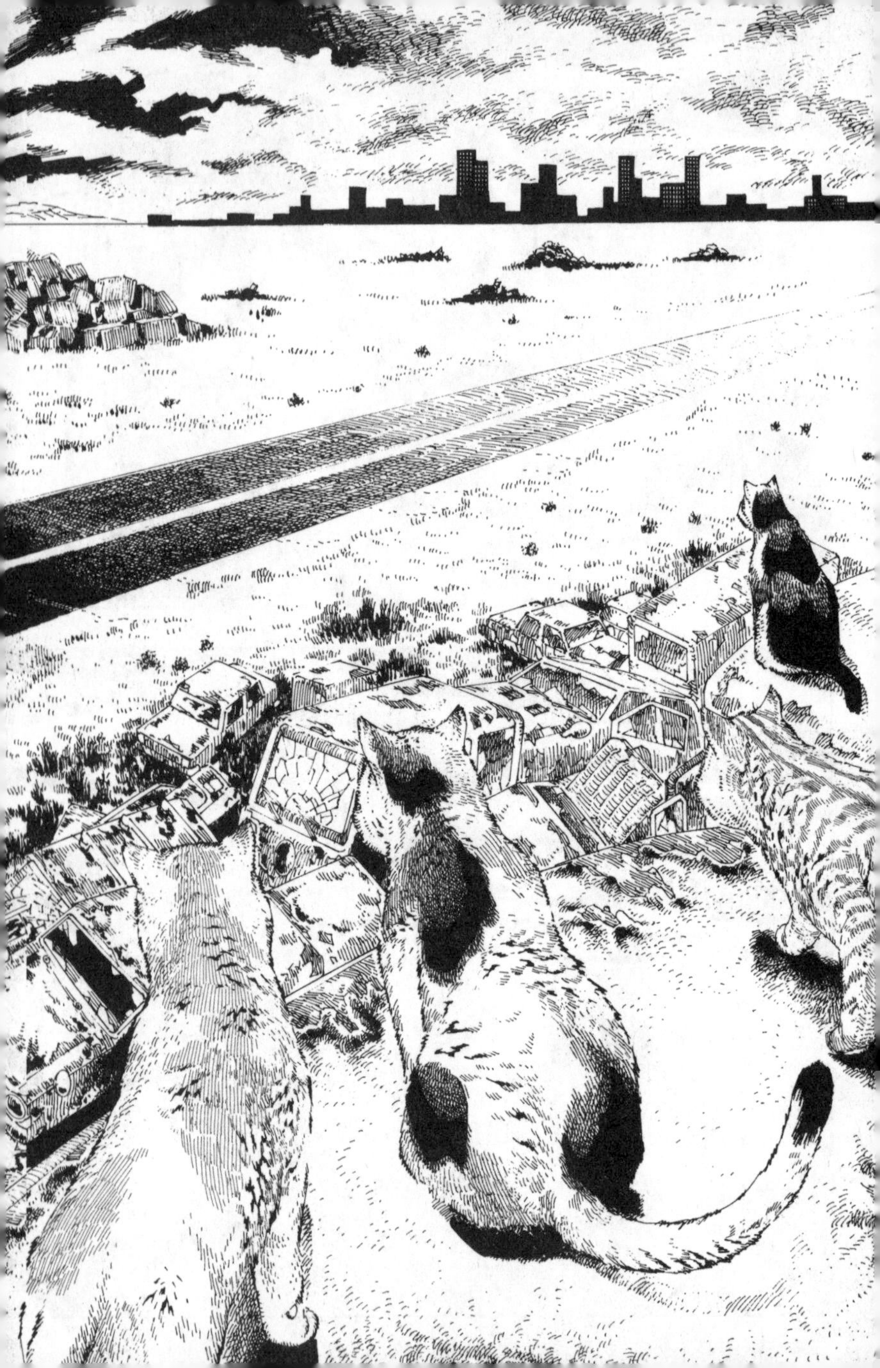

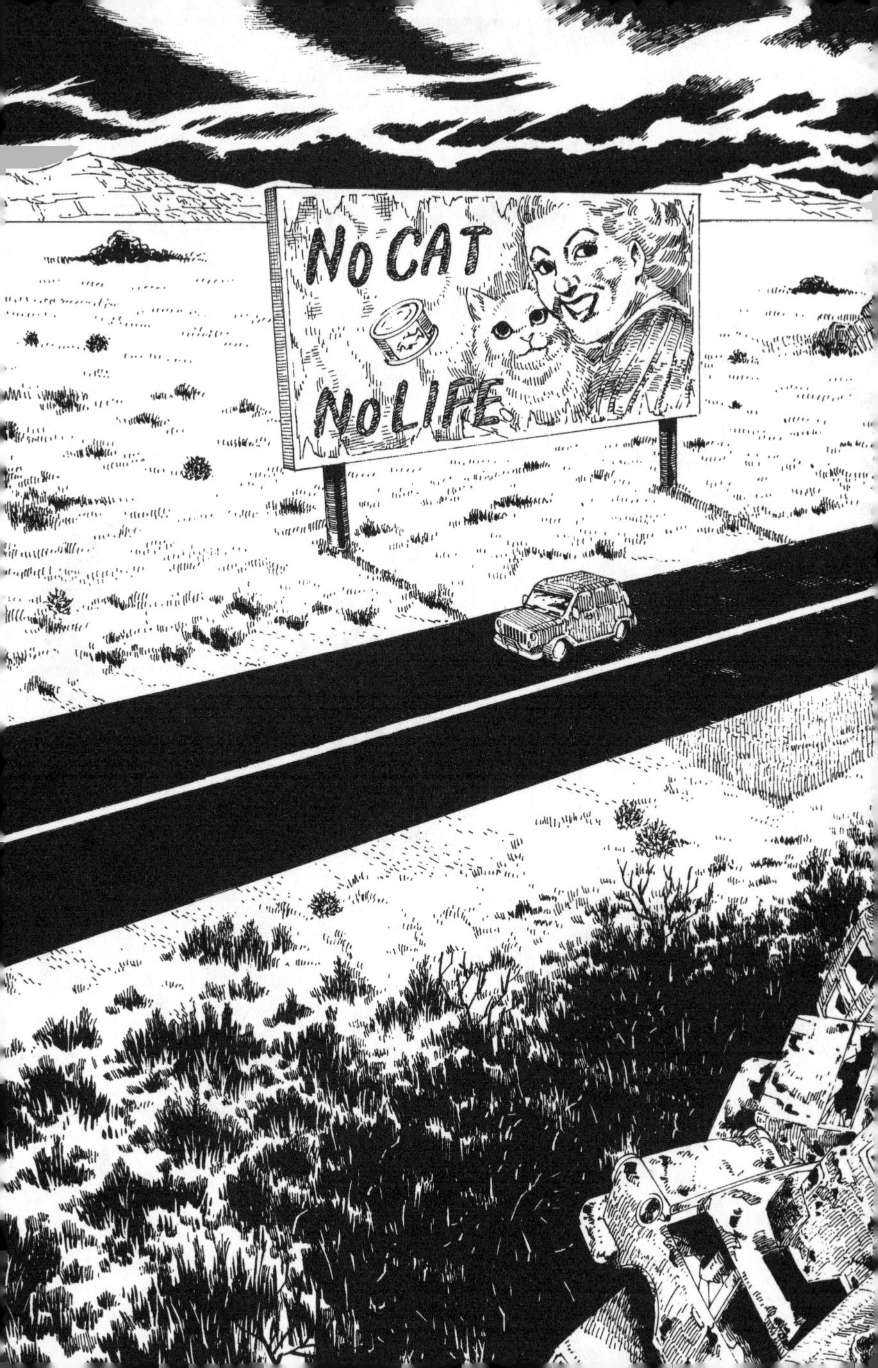
NO CAT
NO LIFE

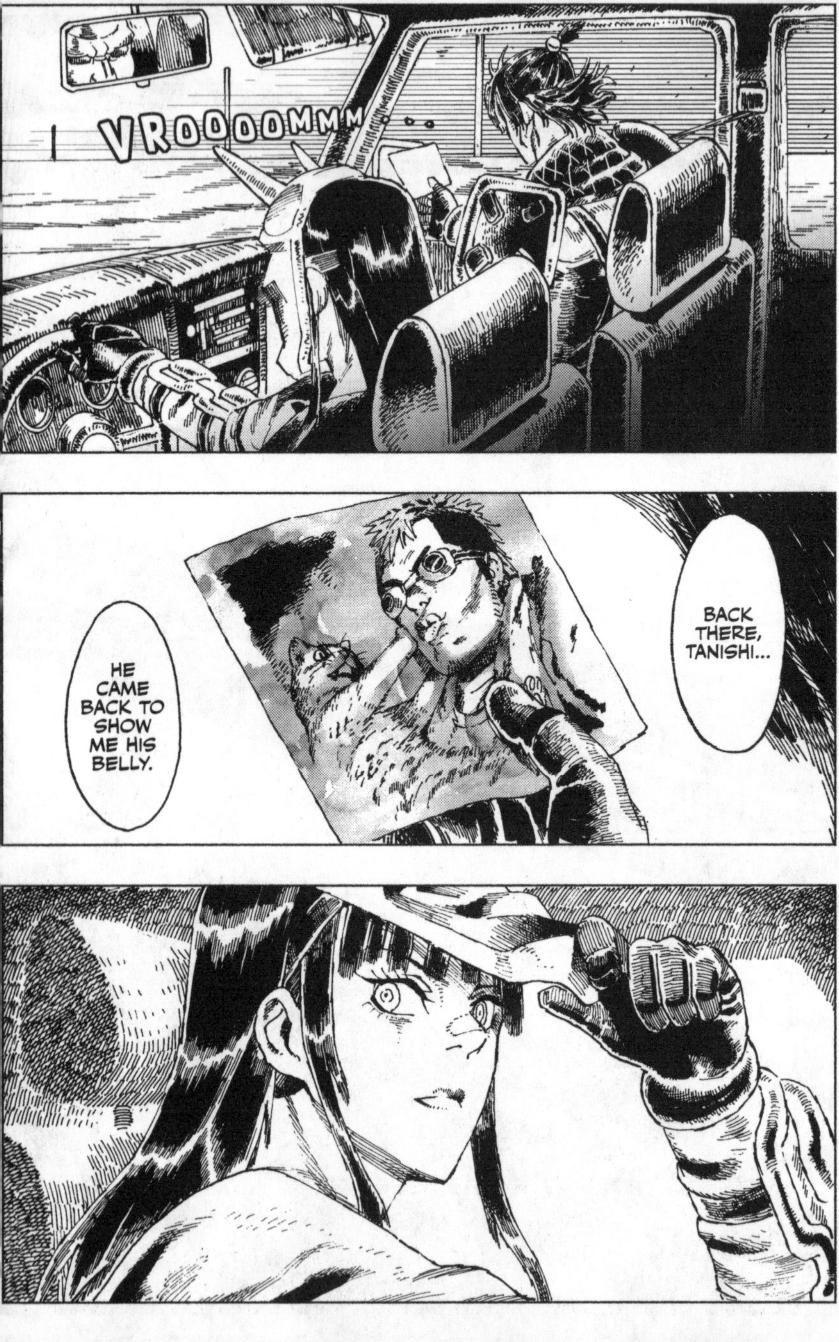
VROOOOMMM
BACK THERE, TANISHI...
HE CAME BACK TO SHOW ME HIS BELLY.

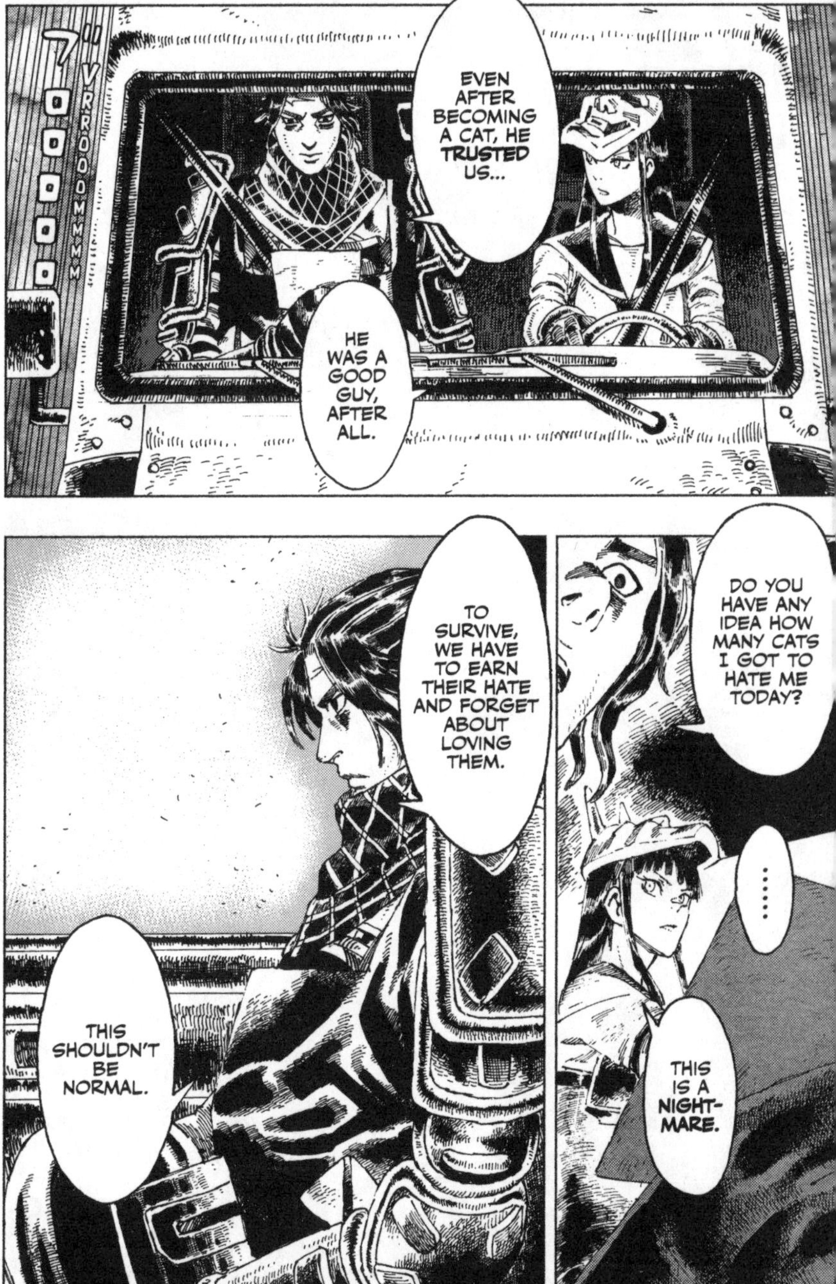
VRROOOOMMMM
EVEN AFTER BECOMING A CAT, HE TRUSTED US...
HE WAS A GOOD GUY, AFTER ALL.
DO YOU HAVE ANY IDEA HOW MANY CATS I GOT TO HATE ME TODAY?
......
THIS IS A NIGHT-MARE.
TO SURVIVE, WE HAVE TO EARN THEIR HATE AND FORGET ABOUT LOVING THEM.
THIS SHOULDN'T BE NORMAL.

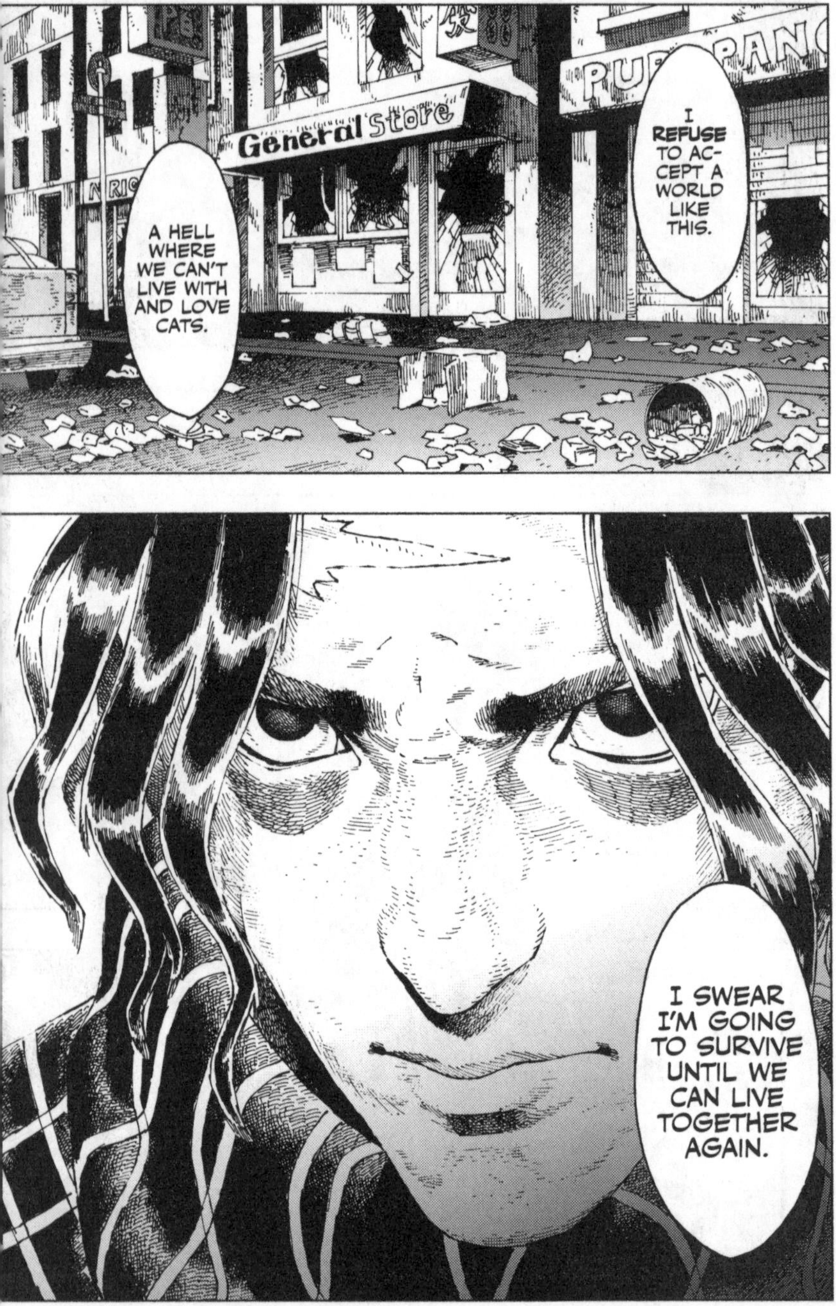
I REFUSE TO ACCEPT A WORLD LIKE THIS.
General Store
A HELL WHERE WE CAN'T LIVE WITH AND LOVE CATS.
I SWEAR I'M GOING TO SURVIVE UNTIL WE CAN LIVE TOGETHER AGAIN.

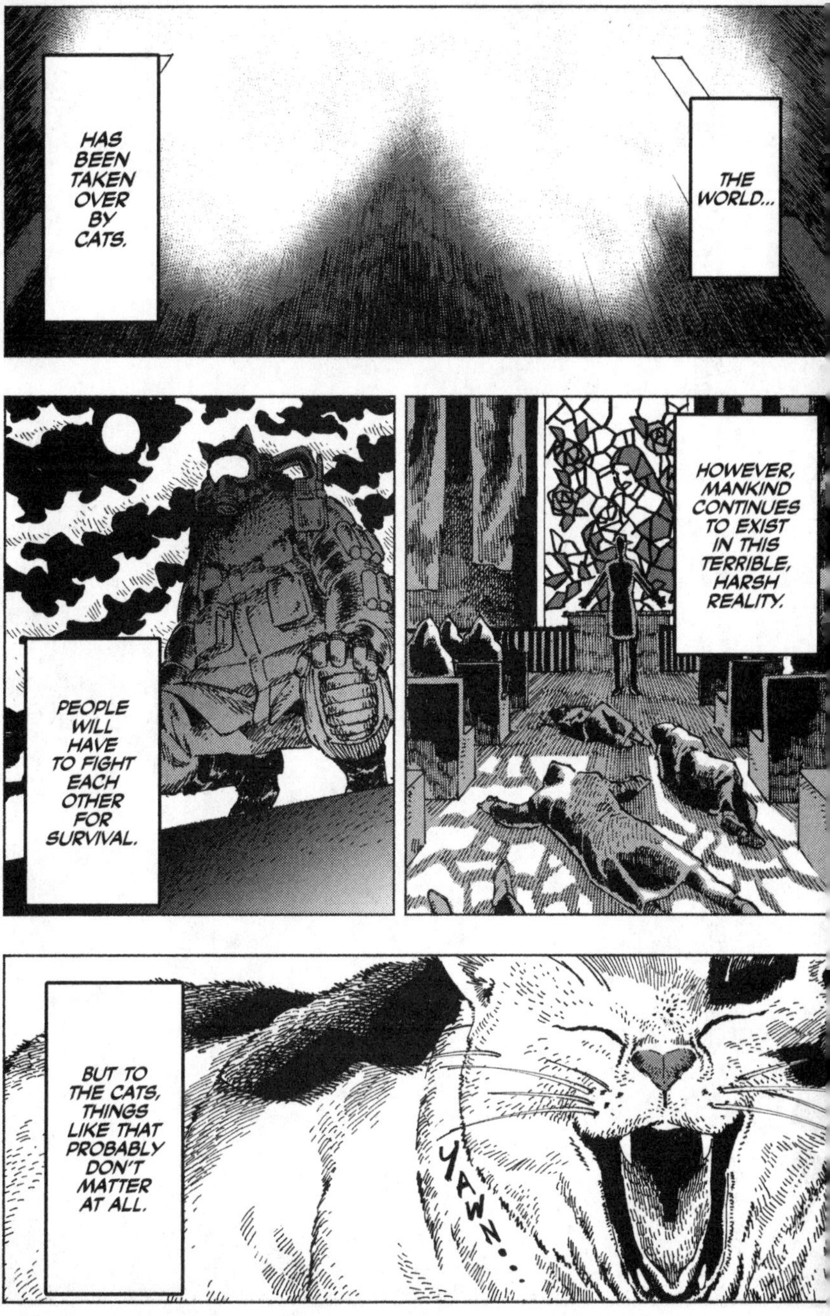
THE WORLD...
HAS BEEN TAKEN OVER BY CATS.
HOWEVER, MANKIND CONTINUES TO EXIST IN THIS TERRIBLE, HARSH REALITY.
PEOPLE WILL HAVE TO FIGHT EACH OTHER FOR SURVIVAL.
BUT TO THE CATS, THINGS LIKE THAT PROBABLY DON'T MATTER AT ALL.
YAWN...

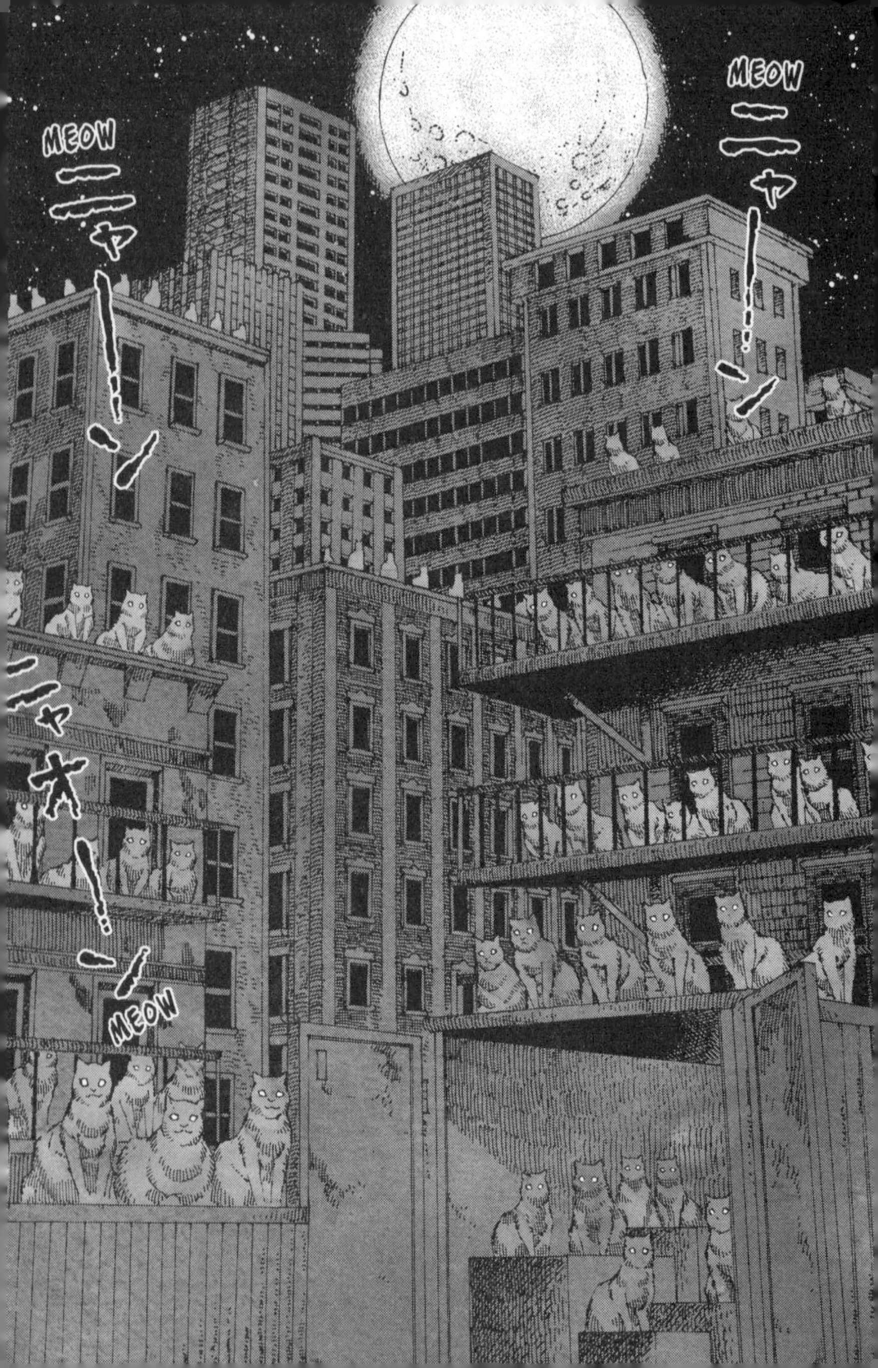
MEOW
ニャー!!
MEOW
ニャー!!
ニャオー!!
MEOW

Brown Tabby/Pheasant Cat

Named so because its coloring resembled that of the pheasant. It is said that the African wildcat, ancestor of the domestic house cat, had similar markings.

NYA IGHT
OF THE
LIVING
CAT 1

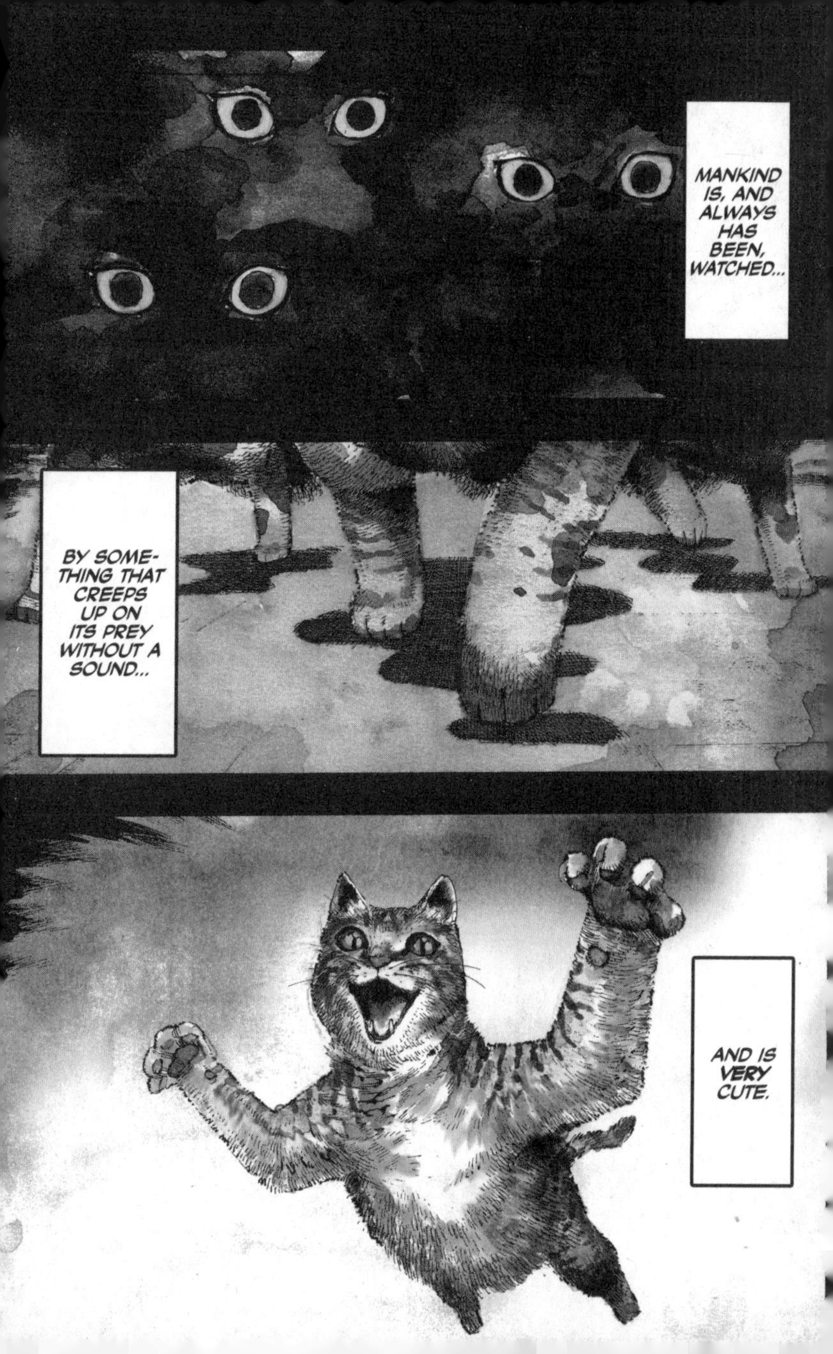
MANKIND IS, AND ALWAYS HAS BEEN, WATCHED...
BY SOMETHING THAT CREEPS UP ON ITS PREY WITHOUT A SOUND...
AND IS VERY CUTE.

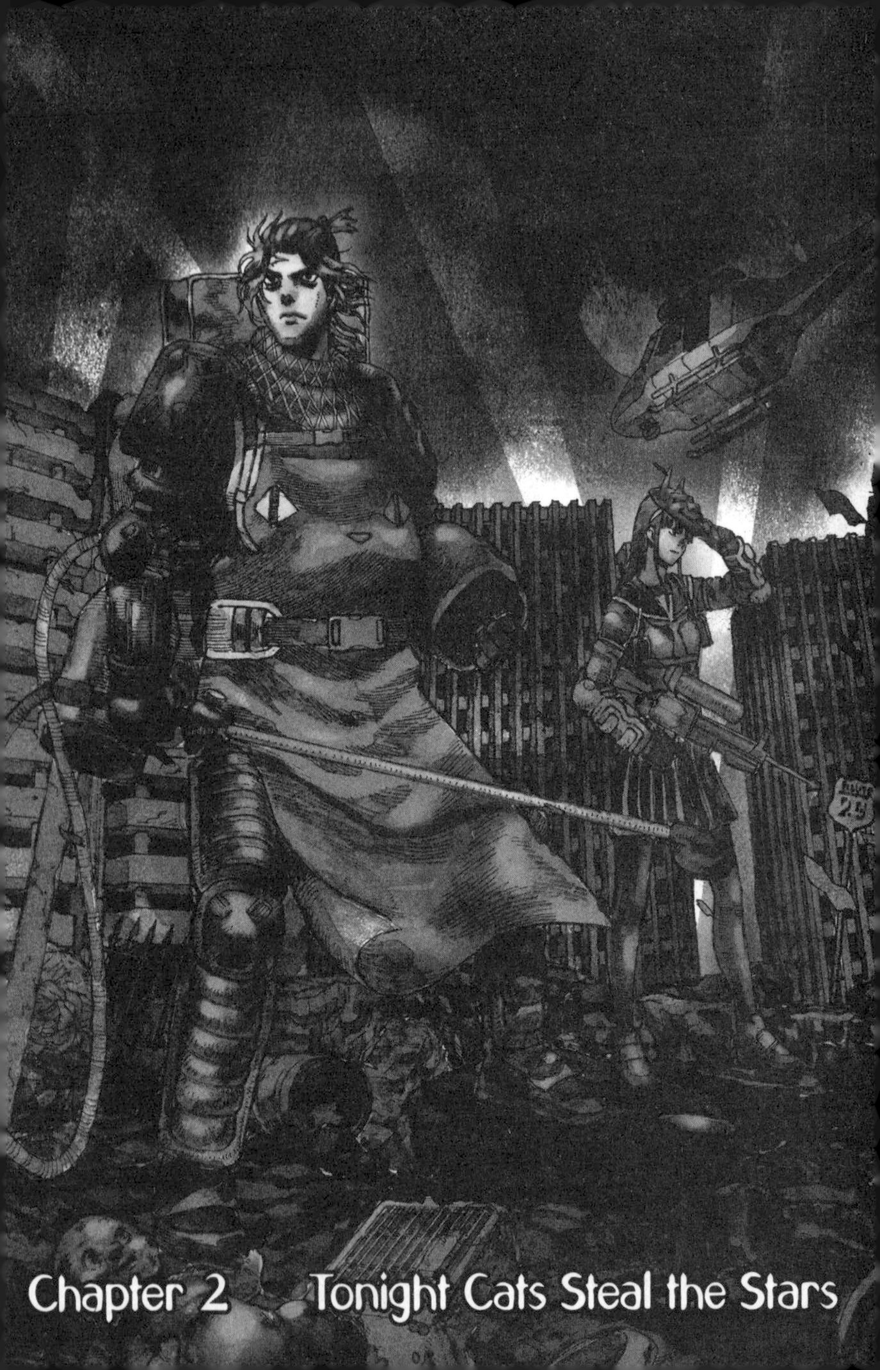

Chapter 2 Tonight Cats Steal the Stars

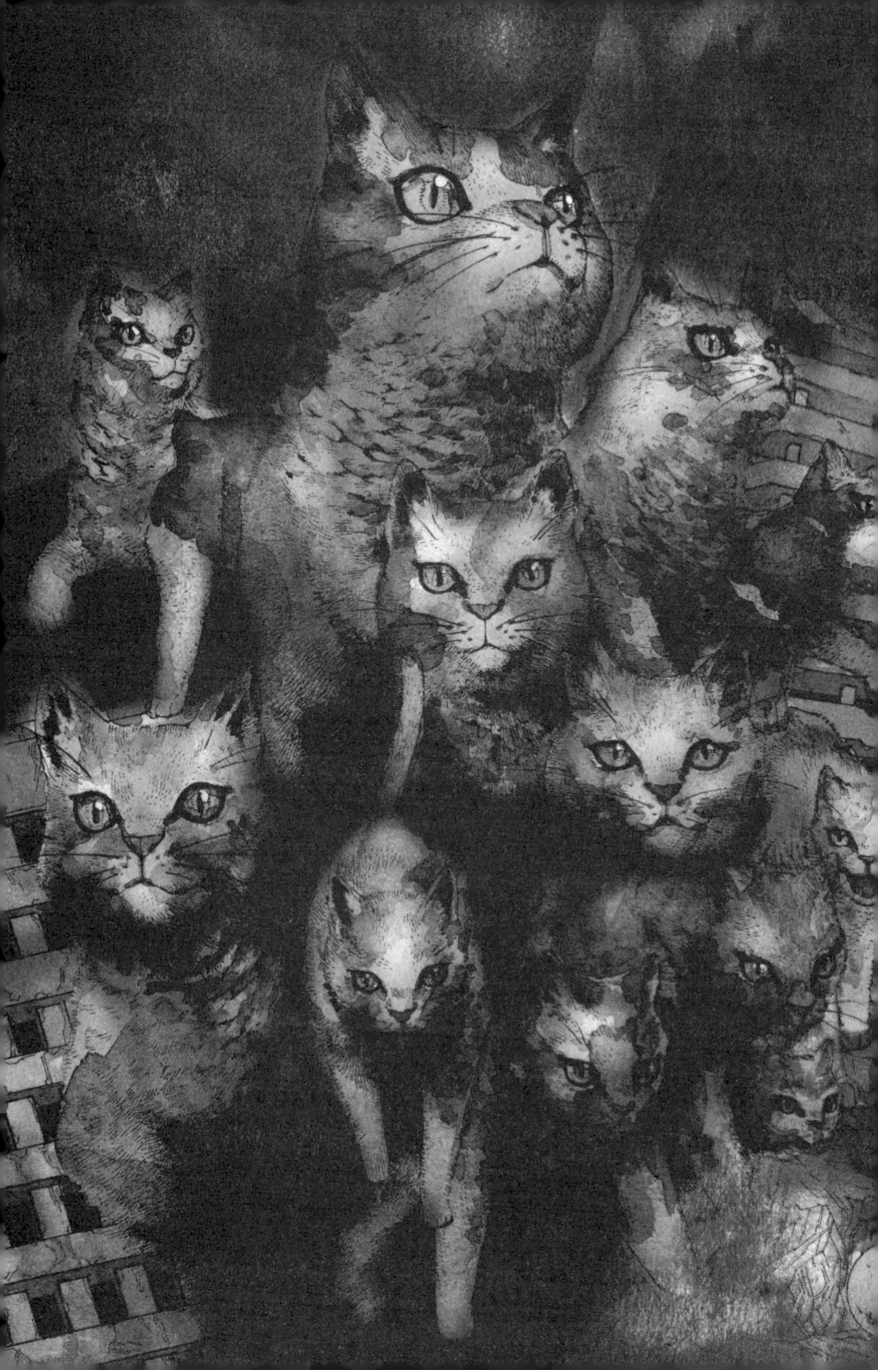

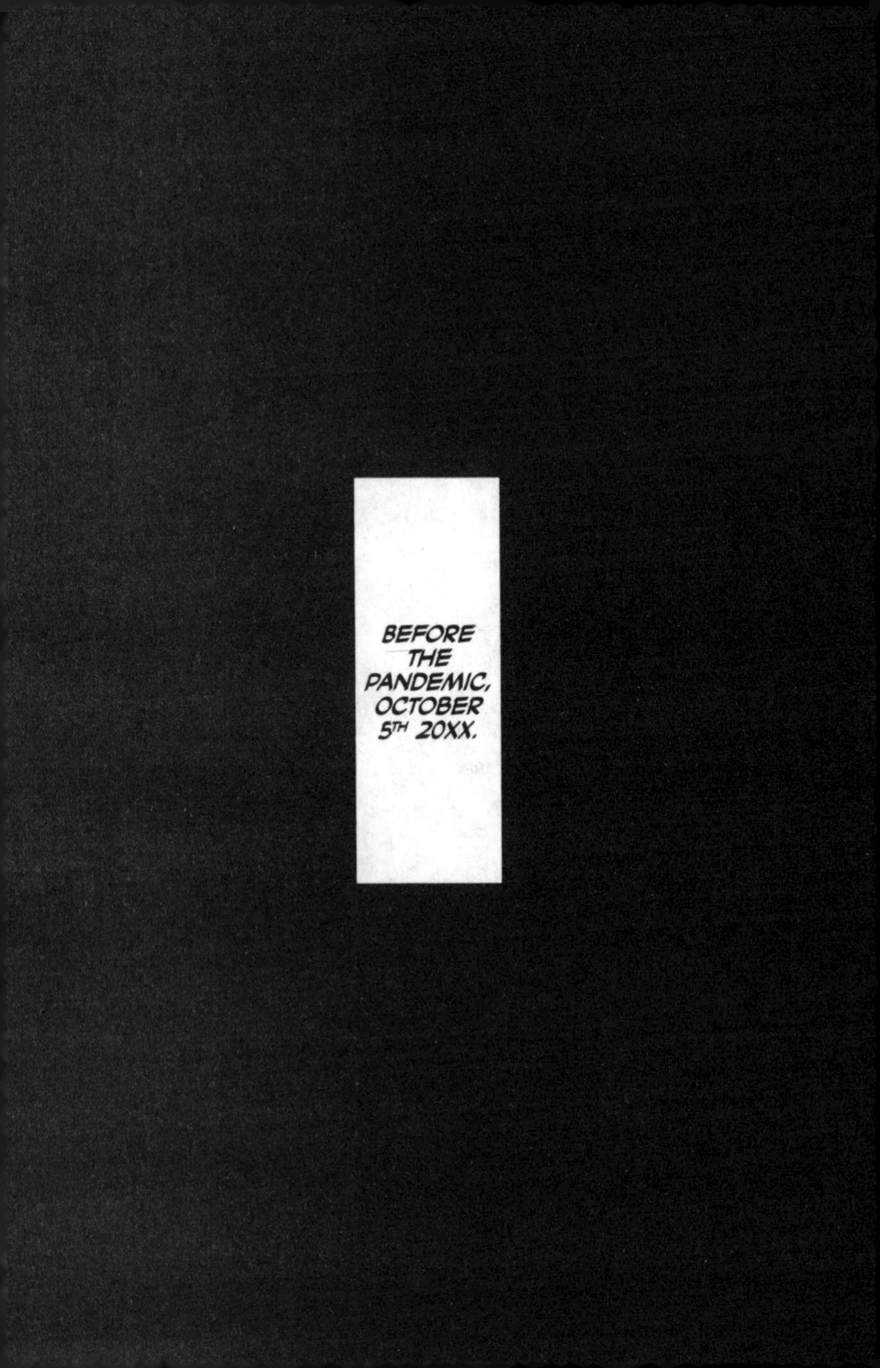
BEFORE THE PANDEMIC, OCTOBER 5TH 20XX.

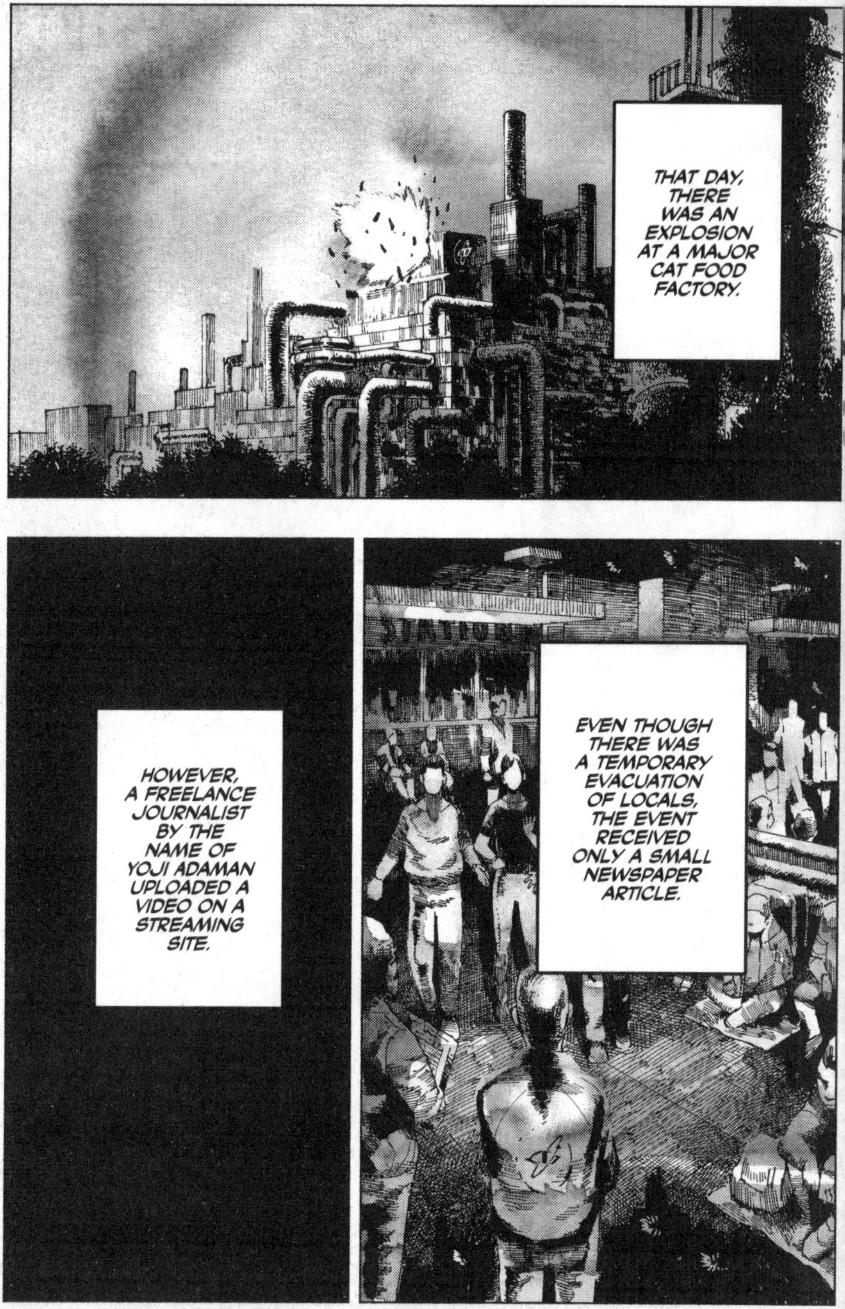
THAT DAY, THERE WAS AN EXPLOSION AT A MAJOR CAT FOOD FACTORY.
EVEN THOUGH THERE WAS A TEMPORARY EVACUATION OF LOCALS, THE EVENT RECEIVED ONLY A SMALL NEWSPAPER ARTICLE.
HOWEVER, A FREELANCE JOURNALIST BY THE NAME OF YOJI ADAMAN UPLOADED A VIDEO ON A STREAMING SITE.

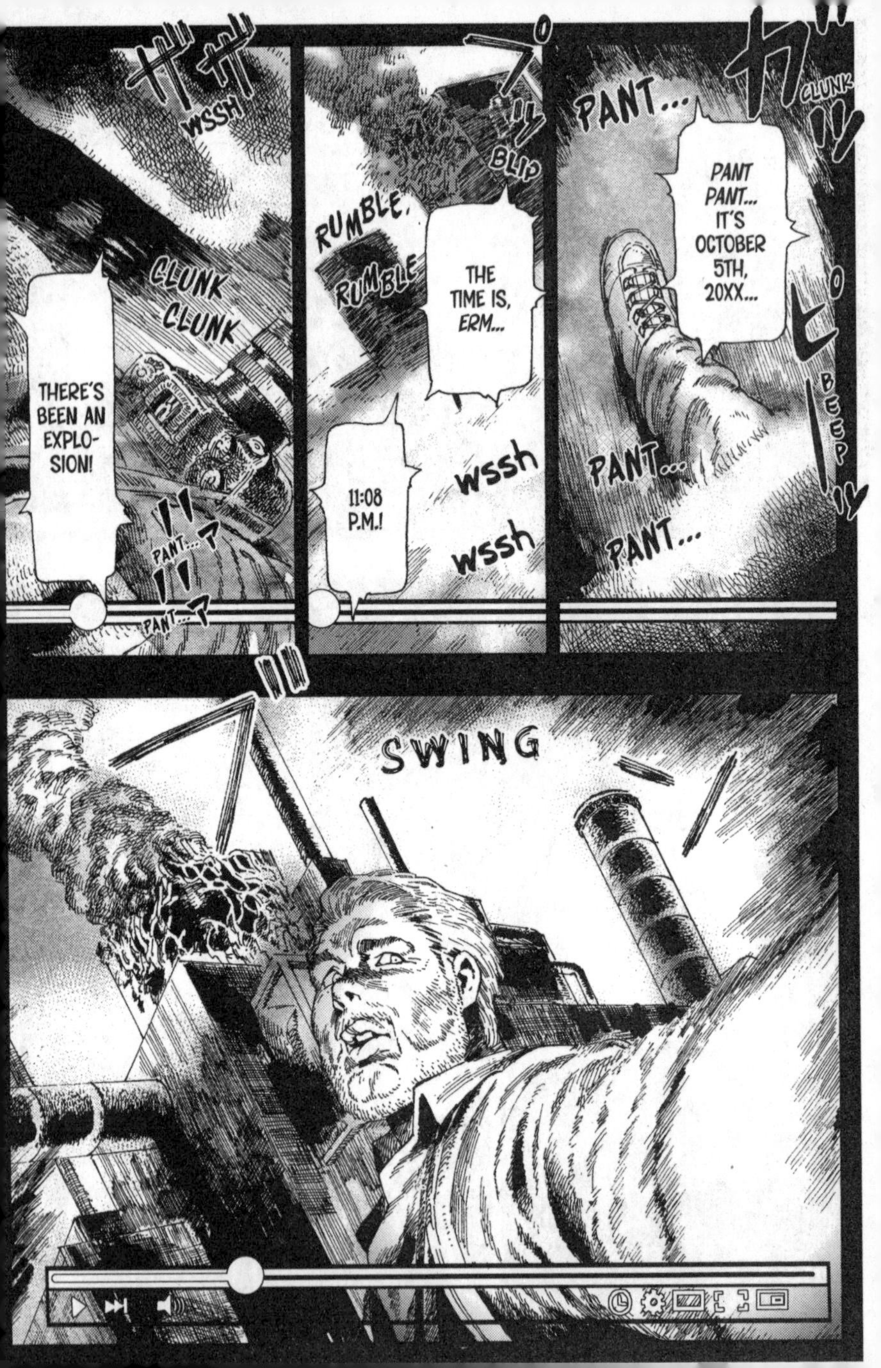
PANT...
CLUNK
PANT PANT... IT'S OCTOBER 5TH, 20XX...
BEEP
PANT...
PANT...
BLIP
RUMBLE, RUMBLE
THE TIME IS, ERM...
11:08 P.M.!
wssh
wssh
WSSH
CLUNK CLUNK
THERE'S BEEN AN EXPLO-SION!
PANT...
PANT...
SWING

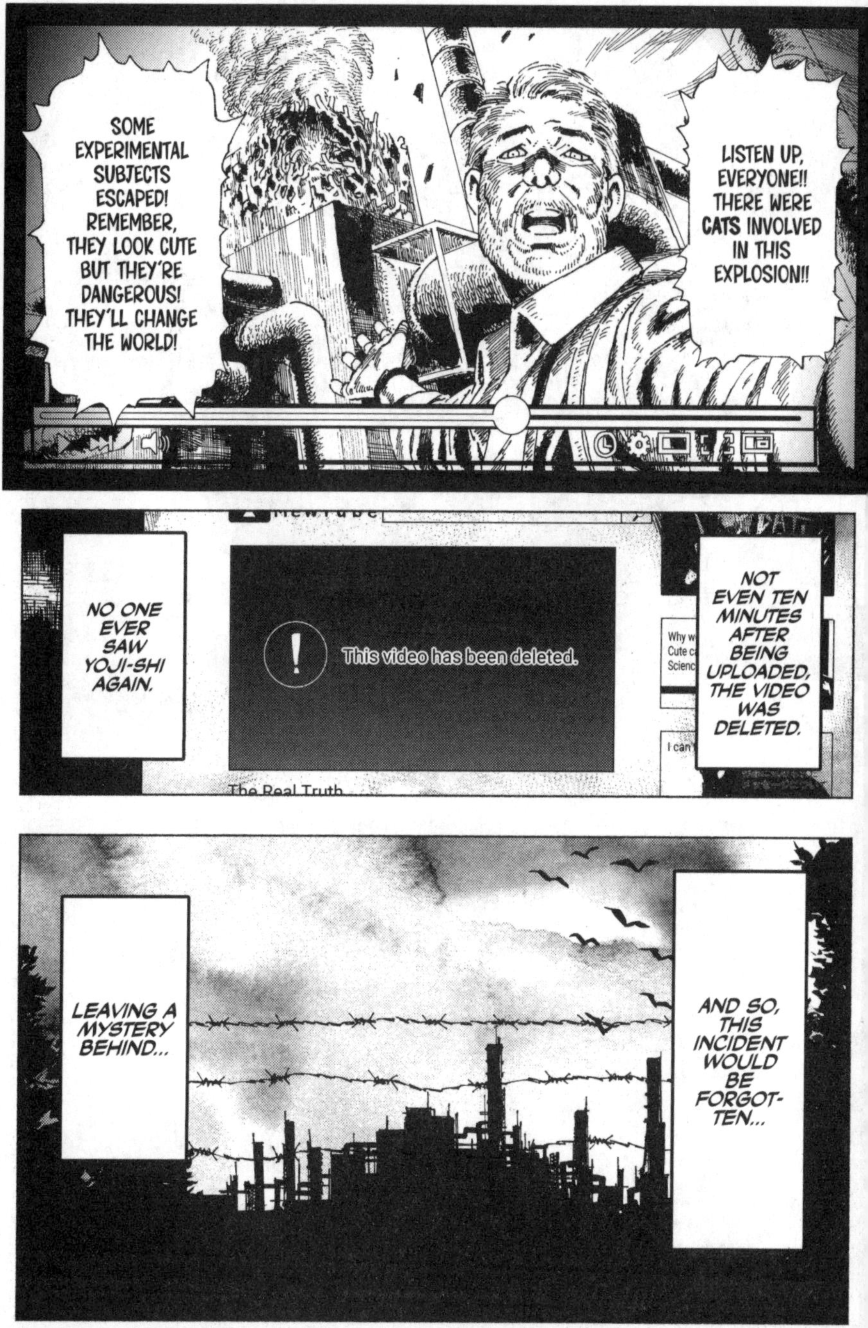
LISTEN UP, EVERYONE!! THERE WERE **CATS** INVOLVED IN THIS EXPLOSION!!
SOME EXPERIMENTAL SUBJECTS ESCAPED! REMEMBER, THEY LOOK CUTE BUT THEY'RE DANGEROUS! THEY'LL CHANGE THE WORLD!
NOT EVEN TEN MINUTES AFTER BEING UPLOADED, THE VIDEO WAS DELETED.
This video has been deleted.
The Real Truth
NO ONE EVER SAW YOJI-SHI AGAIN.
AND SO, THIS INCIDENT WOULD BE FORGOT-TEN...
LEAVING A MYSTERY BEHIND...

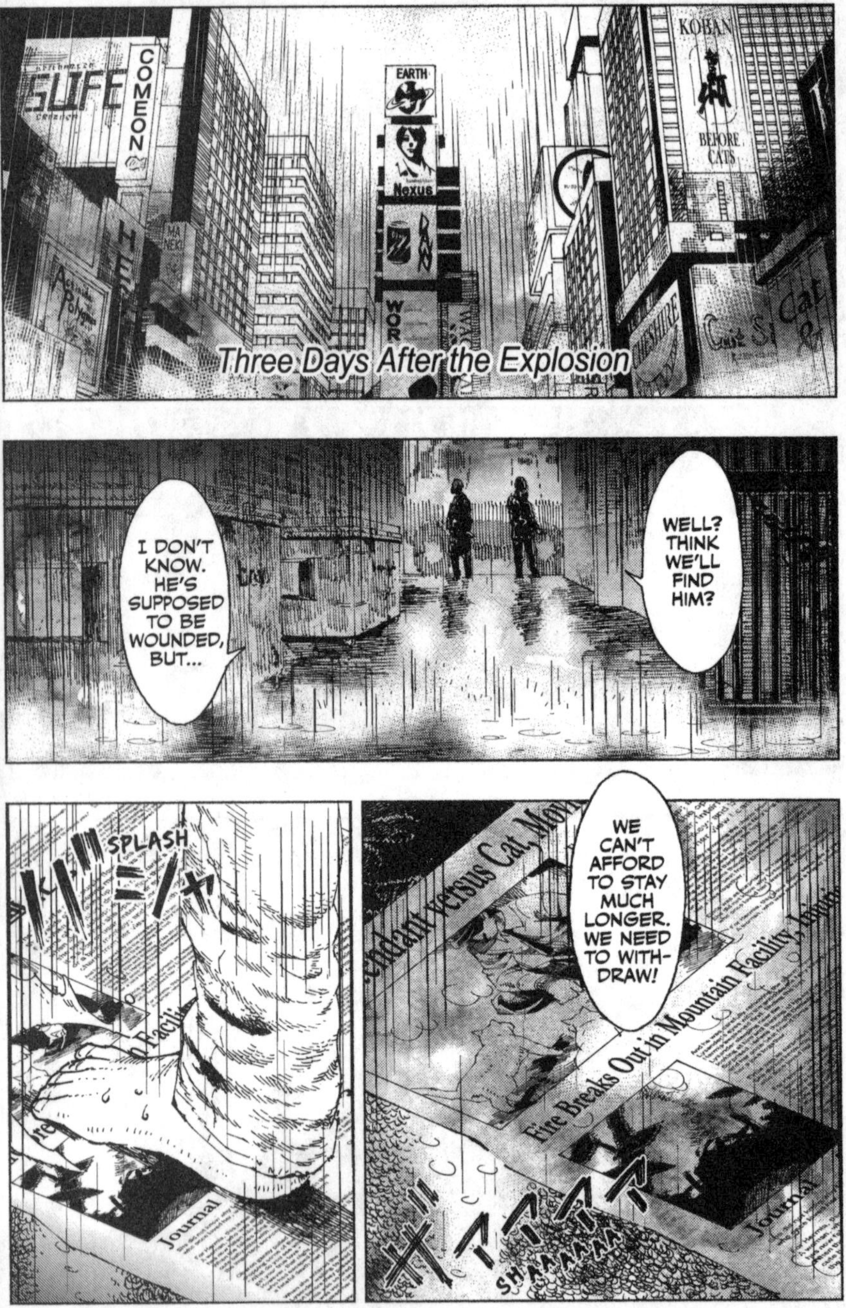
KOBAN
BEFORE CATS
EARTH
Nexus
COMEON
MA NEKI
CHESHIRE
Three Days After the Explosion
WELL? THINK WE'LL FIND HIM?
I DON'T KNOW. HE'S SUPPOSED TO BE WOUNDED, BUT...
WE CAN'T AFFORD TO STAY MUCH LONGER. WE NEED TO WITH-DRAW!
Fire Breaks Out in Mountain Facility, Injur
endant versus Cat, Mov
Journal
SHAAAAAA
SPLASH
Journal

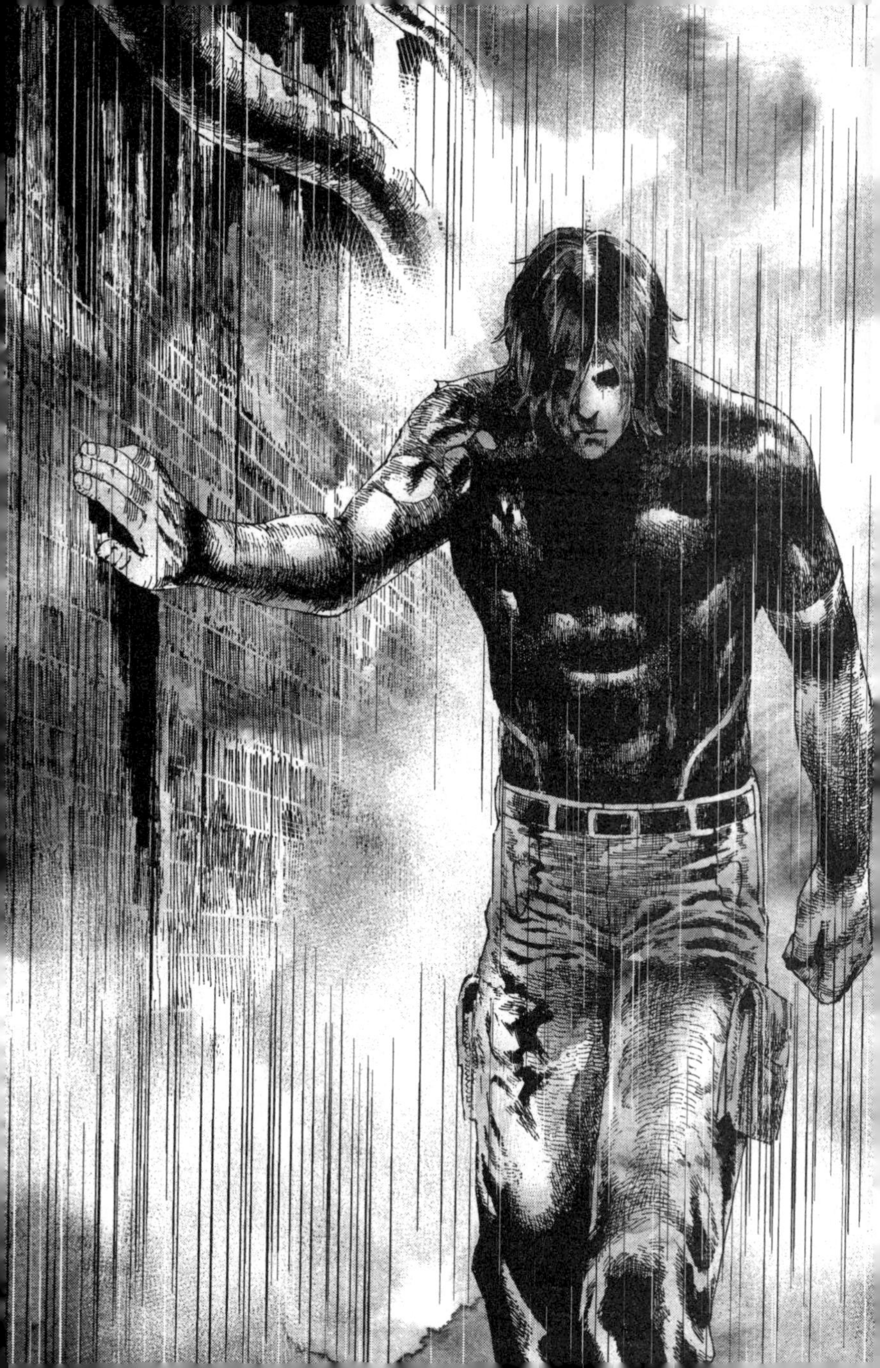

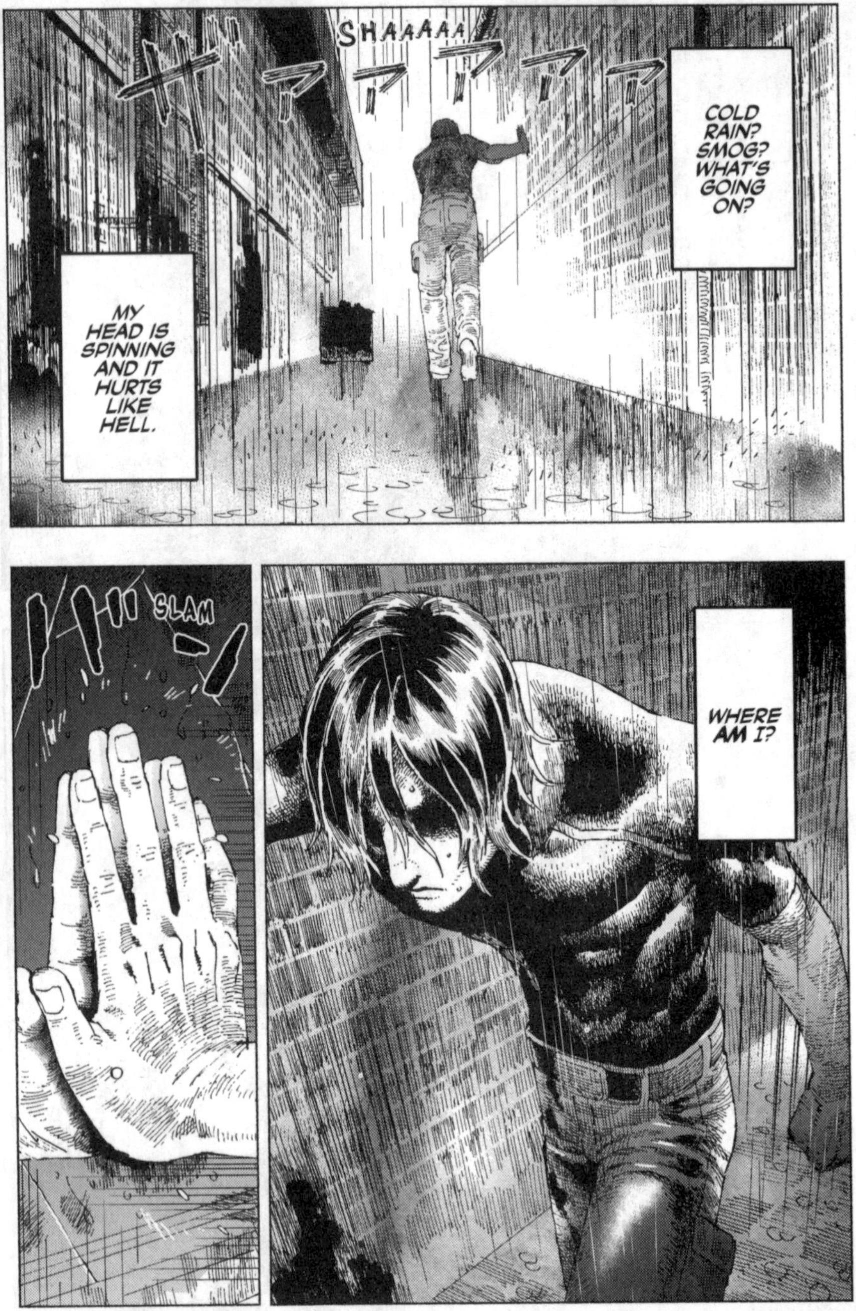
SHAAAAA
COLD RAIN? SMOG? WHAT'S GOING ON?
MY HEAD IS SPINNING AND IT HURTS LIKE HELL.
WHERE AM I?
SLAM

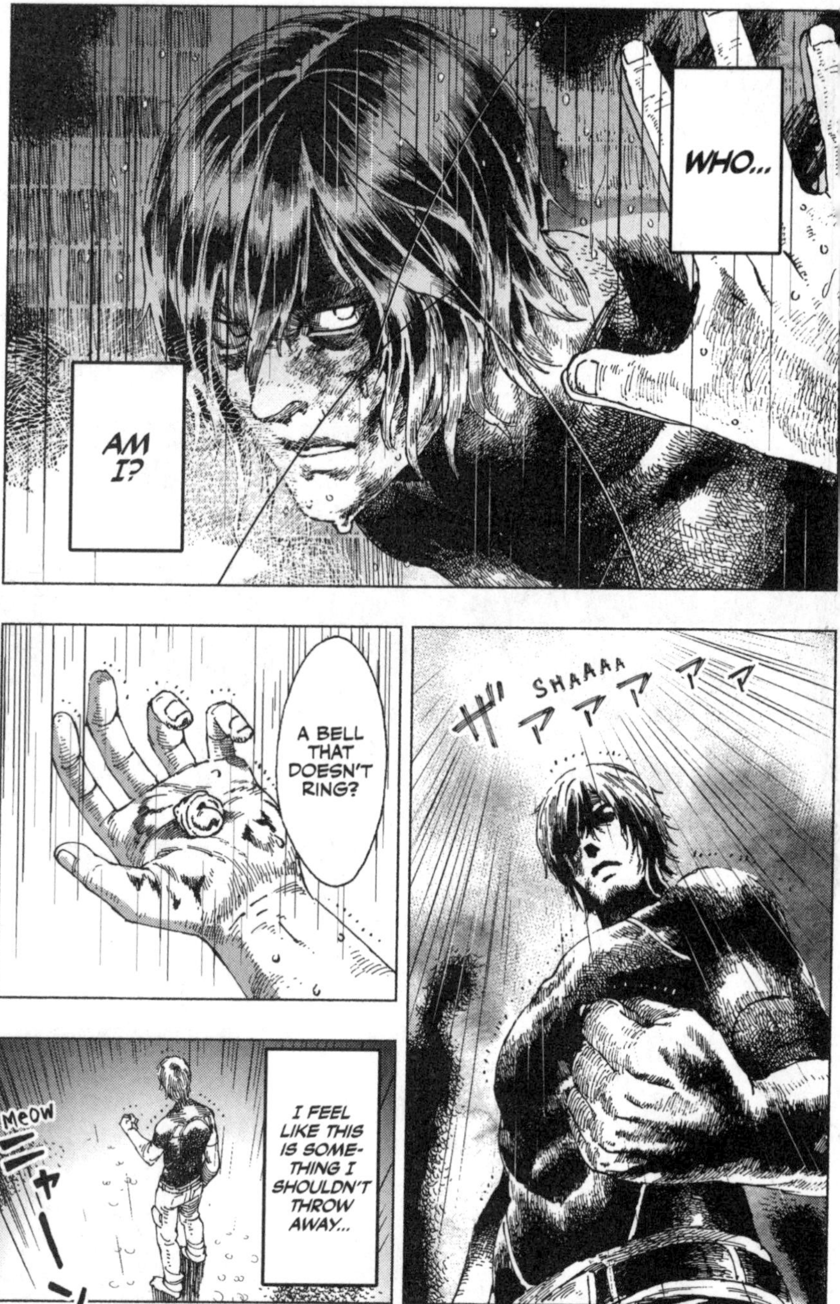
WHO...
AM I?
SHAAAA
A BELL THAT DOESN'T RING?
I FEEL LIKE THIS IS SOMETHING I SHOULDN'T THROW AWAY...
Meow

MYAU

MEOU

dust box

THOSE ARE...

FELIS CATUS, THE DOMESTIC CAT, BELOVED THE WORLD OVER. ONE OF THEIR ANCESTORS IS THE AFRICAN WILDCAT, WHICH THEY EVOLVED APART FROM 131,000 YEARS AGO. THEY BEGAN COEXISTENCE WITH HUMANS WHEN THEY CAME TO CATCH MICE IN OUR FOOD STORES. AS AMBUSH PREDATORS, THEY--

dust box

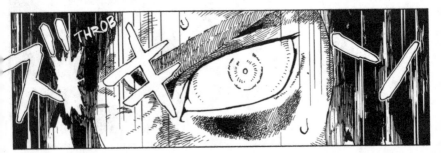

THROB

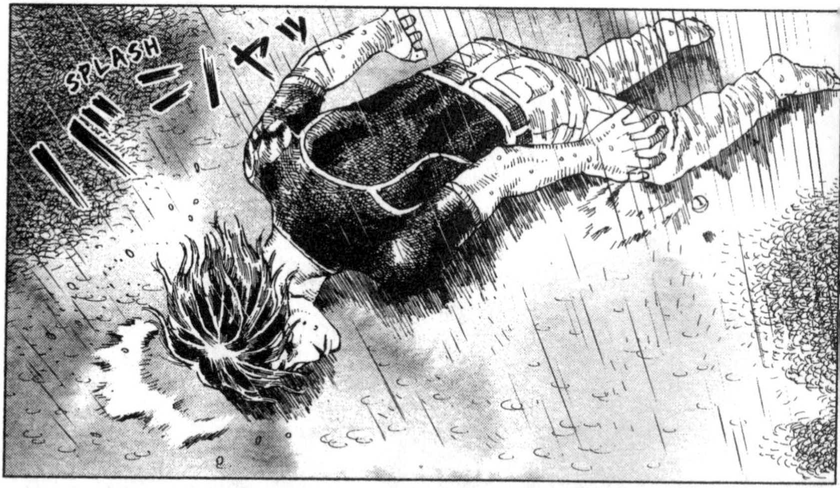
SPLASH
バシャッ

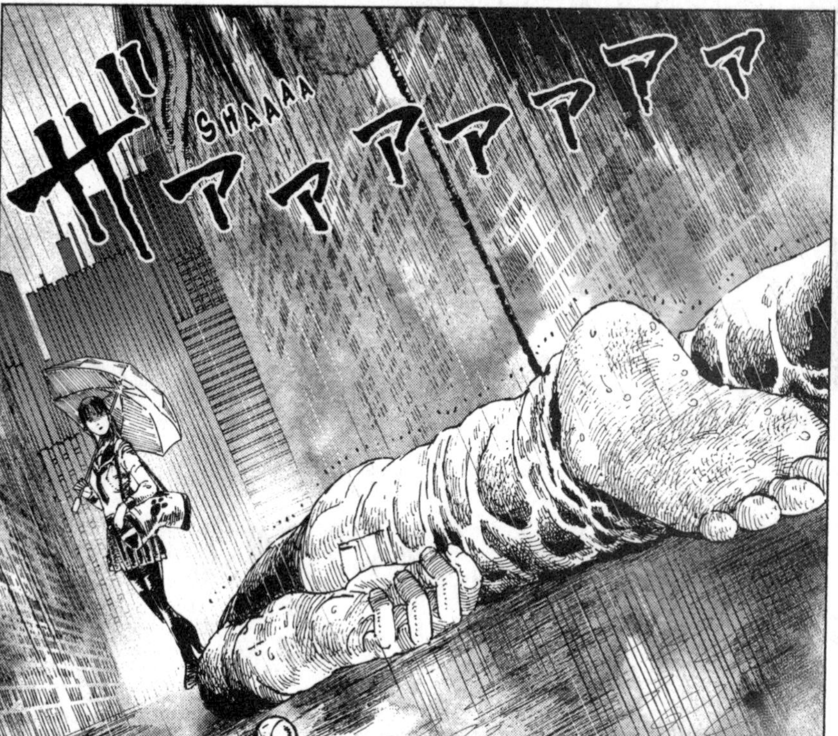
ザアアアアアアア
SHAAAA

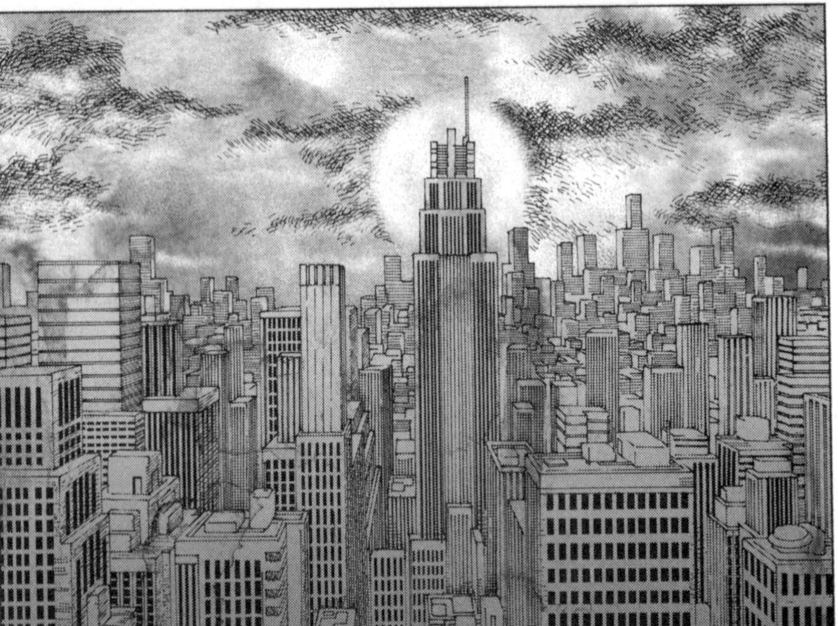

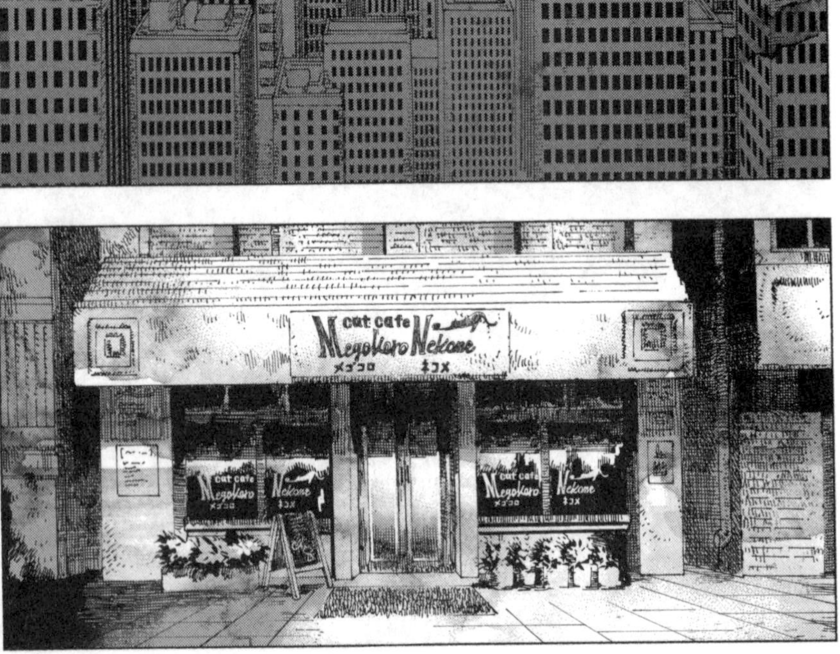
cat cafe
Megokoro Nekome
メゴコロ ネコメ

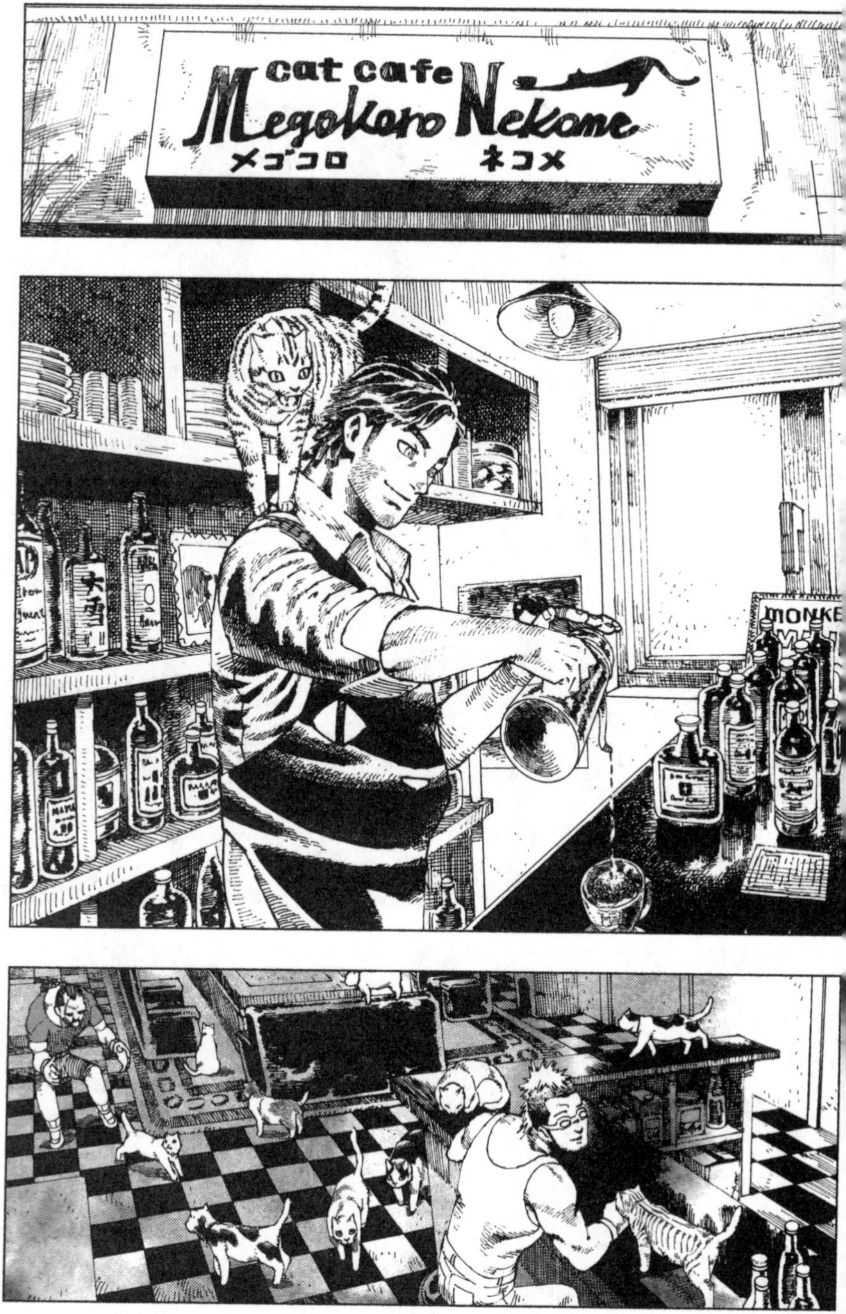
cat cafe
Megokoro Nekome
メゴコロ ネコメ

MEOW

SNUB

I'M SORRY, BUT CONSIDERING YOUR SIZE AND WEIGHT, THIS IS ALL YOU NEED.

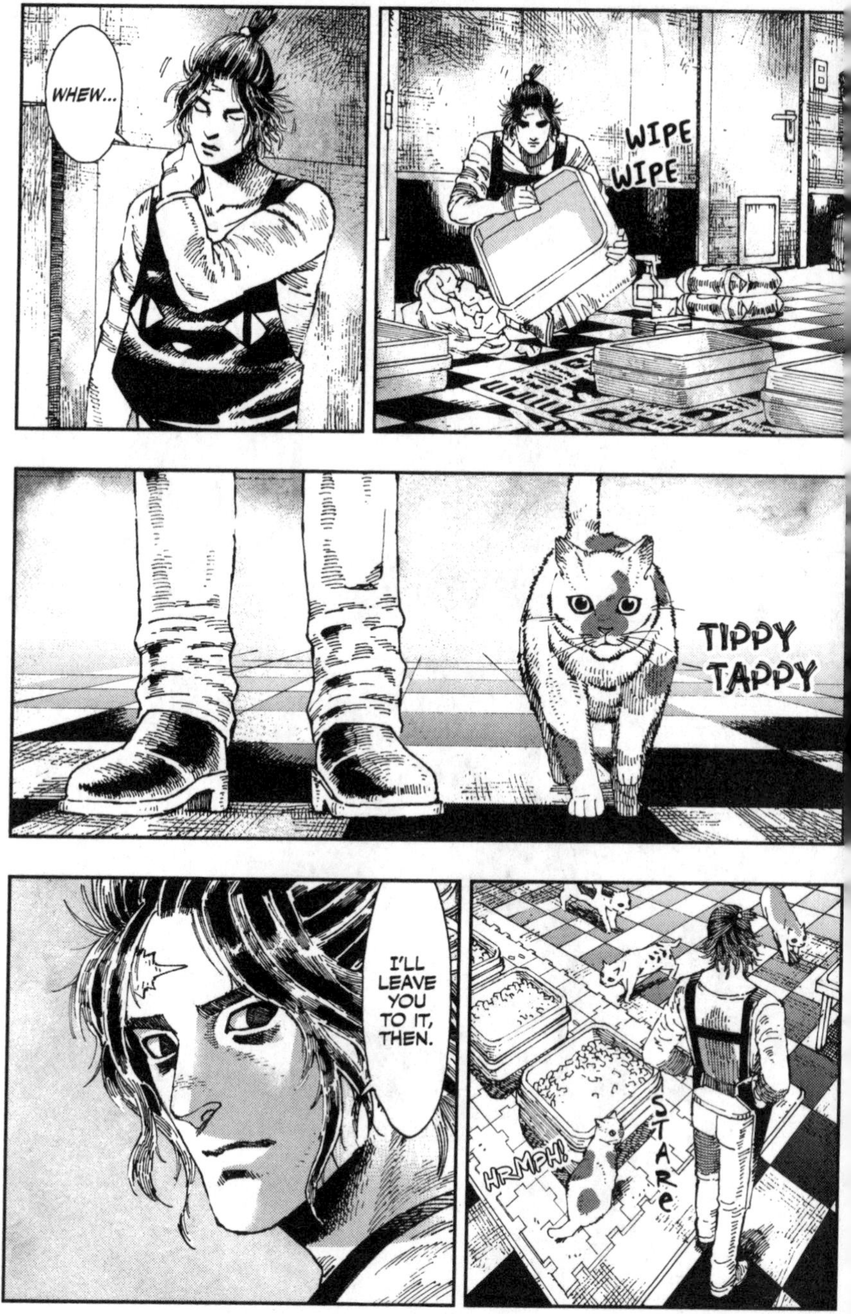
WIPE
WIPE
WHEW...
TIPPY
TAPPY
STARE
HRMPH!
I'LL LEAVE YOU TO IT, THEN.

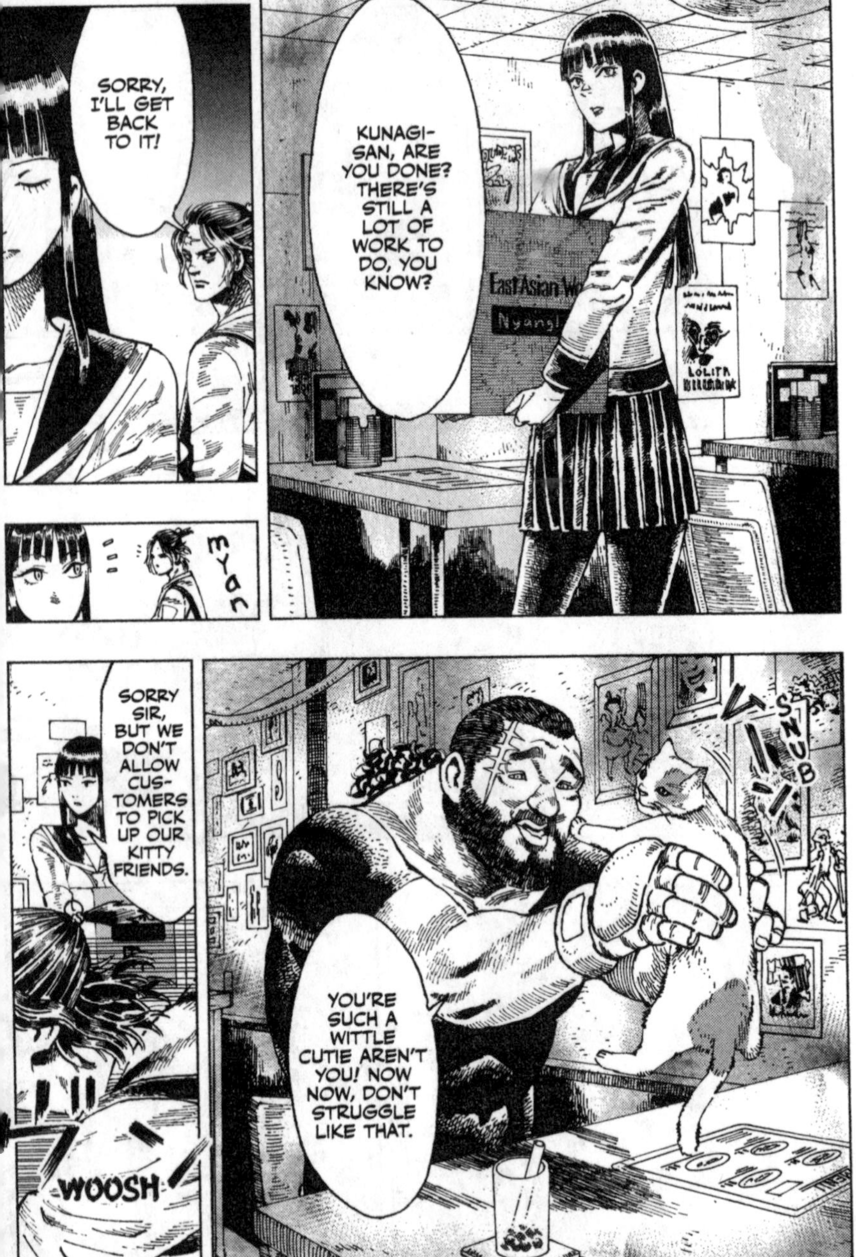
KUNAGI-SAN, ARE YOU DONE? THERE'S STILL A LOT OF WORK TO DO, YOU KNOW?
East Asian Wo
Nyang!
LOLITA
SORRY, I'LL GET BACK TO IT!
myan
YOU'RE SUCH A WITTLE CUTIE AREN'T YOU! NOW NOW, DON'T STRUGGLE LIKE THAT.
SNUB
SORRY SIR, BUT WE DON'T ALLOW CUS-TOMERS TO PICK UP OUR KITTY FRIENDS.
WOOSH

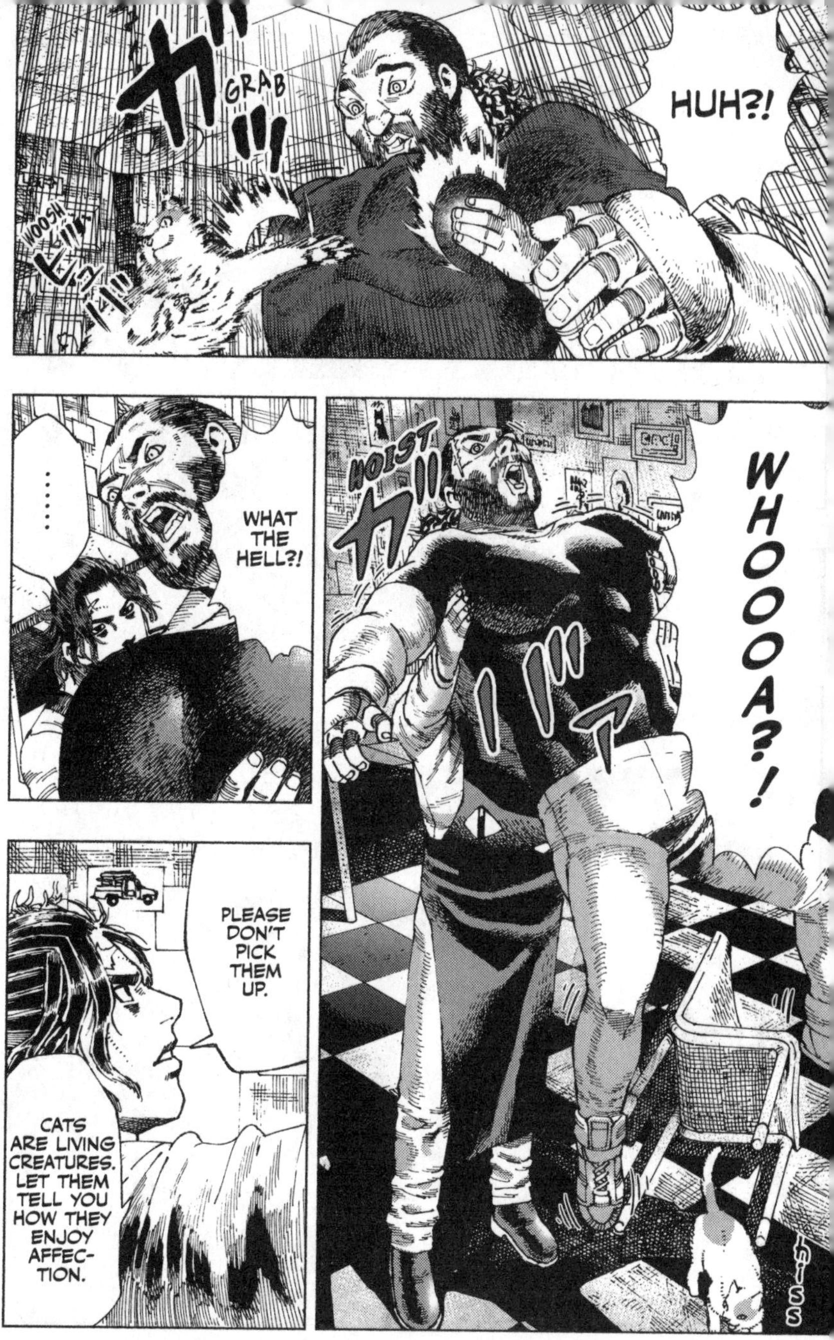
HUH?!
GRAB
WOOSH
WHOOOOA?!
HOIST
hiss
WHAT THE HELL?!
……
PLEASE DON'T PICK THEM UP.
CATS ARE LIVING CREATURES. LET THEM TELL YOU HOW THEY ENJOY AFFEC-TION.

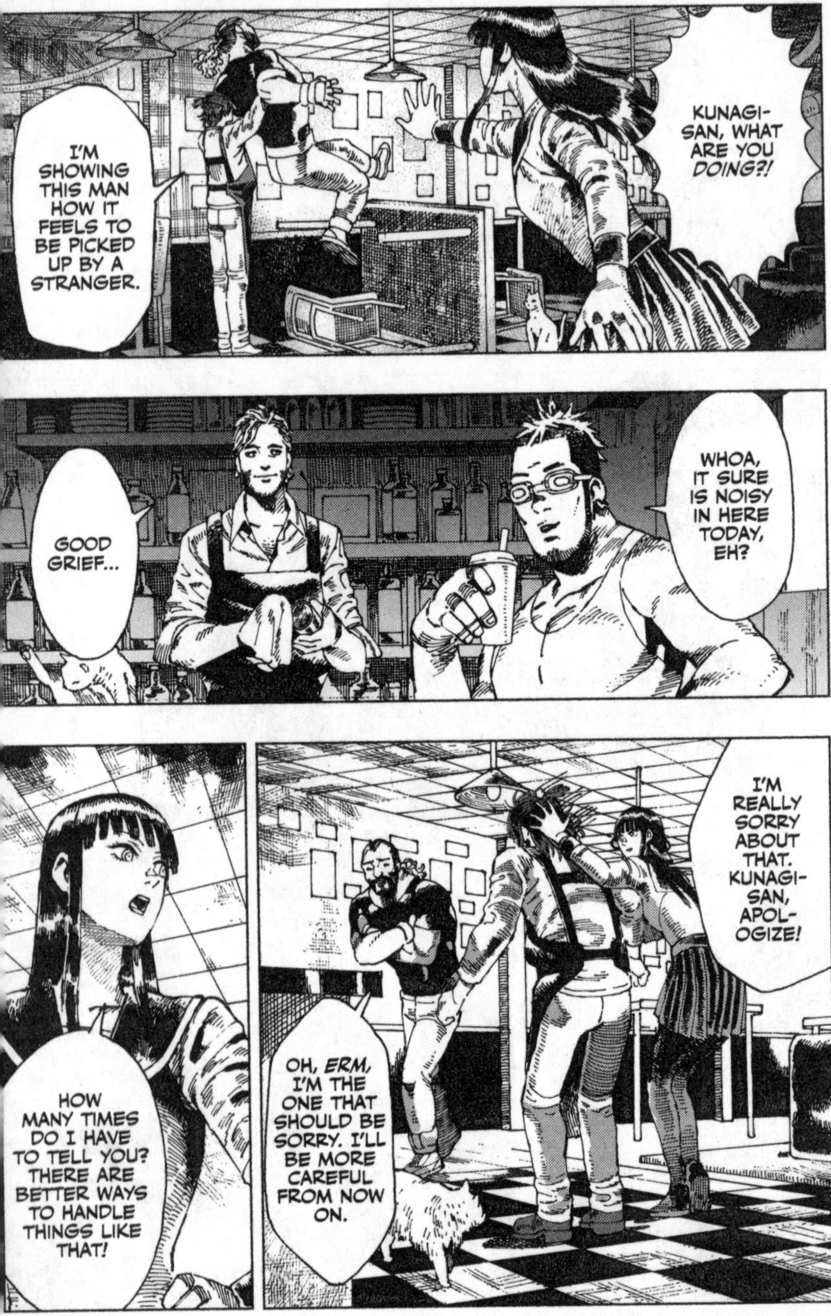
KUNAGI-SAN, WHAT ARE YOU *DOING?!*
I'M SHOWING THIS MAN HOW IT FEELS TO BE PICKED UP BY A STRANGER.
WHOA, IT SURE IS NOISY IN HERE TODAY, EH?
GOOD GRIEF...
I'M REALLY SORRY ABOUT THAT. KUNAGI-SAN, APOLOGIZE!
OH, *ERM,* I'M THE ONE THAT SHOULD BE SORRY. I'LL BE MORE CAREFUL FROM NOW ON.
HOW MANY TIMES DO I HAVE TO TELL YOU? THERE ARE BETTER WAYS TO HANDLE THINGS LIKE THAT!

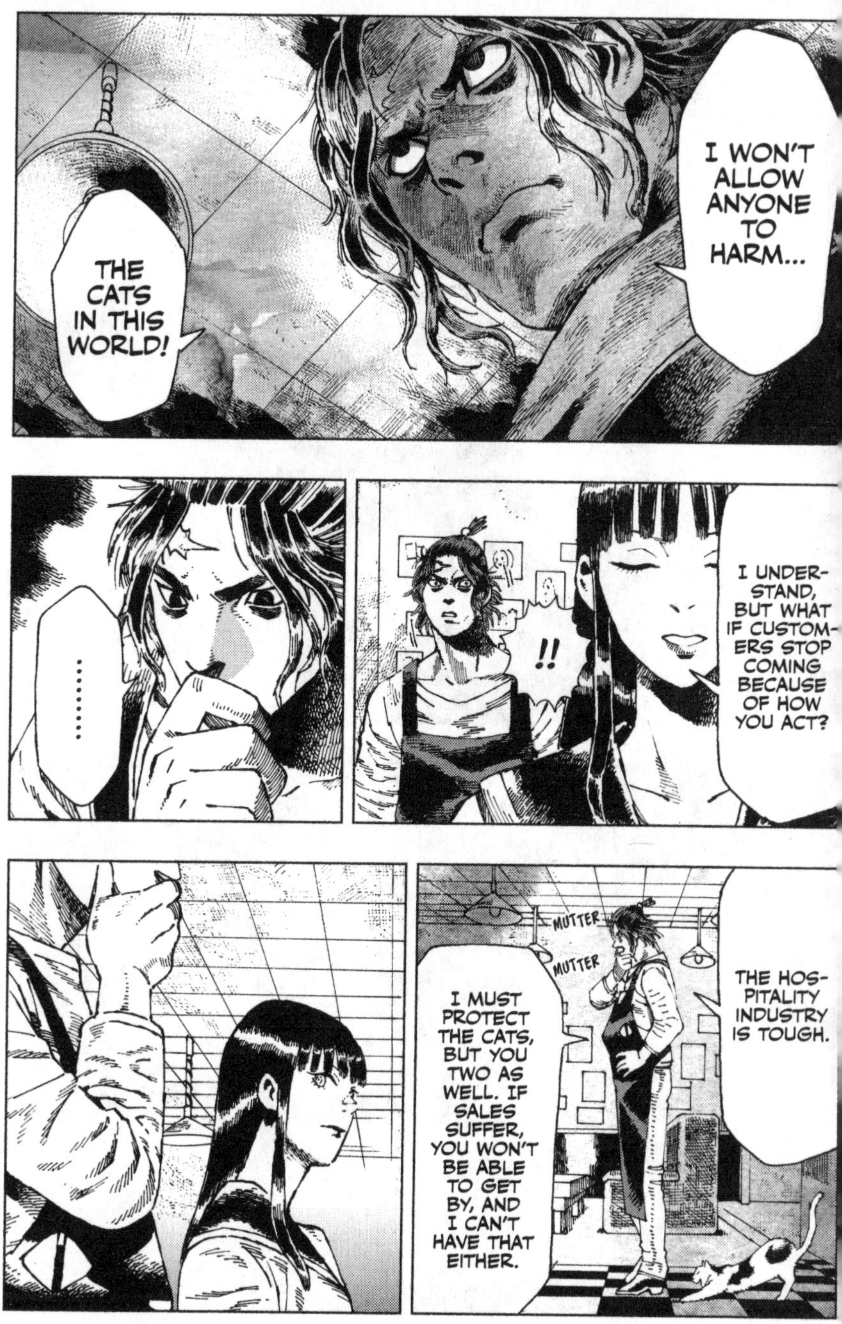
I WON'T ALLOW ANYONE TO HARM...
THE CATS IN THIS WORLD!
I UNDERSTAND, BUT WHAT IF CUSTOMERS STOP COMING BECAUSE OF HOW YOU ACT?
!!
......
THE HOSPITALITY INDUSTRY IS TOUGH.
MUTTER
MUTTER
I MUST PROTECT THE CATS, BUT YOU TWO AS WELL. IF SALES SUFFER, YOU WON'T BE ABLE TO GET BY, AND I CAN'T HAVE THAT EITHER.

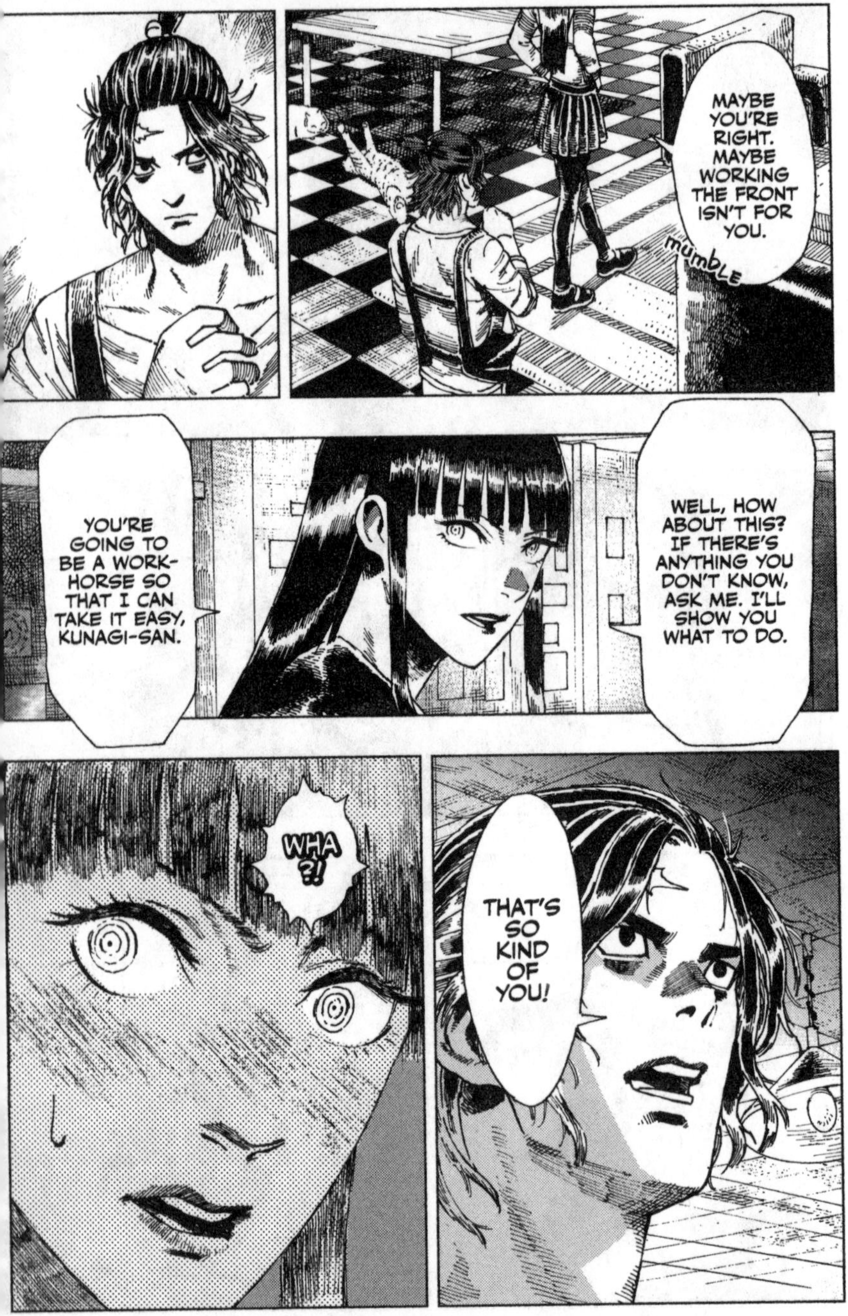
MAYBE YOU'RE RIGHT. MAYBE WORKING THE FRONT ISN'T FOR YOU.
mumble
WELL, HOW ABOUT THIS? IF THERE'S ANYTHING YOU DON'T KNOW, ASK ME. I'LL SHOW YOU WHAT TO DO.
YOU'RE GOING TO BE A WORK-HORSE SO THAT I CAN TAKE IT EASY, KUNAGI-SAN.
THAT'S SO KIND OF YOU!
WHA ?!

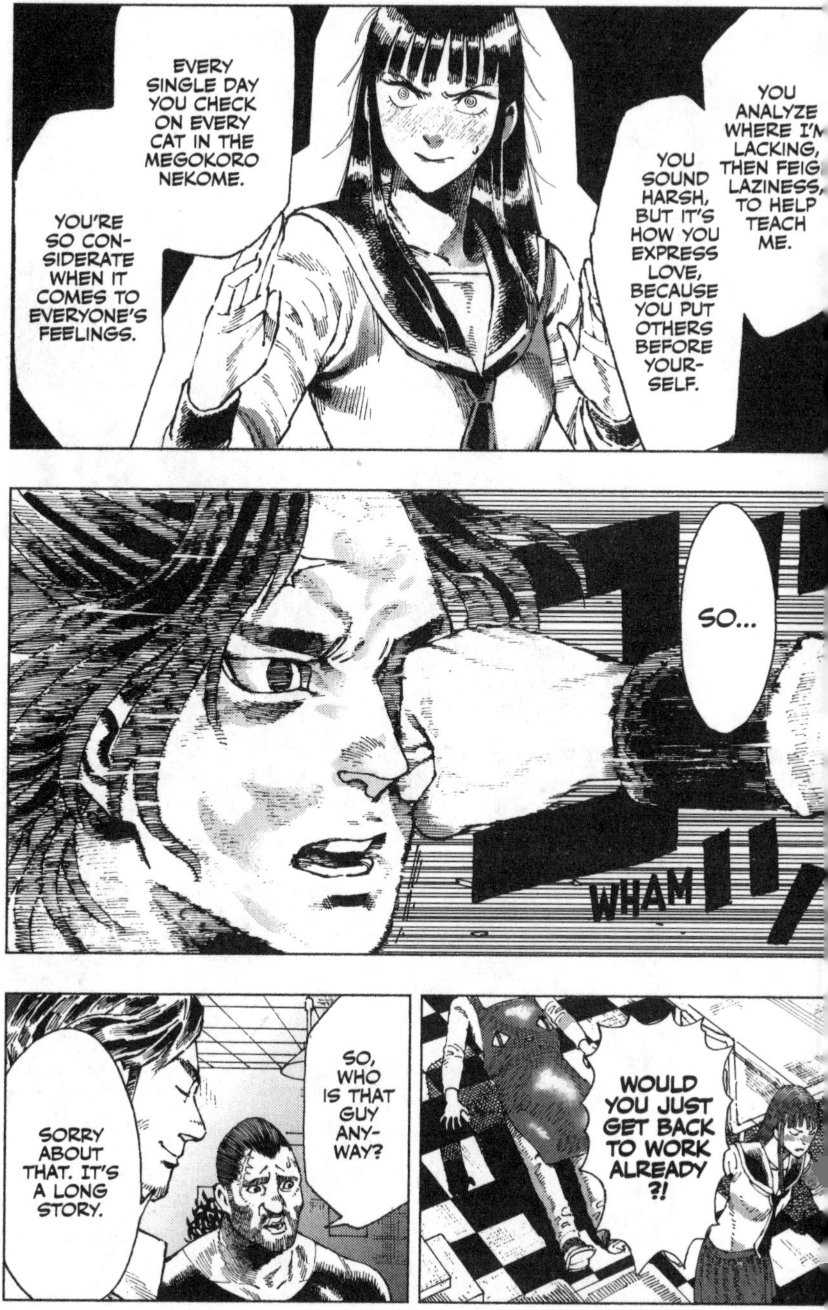
YOU ANALYZE WHERE I'M LACKING, THEN FEIG LAZINESS, TO HELP TEACH ME.
YOU SOUND HARSH, BUT IT'S HOW YOU EXPRESS LOVE, BECAUSE YOU PUT OTHERS BEFORE YOURSELF.
EVERY SINGLE DAY YOU CHECK ON EVERY CAT IN THE MEGOKORO NEKOME.
YOU'RE SO CONSIDERATE WHEN IT COMES TO EVERYONE'S FEELINGS.
SO...
WHAM
WOULD YOU JUST GET BACK TO WORK ALREADY?!
SO, WHO IS THAT GUY ANYWAY?
SORRY ABOUT THAT. IT'S A LONG STORY.

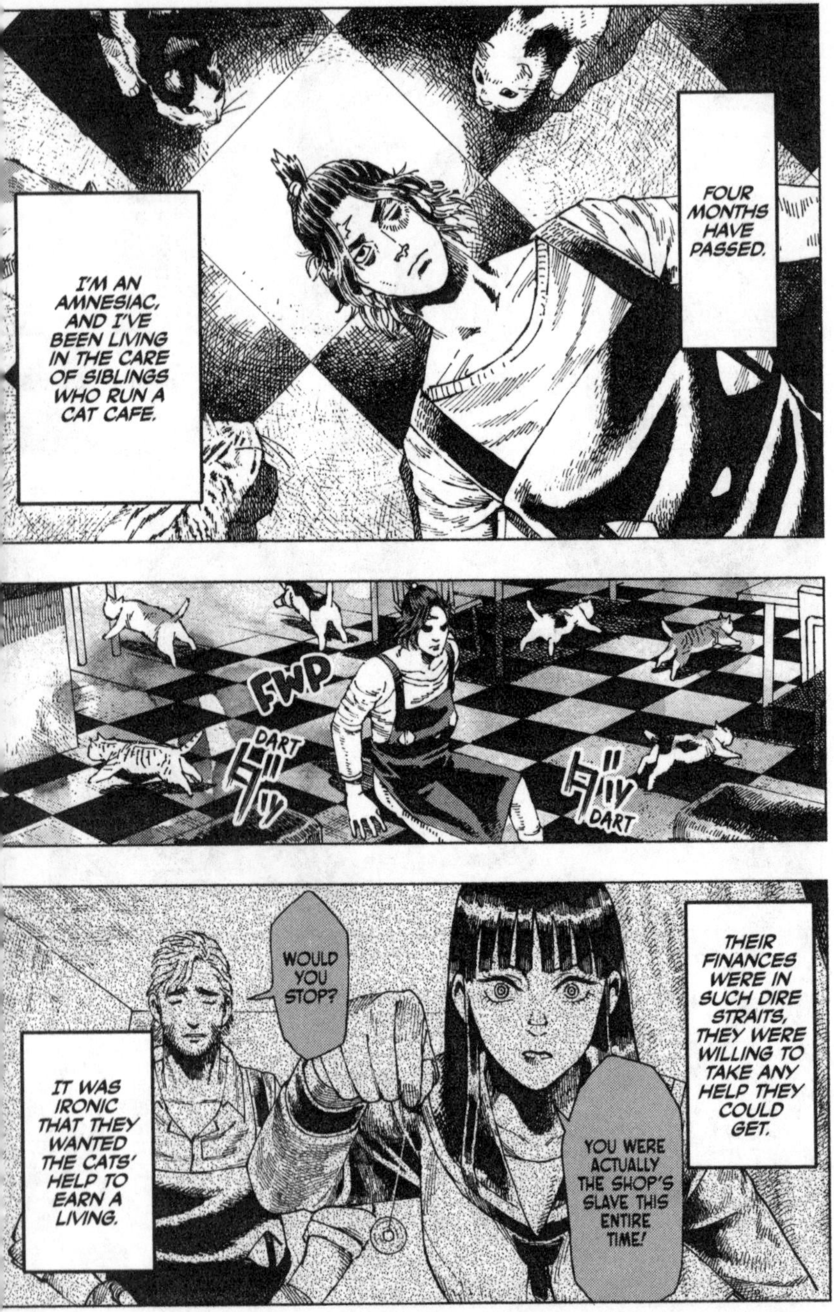
FOUR MONTHS HAVE PASSED.
I'M AN AMNESIAC, AND I'VE BEEN LIVING IN THE CARE OF SIBLINGS WHO RUN A CAT CAFE.
FWP
DART
DART
THEIR FINANCES WERE IN SUCH DIRE STRAITS, THEY WERE WILLING TO TAKE ANY HELP THEY COULD GET.
WOULD YOU STOP?
YOU WERE ACTUALLY THE SHOP'S SLAVE THIS ENTIRE TIME!
IT WAS IRONIC THAT THEY WANTED THE CATS' HELP TO EARN A LIVING.

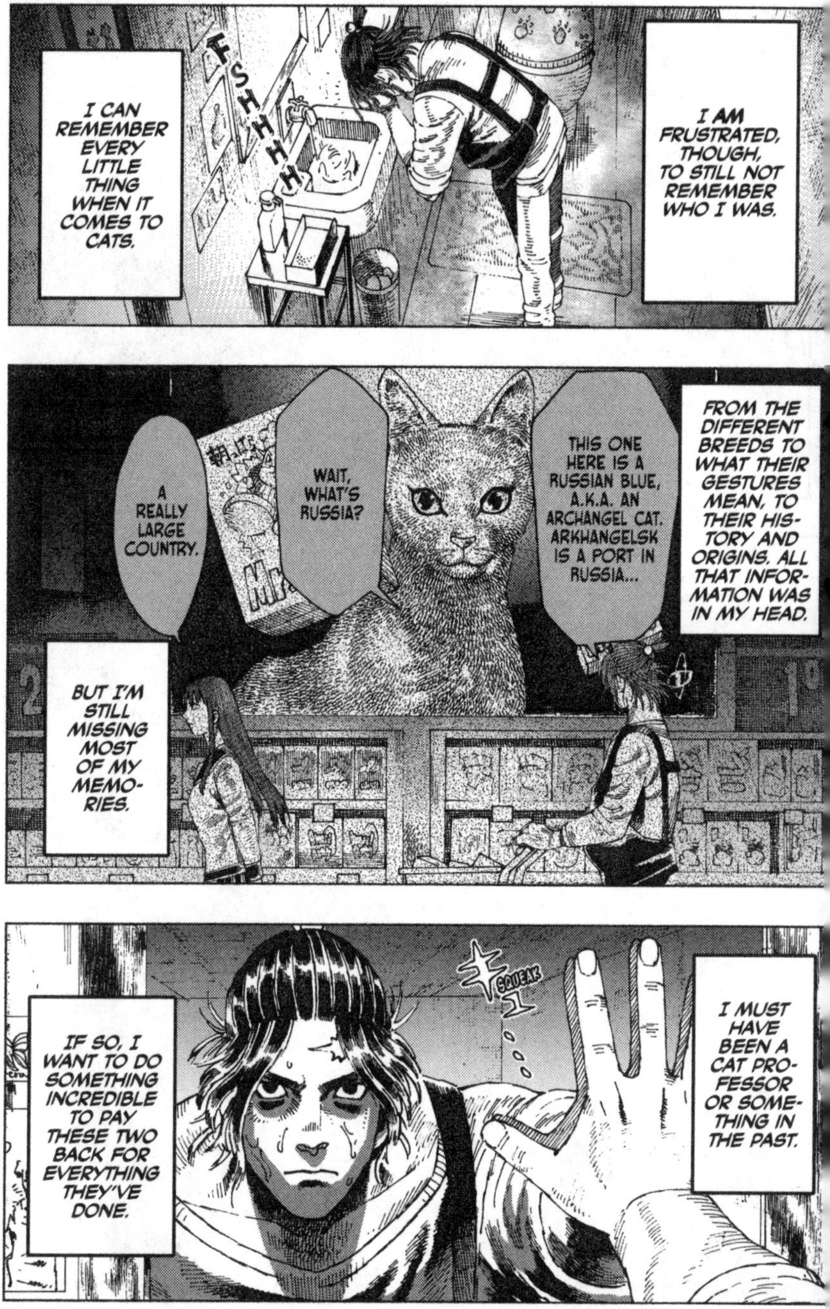
I AM FRUSTRATED, THOUGH, TO STILL NOT REMEMBER WHO I WAS.
FSHHHH
I CAN REMEMBER EVERY LITTLE THING WHEN IT COMES TO CATS.
FROM THE DIFFERENT BREEDS TO WHAT THEIR GESTURES MEAN, TO THEIR HISTORY AND ORIGINS. ALL THAT INFORMATION WAS IN MY HEAD.
THIS ONE HERE IS A RUSSIAN BLUE, A.K.A. AN ARCHANGEL CAT. ARKHANGELSK IS A PORT IN RUSSIA...
WAIT, WHAT'S RUSSIA?
A REALLY LARGE COUNTRY.
BUT I'M STILL MISSING MOST OF MY MEMORIES.
I MUST HAVE BEEN A CAT PROFESSOR OR SOMETHING IN THE PAST.
SQUEAK
IF SO, I WANT TO DO SOMETHING INCREDIBLE TO PAY THESE TWO BACK FOR EVERYTHING THEY'VE DONE.

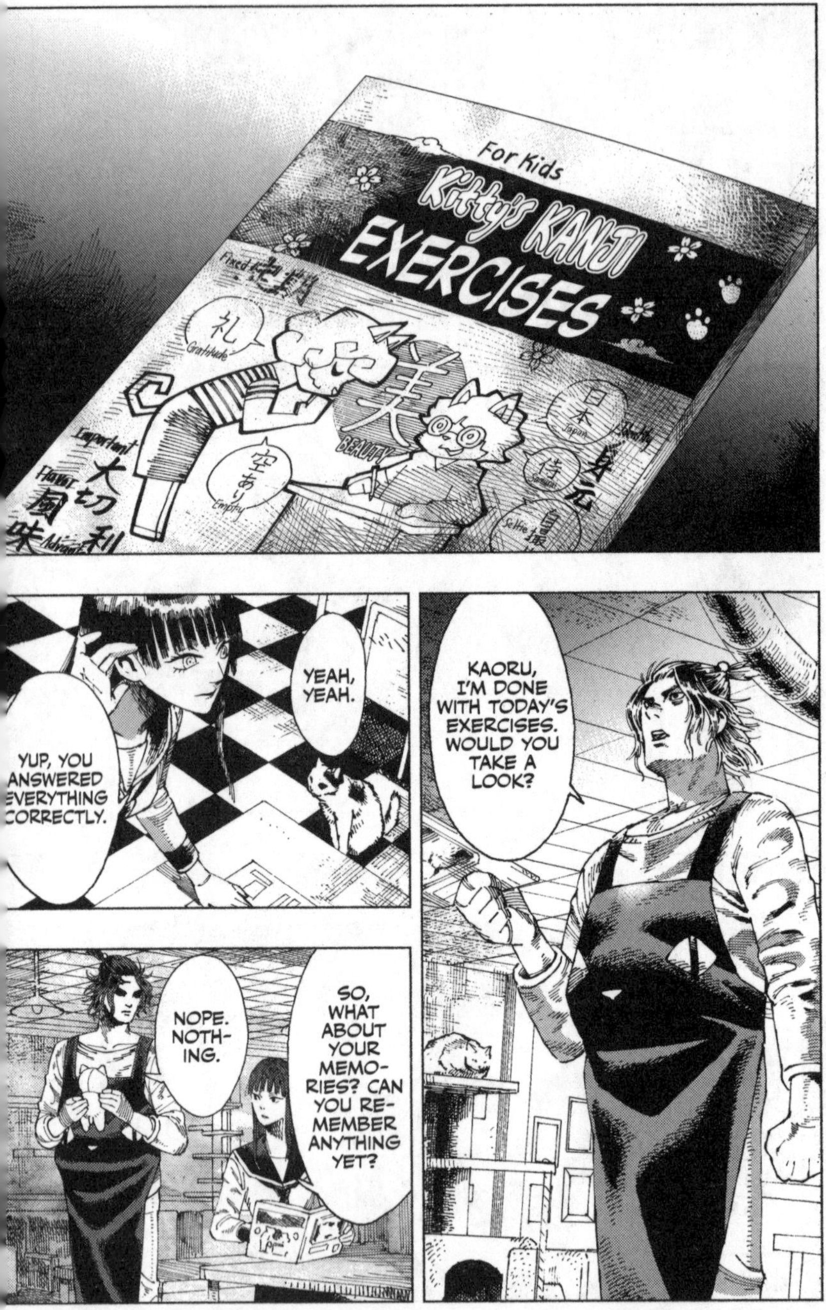
For Kids
Kitty's KANJI EXERCISES
Fixed
礼
Gratitude
美
BEAUTY
空あり
Empty
日本
Japan
侍
Samurai
自撮
Selfie
Important 大切
Flavor
KAORU, I'M DONE WITH TODAY'S EXERCISES. WOULD YOU TAKE A LOOK?
YEAH, YEAH.
YUP, YOU ANSWERED EVERYTHING CORRECTLY.
SO, WHAT ABOUT YOUR MEMO-RIES? CAN YOU RE-MEMBER ANYTHING YET?
NOPE. NOTH-ING.

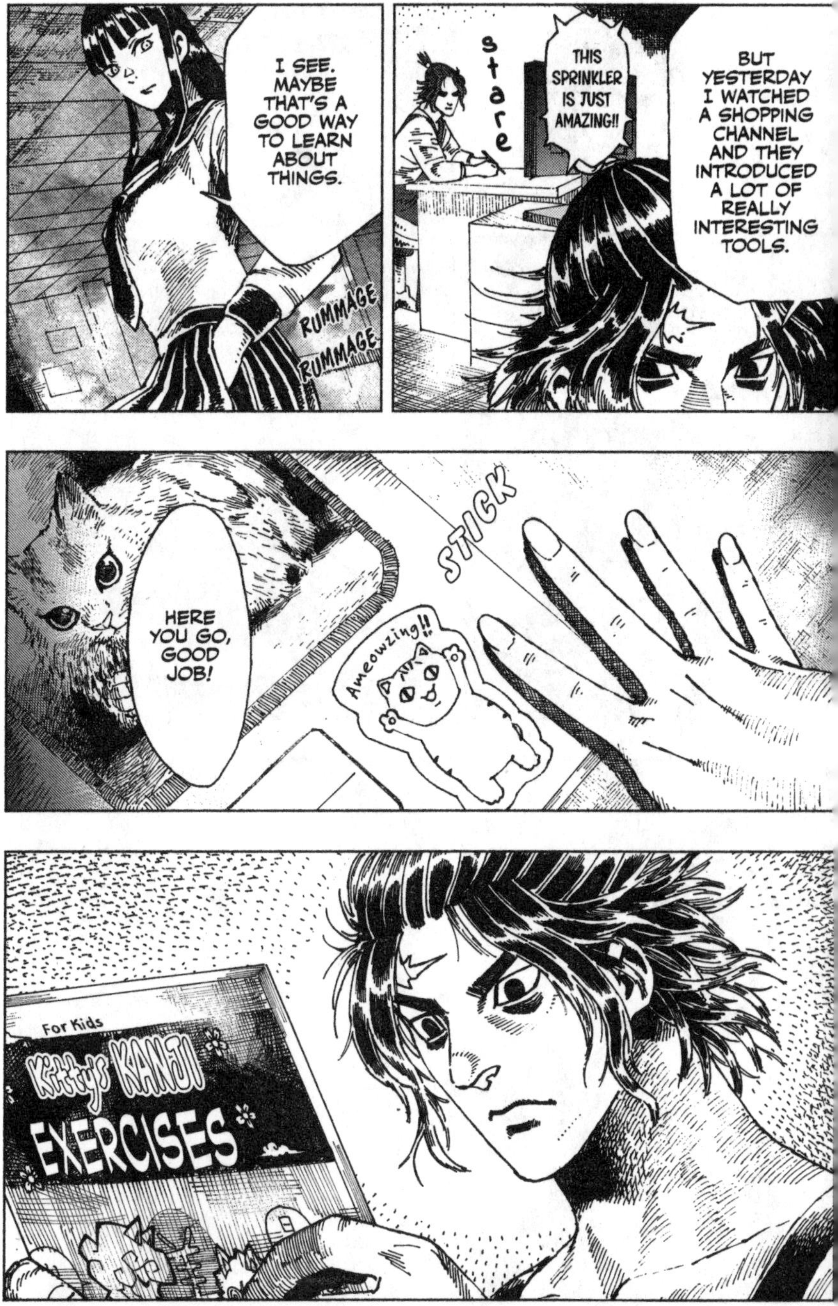
BUT YESTERDAY I WATCHED A SHOPPING CHANNEL AND THEY INTRODUCED A LOT OF REALLY INTERESTING TOOLS.
THIS SPRINKLER IS JUST AMAZING!!
stare
I SEE. MAYBE THAT'S A GOOD WAY TO LEARN ABOUT THINGS.
RUMMAGE
RUMMAGE
STICK
Ameowzing!!
HERE YOU GO, GOOD JOB!
For Kids
Kitty's KANJI
EXERCISES

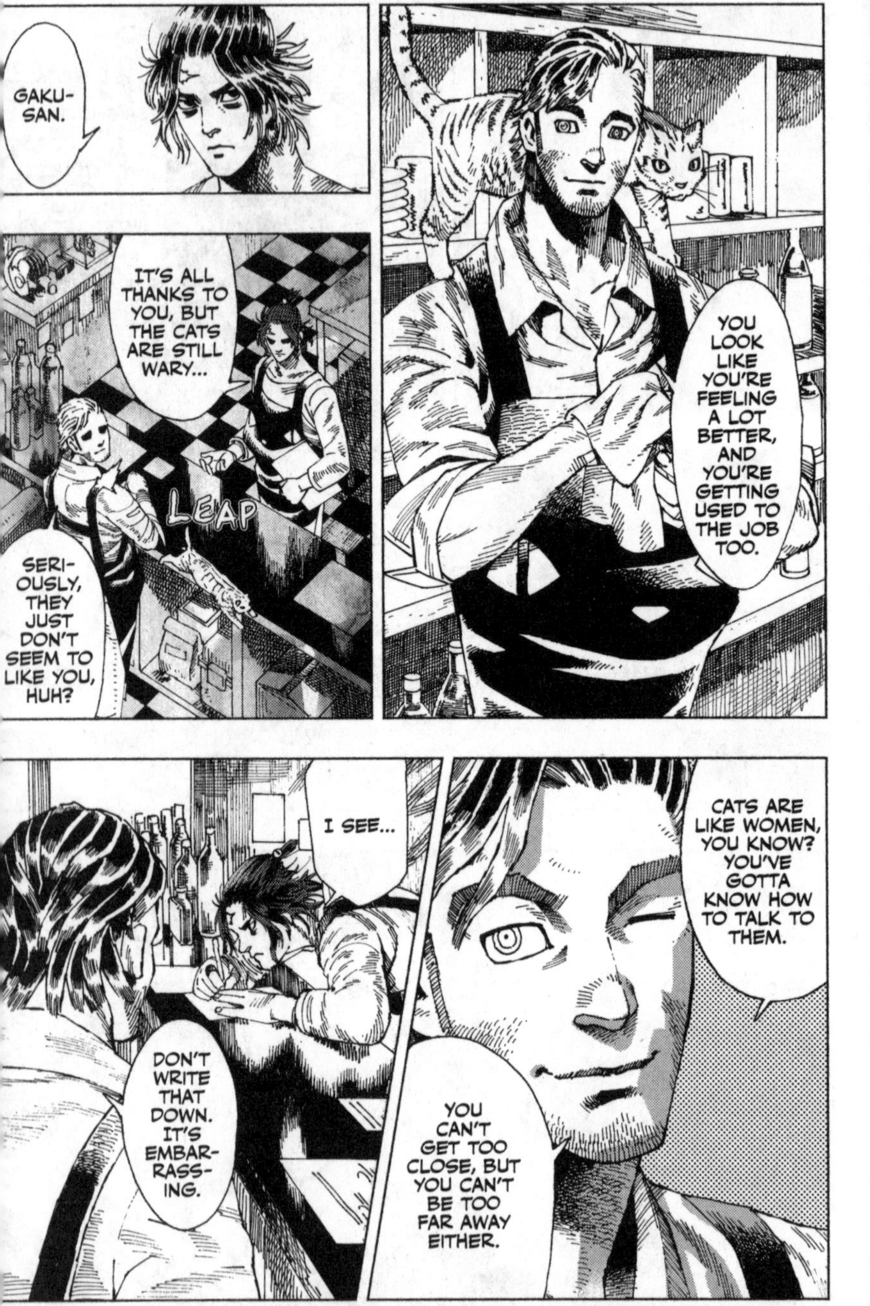
YOU LOOK LIKE YOU'RE FEELING A LOT BETTER, AND YOU'RE GETTING USED TO THE JOB TOO.
GAKU-SAN.
IT'S ALL THANKS TO YOU, BUT THE CATS ARE STILL WARY...
LEAP
SERIOUSLY, THEY JUST DON'T SEEM TO LIKE YOU, HUH?
CATS ARE LIKE WOMEN, YOU KNOW? YOU'VE GOTTA KNOW HOW TO TALK TO THEM.
YOU CAN'T GET TOO CLOSE, BUT YOU CAN'T BE TOO FAR AWAY EITHER.
I SEE...
DON'T WRITE THAT DOWN. IT'S EMBARRASSING.

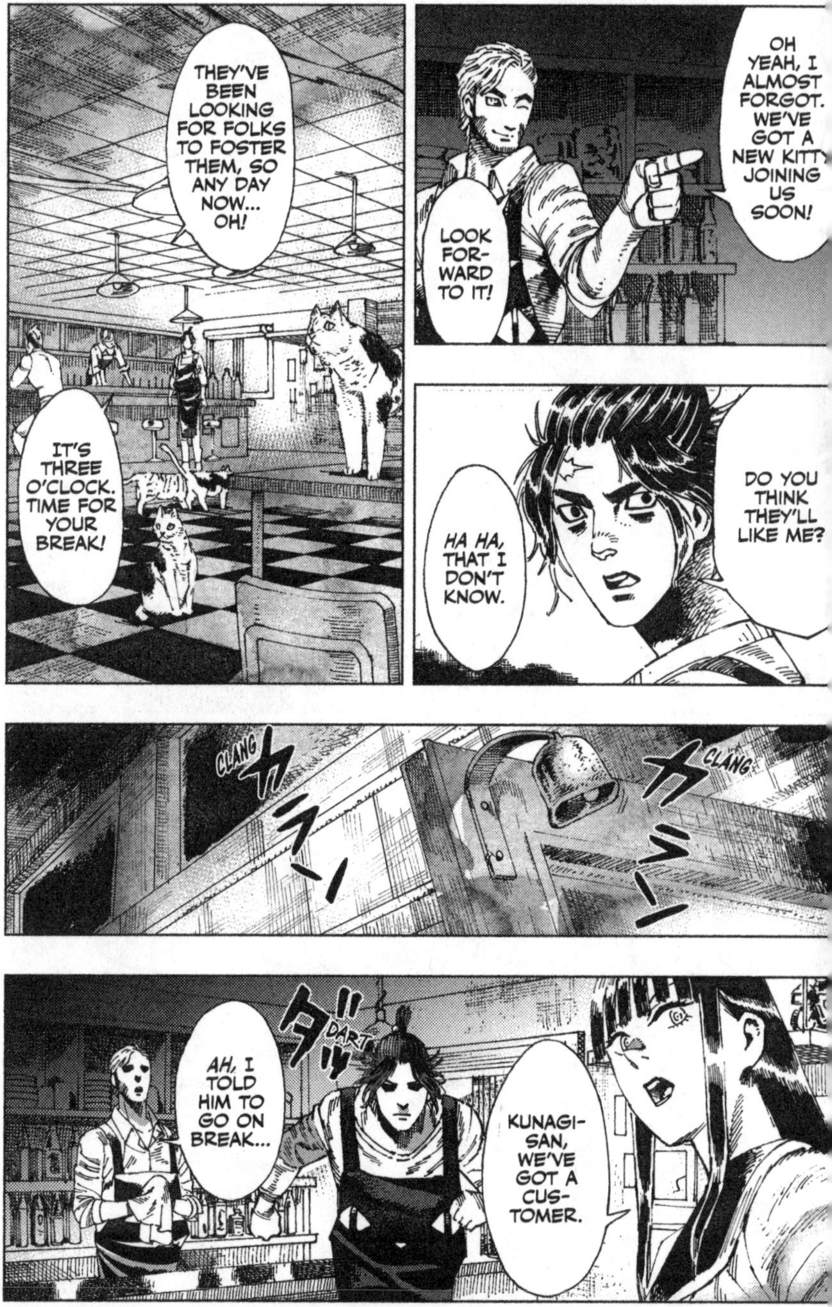
OH YEAH, I ALMOST FORGOT. WE'VE GOT A NEW KITT JOINING US SOON!
LOOK FORWARD TO IT!
DO YOU THINK THEY'LL LIKE ME?
HA HA, THAT I DON'T KNOW.
THEY'VE BEEN LOOKING FOR FOLKS TO FOSTER THEM, SO ANY DAY NOW... OH!
IT'S THREE O'CLOCK. TIME FOR YOUR BREAK!
CLANG
CLANG
KUNAGI-SAN, WE'VE GOT A CUS-TOMER.
DART
AH, I TOLD HIM TO GO ON BREAK...

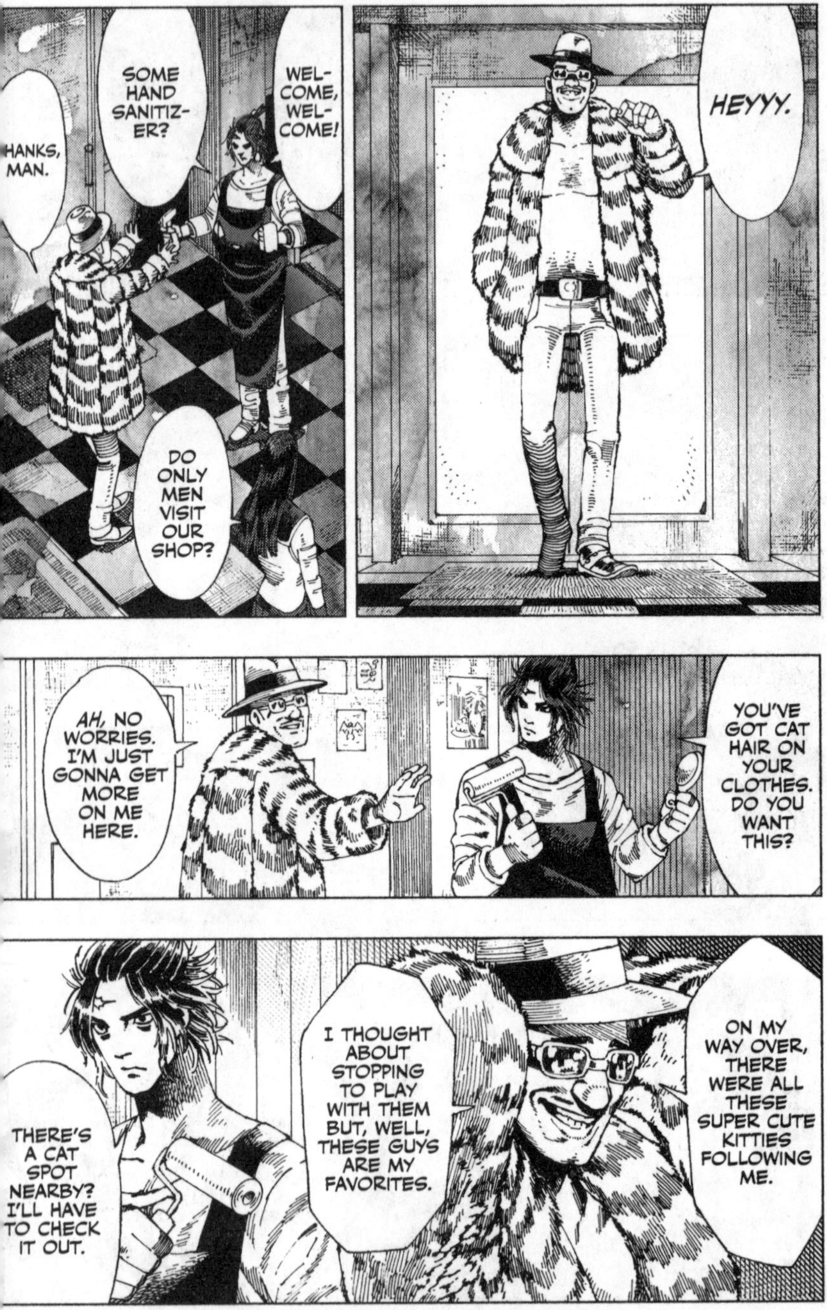
HEYYY.
WEL-COME, WEL-COME!
SOME HAND SANITIZ-ER?
HANKS, MAN.
DO ONLY MEN VISIT OUR SHOP?
YOU'VE GOT CAT HAIR ON YOUR CLOTHES. DO YOU WANT THIS?
AH, NO WORRIES. I'M JUST GONNA GET MORE ON ME HERE.
ON MY WAY OVER, THERE WERE ALL THESE SUPER CUTE KITTIES FOLLOWING ME.
I THOUGHT ABOUT STOPPING TO PLAY WITH THEM BUT, WELL, THESE GUYS ARE MY FAVORITES.
THERE'S A CAT SPOT NEARBY? I'LL HAVE TO CHECK IT OUT.

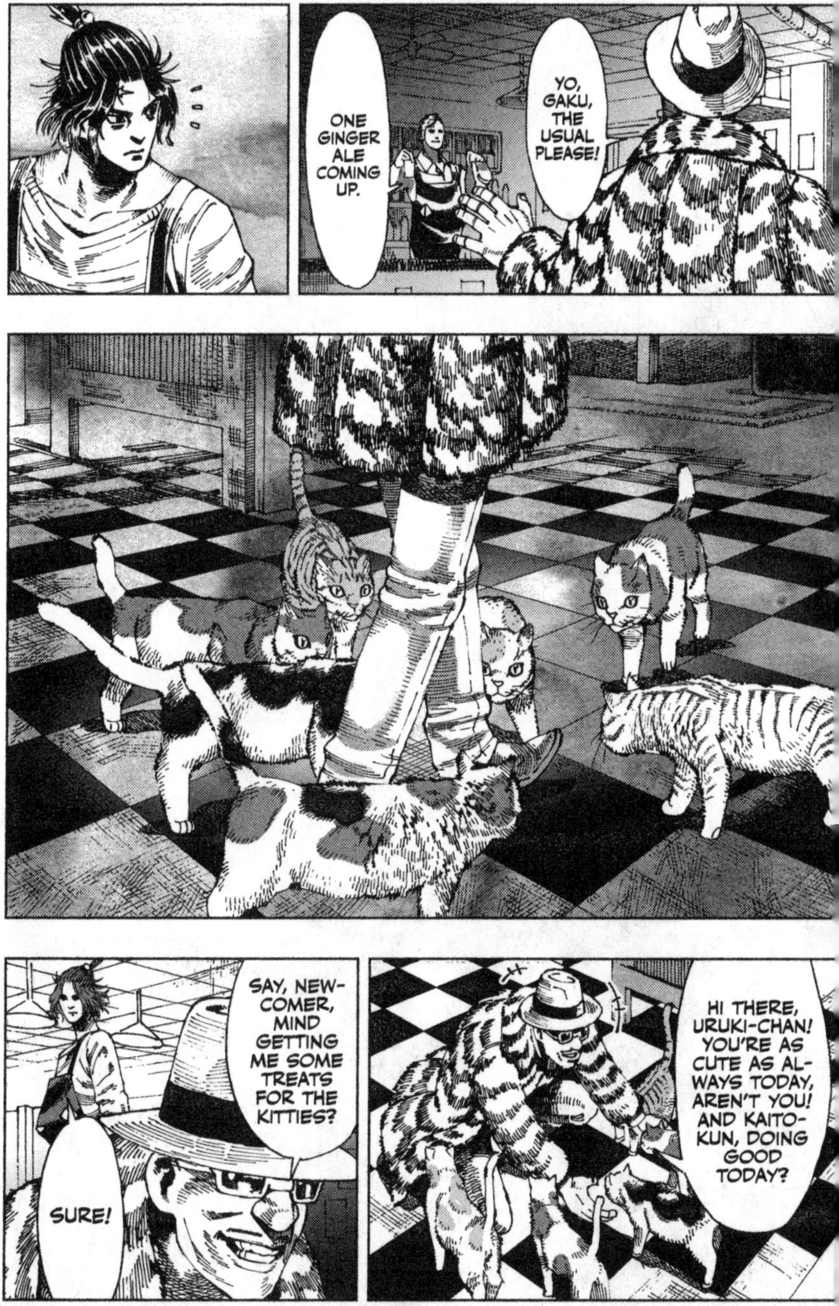
YO, GAKU, THE USUAL PLEASE!
ONE GINGER ALE COMING UP.
HI THERE, URUKI-CHAN! YOU'RE AS CUTE AS AL-WAYS TODAY, AREN'T YOU! AND KAITO-KUN, DOING GOOD TODAY?
SAY, NEW-COMER, MIND GETTING ME SOME TREATS FOR THE KITTIES?
SURE!

THANKS, MAN.

HERE.

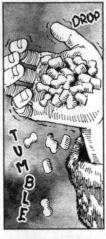

DROP

TUMBLE

SPRINKLE °°°

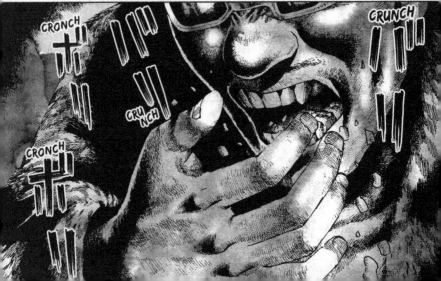

CRONCH

CRUNCH

GRU NCH

CRONCH

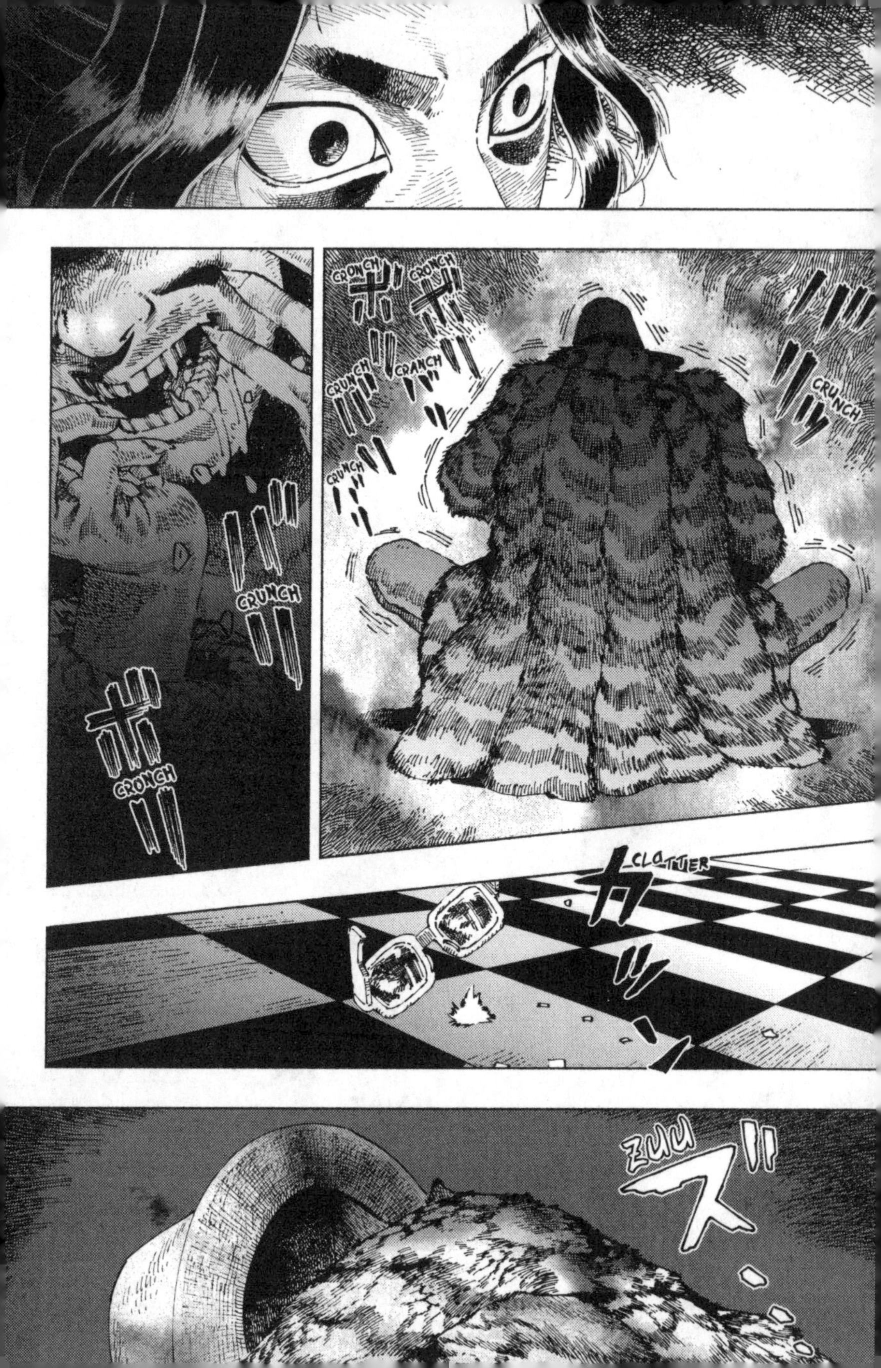
CRUNCH
CRONCH
CRONCH
CRANCH
CRUNCH
CRUNCH
CRUNCH
CRONCH
CLOTTER
ZUU

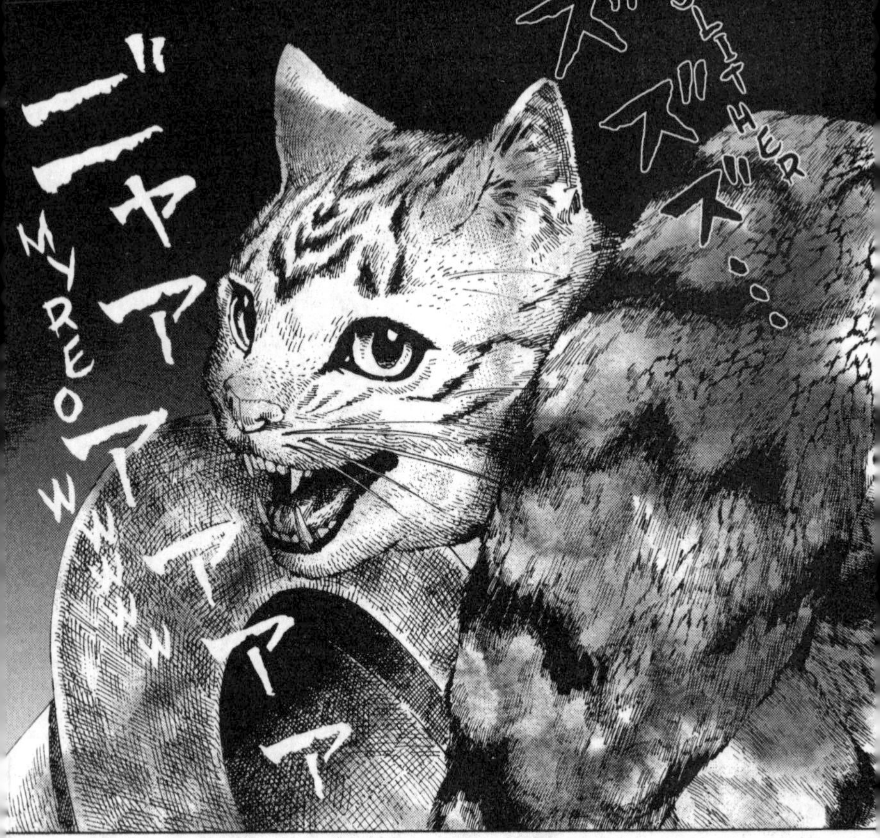
SLITHER
MYREOW
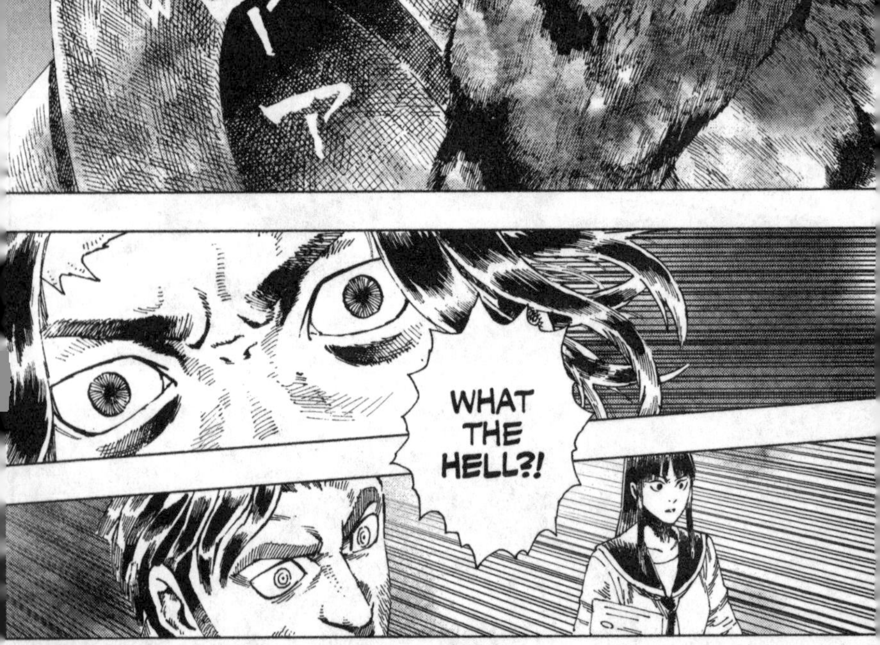
WHAT THE HELL?!

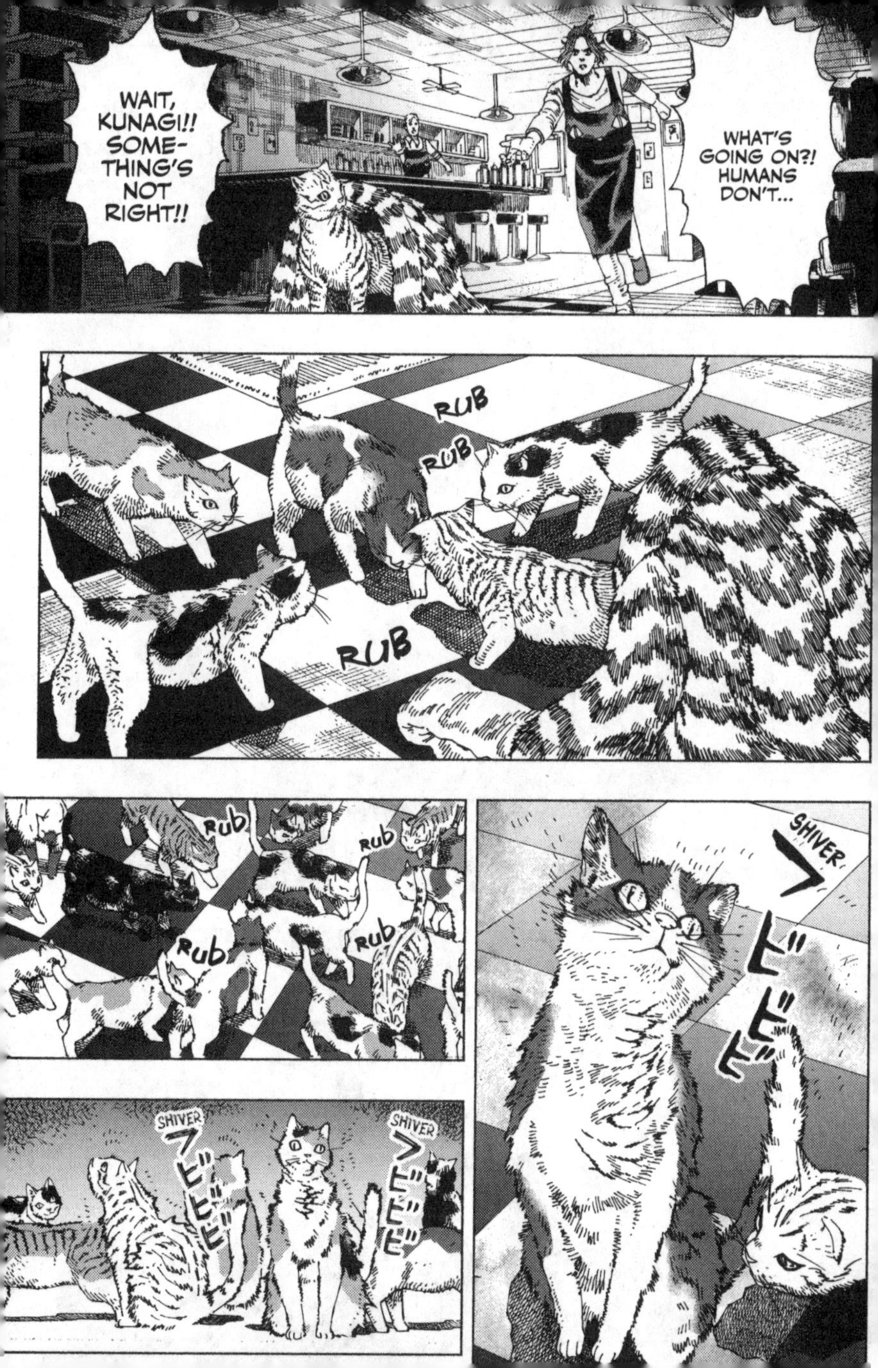
WHAT'S GOING ON?! HUMANS DON'T...
WAIT, KUNAGI!! SOME-THING'S NOT RIGHT!!
RUB
RUB
RUB
SHIVER
Rub
Rub
Rub
Rub
SHIVER
SHIVER

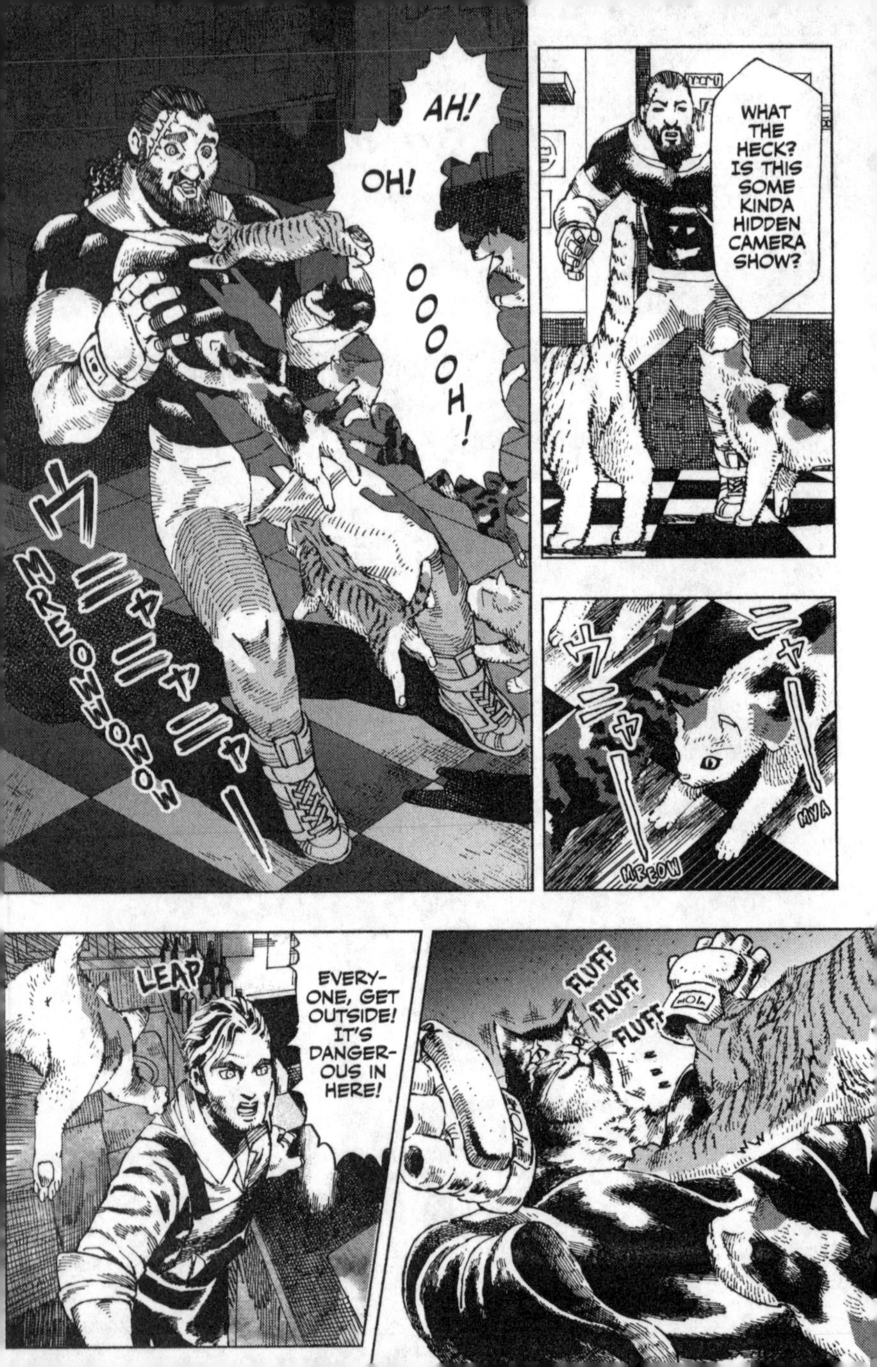
WHAT THE HECK? IS THIS SOME KINDA HIDDEN CAMERA SHOW?
MYA
MREOW
AH!
OH!
OOOOOH!
MREOWWOWOW
FLUFF
FLUFF
FLUFF
LEAP
EVERY-ONE, GET OUTSIDE! IT'S DANGER-OUS IN HERE!

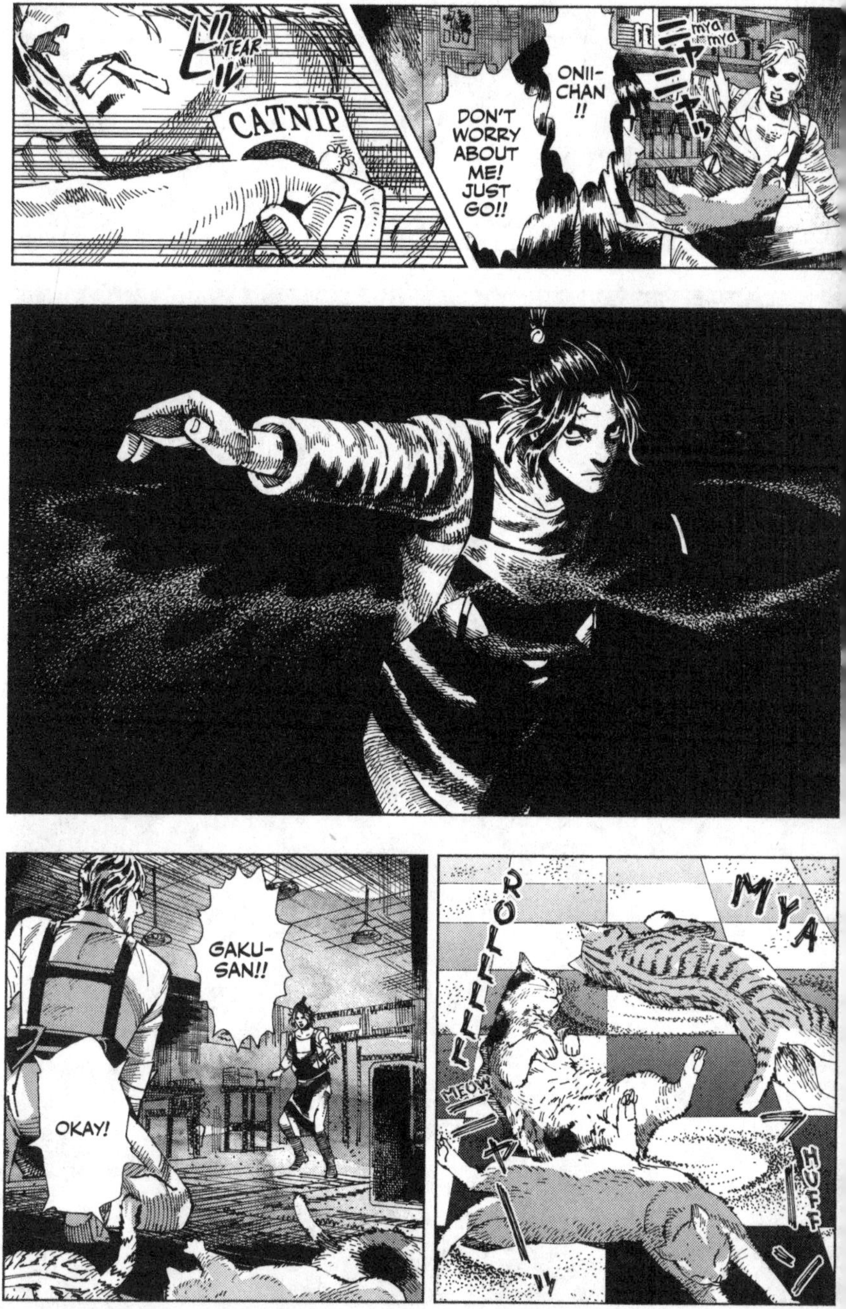
mya mya
ONII-CHAN!!
DON'T WORRY ABOUT ME! JUST GO!!
TEAR
CATNIP
MYA
ROLLLLL
MEOW
HUFF
GAKU-SAN!!
OKAY!

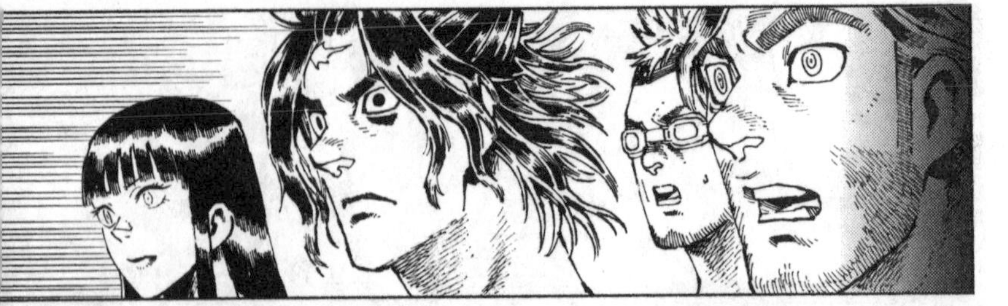

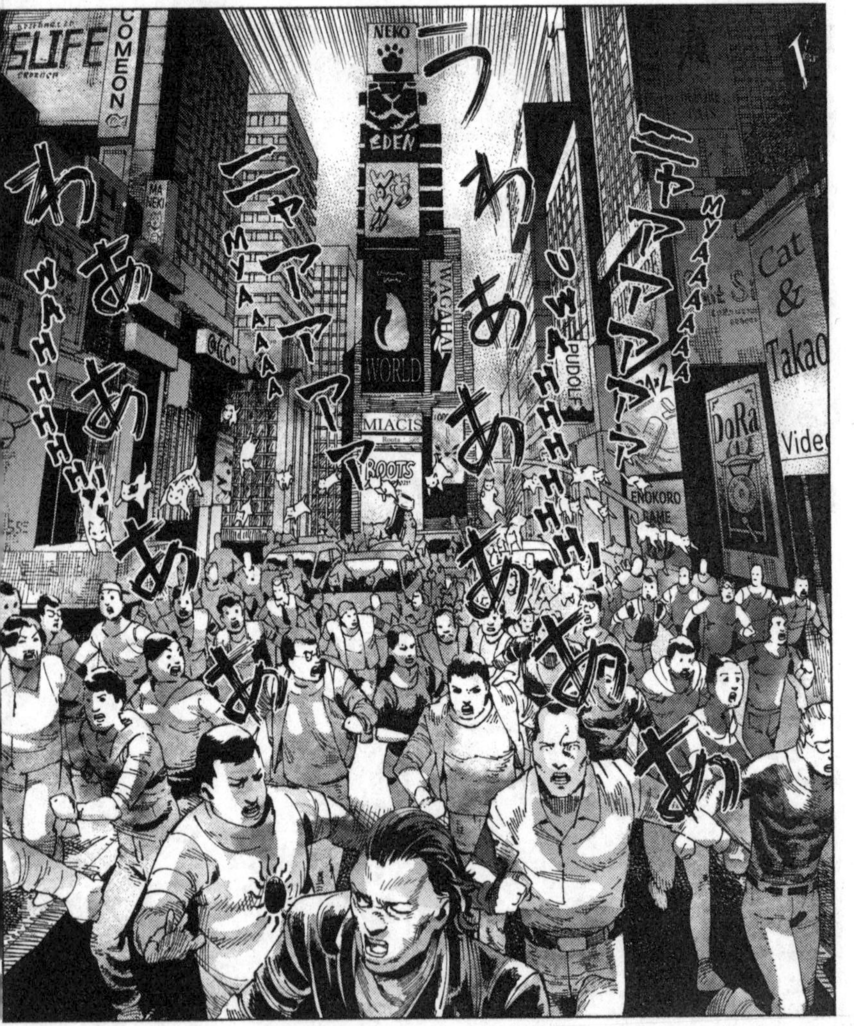
ニャアアアアア
MYAAAAAAAA
うわあああああ
UWAHHHHHHH!
ニャアアアア
MYAAAAA
わあああ
WAHHHHHH!
Cat & Takao
DoRa
NEKO
EDEN
WORLD
MIACIS
ROOTS
WAGAHAI
COMEON

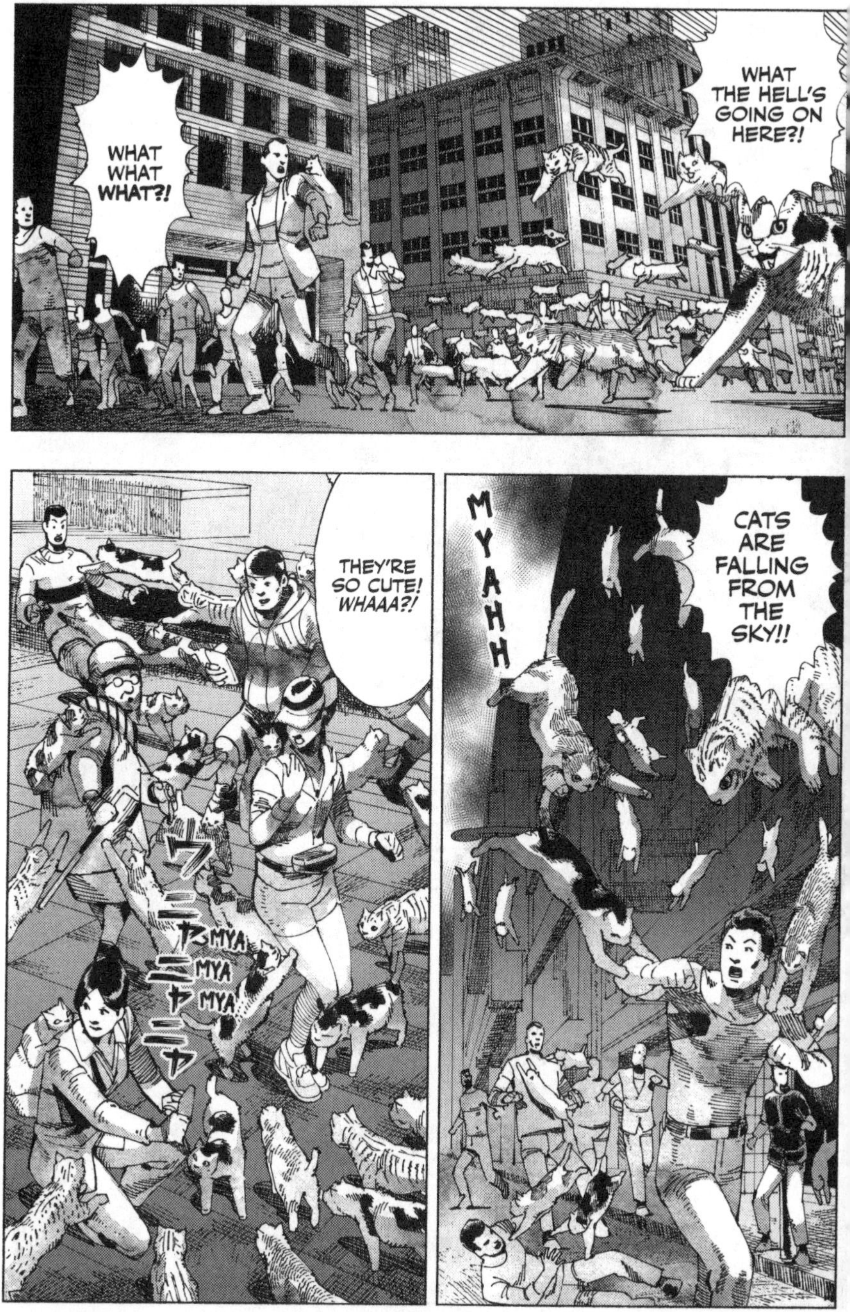
WHAT THE HELL'S GOING ON HERE?!
WHAT WHAT WHAT?!
CATS ARE FALLING FROM THE SKY!!
MYAHH
THEY'RE SO CUTE! WHAAA?!
MYA
MYA
MYA

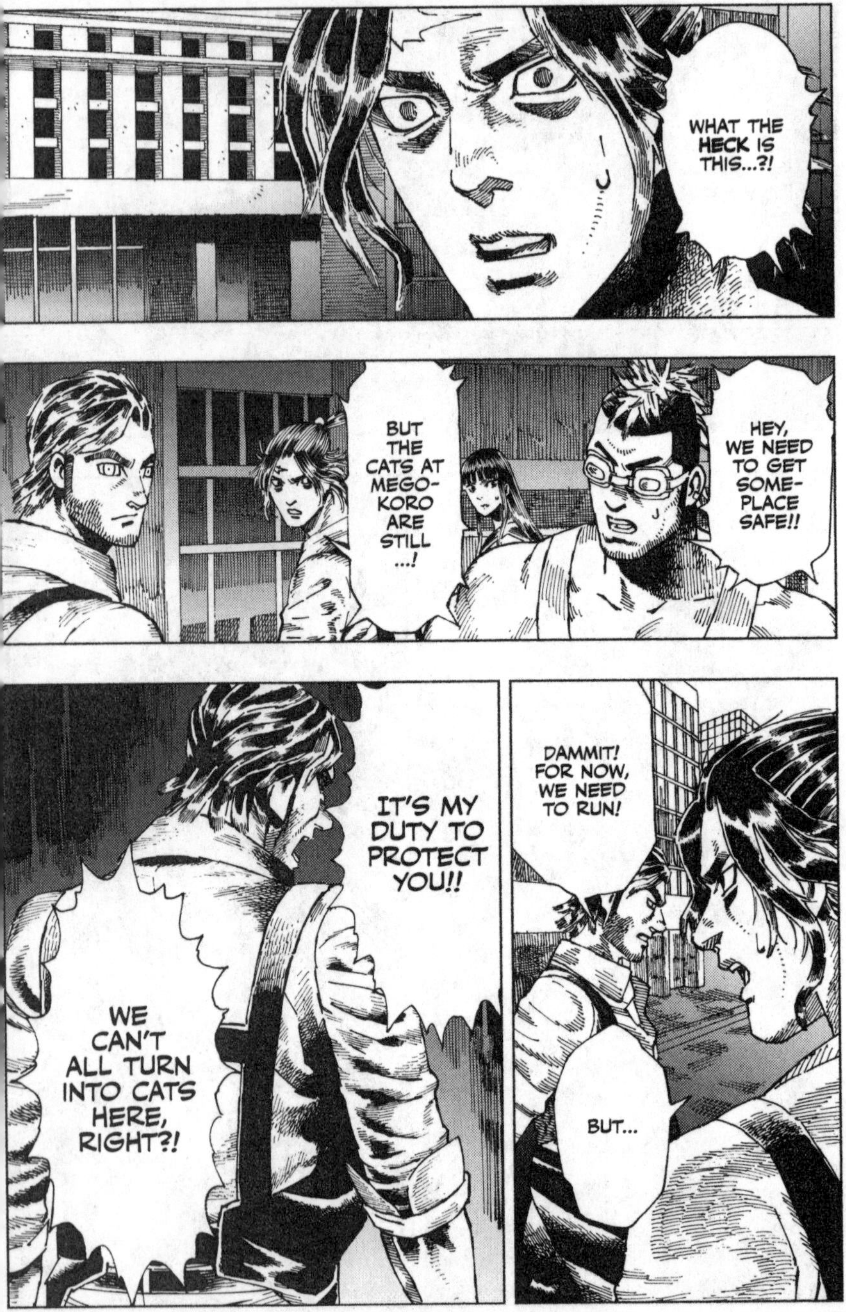
WHAT THE HECK IS THIS...?!
HEY, WE NEED TO GET SOME-PLACE SAFE!!
BUT THE CATS AT MEGO-KORO ARE STILL ...!
DAMMIT! FOR NOW, WE NEED TO RUN!
BUT...
IT'S MY DUTY TO PROTECT YOU!!
WE CAN'T ALL TURN INTO CATS HERE, RIGHT?!

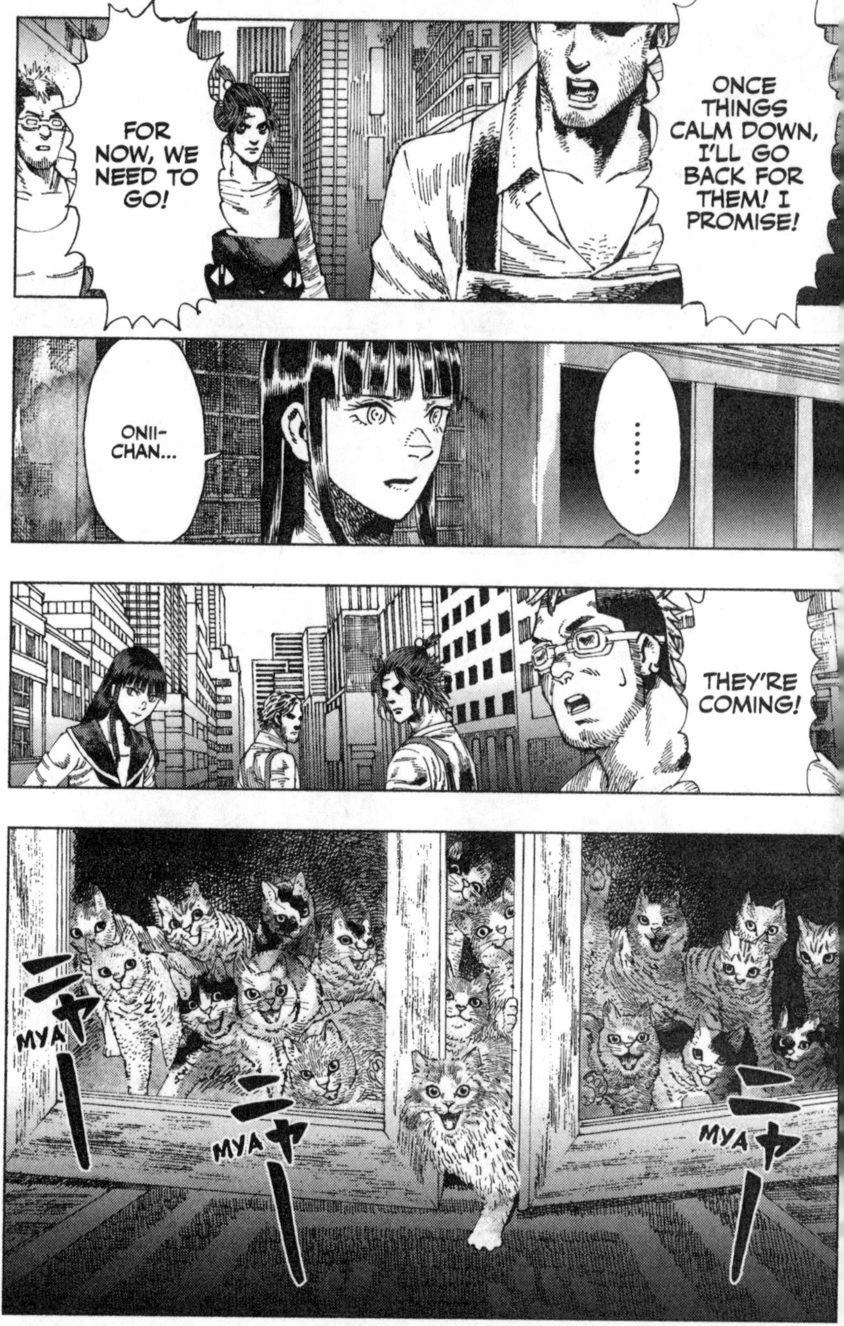
ONCE THINGS CALM DOWN, I'LL GO BACK FOR THEM! I PROMISE!
FOR NOW, WE NEED TO GO!
......
ONII-CHAN...
THEY'RE COMING!
ニャー
MYA
ニャー
MYA
ニャー
MYA

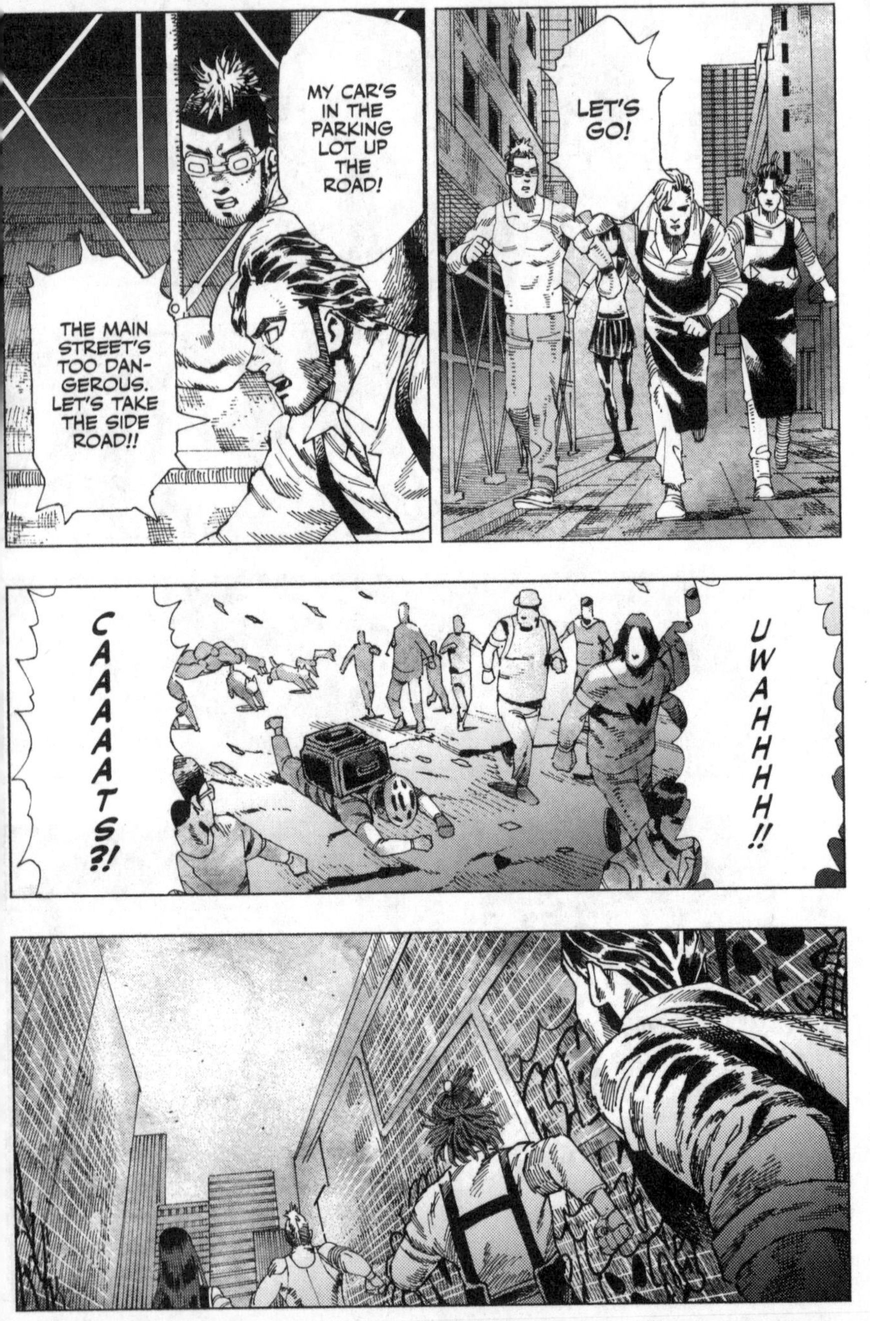
LET'S GO!
MY CAR'S IN THE PARKING LOT UP THE ROAD!
THE MAIN STREET'S TOO DANGEROUS. LET'S TAKE THE SIDE ROAD!!
UWAHHHHH!!
CAAAAATS?!

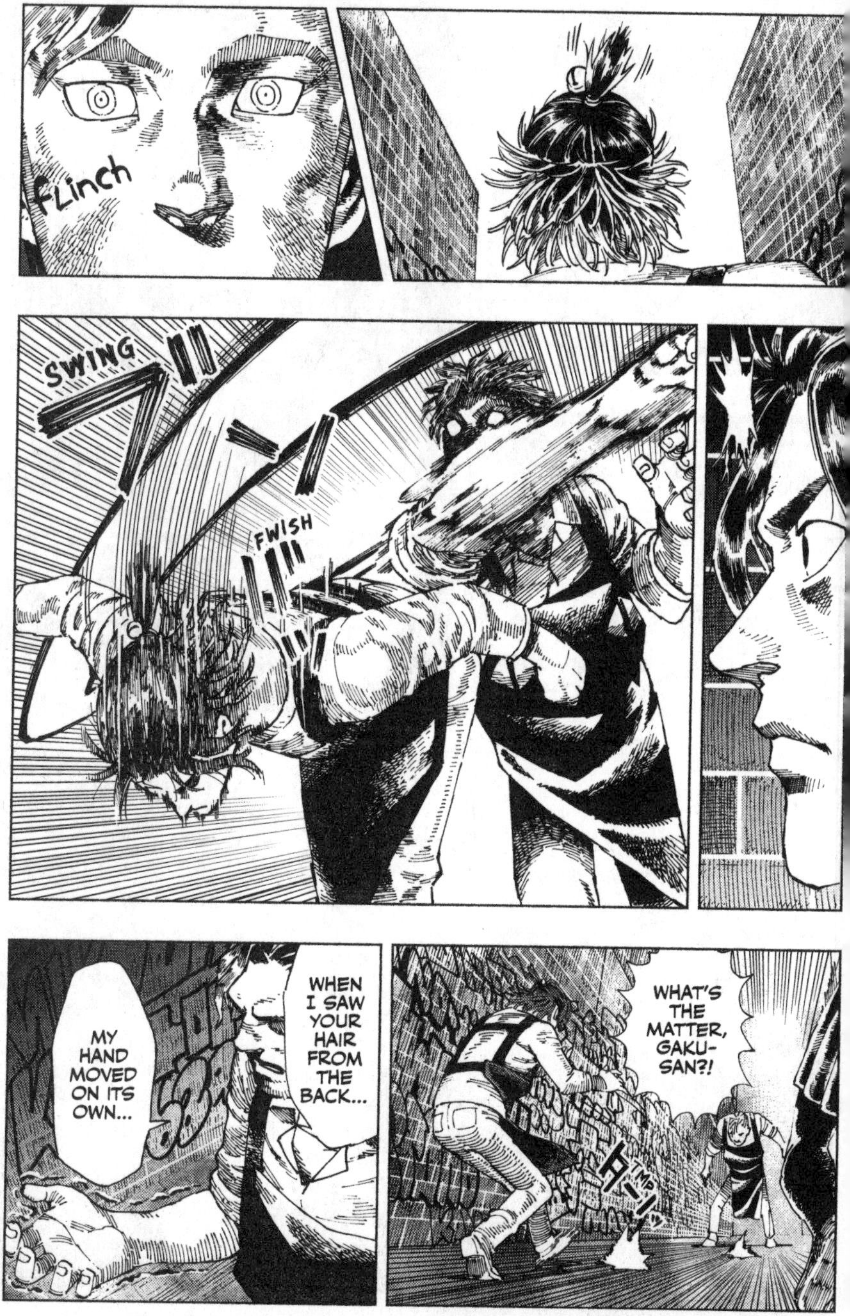
FLINCH
SWING
FWISH
WHAT'S THE MATTER, GAKU-SAN?!
TMP
WHEN I SAW YOUR HAIR FROM THE BACK...
MY HAND MOVED ON ITS OWN...

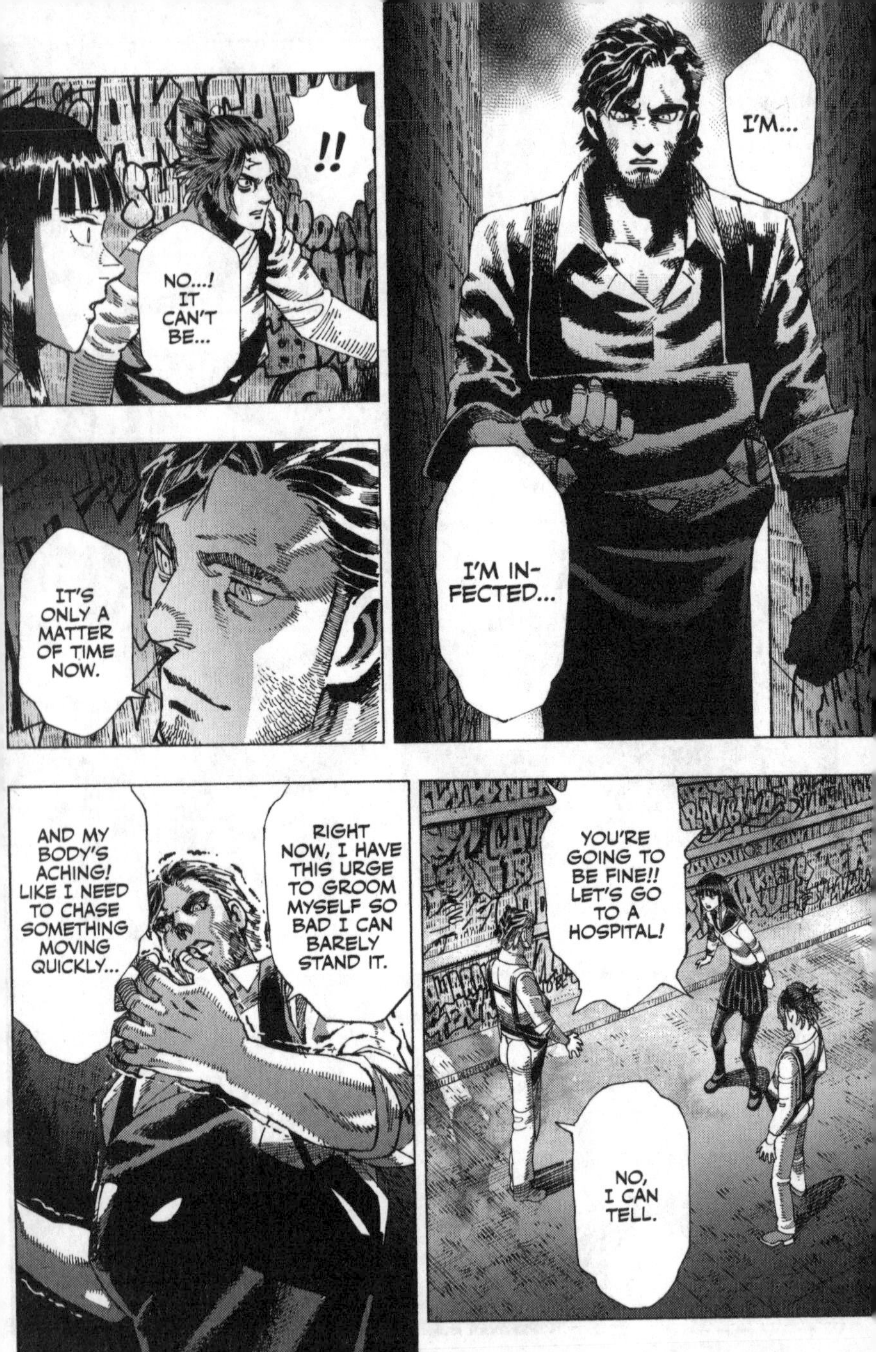
I'M...
I'M IN-FECTED...
!!
NO...! IT CAN'T BE...
IT'S ONLY A MATTER OF TIME NOW.
YOU'RE GOING TO BE FINE!! LET'S GO TO A HOSPITAL!
NO, I CAN TELL.
RIGHT NOW, I HAVE THIS URGE TO GROOM MYSELF SO BAD I CAN BARELY STAND IT.
AND MY BODY'S ACHING! LIKE I NEED TO CHASE SOMETHING MOVING QUICKLY...

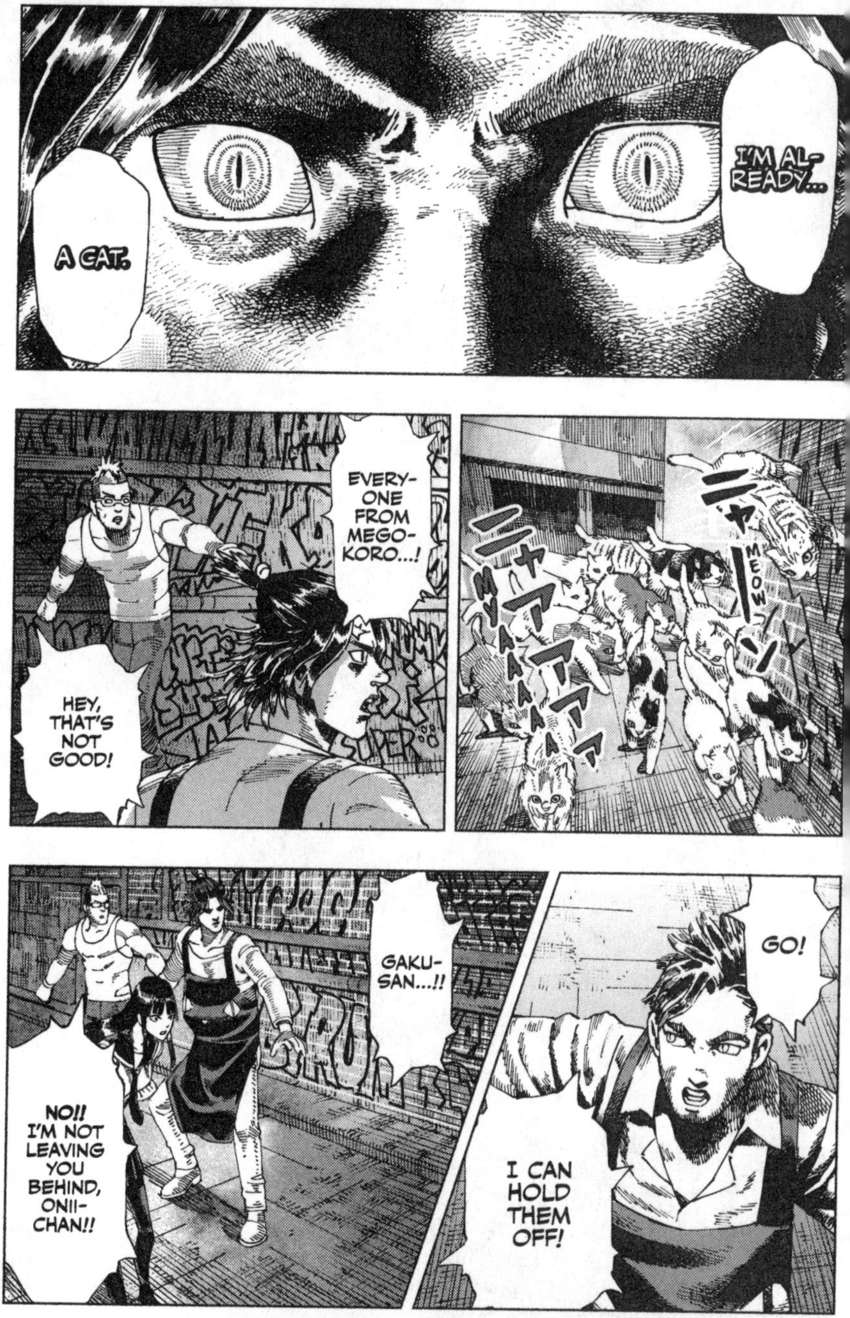
I'M AL-READY...
A CAT.
ニャーン
MEOW
ニャアアアア
MYAAAAAA
EVERY-ONE FROM MEGO-KORO...!
HEY, THAT'S NOT GOOD!
GO!
I CAN HOLD THEM OFF!
GAKU-SAN...!!
NO!! I'M NOT LEAVING YOU BEHIND, ONII-CHAN!!

PROMISE ME YOU'LL SURVIVE THIS.

KAORU...

KU-NAGI...

I'M SORRY.

TANI-SHI.

DON'T THINK I'LL FORGET YOUR TAB.

TAKE CARE OF KAORU FOR ME?

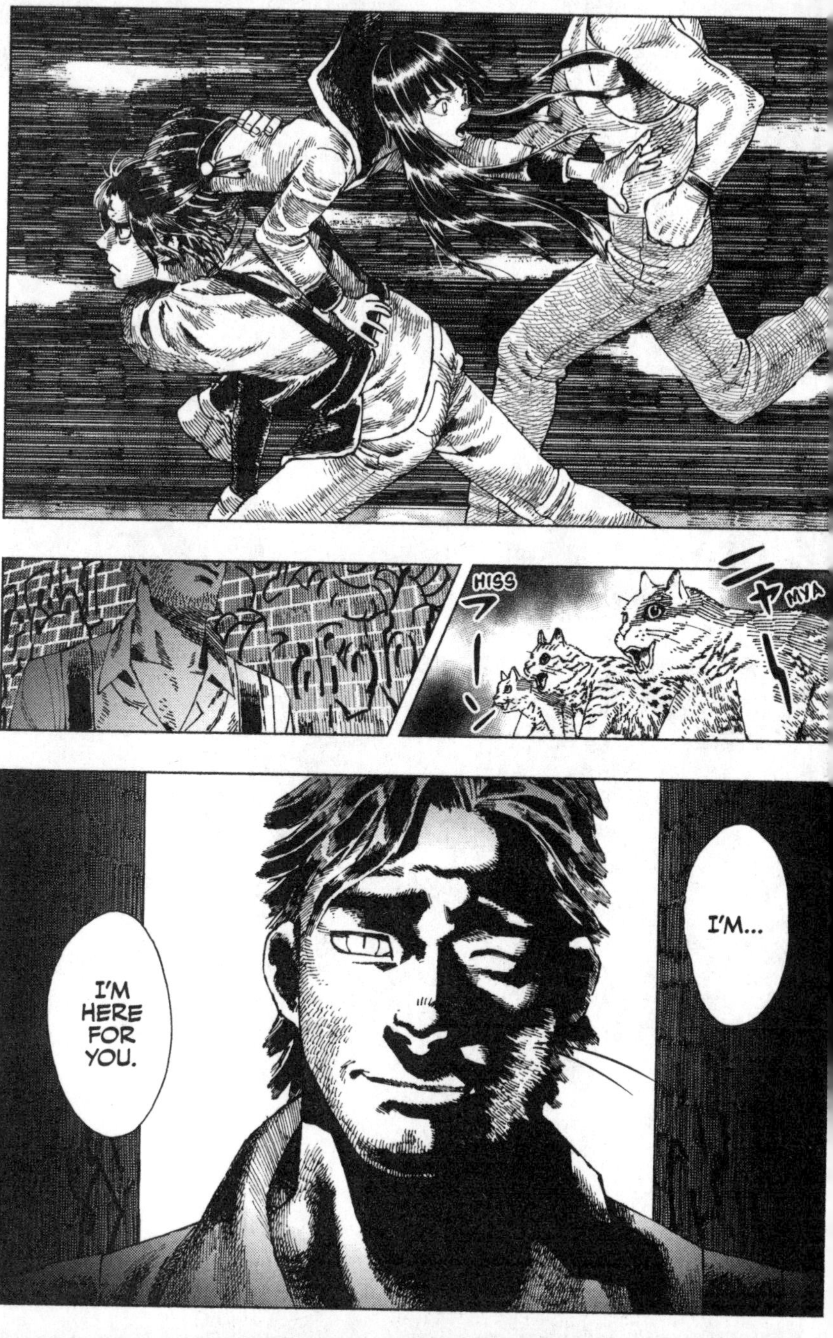
MYA
HISS
I'M...
I'M HERE FOR YOU.

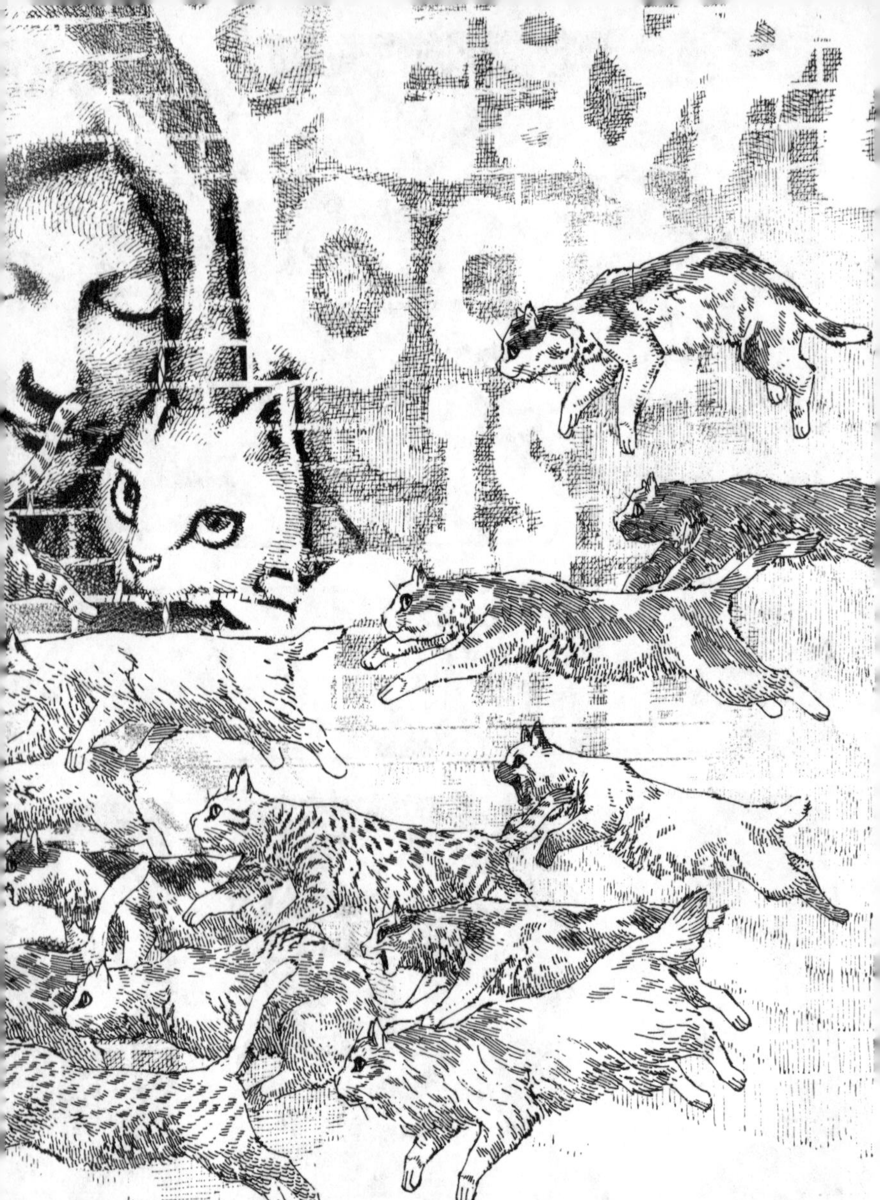

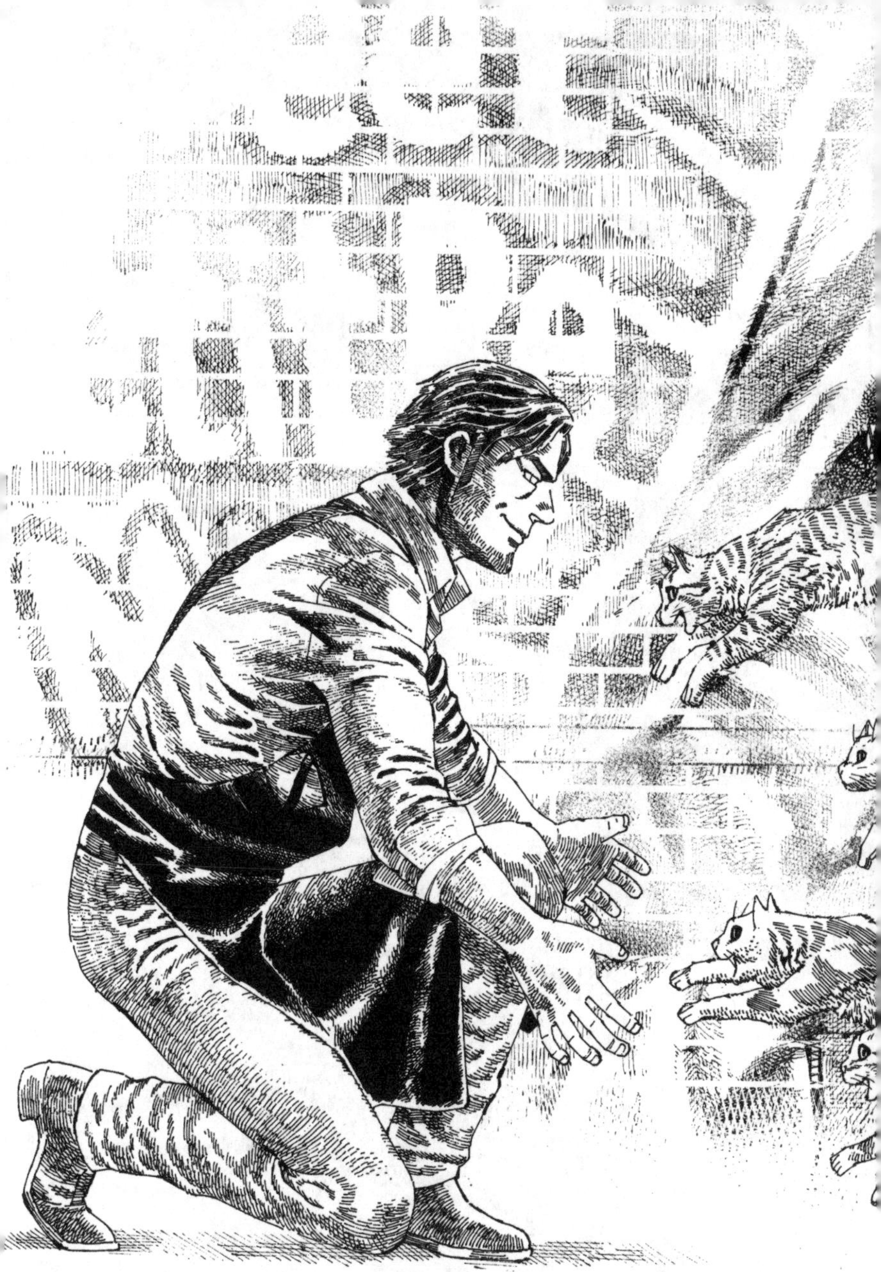

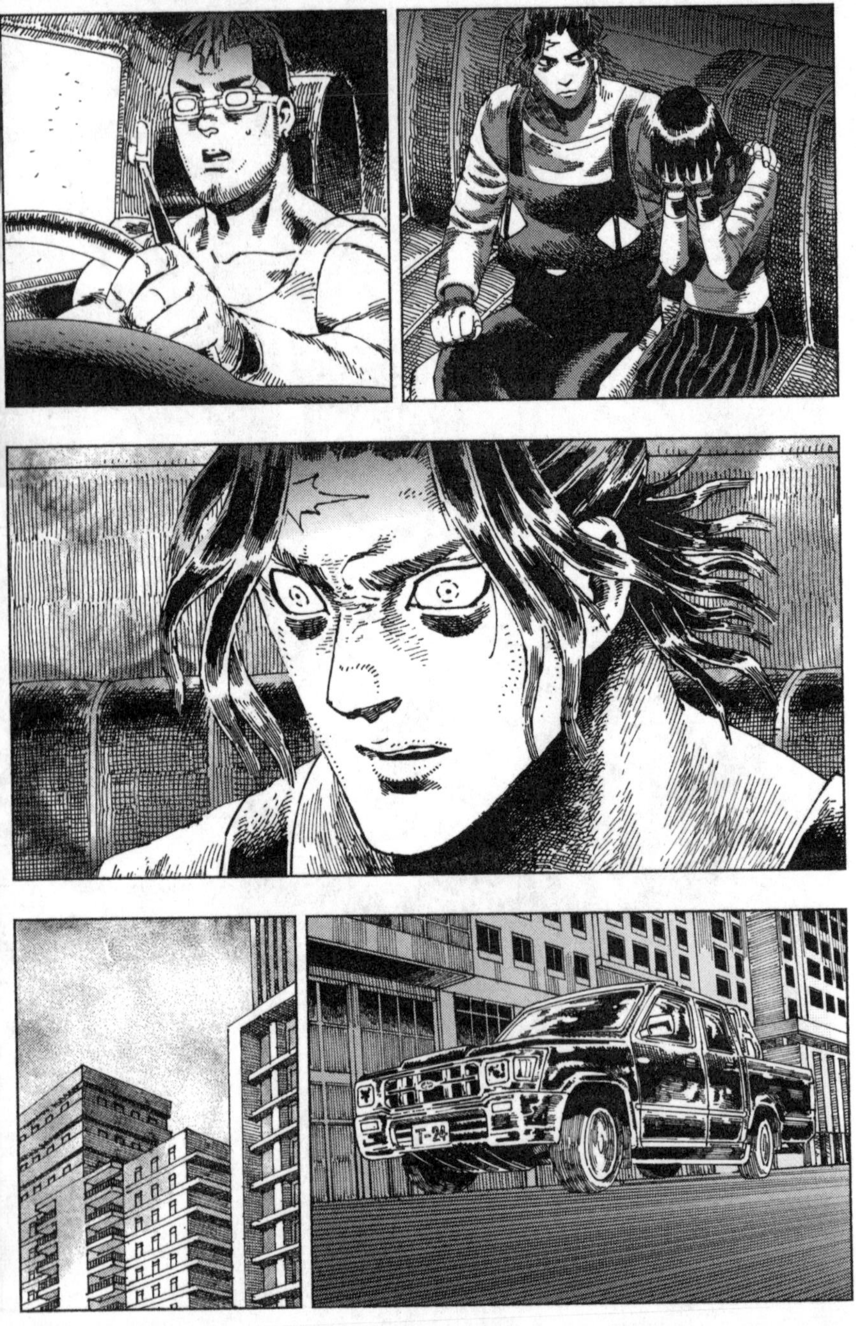
T-24

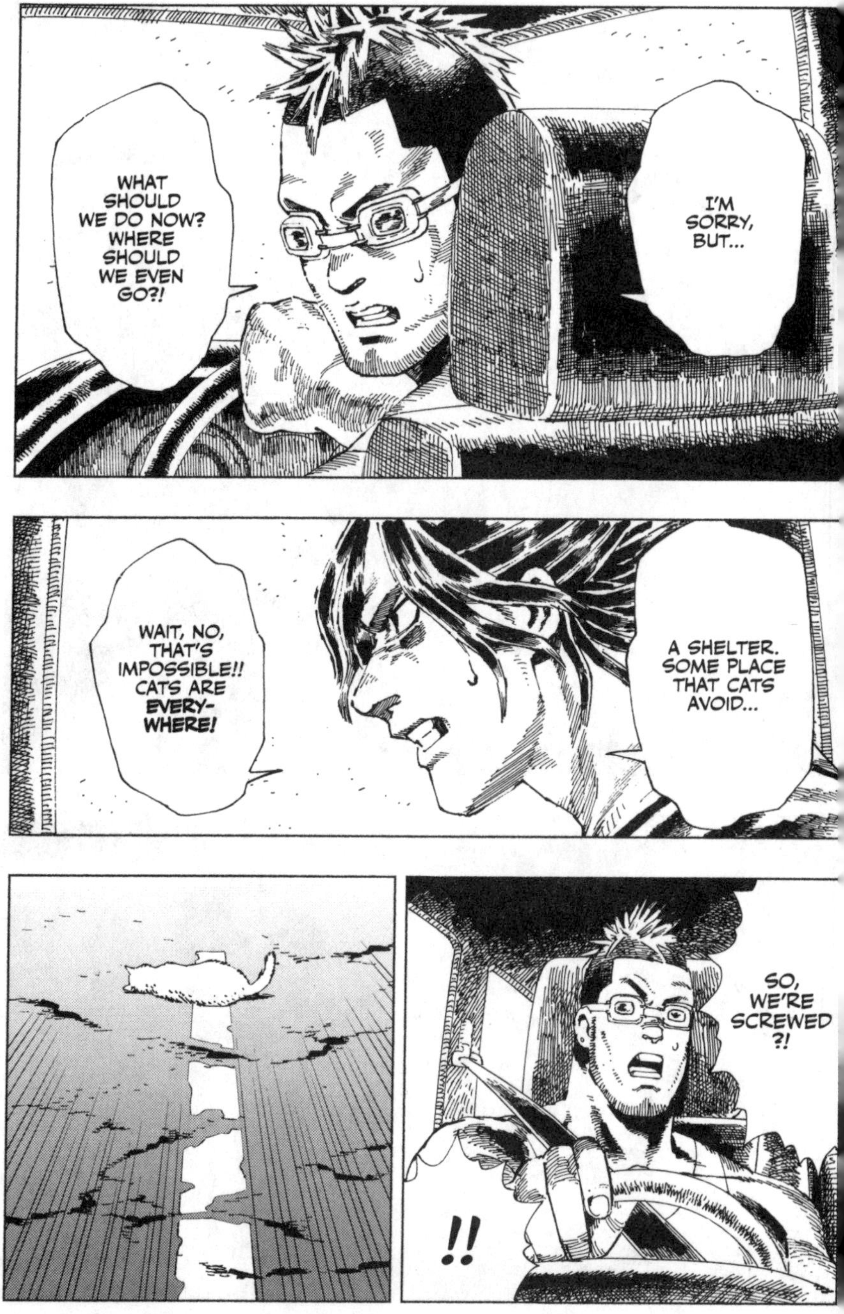
I'M SORRY, BUT...
WHAT SHOULD WE DO NOW? WHERE SHOULD WE EVEN GO?!
A SHELTER. SOME PLACE THAT CATS AVOID...
WAIT, NO, THAT'S IMPOSSIBLE!! CATS ARE EVERYWHERE!
SO, WE'RE SCREWED?!
!!

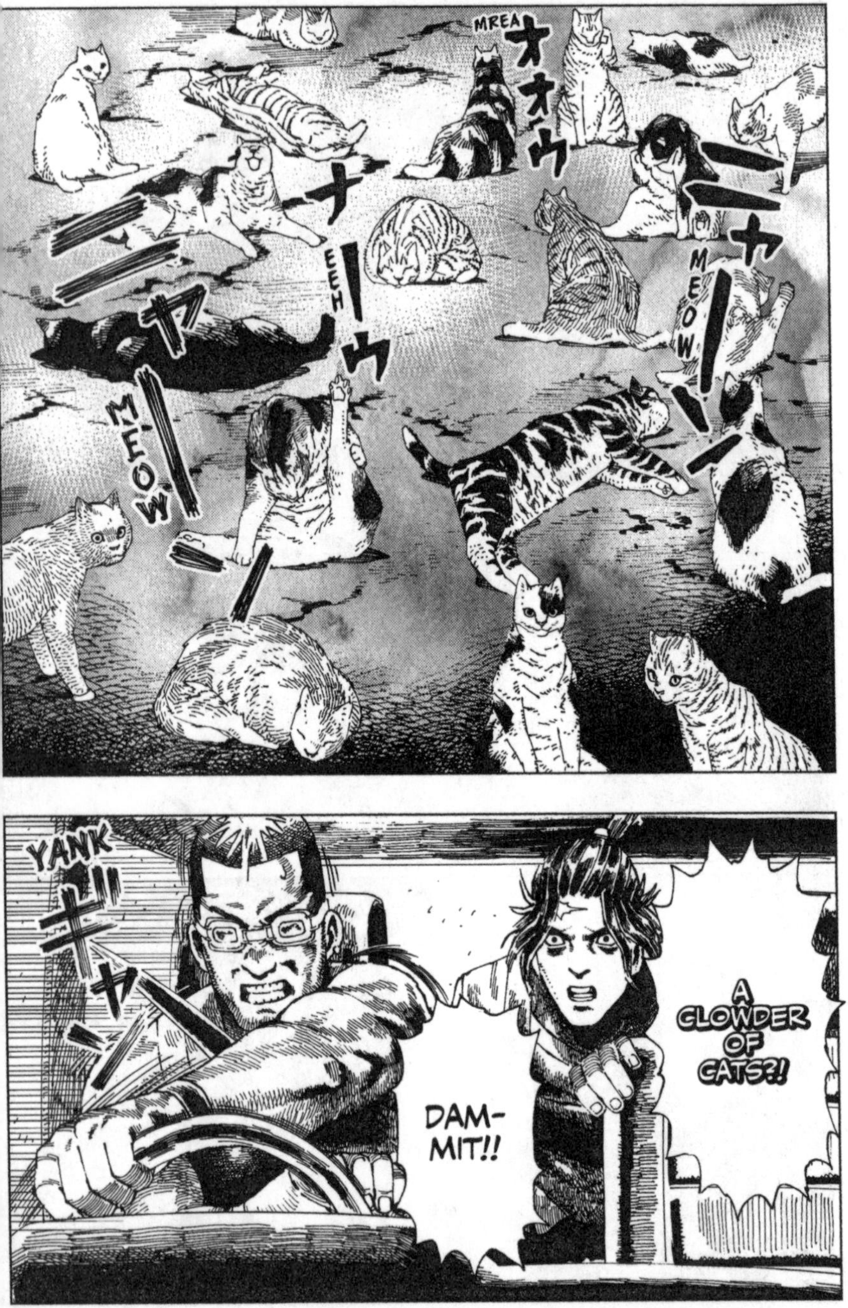
MREA
オオウ
ニャー
MEOW
ナーウ
EEEH
ニャー
MEOW
A CLOWDER OF CATS?!
DAM-MIT!!
YANK

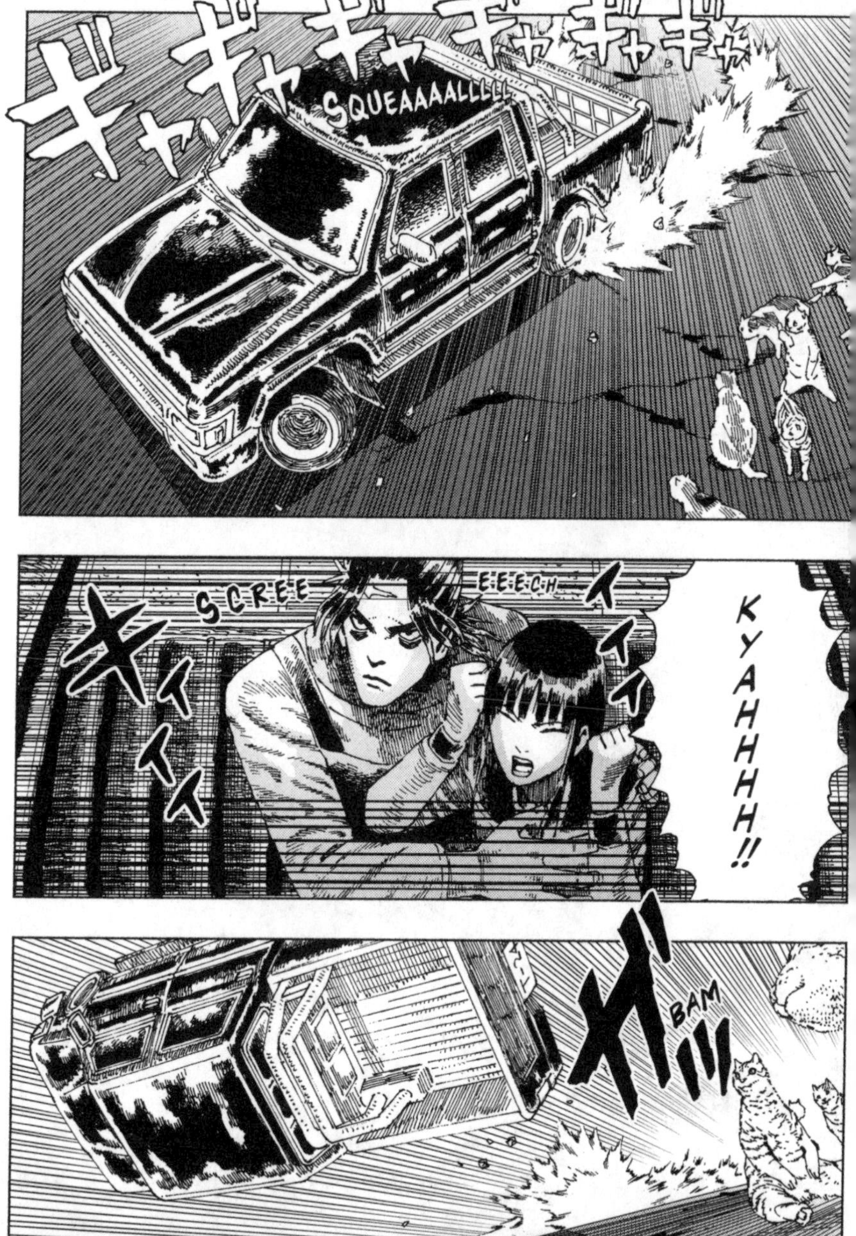
ギャギャギャギャギャギャ
SQUEAAAALLLLL
KYAHHHHH!!
SCREE
EEECH
BAM

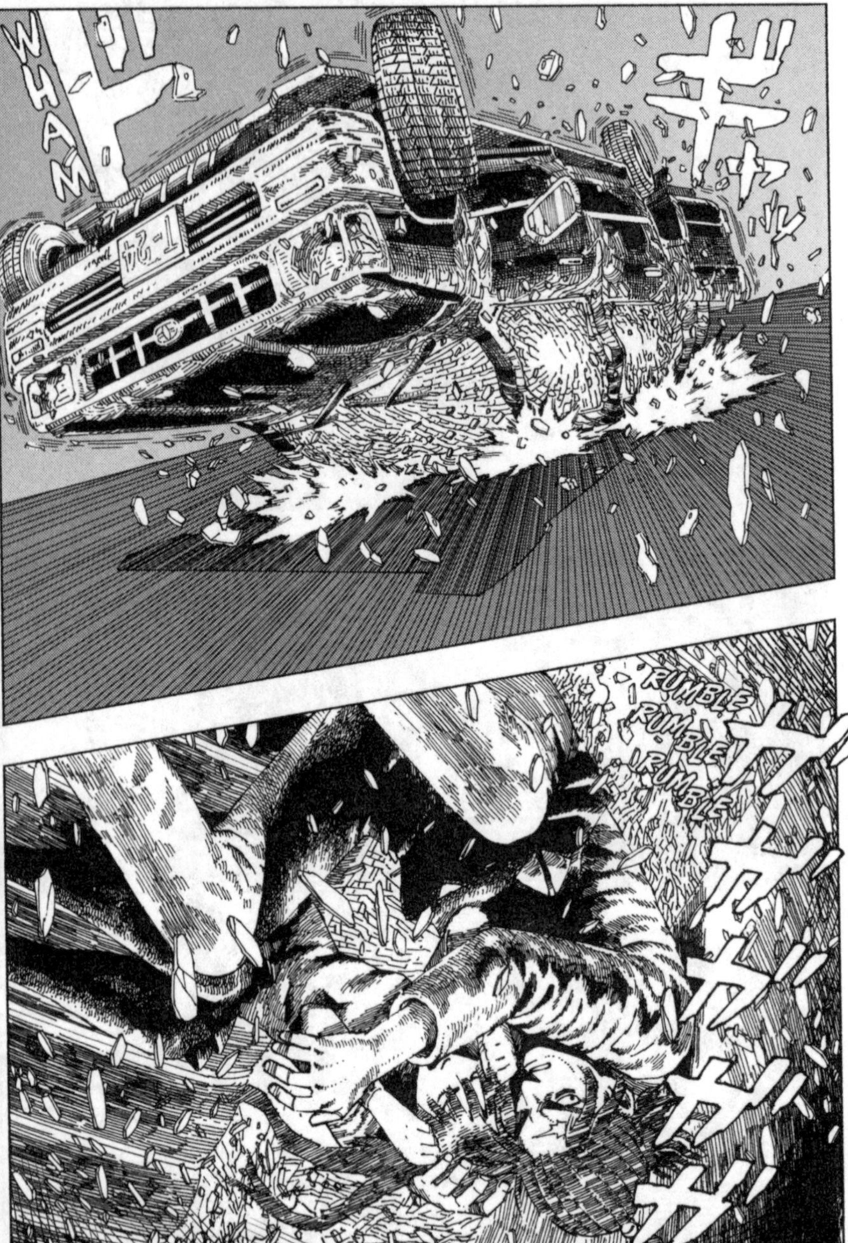
WHAM
RUMBLE
RUMBLE
RUMBLE

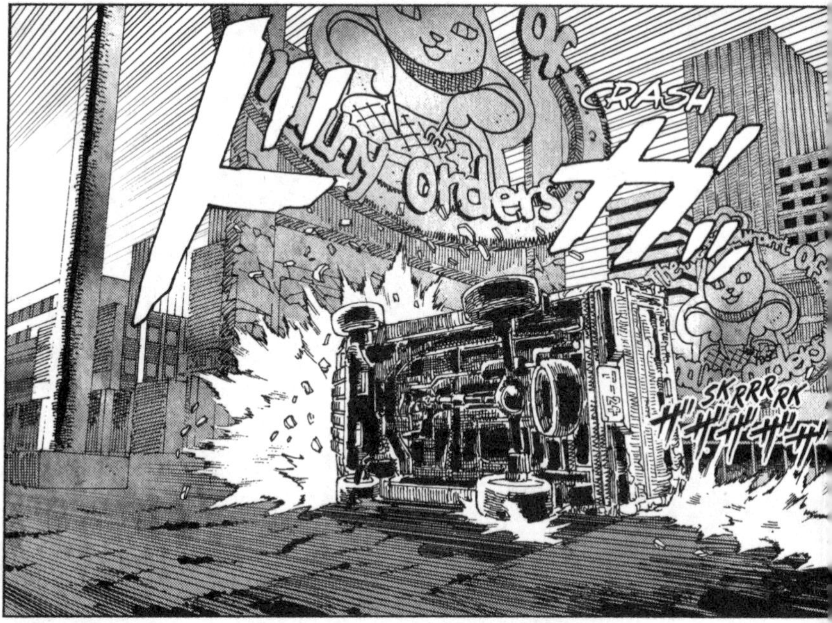
Orders
CRASH
SKRRRRK
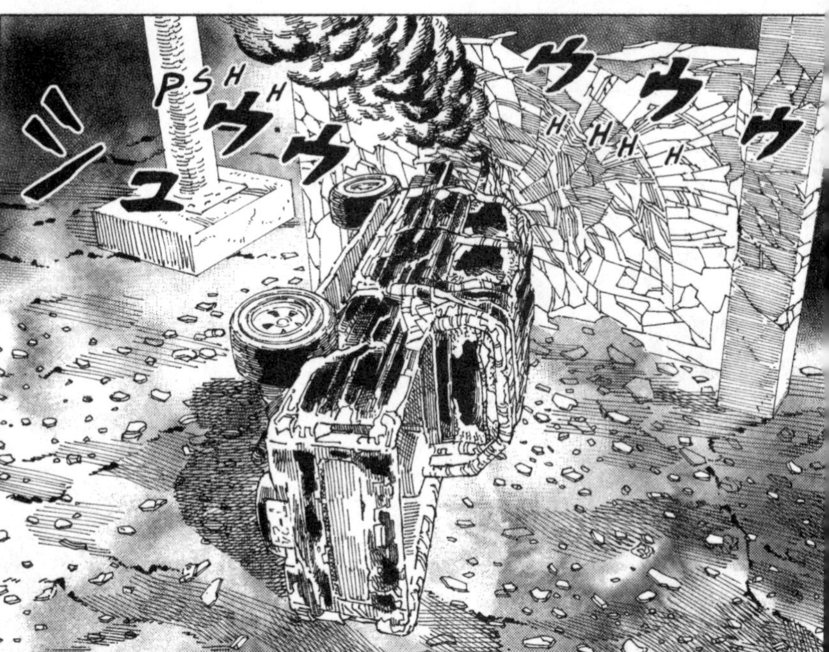
PSHHHHHH

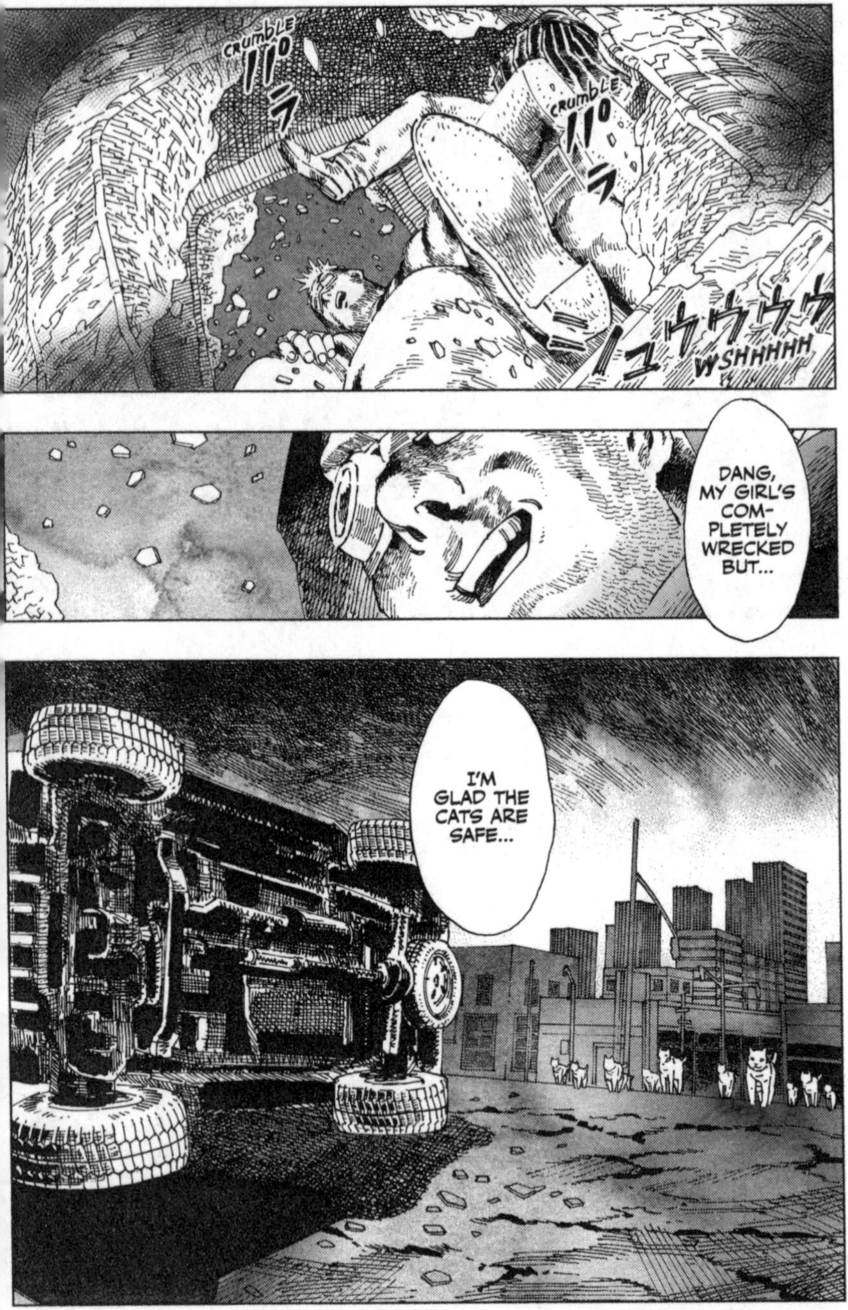
CRUMBLE
CRUMBLE
WSHHHHH
DANG, MY GIRL'S COM-PLETELY WRECKED BUT...
I'M GLAD THE CATS ARE SAFE...

Russian Blue

As the name implies, this is a breed with a gray-blue coat believed to have originated in Russia. Although they almost went extinct towards the end of World War II, their numbers have recovered in recent years.

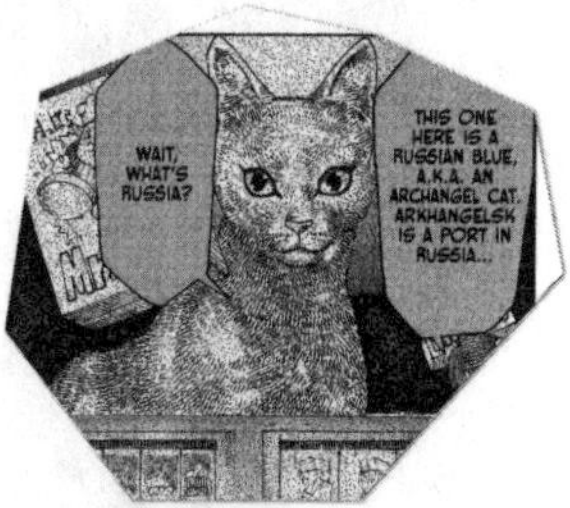
THIS ONE HERE IS A RUSSIAN BLUE, A.K.A. AN ARCHANGEL CAT. ARKHANGELSK IS A PORT IN RUSSIA...
WAIT, WHAT'S RUSSIA?

NYAIGHT
OF THE
LIVING
CAT
1

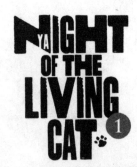

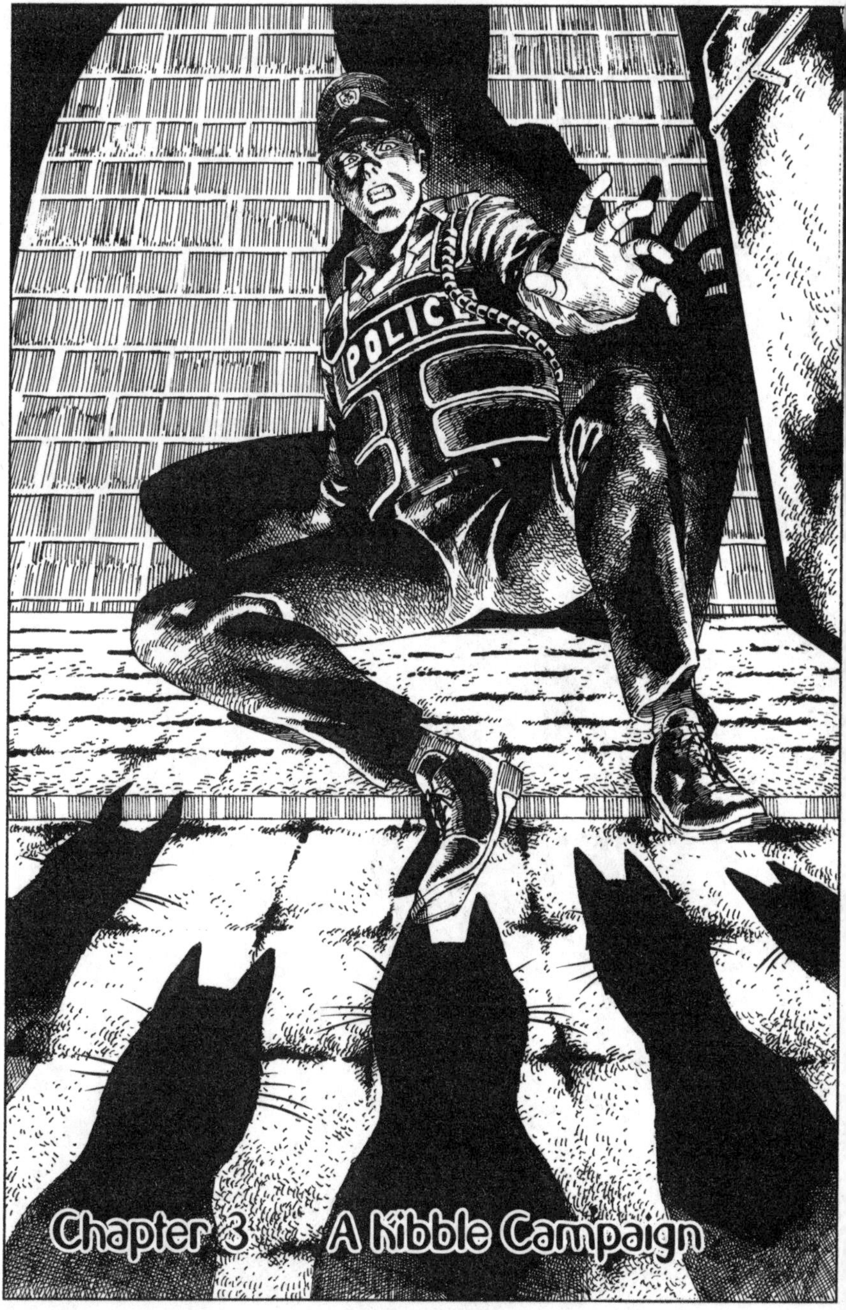
POLICE
Chapter 3 A Kibble Campaign

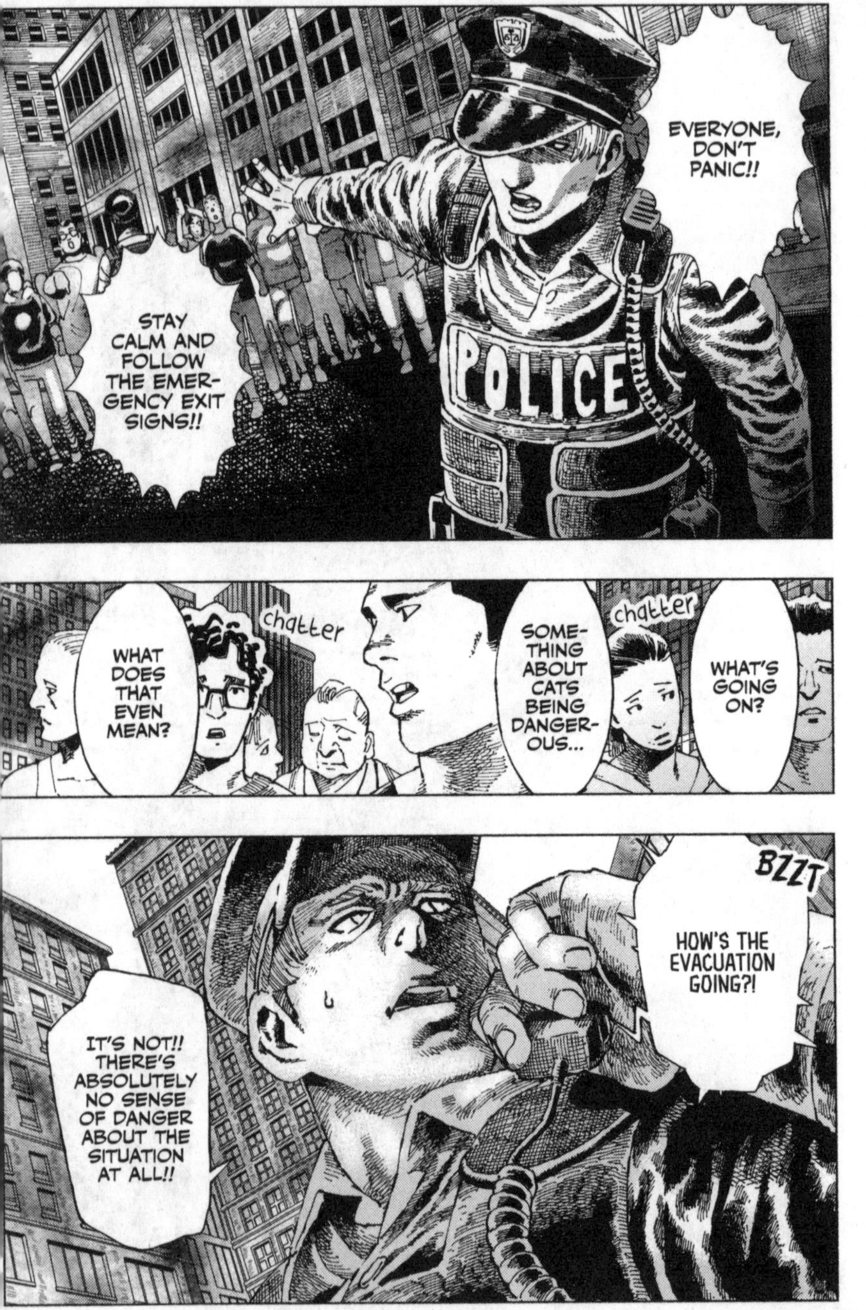
EVERYONE, DON'T PANIC!!
STAY CALM AND FOLLOW THE EMERGENCY EXIT SIGNS!!
chatter
WHAT'S GOING ON?
SOMETHING ABOUT CATS BEING DANGEROUS...
chatter
WHAT DOES THAT EVEN MEAN?
BZZT
HOW'S THE EVACUATION GOING?!
IT'S NOT!! THERE'S ABSOLUTELY NO SENSE OF DANGER ABOUT THE SITUATION AT ALL!!

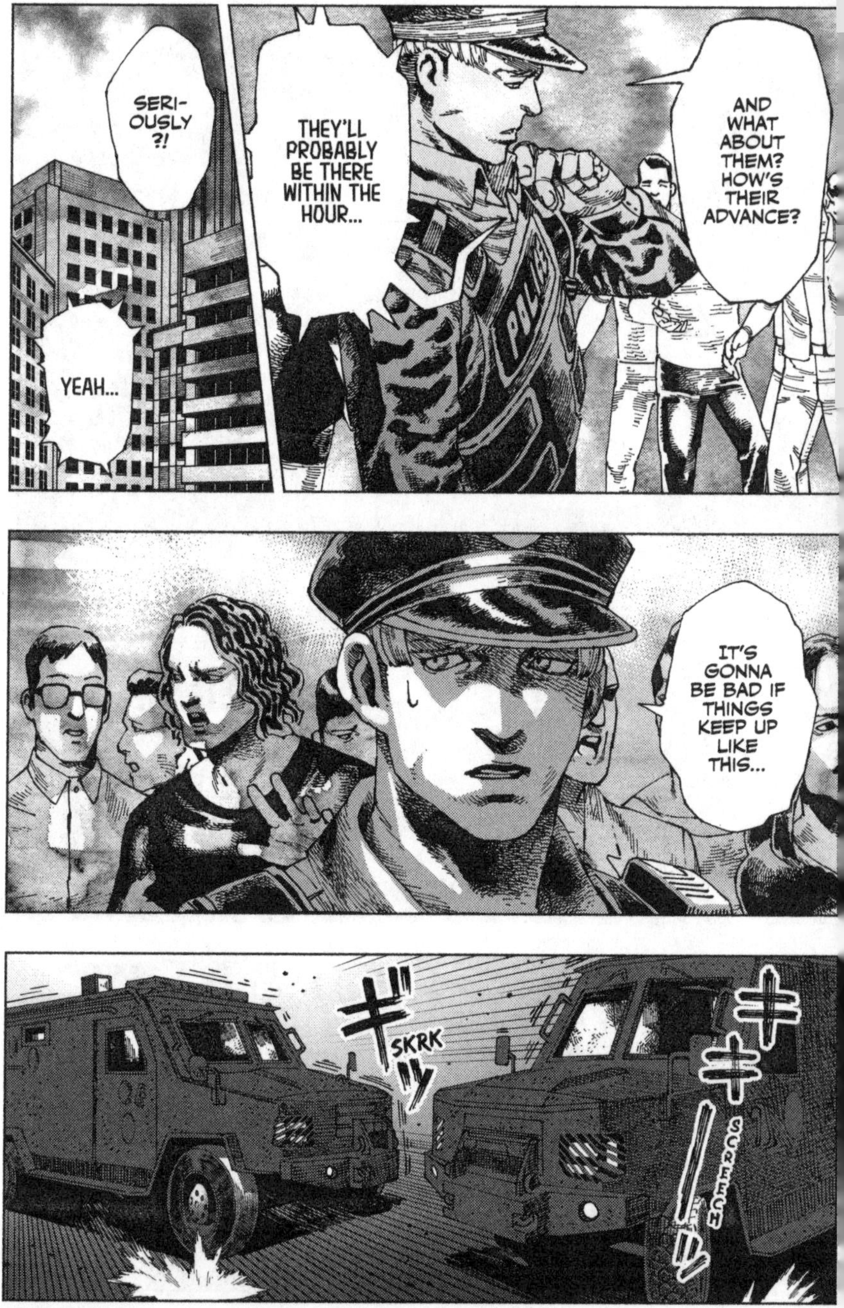
AND WHAT ABOUT THEM? HOW'S THEIR ADVANCE?
THEY'LL PROBABLY BE THERE WITHIN THE HOUR...
SERI-OUSLY ?!
YEAH...
IT'S GONNA BE BAD IF THINGS KEEP UP LIKE THIS...
SCREECH
SKRK

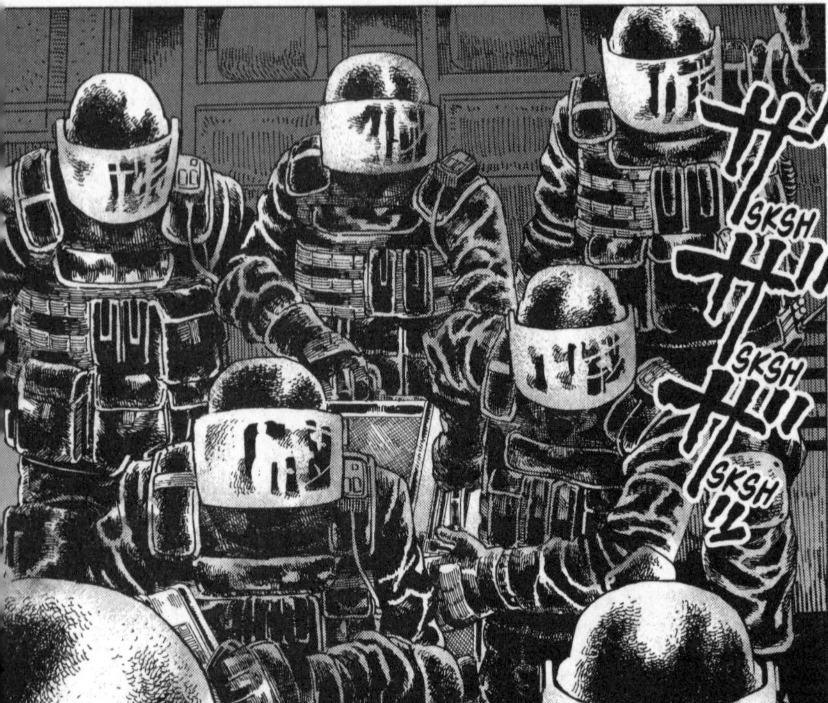
SKSH
SKSH
SKSH
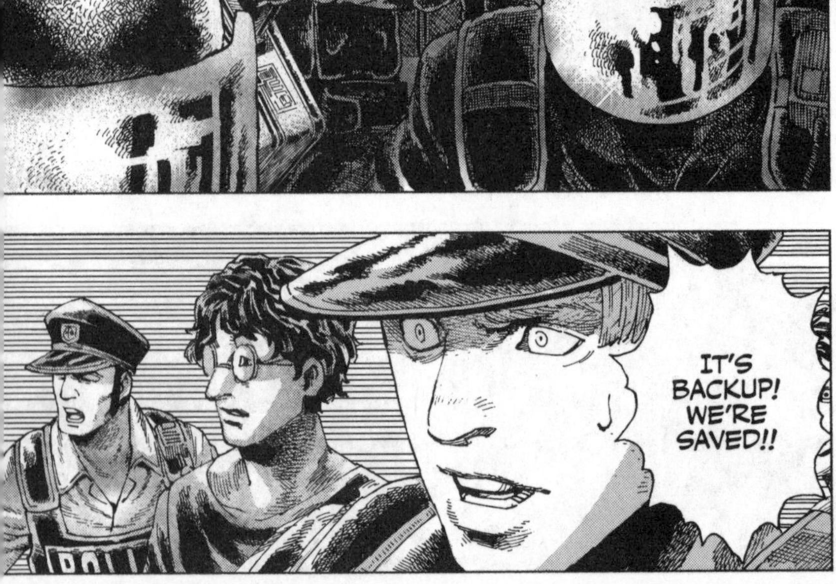
IT'S BACKUP! WE'RE SAVED!!

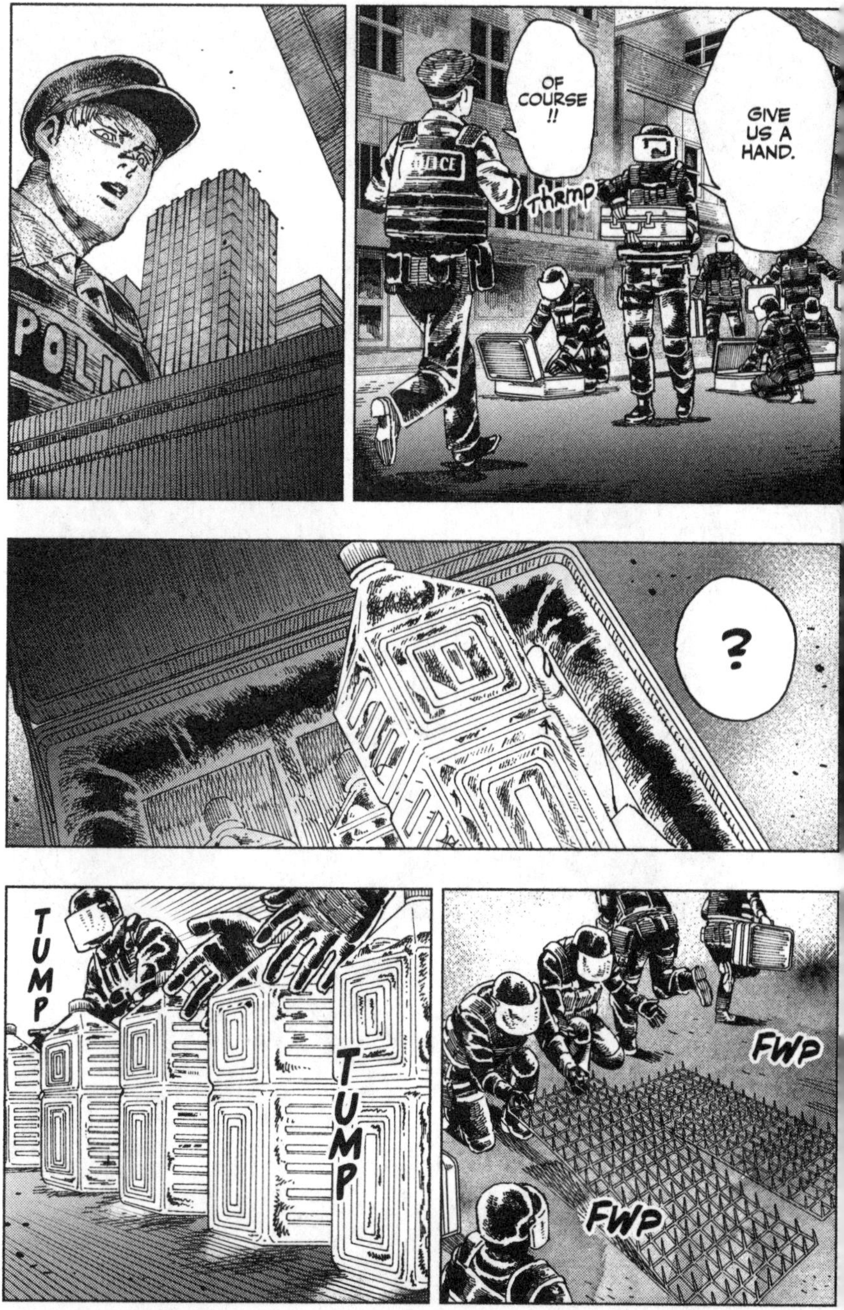
GIVE US A HAND.
OF COURSE !!
thrmp
?
FWP
FWP
TUMP
TUMP

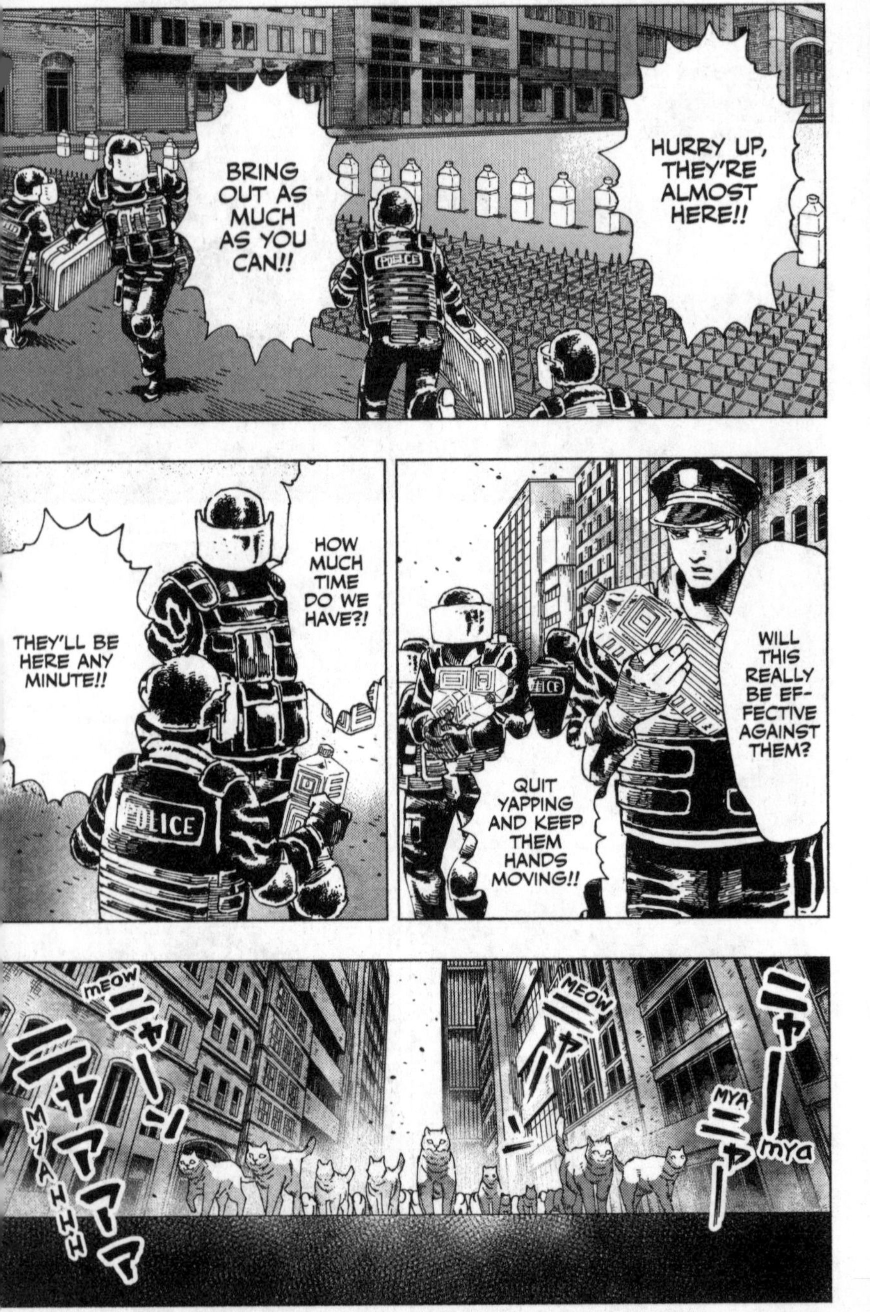
HURRY UP, THEY'RE ALMOST HERE!!
BRING OUT AS MUCH AS YOU CAN!!
WILL THIS REALLY BE EF-FECTIVE AGAINST THEM?
QUIT YAPPING AND KEEP THEM HANDS MOVING!!
HOW MUCH TIME DO WE HAVE?!
THEY'LL BE HERE ANY MINUTE!!
ニャーー
mya
ニャー
MYA
ニャー
MEOW
ニャー
MEOW
ニャアアア
MYAHHHH

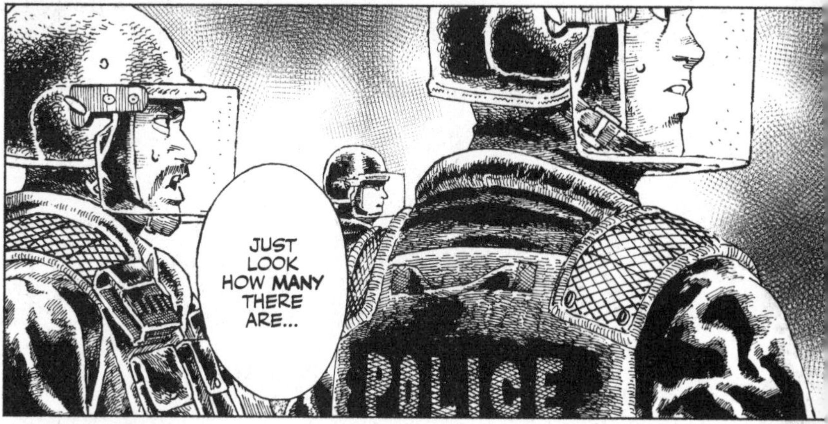
JUST LOOK HOW **MANY** THERE ARE...
POLICE

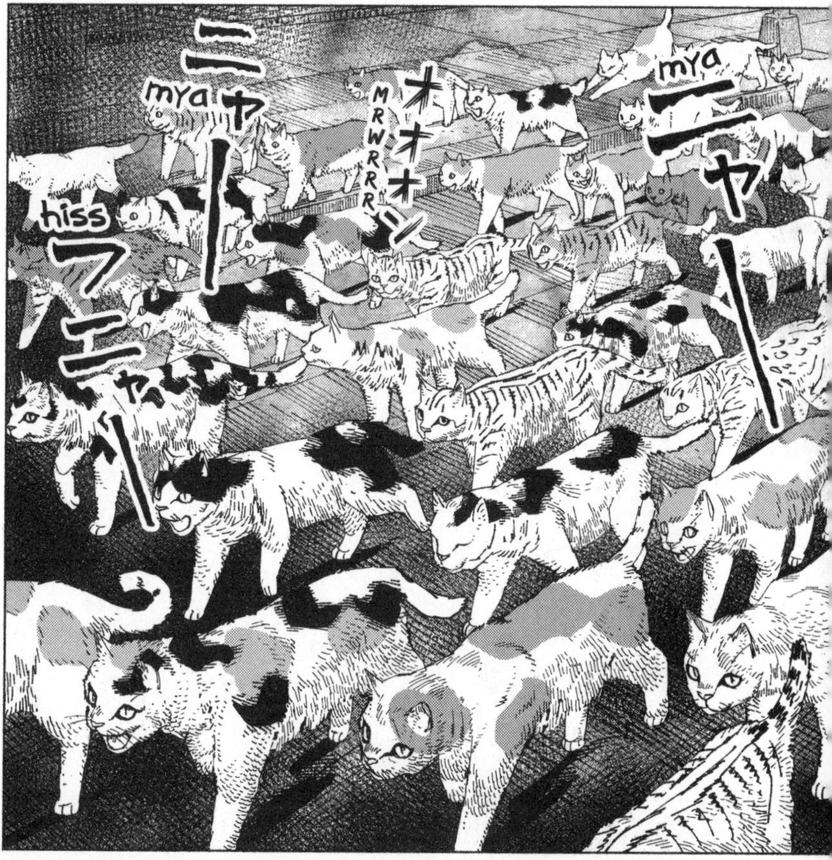
mya
ニャー
MRWRRRR
オオオーン
mya
ニャー
hiss

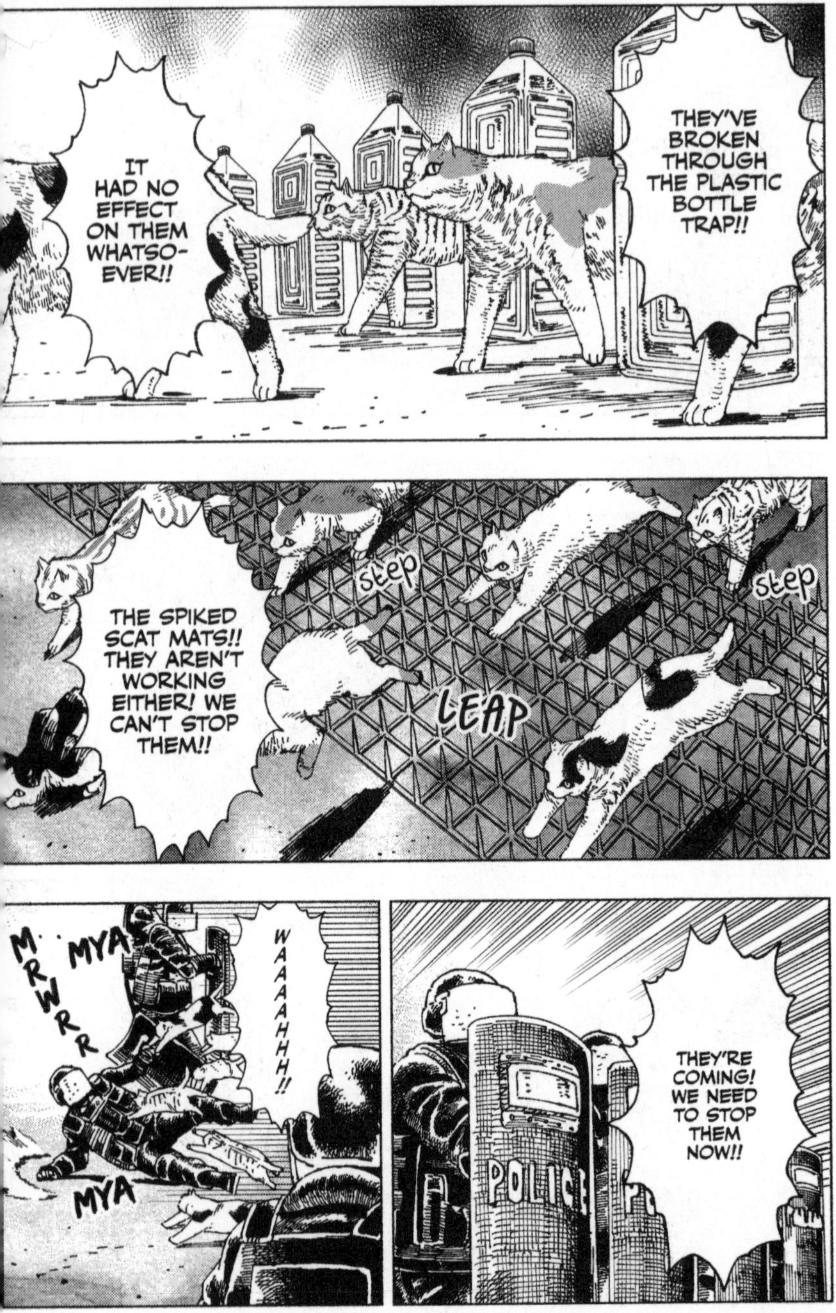
THEY'VE BROKEN THROUGH THE PLASTIC BOTTLE TRAP!!
IT HAD NO EFFECT ON THEM WHATSO-EVER!!
step
step
THE SPIKED SCAT MATS!! THEY AREN'T WORKING EITHER! WE CAN'T STOP THEM!!
LEAP
THEY'RE COMING! WE NEED TO STOP THEM NOW!!
POLICE
WAAAAAHHH!!
MYA
MRWRR
MYA

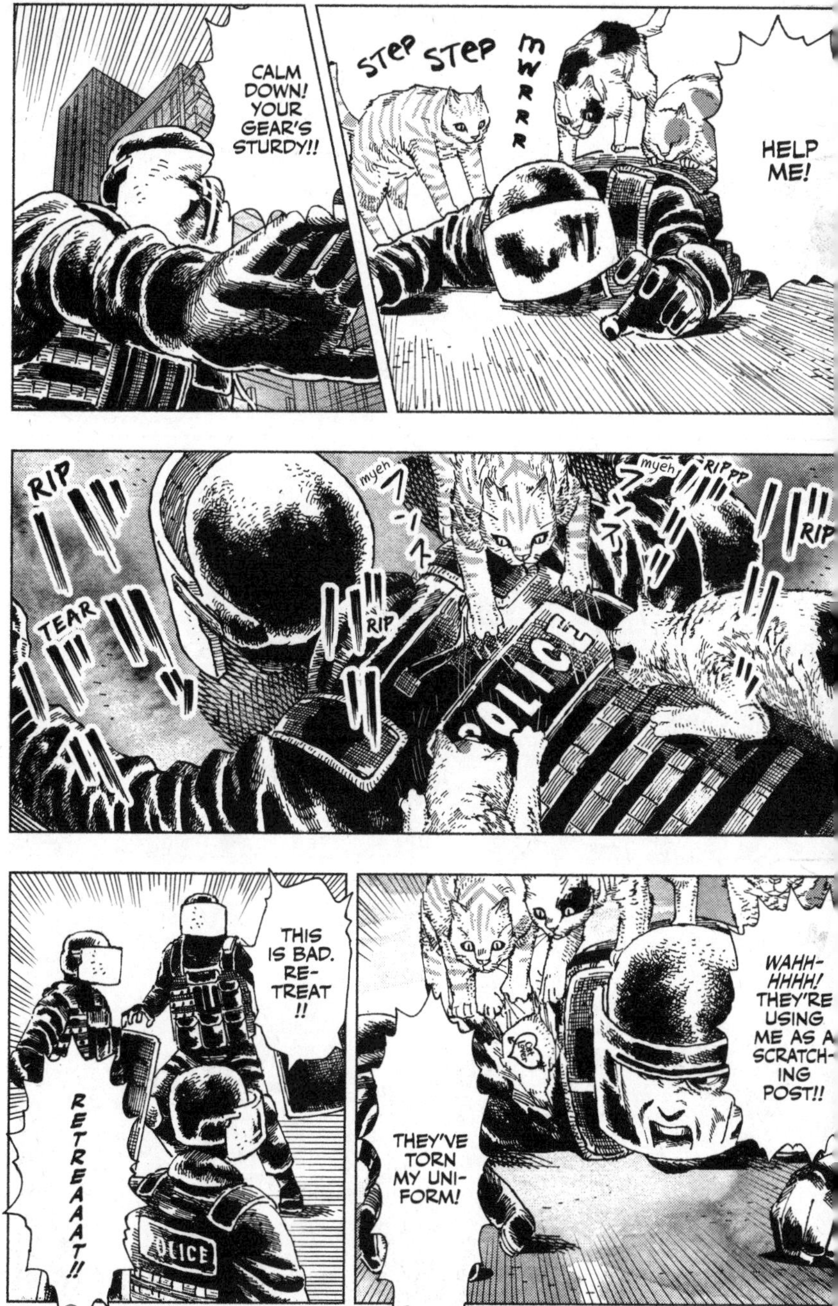
STEP STEP
MWRRR
HELP ME!
CALM DOWN! YOUR GEAR'S STURDY!!
RIP
RIPPP
myeh
myeh
RIP
TEAR
RIP
POLICE
WAHH-HHHH! THEY'RE USING ME AS A SCRATCH-ING POST!!
THEY'VE TORN MY UNI-FORM!
THIS IS BAD. RE-TREAT!!
RETREAAAAT!!
OLICE

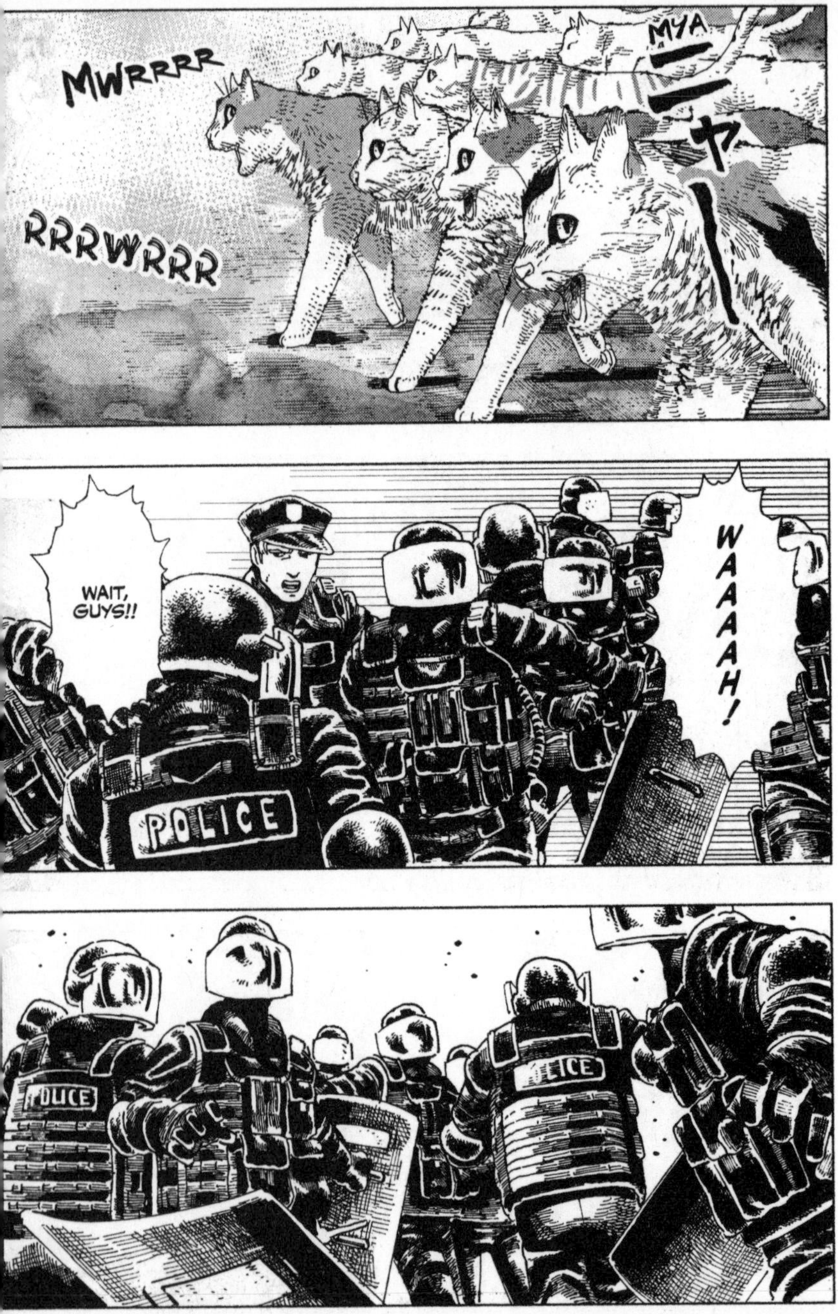
MYA
ヤ
MWRRRR
RRRWRRRR
WAAAAAH!
WAIT, GUYS!!
POLICE

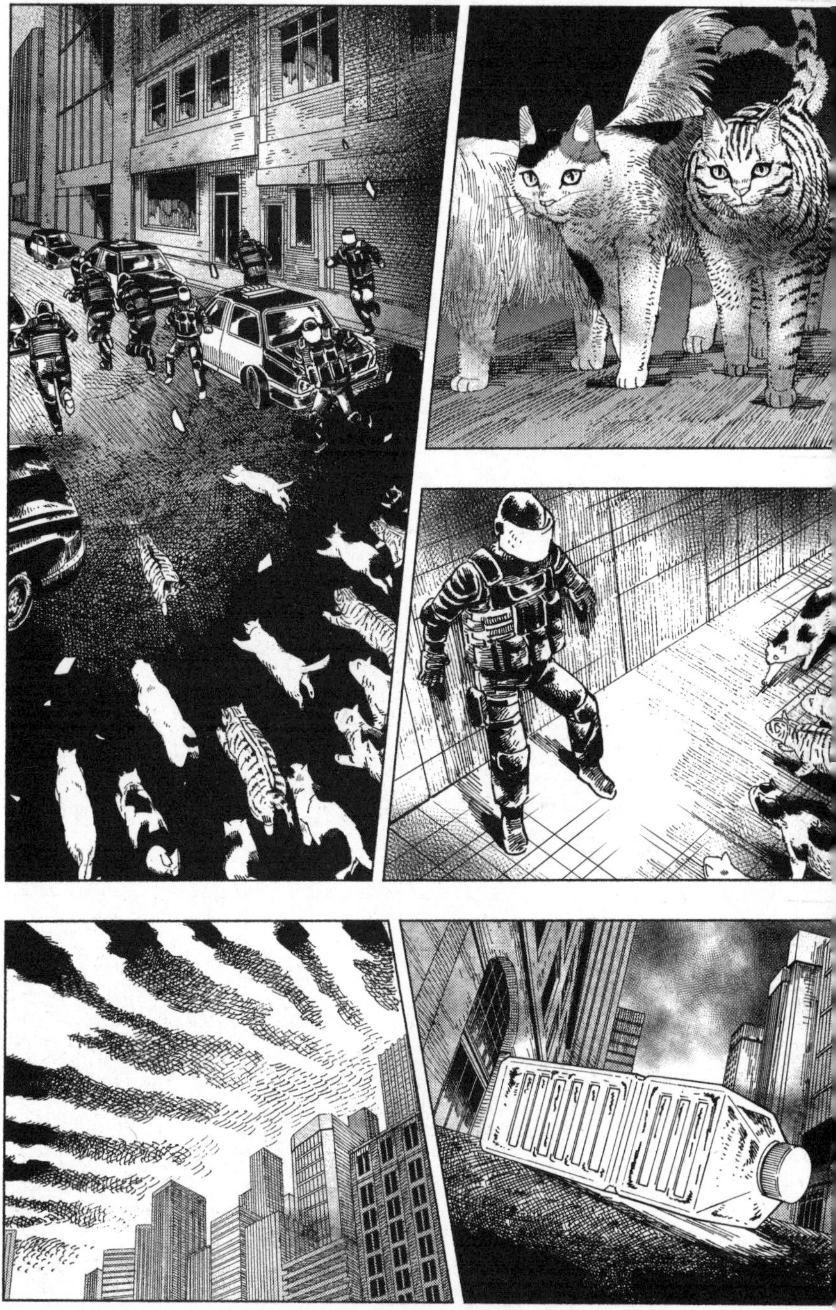

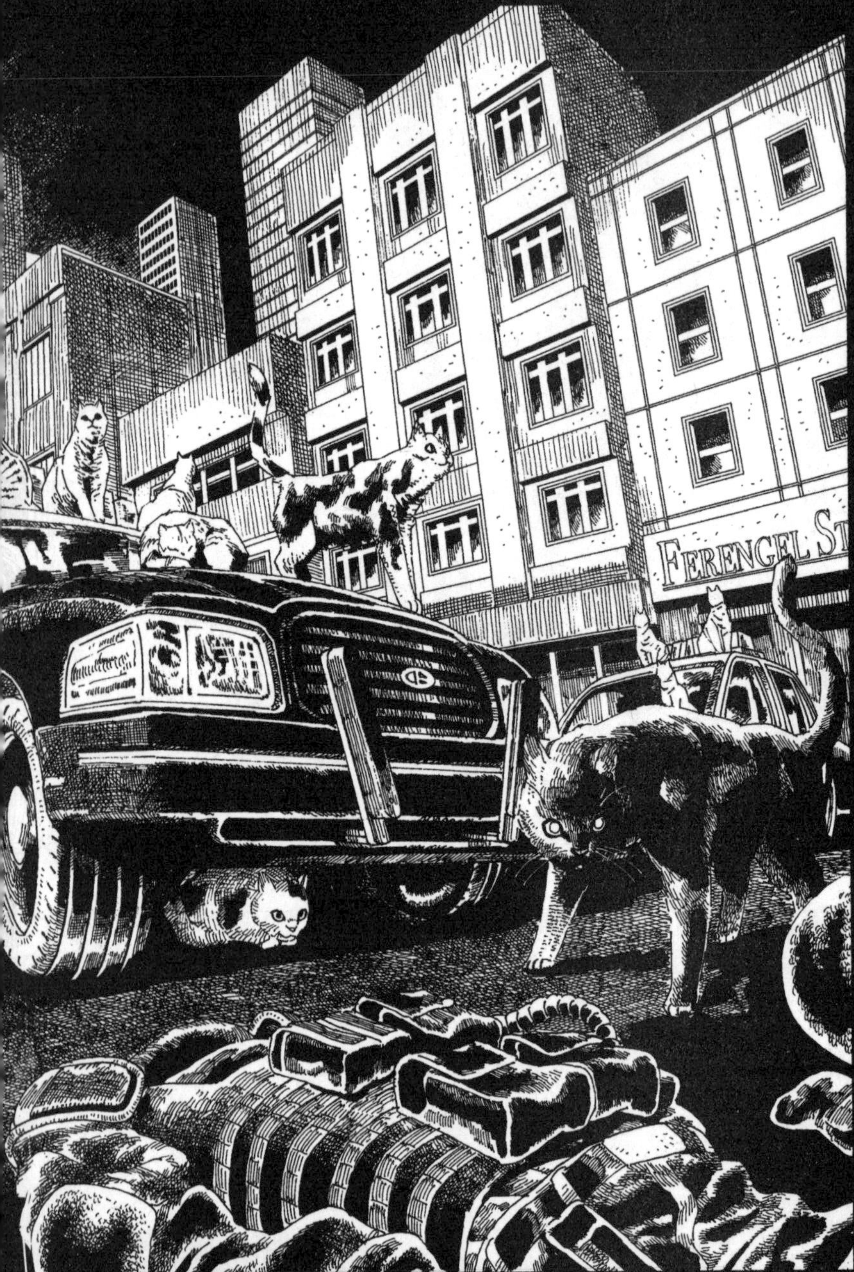
FERENGEL ST

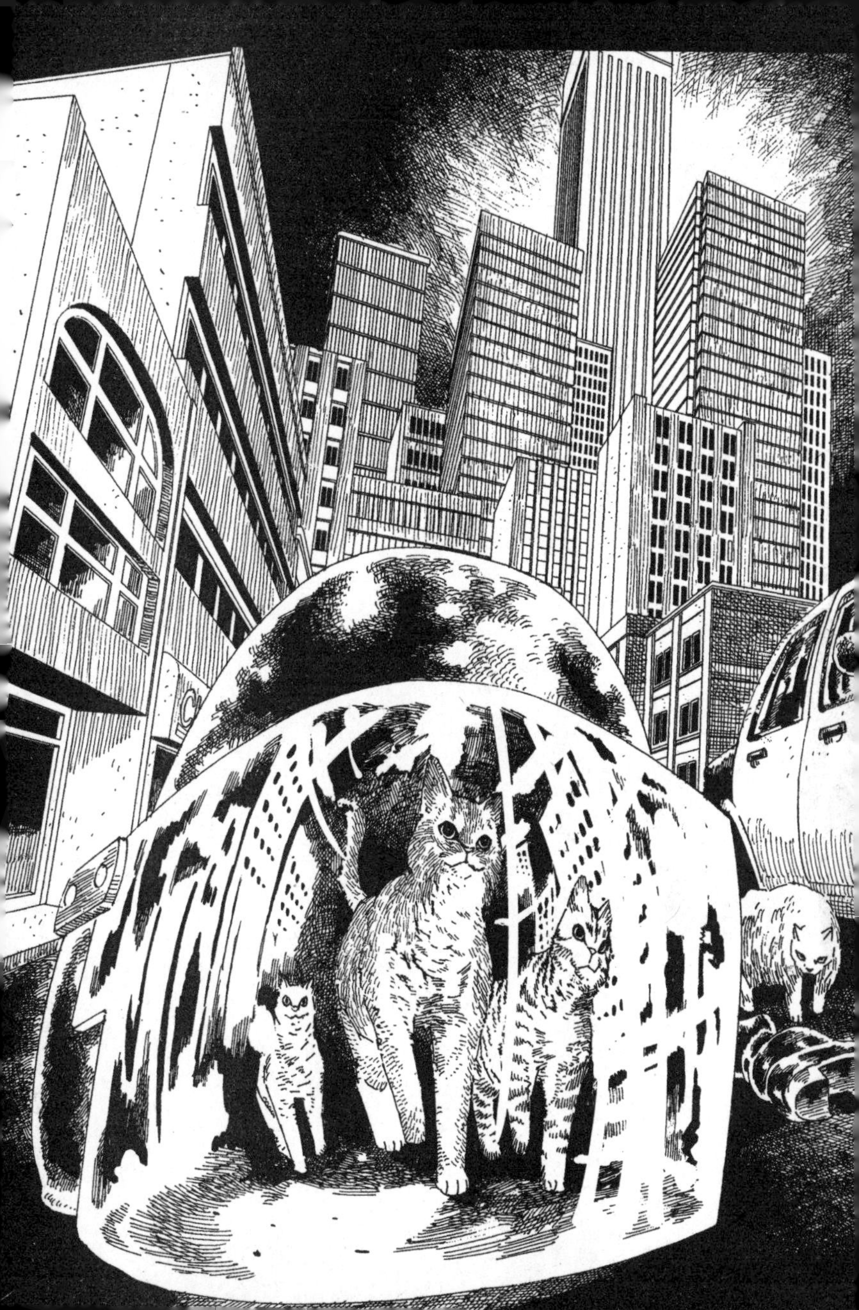

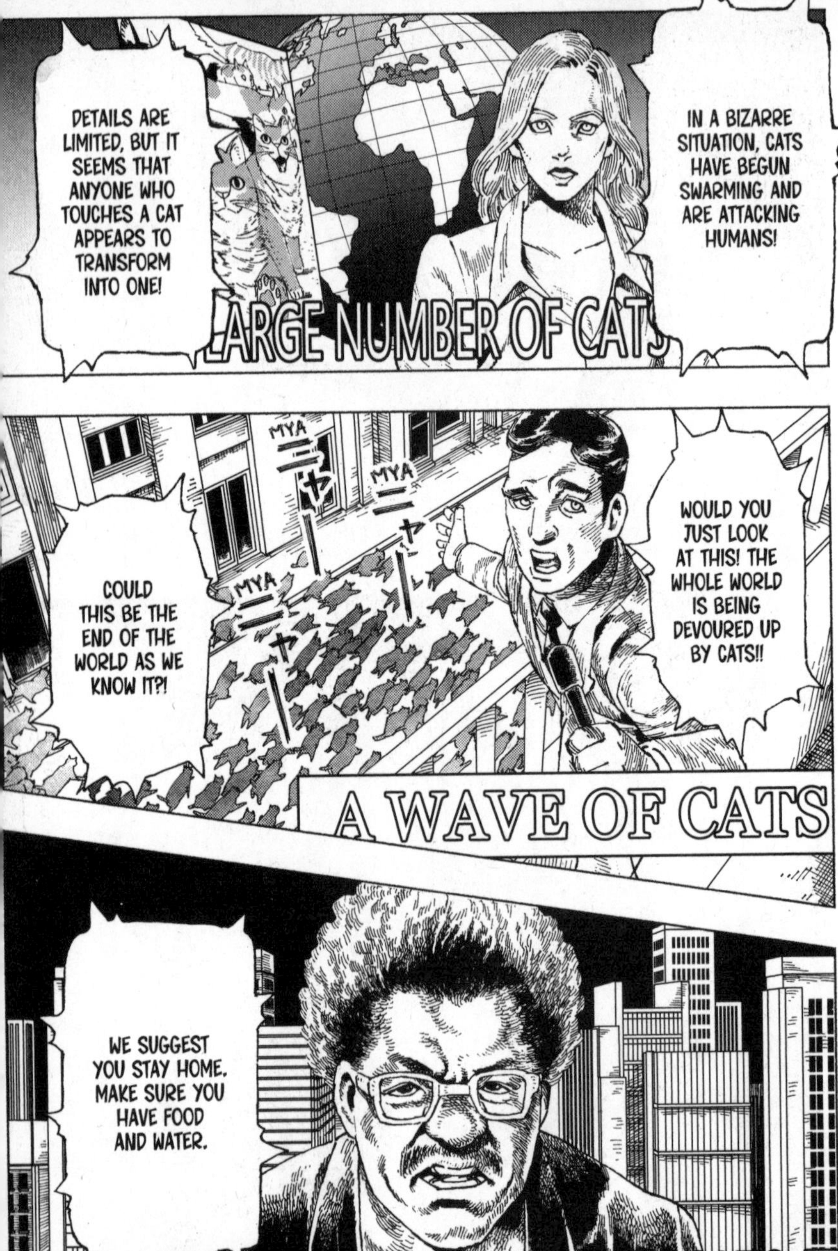
IN A BIZARRE SITUATION, CATS HAVE BEGUN SWARMING AND ARE ATTACKING HUMANS!
DETAILS ARE LIMITED, BUT IT SEEMS THAT ANYONE WHO TOUCHES A CAT APPEARS TO TRANSFORM INTO ONE!
LARGE NUMBER OF CATS
WOULD YOU JUST LOOK AT THIS! THE WHOLE WORLD IS BEING DEVOURED UP BY CATS!!
MYA
MYA
MYA
COULD THIS BE THE END OF THE WORLD AS WE KNOW IT?!
A WAVE OF CATS
WE SUGGEST YOU STAY HOME. MAKE SURE YOU HAVE FOOD AND WATER.
A HUGE NUMBER OF CATS

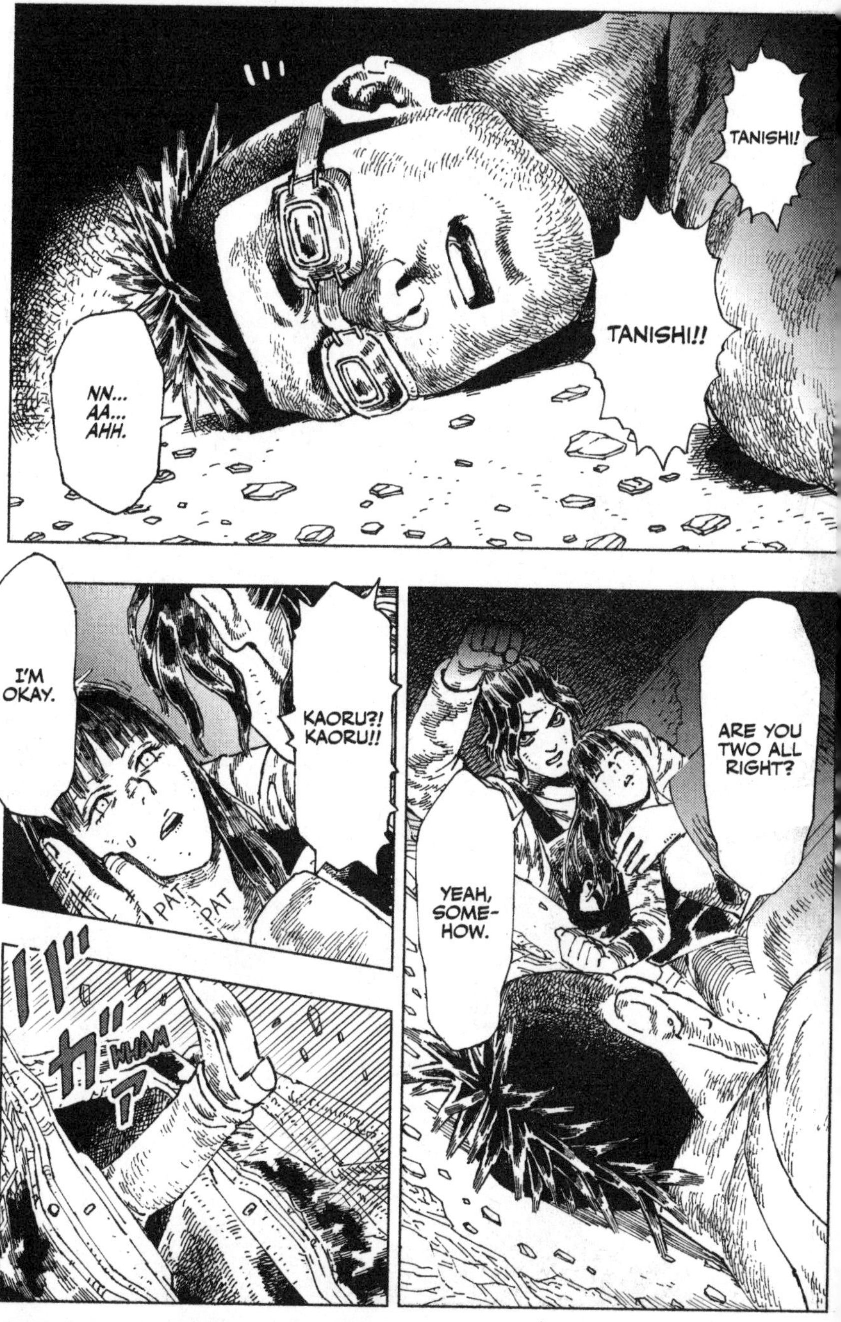
TANISHI!
TANISHI!!
NN... AA... AHH.
ARE YOU TWO ALL RIGHT?
YEAH, SOMEHOW.
KAORU?! KAORU!!
I'M OKAY.
PAT PAT
WHAM

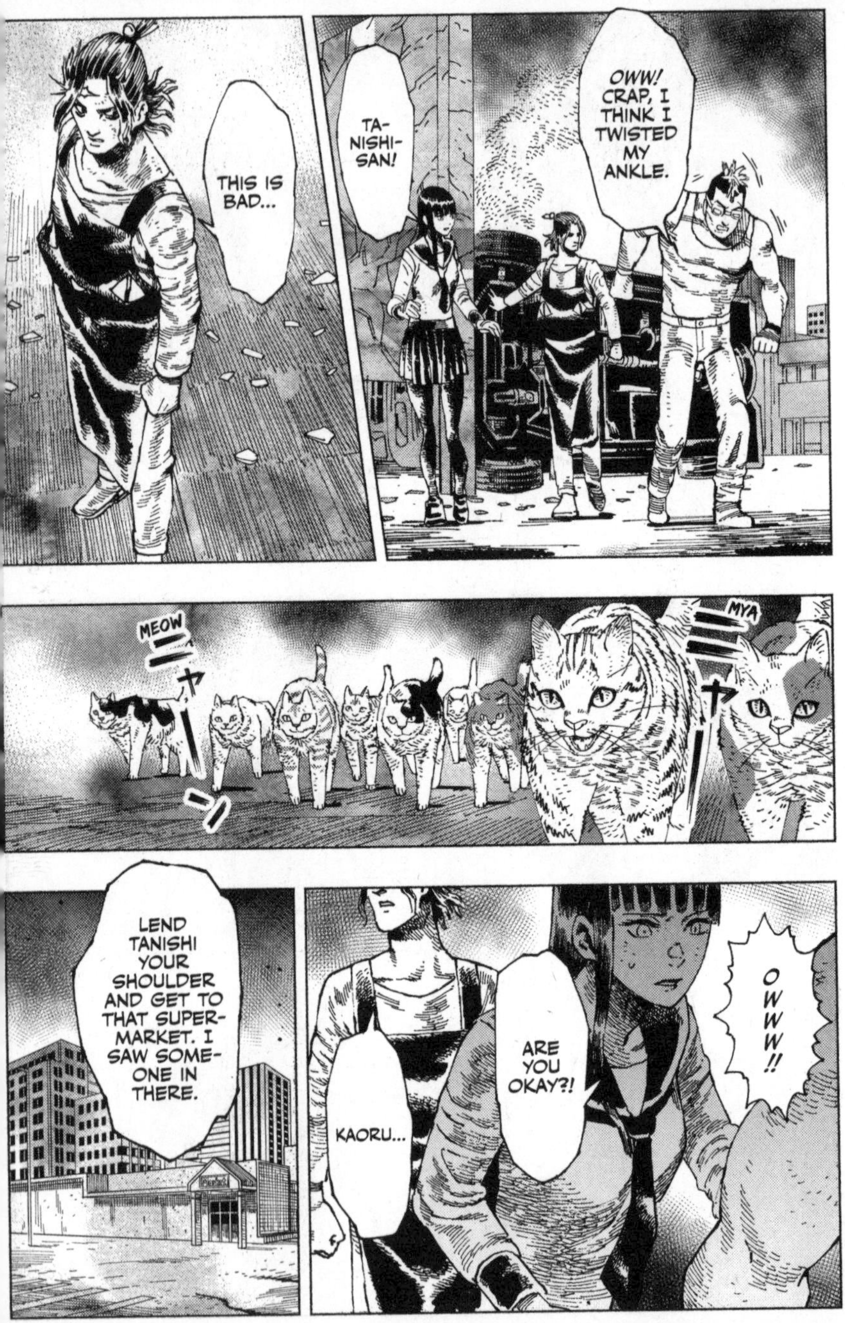
OWW! CRAP, I THINK I TWISTED MY ANKLE.
TA-NISHI-SAN!
THIS IS BAD...
MYA
MEOW
OWWW!!
ARE YOU OKAY?!
KAORU...
LEND TANISHI YOUR SHOULDER AND GET TO THAT SUPER-MARKET. I SAW SOME-ONE IN THERE.

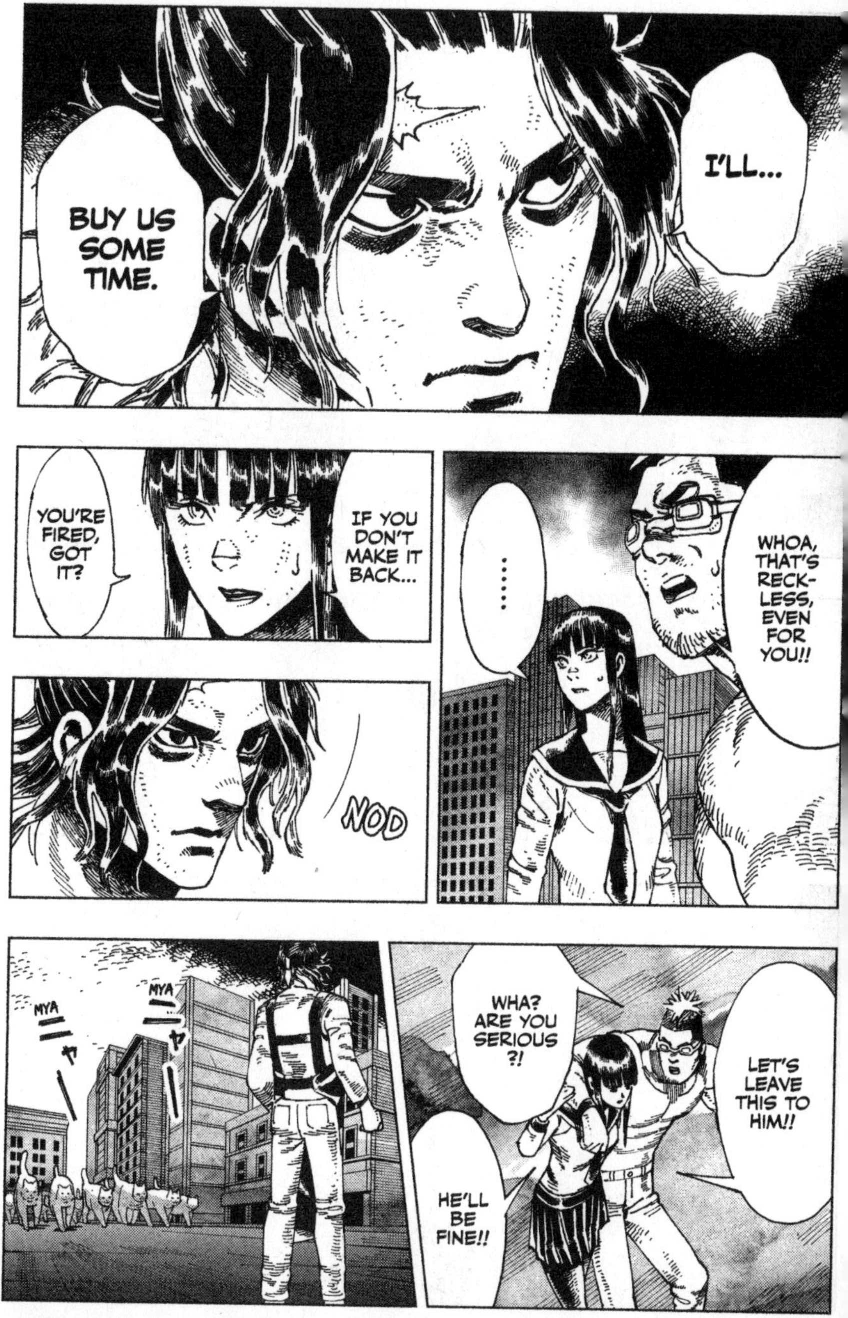
I'LL...
BUY US SOME TIME.
WHOA, THAT'S RECK-LESS, EVEN FOR YOU!!
......
IF YOU DON'T MAKE IT BACK...
YOU'RE FIRED, GOT IT?
NOD
LET'S LEAVE THIS TO HIM!!
WHA? ARE YOU SERIOUS?!
HE'LL BE FINE!!
MYA
MYA

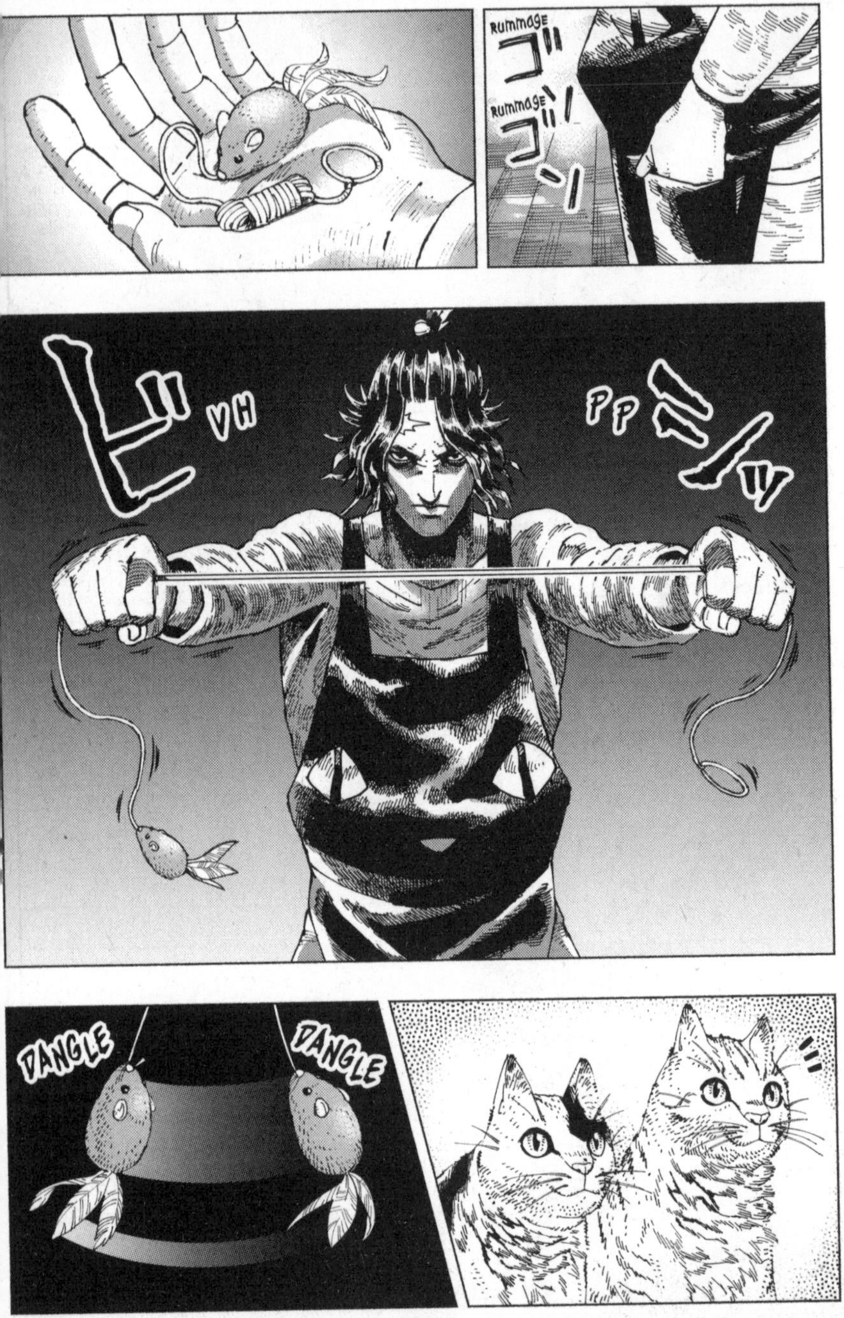
RUMMAGE
RUMMAGE
PP
VH
DANGLE
DANGLE

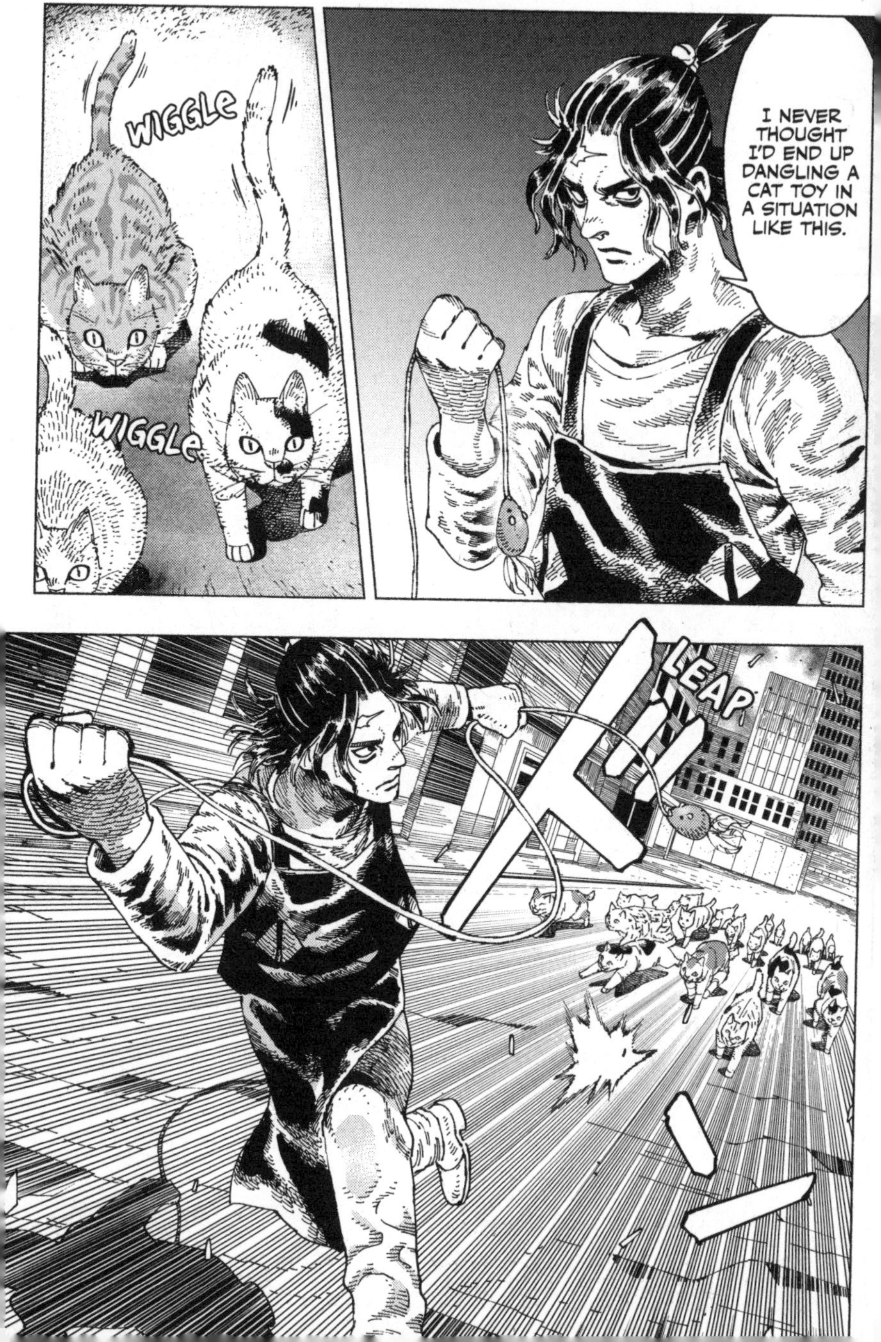
I NEVER THOUGHT I'D END UP DANGLING A CAT TOY IN A SITUATION LIKE THIS.
WIGGLE
WIGGLE
LEAP

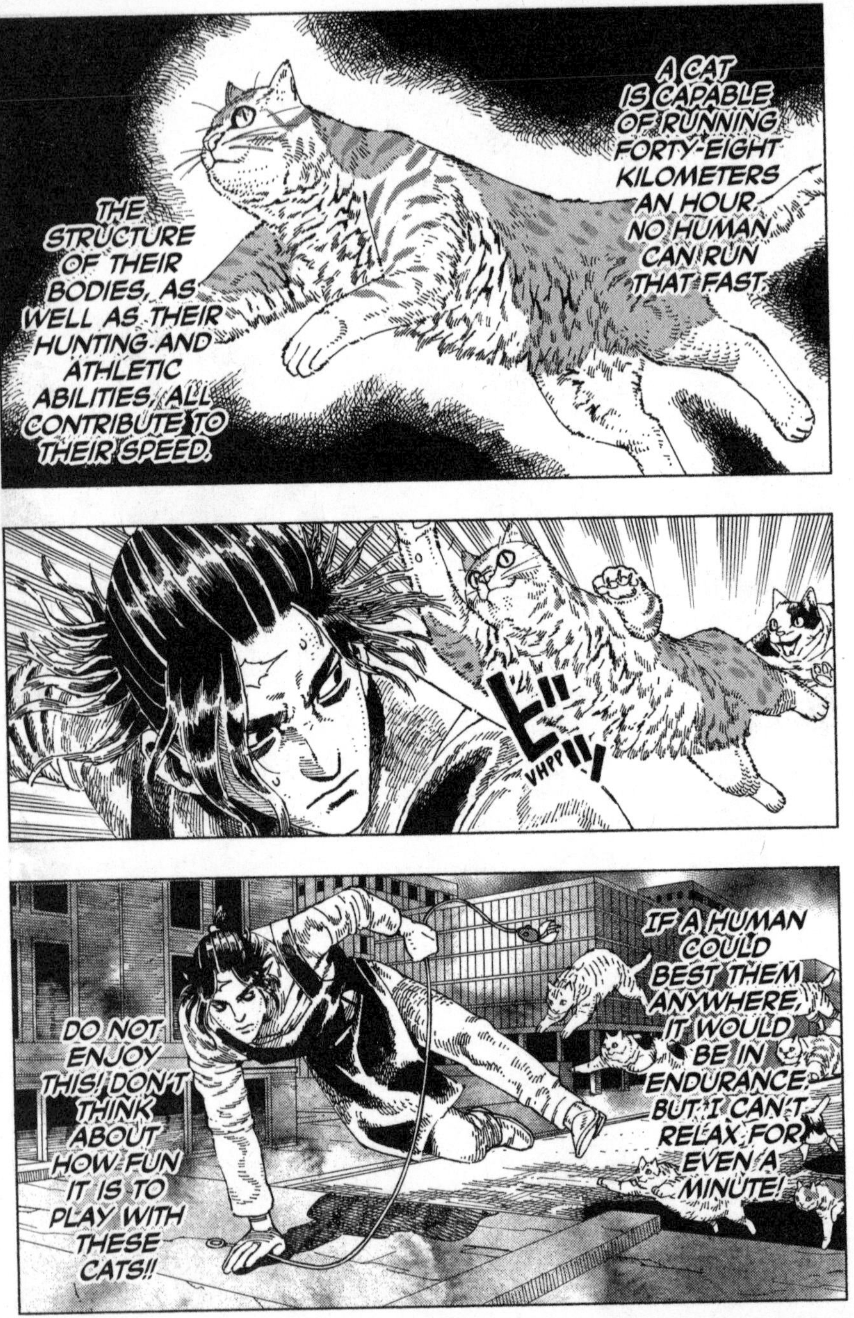
A CAT IS CAPABLE OF RUNNING FORTY-EIGHT KILOMETERS AN HOUR. NO HUMAN CAN RUN THAT FAST.
THE STRUCTURE OF THEIR BODIES, AS WELL AS THEIR HUNTING AND ATHLETIC ABILITIES, ALL CONTRIBUTE TO THEIR SPEED.
VHPP
IF A HUMAN COULD BEST THEM ANYWHERE, IT WOULD BE IN ENDURANCE. BUT I CAN'T RELAX FOR EVEN A MINUTE!
DO NOT ENJOY THIS! DON'T THINK ABOUT HOW FUN IT IS TO PLAY WITH THESE CATS!!

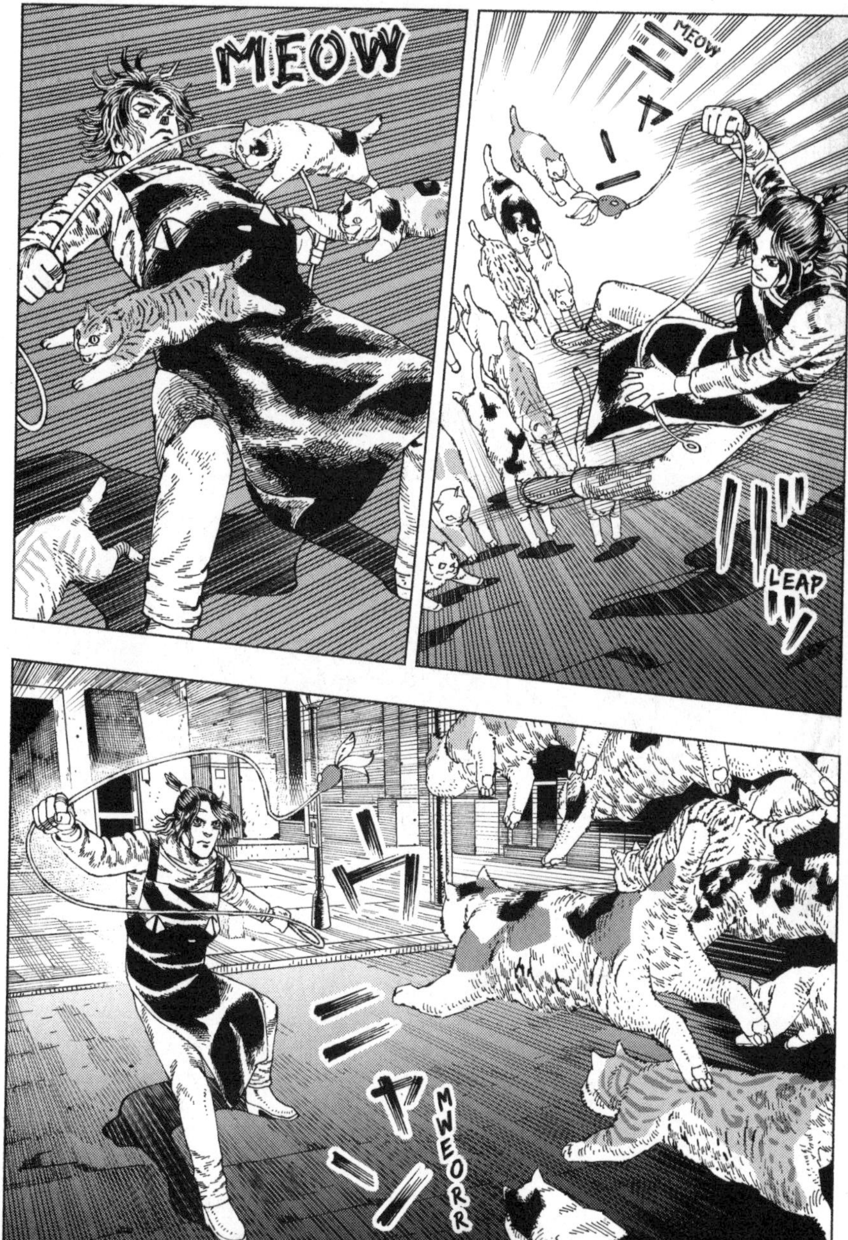
MEOW
LEAP
MEOW
MWEORR

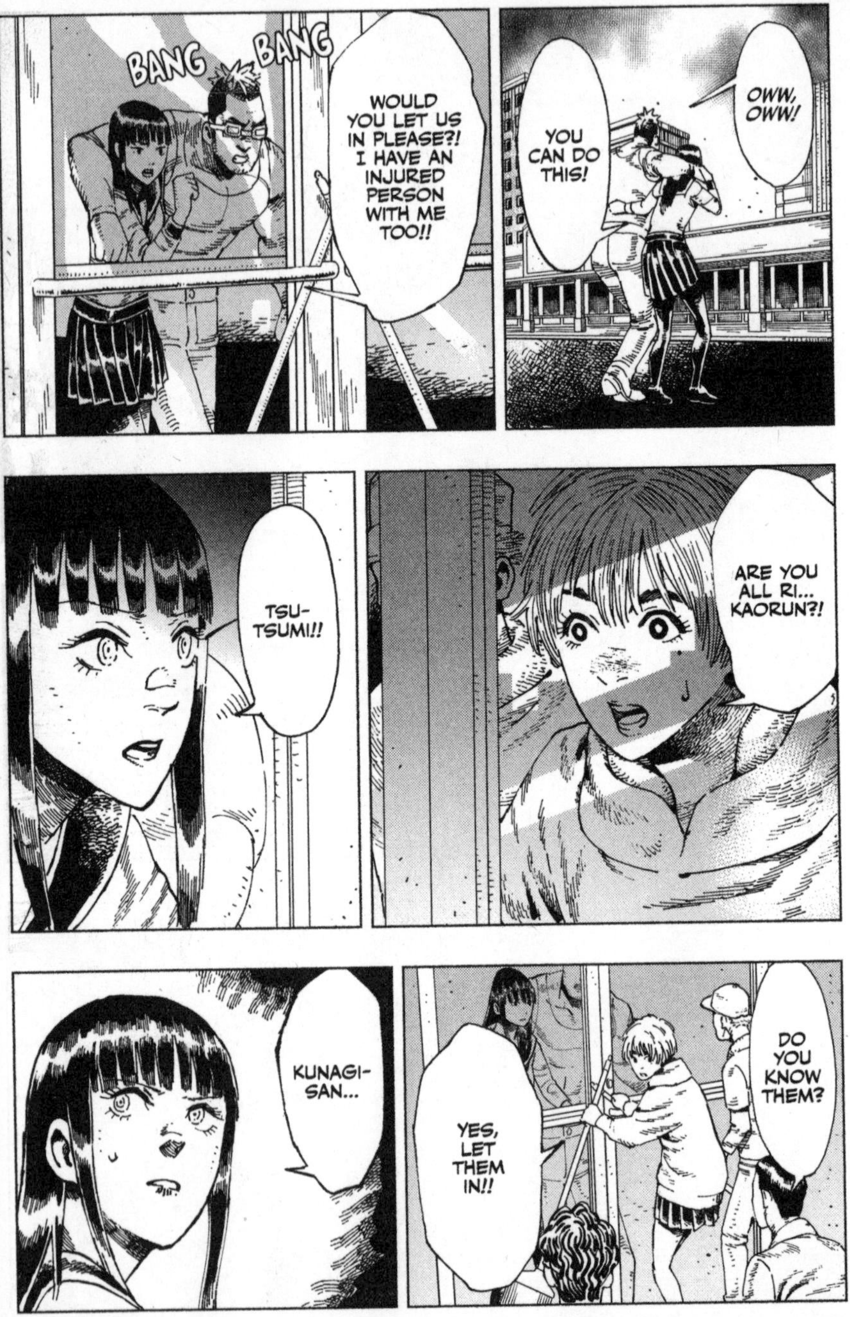
OWW, OWW!
YOU CAN DO THIS!
BANG BANG
WOULD YOU LET US IN PLEASE?! I HAVE AN INJURED PERSON WITH ME TOO!!
ARE YOU ALL RI... KAORUN?!
TSU-TSUMI!!
DO YOU KNOW THEM?
YES, LET THEM IN!!
KUNAGI-SAN...

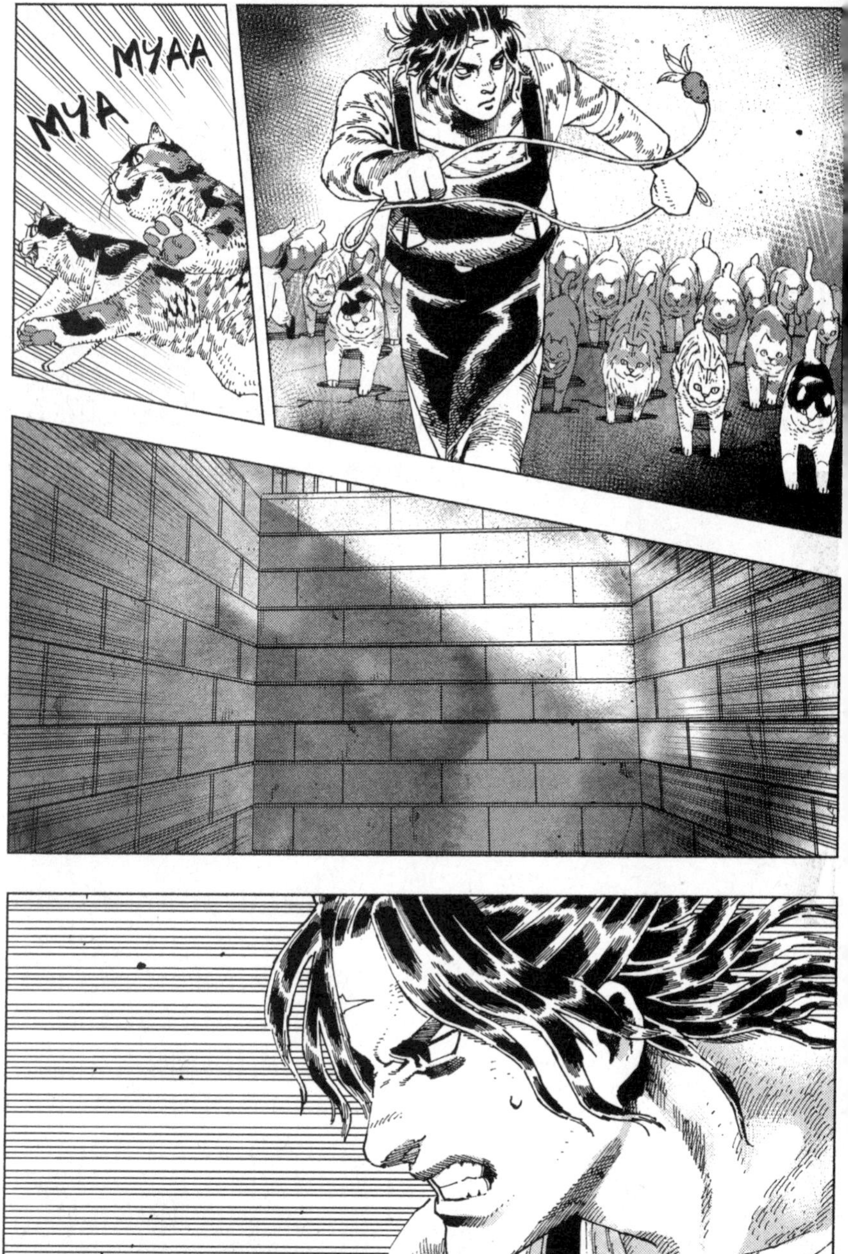
MYAA
MYA

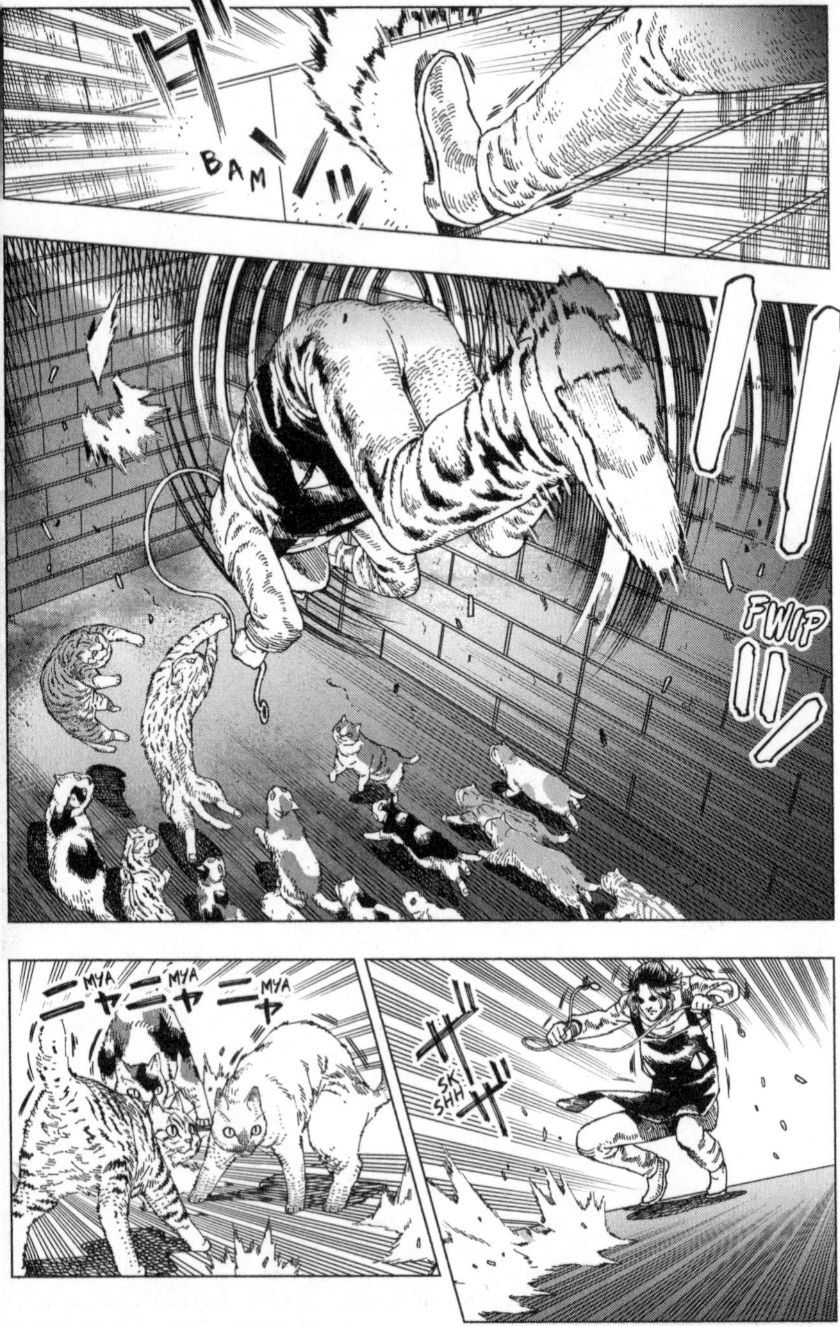
BAM
FWIP
SK SHH
ニャ MYA
ニャ MYA
ニャ MYA

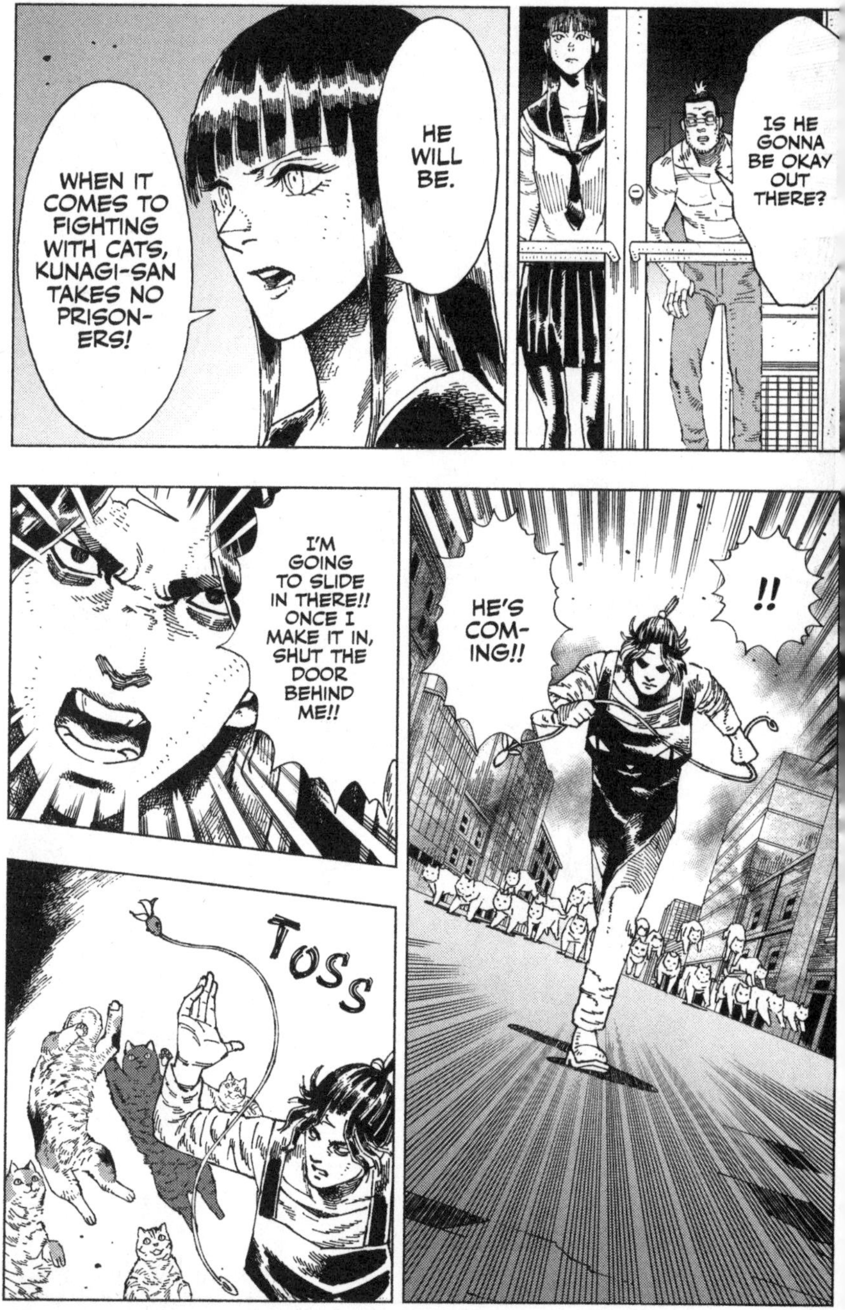
IS HE GONNA BE OKAY OUT THERE?
HE WILL BE.
WHEN IT COMES TO FIGHTING WITH CATS, KUNAGI-SAN TAKES NO PRISONERS!
!!
HE'S COMING!!
I'M GOING TO SLIDE IN THERE!! ONCE I MAKE IT IN, SHUT THE DOOR BEHIND ME!!
TOSS

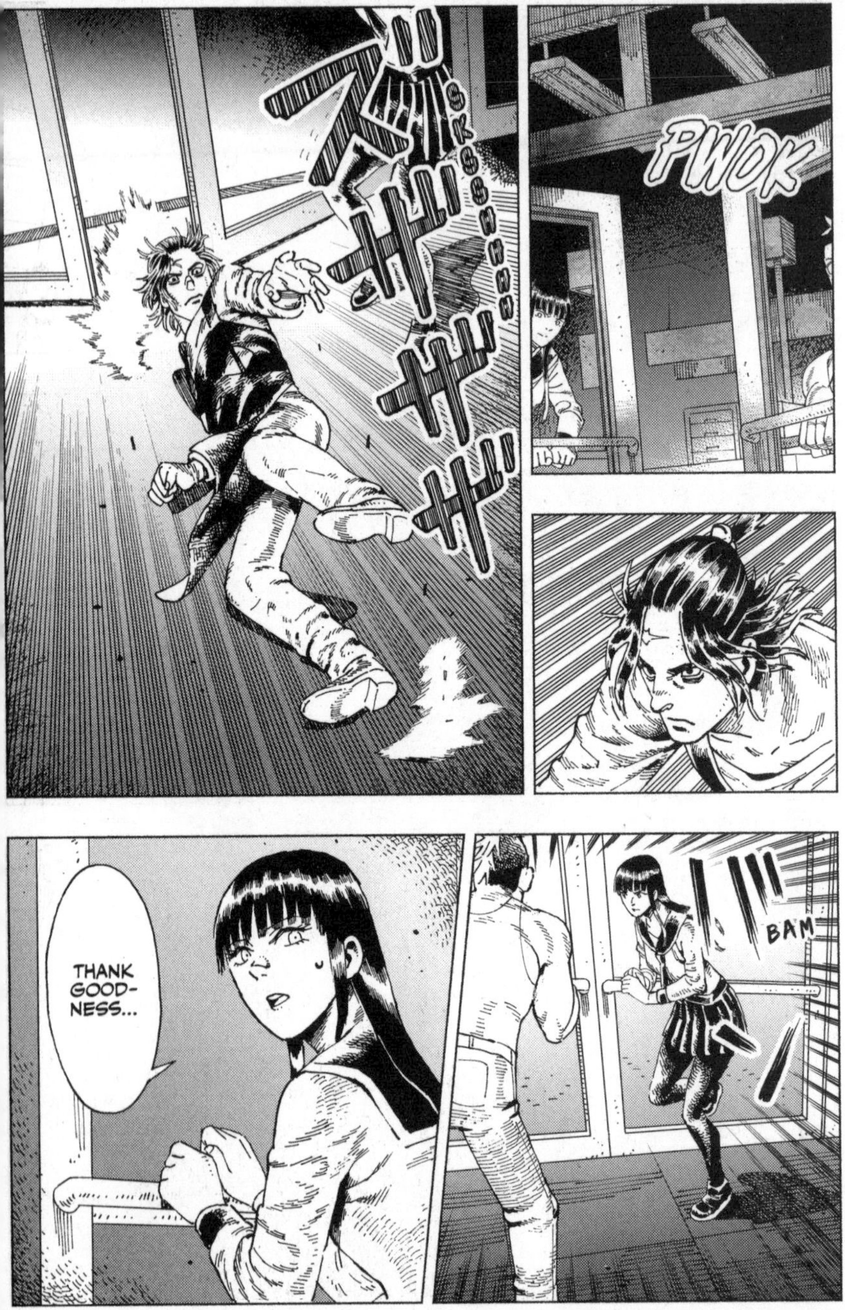
PWOK
SKSSHHHH
BAM
THANK GOODNESS...

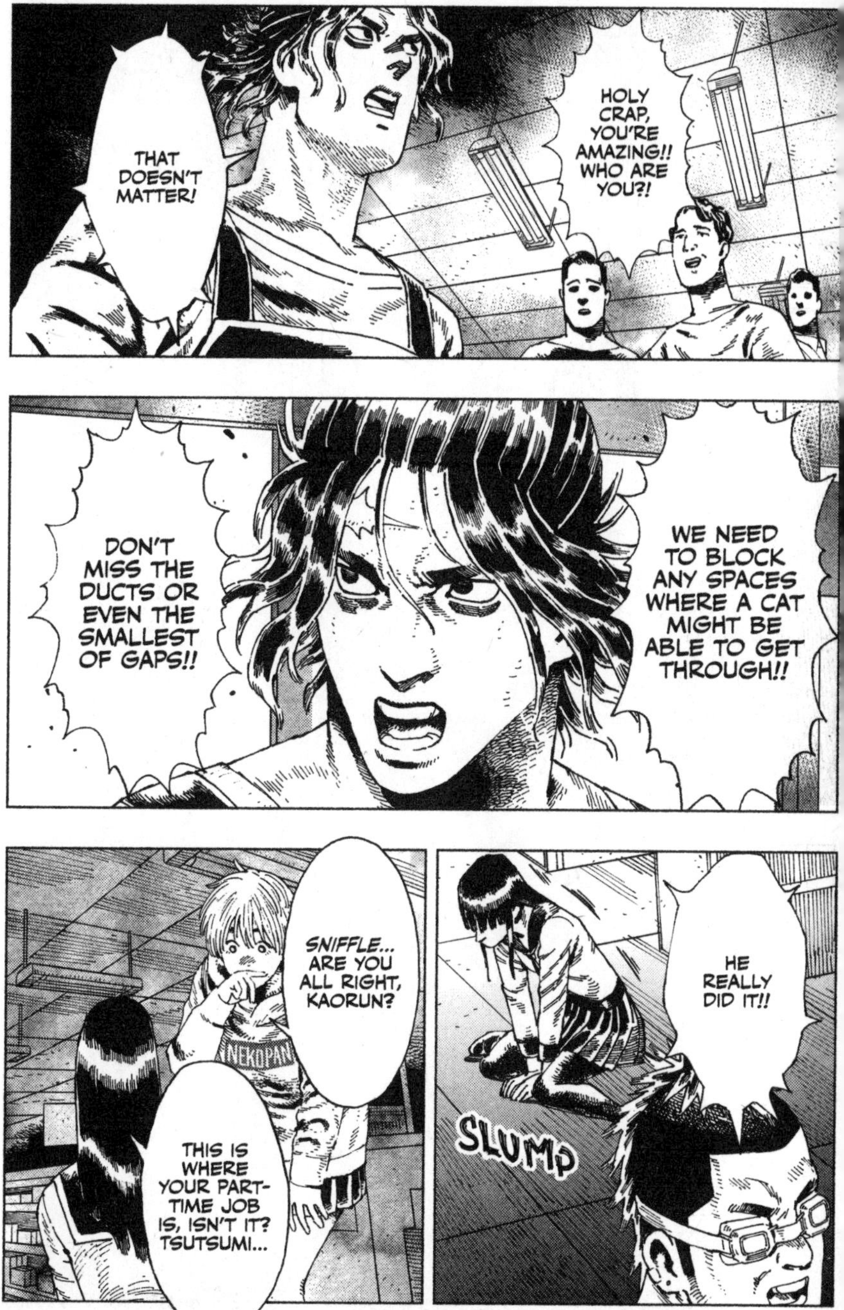
HOLY CRAP, YOU'RE AMAZING!! WHO ARE YOU?!
THAT DOESN'T MATTER!
WE NEED TO BLOCK ANY SPACES WHERE A CAT MIGHT BE ABLE TO GET THROUGH!!
DON'T MISS THE DUCTS OR EVEN THE SMALLEST OF GAPS!!
HE REALLY DID IT!!
SLUMP
SNIFFLE... ARE YOU ALL RIGHT, KAORUN?
NEKOPAN
THIS IS WHERE YOUR PART-TIME JOB IS, ISN'T IT? TSUTSUMI...

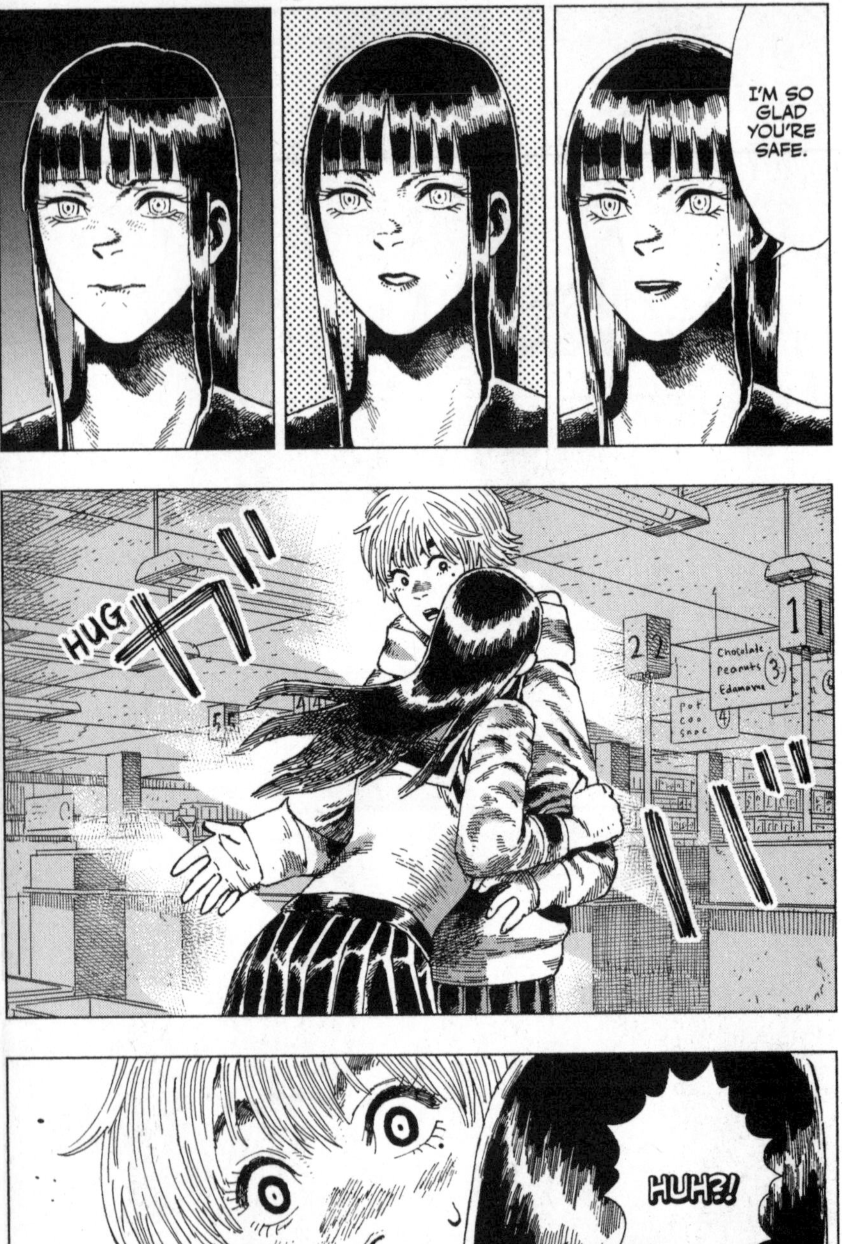
I'M SO GLAD YOU'RE SAFE.
HUG
Chocolate Peanuts Edamame
HUH?!

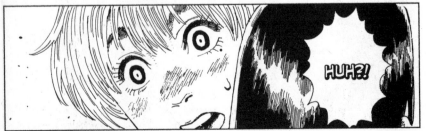

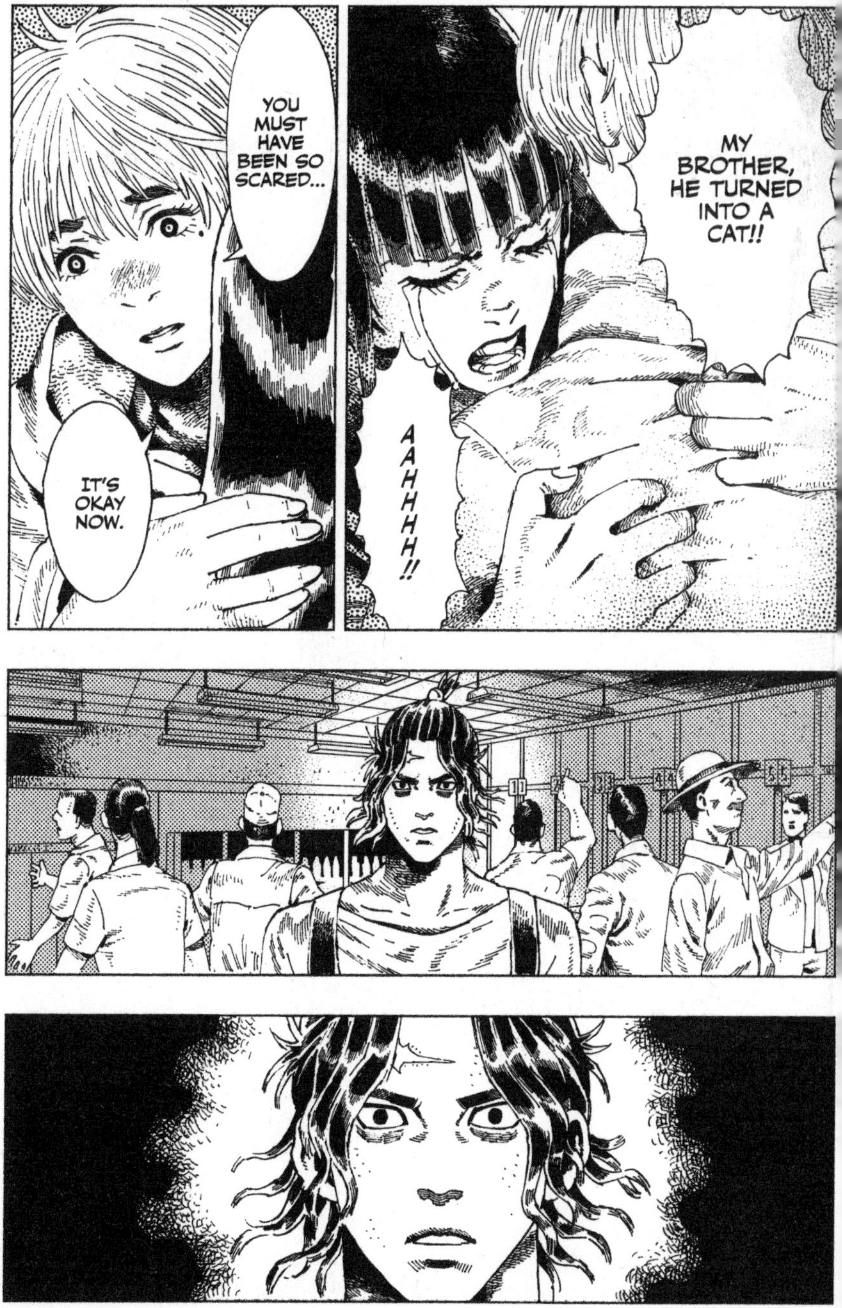
MY BROTHER, HE TURNED INTO A CAT!!
AAHHHHH!!
YOU MUST HAVE BEEN SO SCARED...
IT'S OKAY NOW.

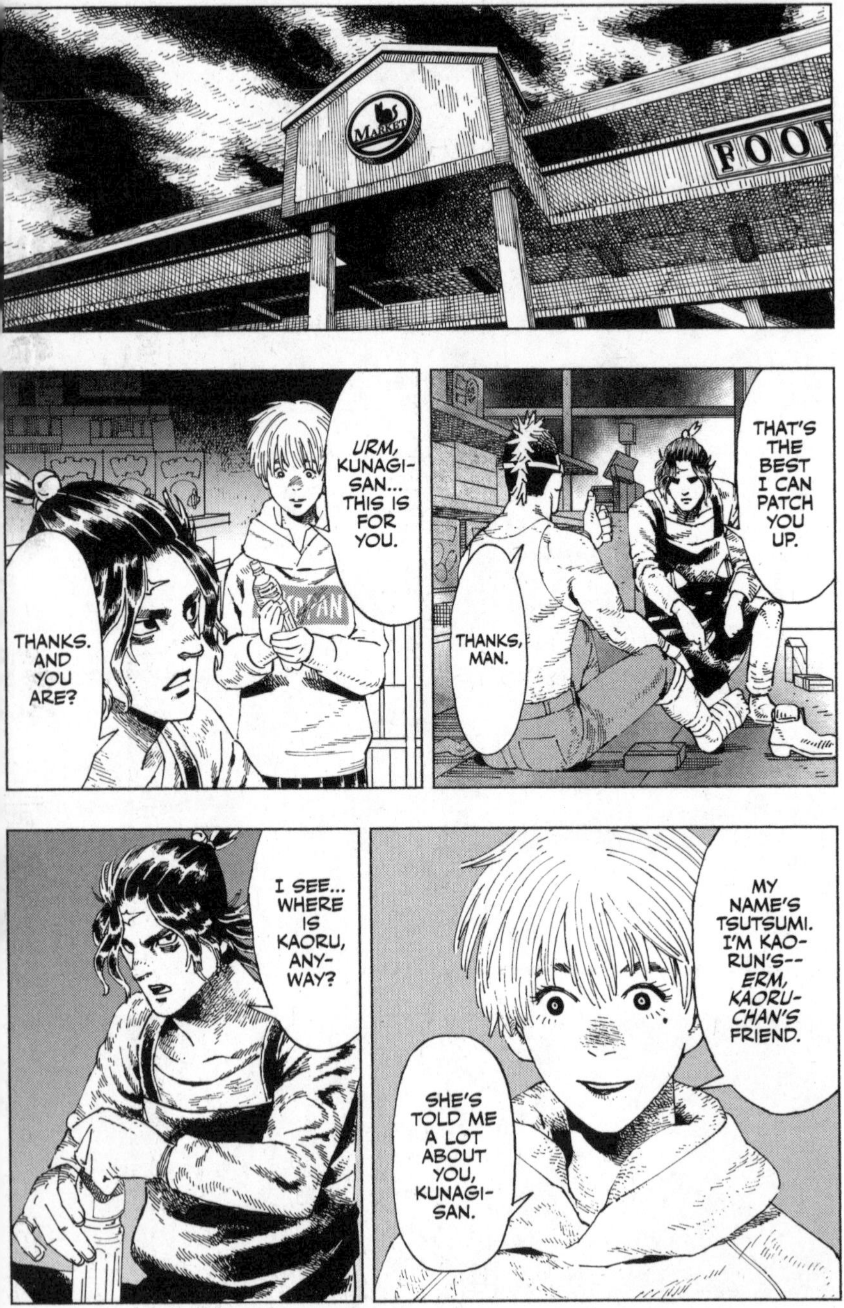
MARKET
THAT'S THE BEST I CAN PATCH YOU UP.
THANKS, MAN.
URM, KUNAGI-SAN... THIS IS FOR YOU.
THANKS. AND YOU ARE?
MY NAME'S TSUTSUMI. I'M KAO-RUN'S-- *ERM,* KAORU-CHAN'S FRIEND.
SHE'S TOLD ME A LOT ABOUT YOU, KUNAGI-SAN.
I SEE... WHERE IS KAORU, ANYWAY?

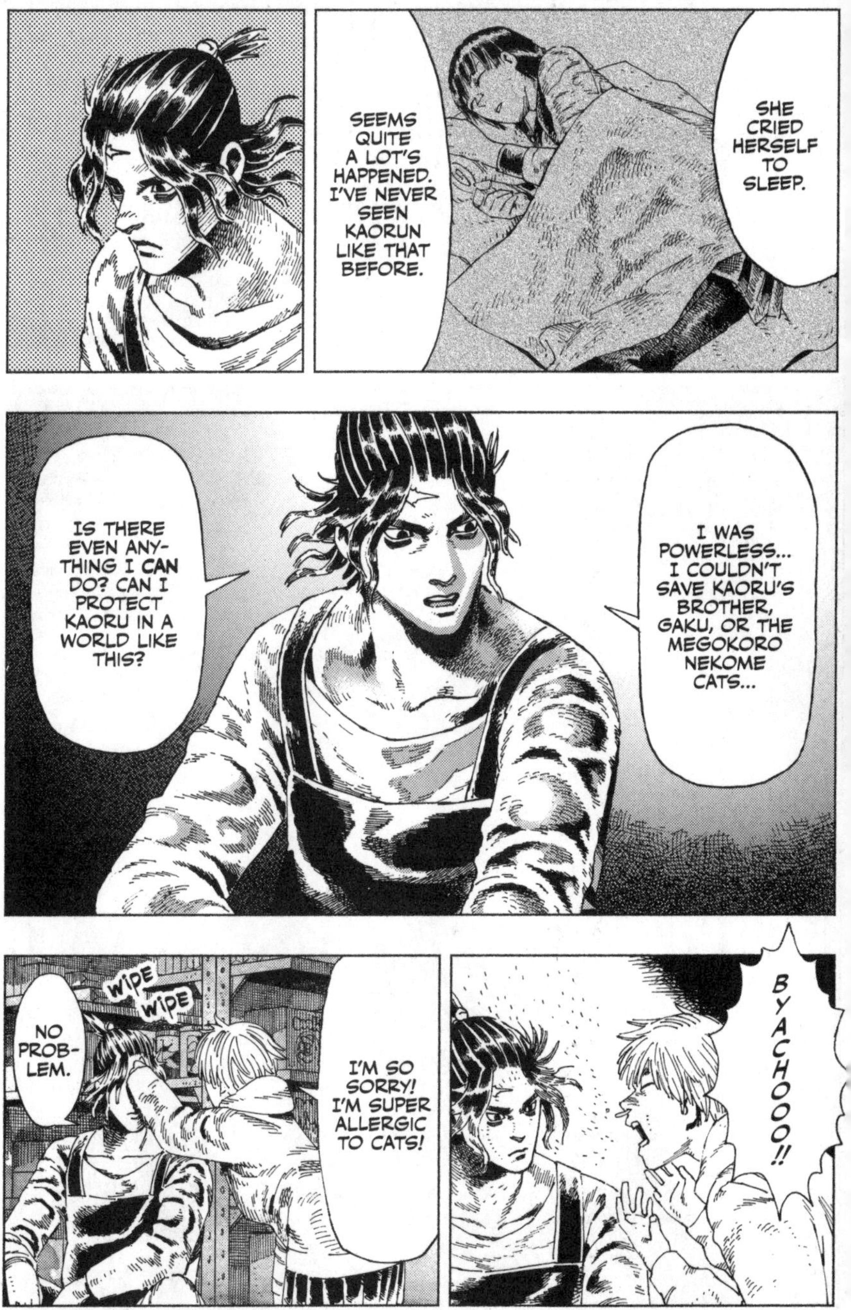
SHE CRIED HERSELF TO SLEEP.
SEEMS QUITE A LOT'S HAPPENED. I'VE NEVER SEEN KAORUN LIKE THAT BEFORE.
I WAS POWERLESS... I COULDN'T SAVE KAORU'S BROTHER, GAKU, OR THE MEGOKORO NEKOME CATS...
IS THERE EVEN ANY-THING I CAN DO? CAN I PROTECT KAORU IN A WORLD LIKE THIS?
BYACHOOOO!!
I'M SO SORRY! I'M SUPER ALLERGIC TO CATS!
wipe wipe
NO PROB-LEM.

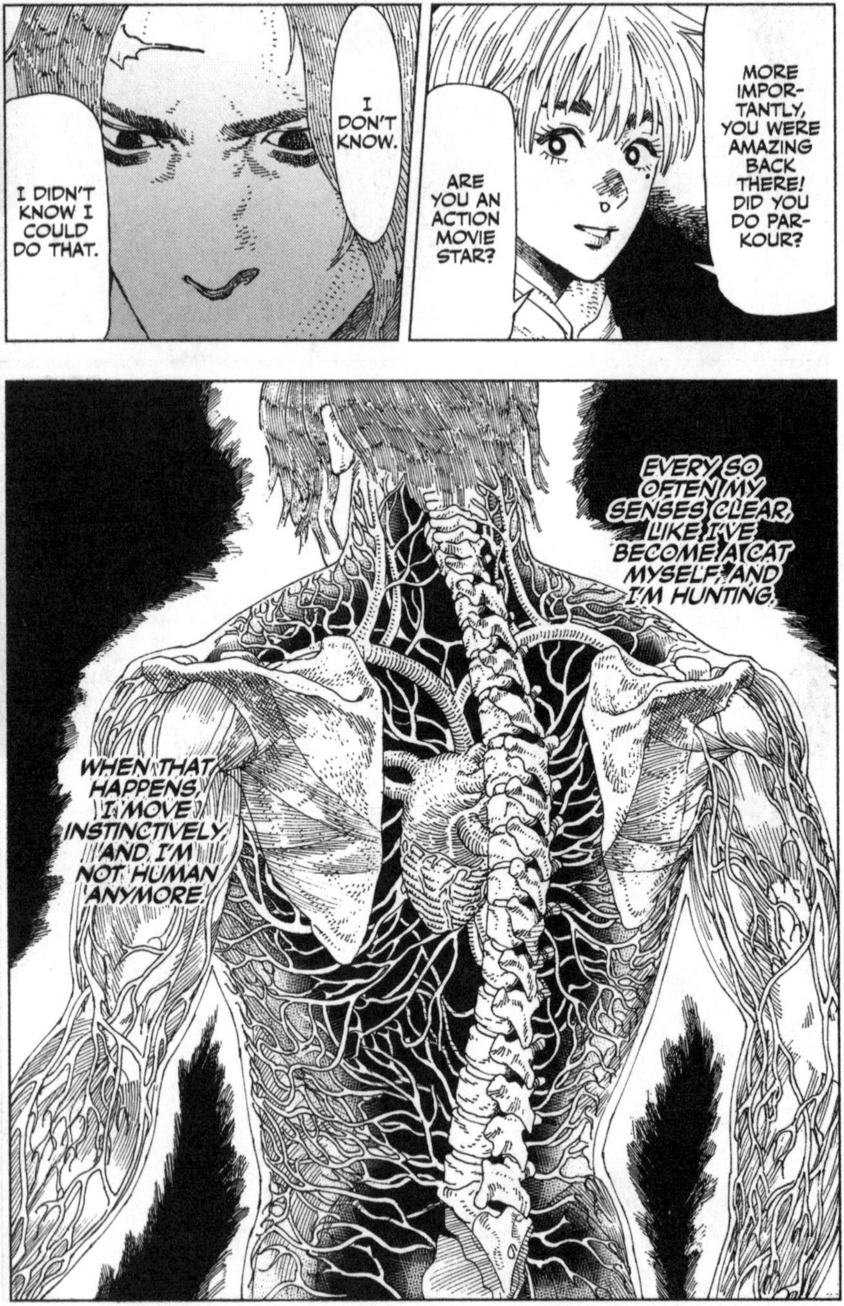
MORE IMPORTANTLY, YOU WERE AMAZING BACK THERE! DID YOU DO PARKOUR?
ARE YOU AN ACTION MOVIE STAR?
I DON'T KNOW.
I DIDN'T KNOW I COULD DO THAT.
EVERY SO OFTEN MY SENSES CLEAR, LIKE I'VE BECOME A CAT MYSELF, AND I'M HUNTING.
WHEN THAT HAPPENS, I MOVE INSTINCTIVELY AND I'M NOT HUMAN ANYMORE.

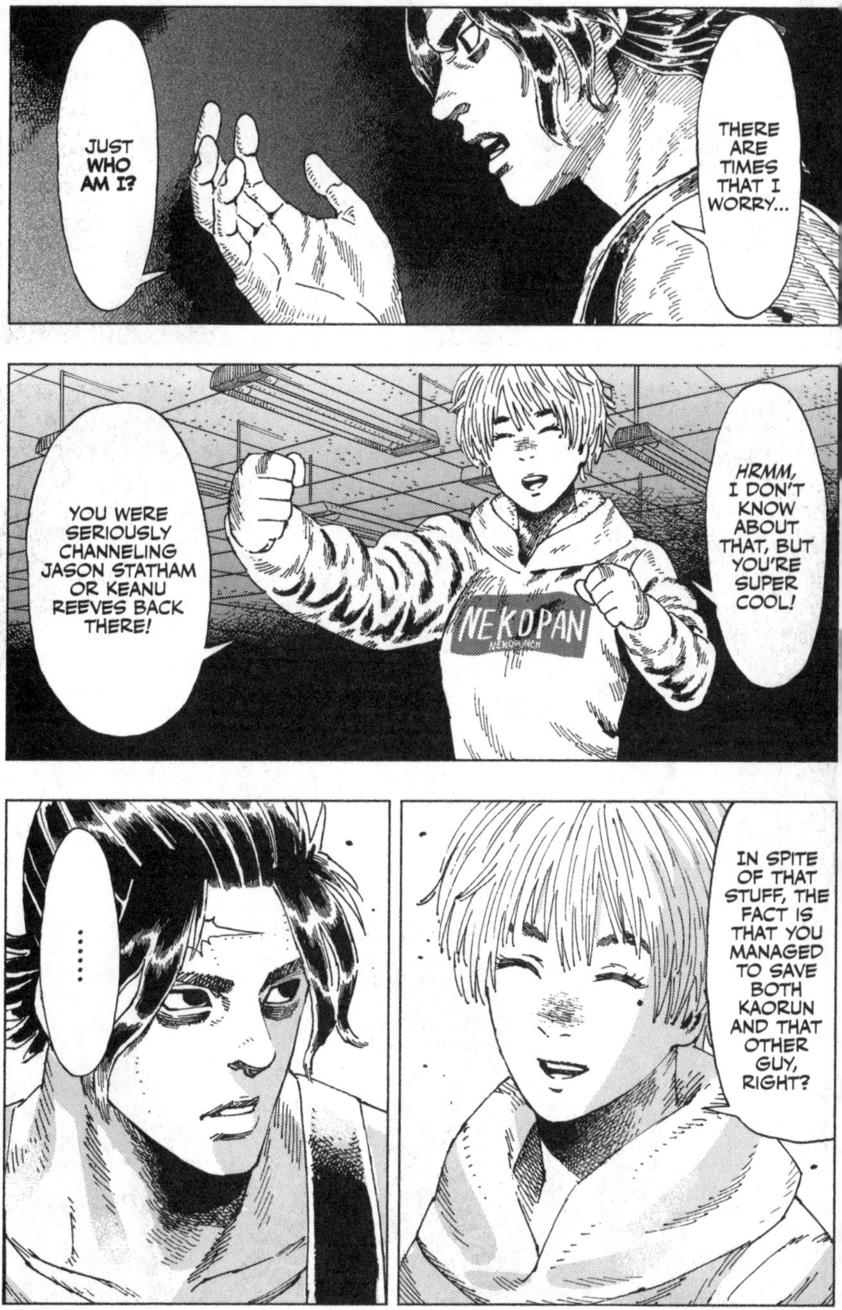
THERE ARE TIMES THAT I WORRY...
JUST WHO AM I?
HRMM, I DON'T KNOW ABOUT THAT, BUT YOU'RE SUPER COOL!
NEKOPAN
YOU WERE SERIOUSLY CHANNELING JASON STATHAM OR KEANU REEVES BACK THERE!
IN SPITE OF THAT STUFF, THE FACT IS THAT YOU MANAGED TO SAVE BOTH KAORUN AND THAT OTHER GUY, RIGHT?
......

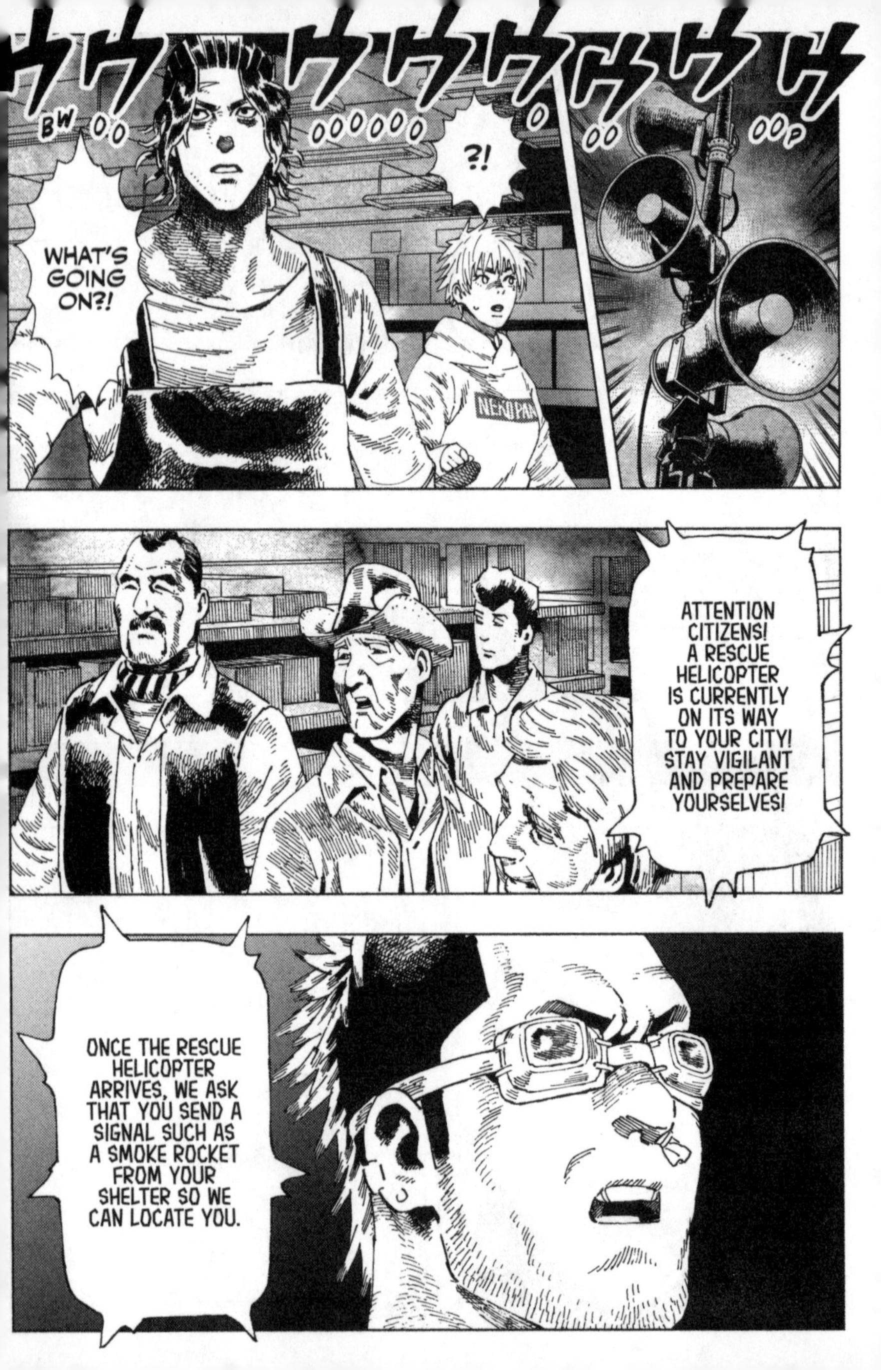
BWOOOOOOOOOOOOOP
?!
WHAT'S GOING ON?!
ATTENTION CITIZENS! A RESCUE HELICOPTER IS CURRENTLY ON ITS WAY TO YOUR CITY! STAY VIGILANT AND PREPARE YOURSELVES!
ONCE THE RESCUE HELICOPTER ARRIVES, WE ASK THAT YOU SEND A SIGNAL SUCH AS A SMOKE ROCKET FROM YOUR SHELTER SO WE CAN LOCATE YOU.

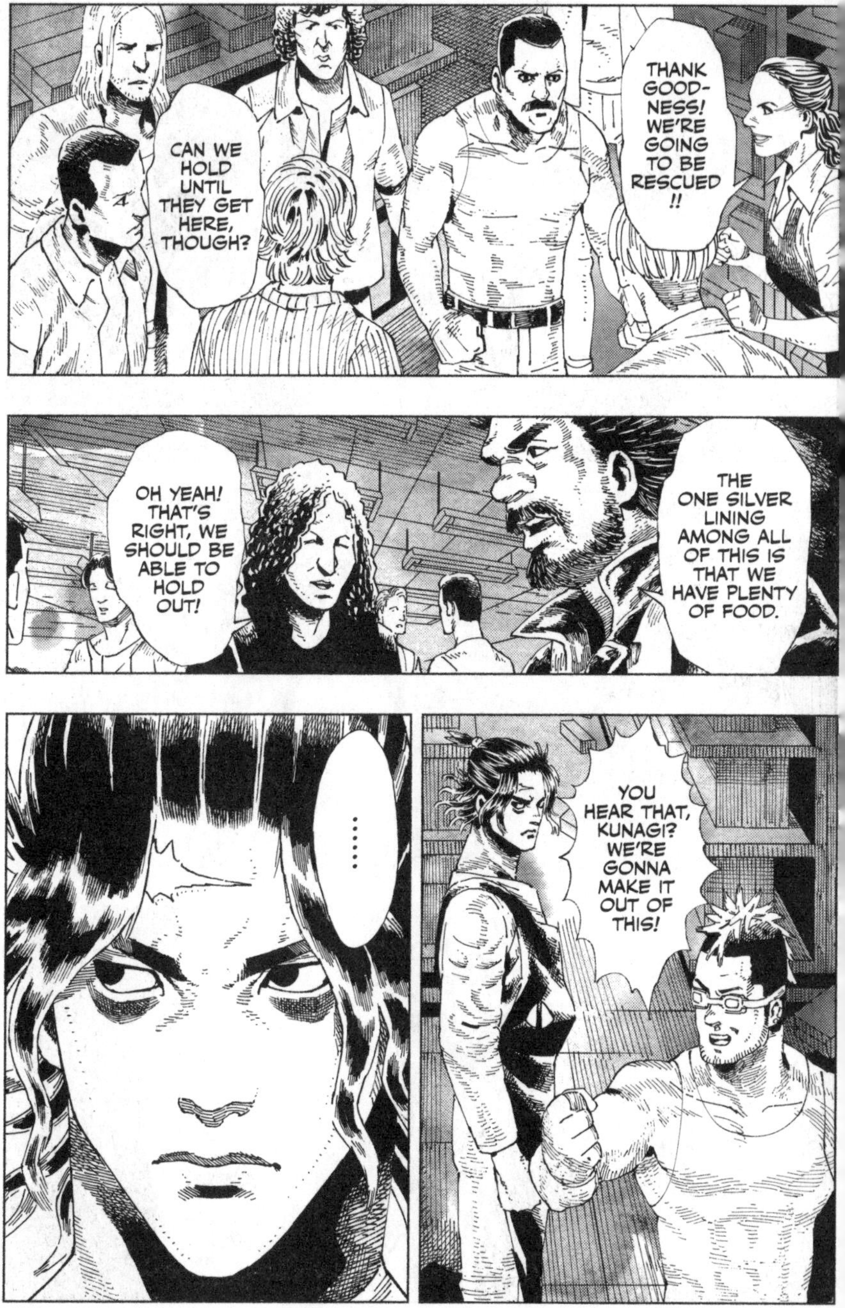
THANK GOODNESS! WE'RE GOING TO BE RESCUED !!
CAN WE HOLD UNTIL THEY GET HERE, THOUGH?
THE ONE SILVER LINING AMONG ALL OF THIS IS THAT WE HAVE PLENTY OF FOOD.
OH YEAH! THAT'S RIGHT, WE SHOULD BE ABLE TO HOLD OUT!
YOU HEAR THAT, KUNAGI? WE'RE GONNA MAKE IT OUT OF THIS!
......

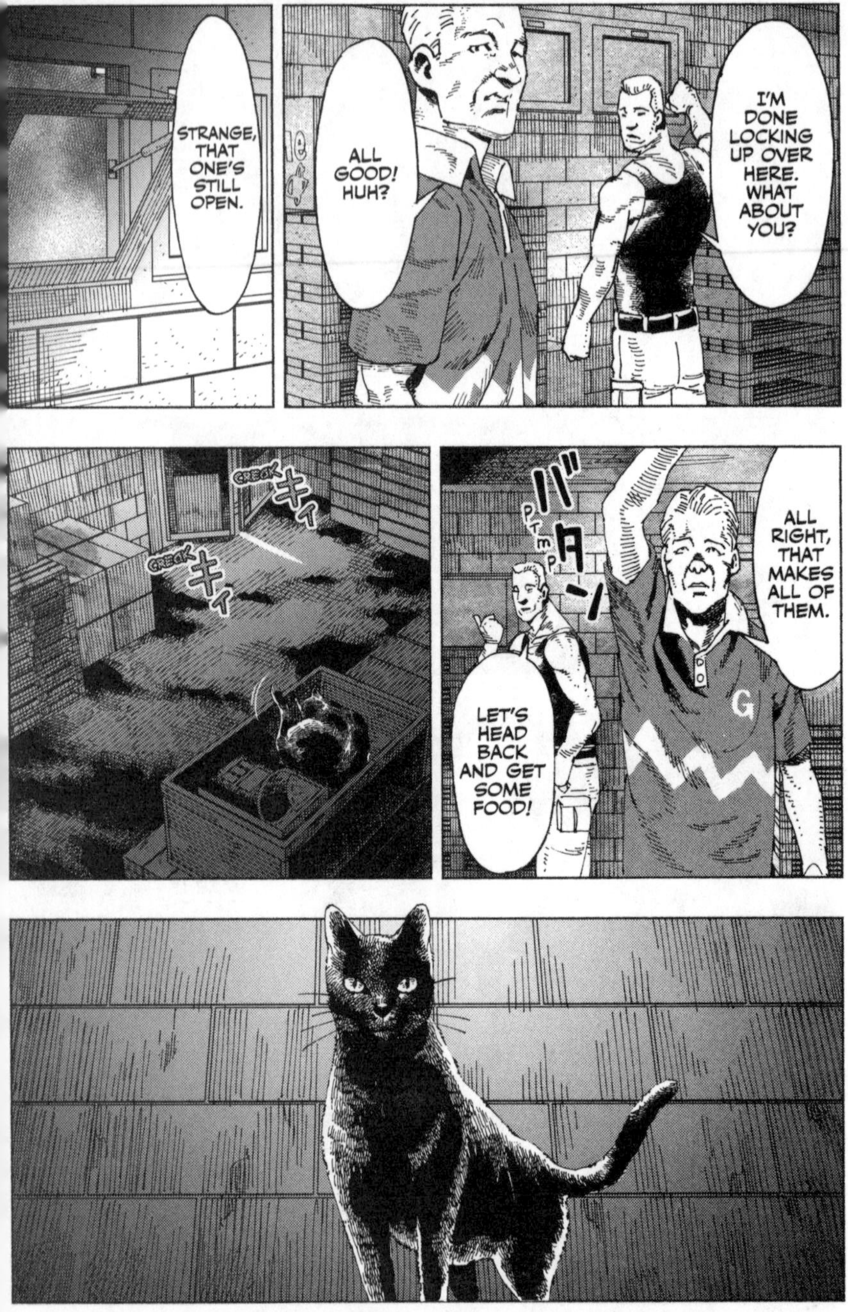
I'M DONE LOCKING UP OVER HERE. WHAT ABOUT YOU?
ALL GOOD! HUH?
STRANGE, THAT ONE'S STILL OPEN.
ALL RIGHT, THAT MAKES ALL OF THEM.
バタン
PTMP
LET'S HEAD BACK AND GET SOME FOOD!
CREAK キィ
CREAK キィ

Black Cat

A generic name for cats covered in a black coat from tail to snout. Whether they're considered lucky or unlucky varies from country to country. A black beckoning cat is said to possess the benefit of warding off evil spirits and misfortune.

NIGHT
A
OF THE
LIVING
CAT 1

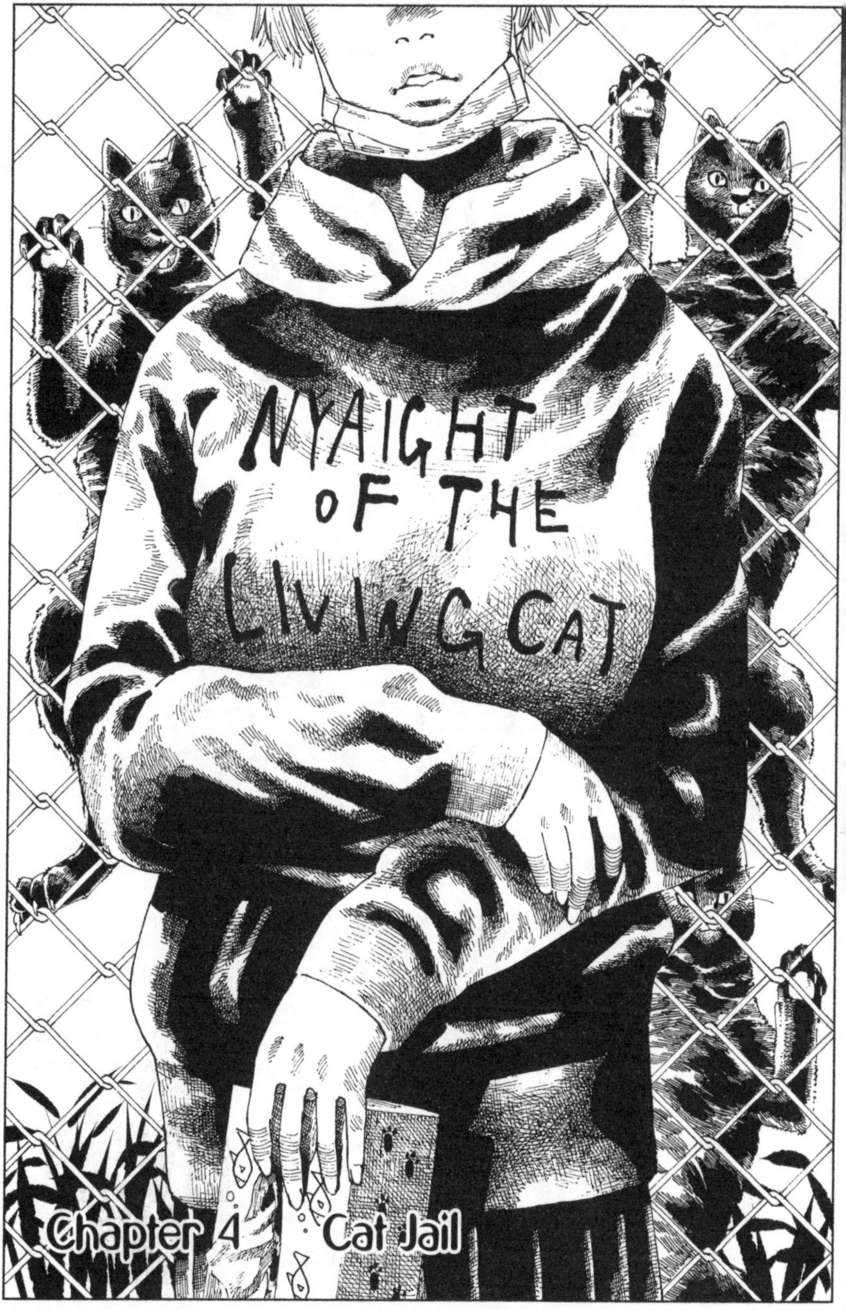
NYAIGHT OF THE LIVING CAT
Chapter 4 Cat Jail

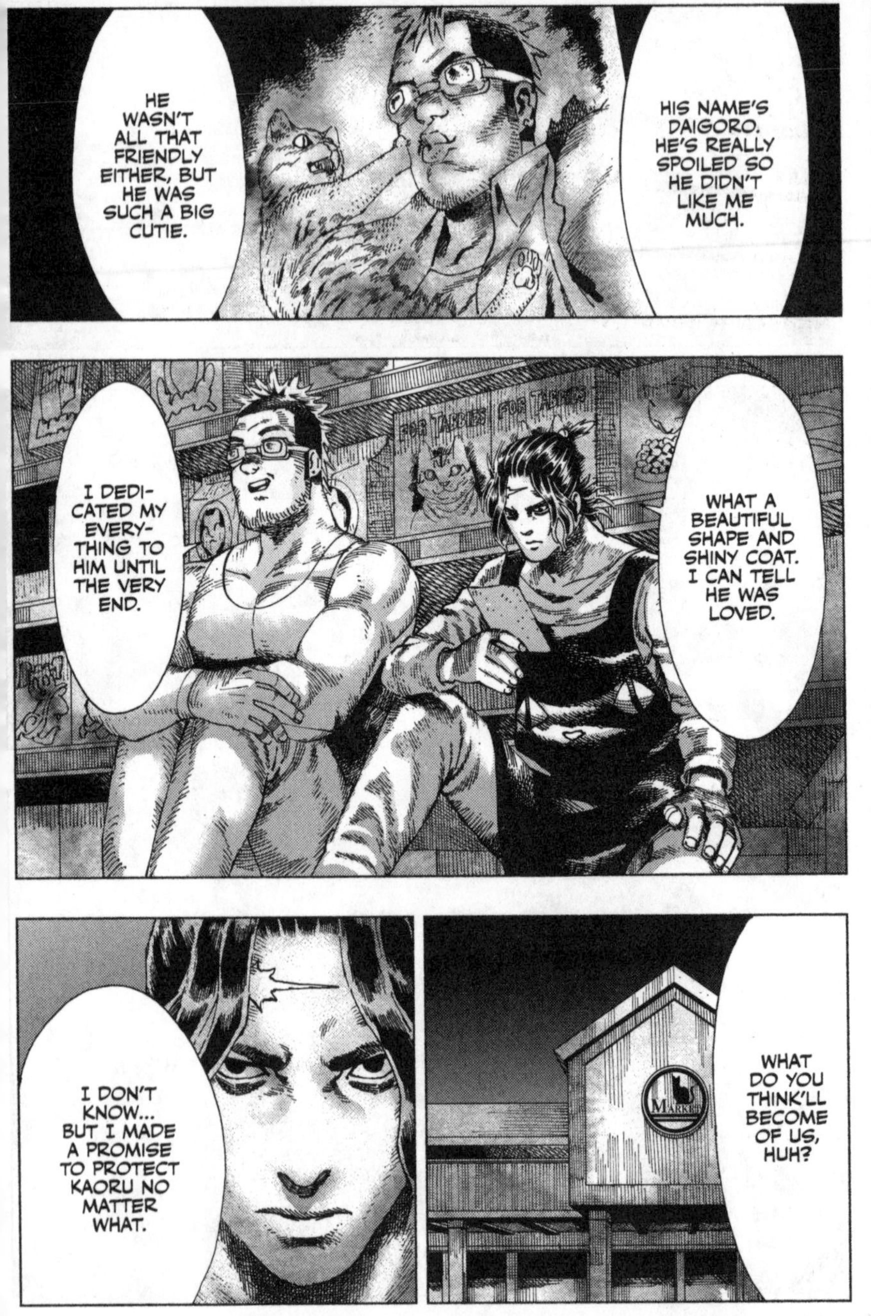
HIS NAME'S DAIGORO. HE'S REALLY SPOILED SO HE DIDN'T LIKE ME MUCH.
HE WASN'T ALL THAT FRIENDLY EITHER, BUT HE WAS SUCH A BIG CUTIE.
WHAT A BEAUTIFUL SHAPE AND SHINY COAT. I CAN TELL HE WAS LOVED.
I DEDI-CATED MY EVERY-THING TO HIM UNTIL THE VERY END.
WHAT DO YOU THINK'LL BECOME OF US, HUH?
I DON'T KNOW... BUT I MADE A PROMISE TO PROTECT KAORU NO MATTER WHAT.

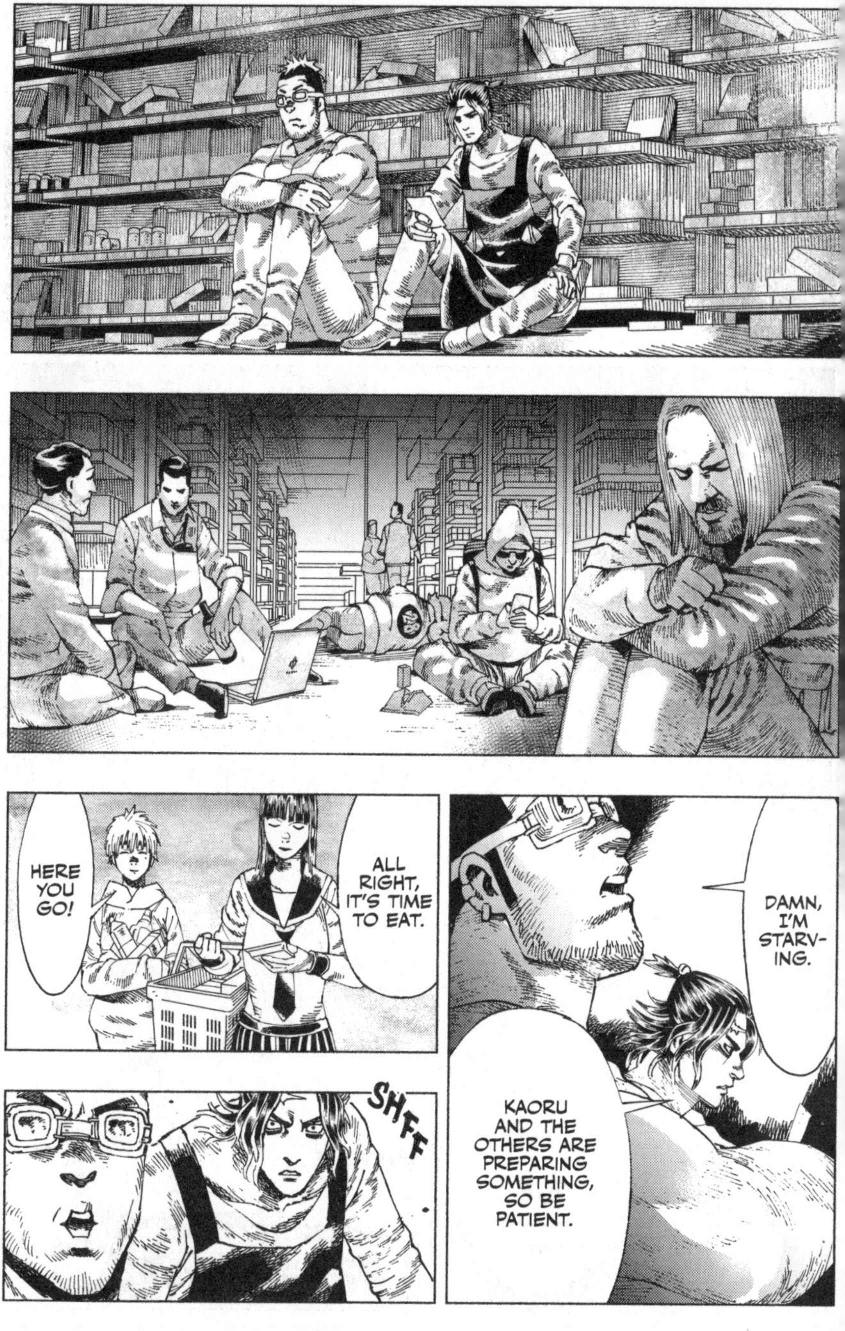
DAMN, I'M STARVING.
KAORU AND THE OTHERS ARE PREPARING SOMETHING, SO BE PATIENT.
ALL RIGHT, IT'S TIME TO EAT.
HERE YOU GO!
SHFF

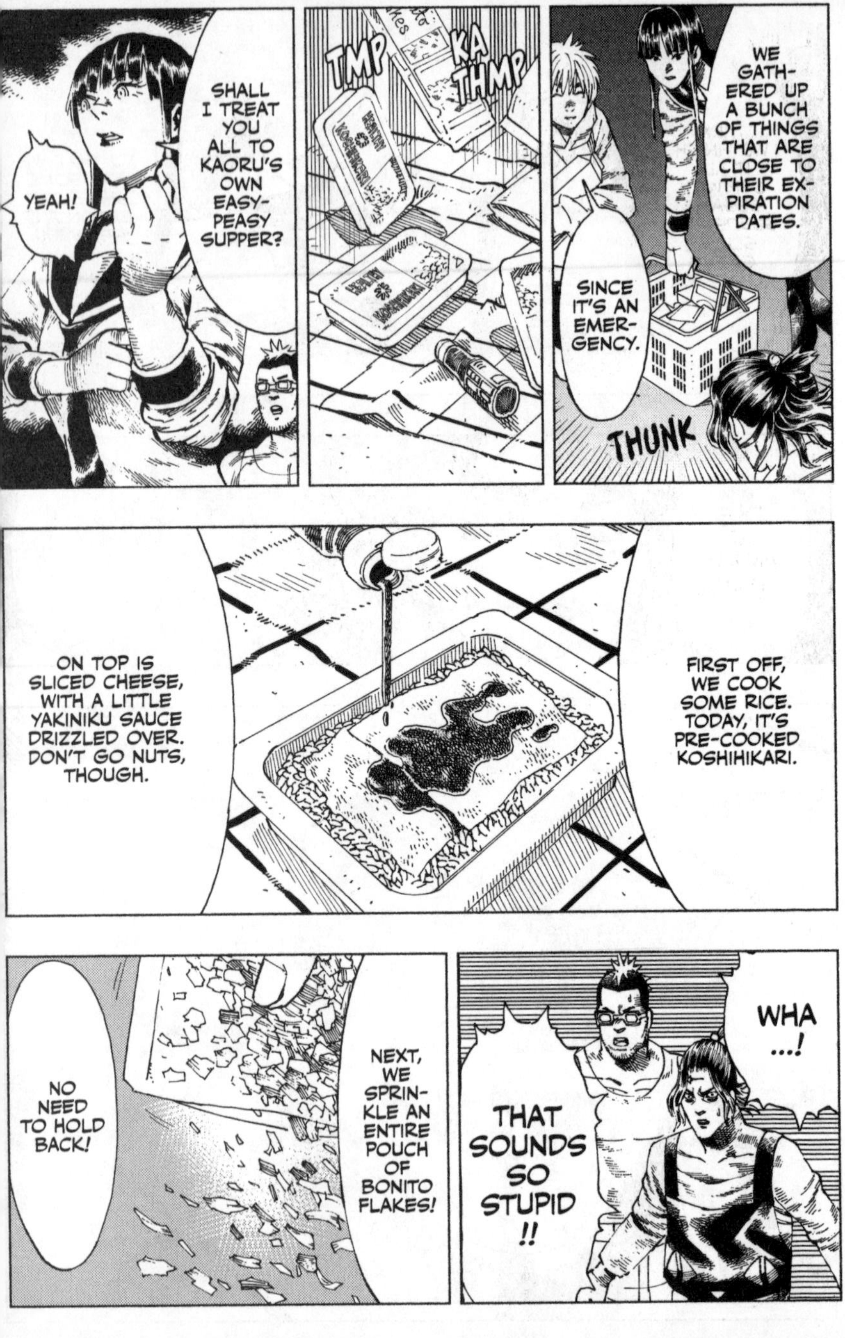
WE GATHERED UP A BUNCH OF THINGS THAT ARE CLOSE TO THEIR EXPIRATION DATES.
SINCE IT'S AN EMERGENCY.
THUNK
KA THMP
TMP
SHALL I TREAT YOU ALL TO KAORU'S OWN EASY-PEASY SUPPER?
YEAH!
FIRST OFF, WE COOK SOME RICE. TODAY, IT'S PRE-COOKED KOSHIHIKARI.
ON TOP IS SLICED CHEESE, WITH A LITTLE YAKINIKU SAUCE DRIZZLED OVER. DON'T GO NUTS, THOUGH.
WHA ...!
THAT SOUNDS SO STUPID !!
NEXT, WE SPRINKLE AN ENTIRE POUCH OF BONITO FLAKES!
NO NEED TO HOLD BACK!

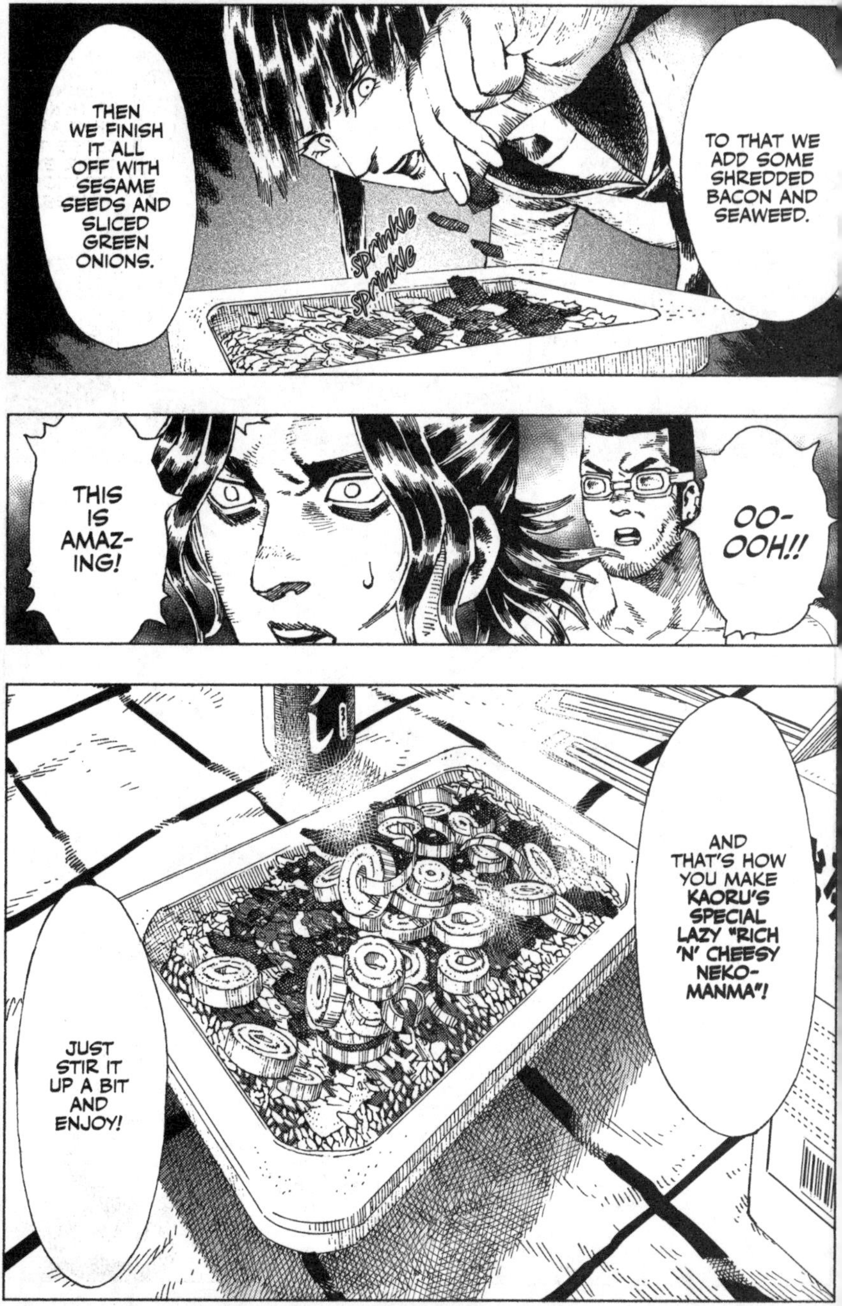
TO THAT WE ADD SOME SHREDDED BACON AND SEAWEED.
sprinkle sprinkle
THEN WE FINISH IT ALL OFF WITH SESAME SEEDS AND SLICED GREEN ONIONS.
OO-OOH!!
THIS IS AMAZ-ING!
AND THAT'S HOW YOU MAKE KAORU'S SPECIAL LAZY "RICH 'N' CHEESY NEKO-MANMA"!
JUST STIR IT UP A BIT AND ENJOY!

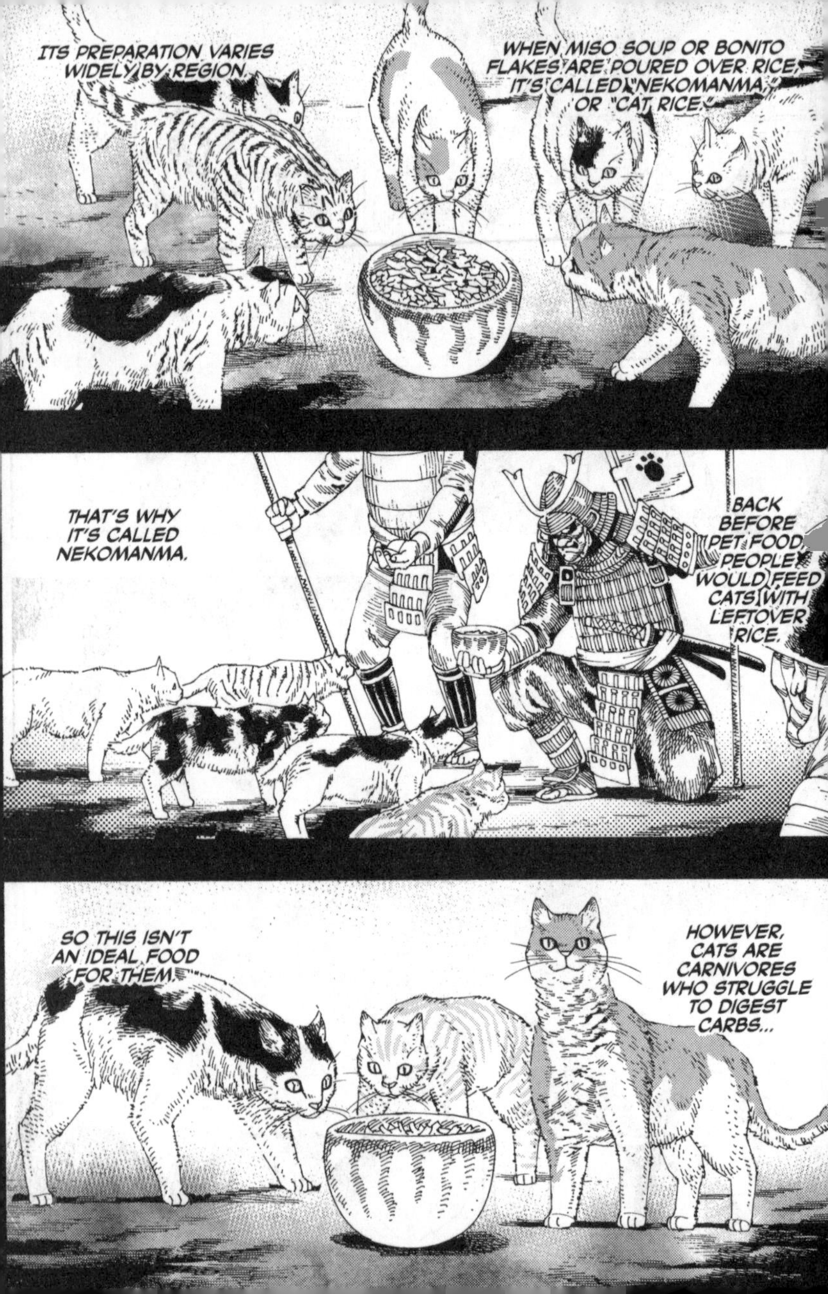
WHEN MISO SOUP OR BONITO FLAKES ARE POURED OVER RICE, IT'S CALLED "NEKOMANMA," OR "CAT RICE."
ITS PREPARATION VARIES WIDELY BY REGION.
BACK BEFORE PET FOOD, PEOPLE WOULD FEED CATS WITH LEFTOVER RICE.
THAT'S WHY IT'S CALLED NEKOMANMA.
HOWEVER, CATS ARE CARNIVORES WHO STRUGGLE TO DIGEST CARBS...
SO THIS ISN'T AN IDEAL FOOD FOR THEM.

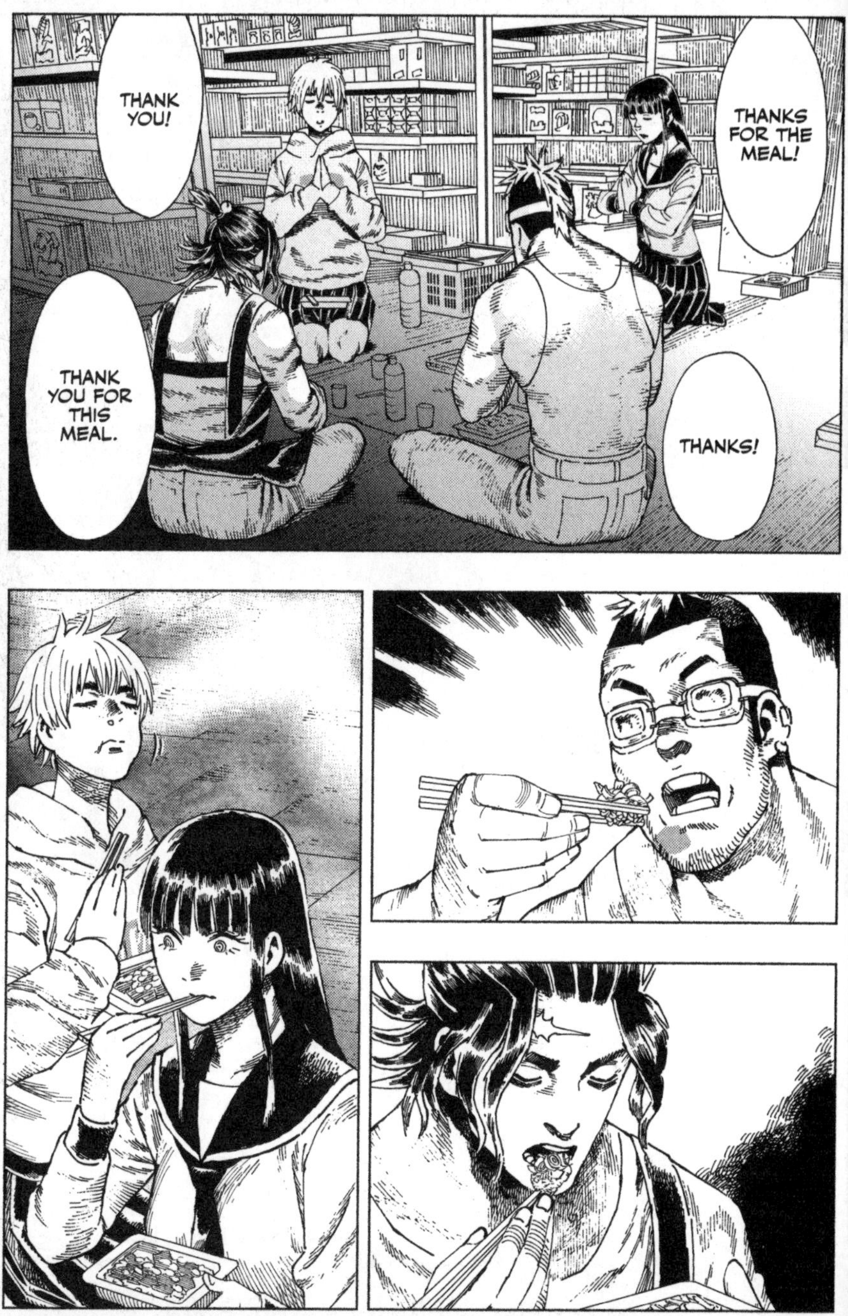
THANKS FOR THE MEAL!
THANK YOU!
THANKS!
THANK YOU FOR THIS MEAL.

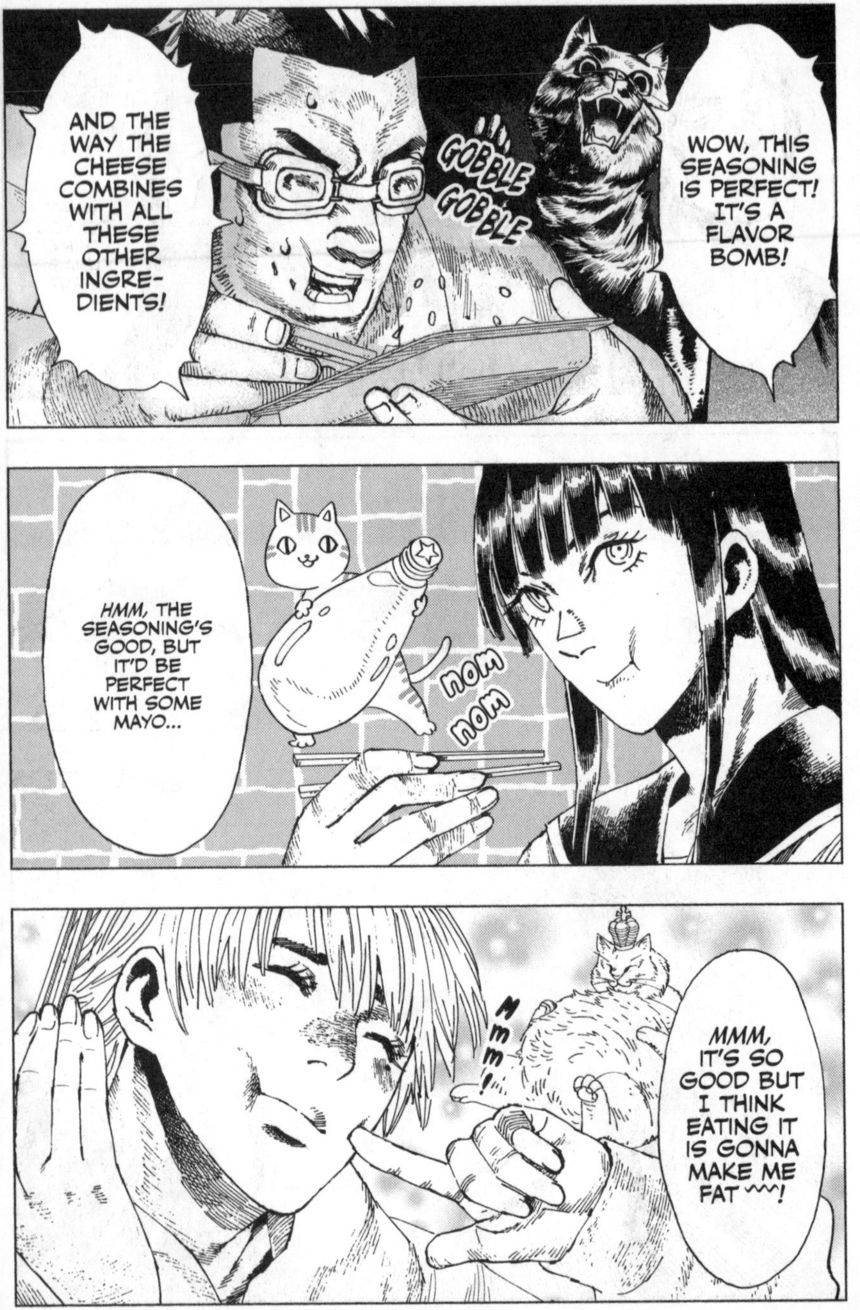
WOW, THIS SEASONING IS PERFECT! IT'S A FLAVOR BOMB!
GOBBLE GOBBLE
AND THE WAY THE CHEESE COMBINES WITH ALL THESE OTHER INGRE- DIENTS!
nom nom
HMM, THE SEASONING'S GOOD, BUT IT'D BE PERFECT WITH SOME MAYO...
MMM, IT'S SO GOOD BUT I THINK EATING IT IS GONNA MAKE ME FAT~!
MMM!

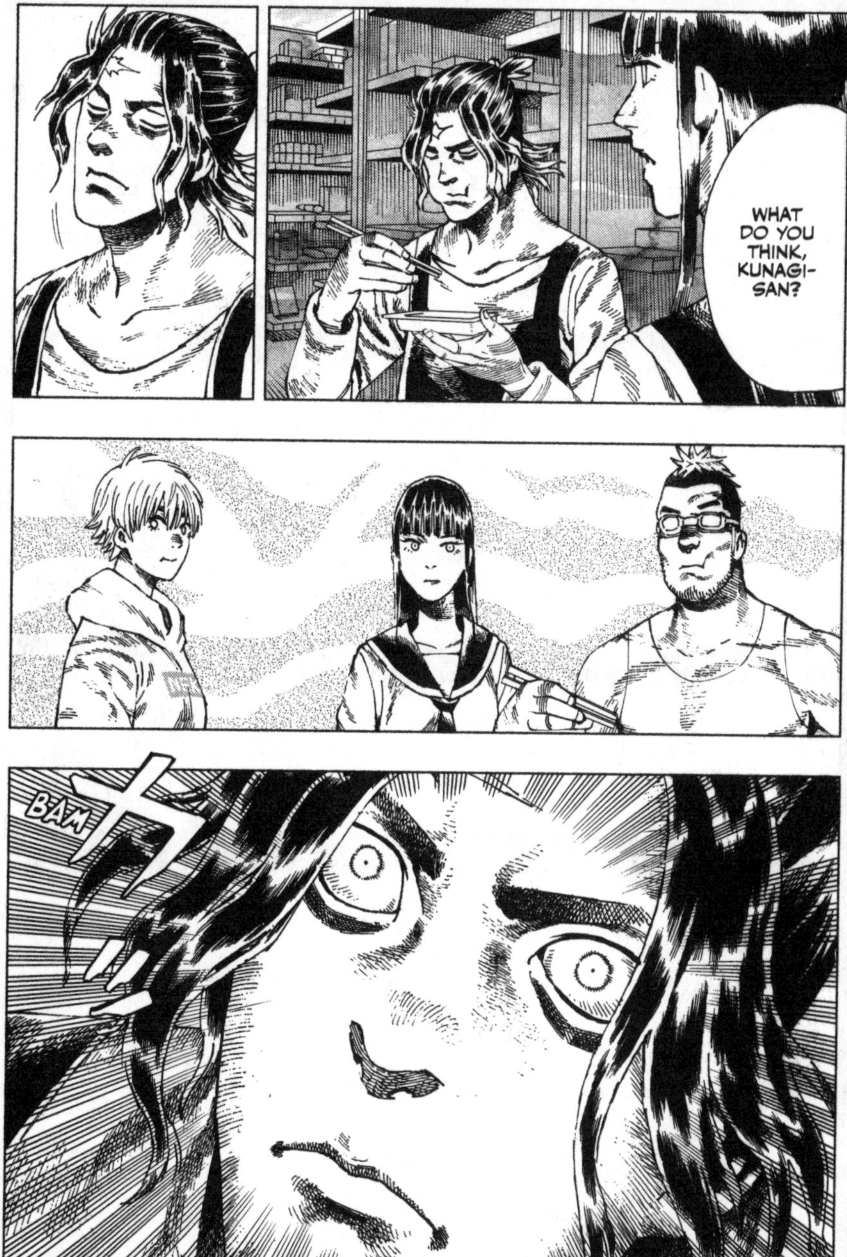
WHAT DO YOU THINK, KUNAGI-SAN?
BAM

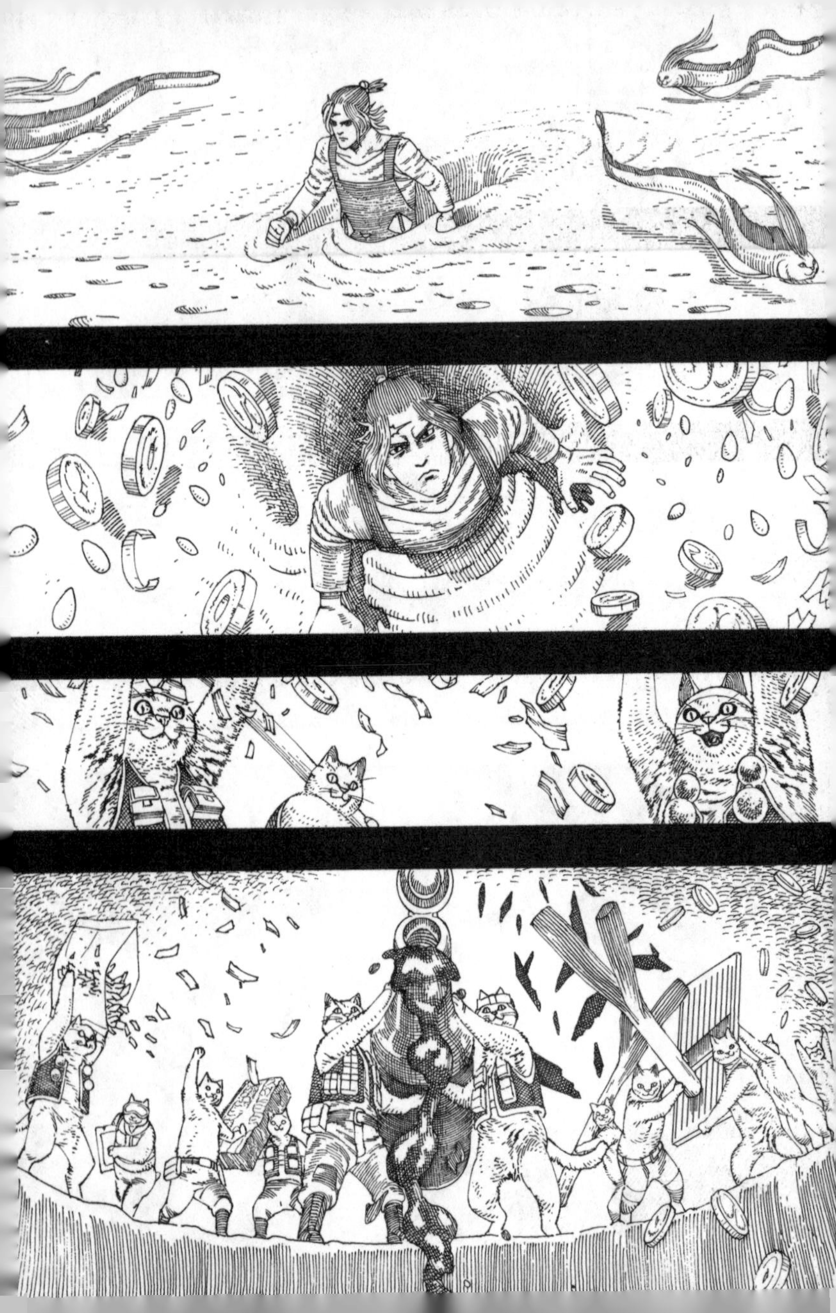

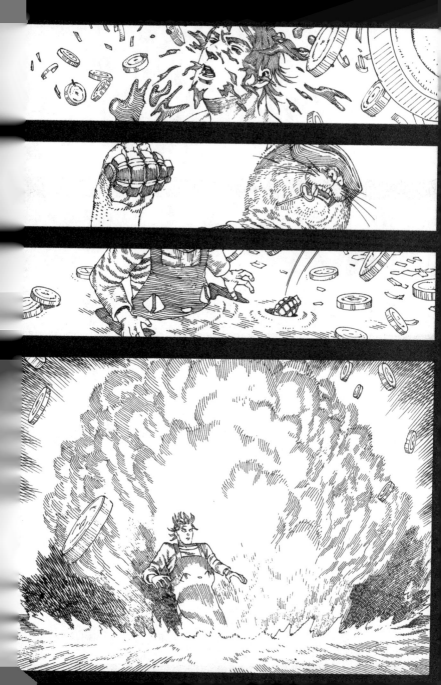

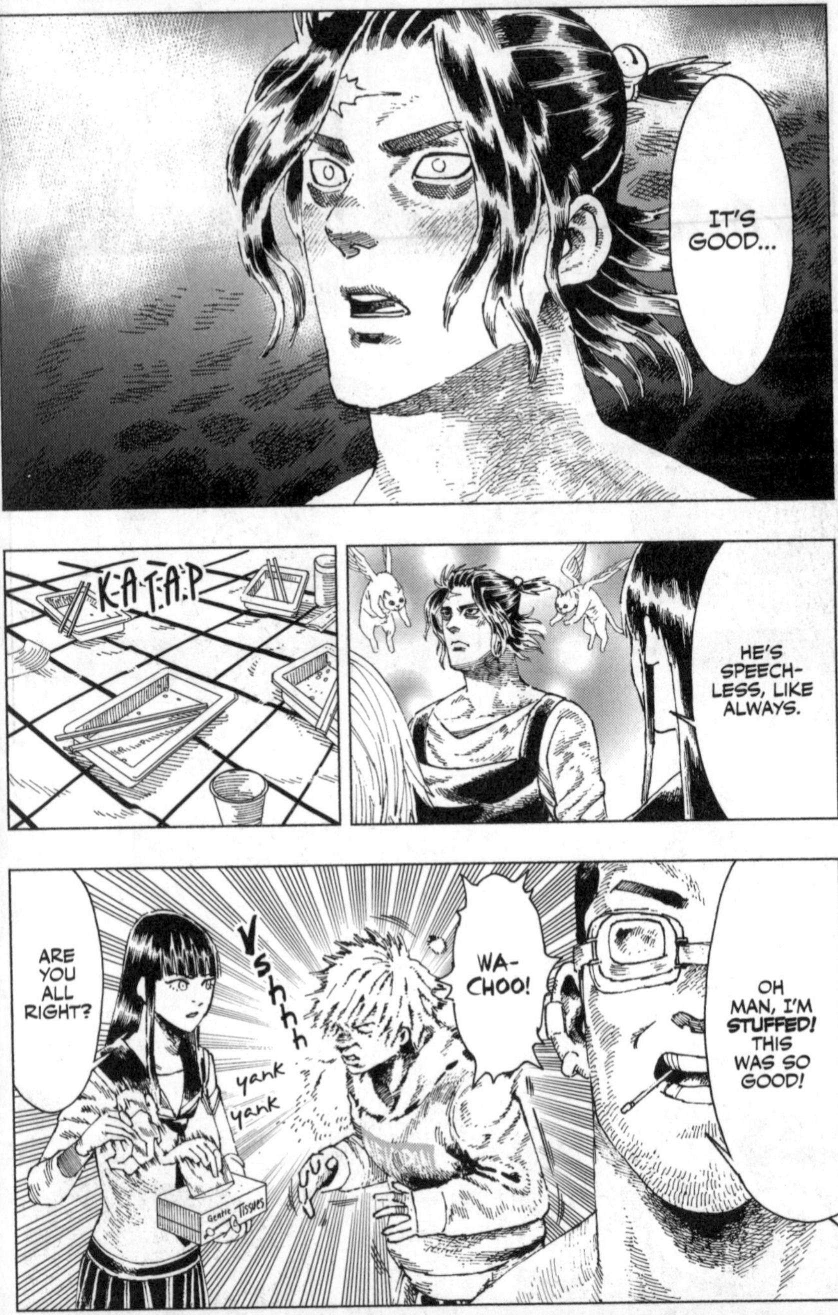
IT'S GOOD...
HE'S SPEECH-LESS, LIKE ALWAYS.
K-A-T-A-P
OH MAN, I'M **STUFFED!** THIS WAS SO GOOD!
WA-CHOO!
Vshhhh
yank yank
Gentle Tissues
ARE YOU ALL RIGHT?

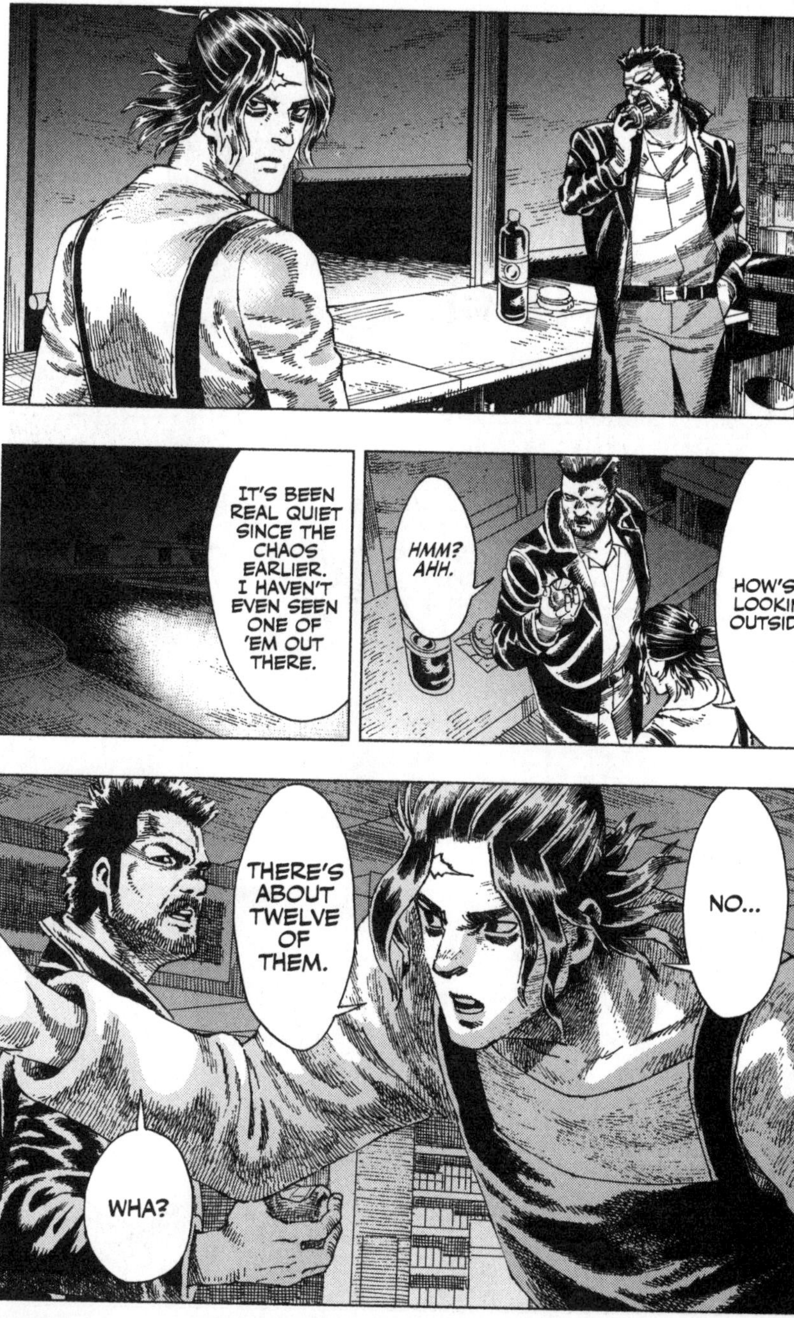
HOW'S IT LOOKING OUTSIDE?
HMM? AHH.
IT'S BEEN REAL QUIET SINCE THE CHAOS EARLIER. I HAVEN'T EVEN SEEN ONE OF 'EM OUT THERE.
NO...
THERE'S ABOUT TWELVE OF THEM.
WHA?

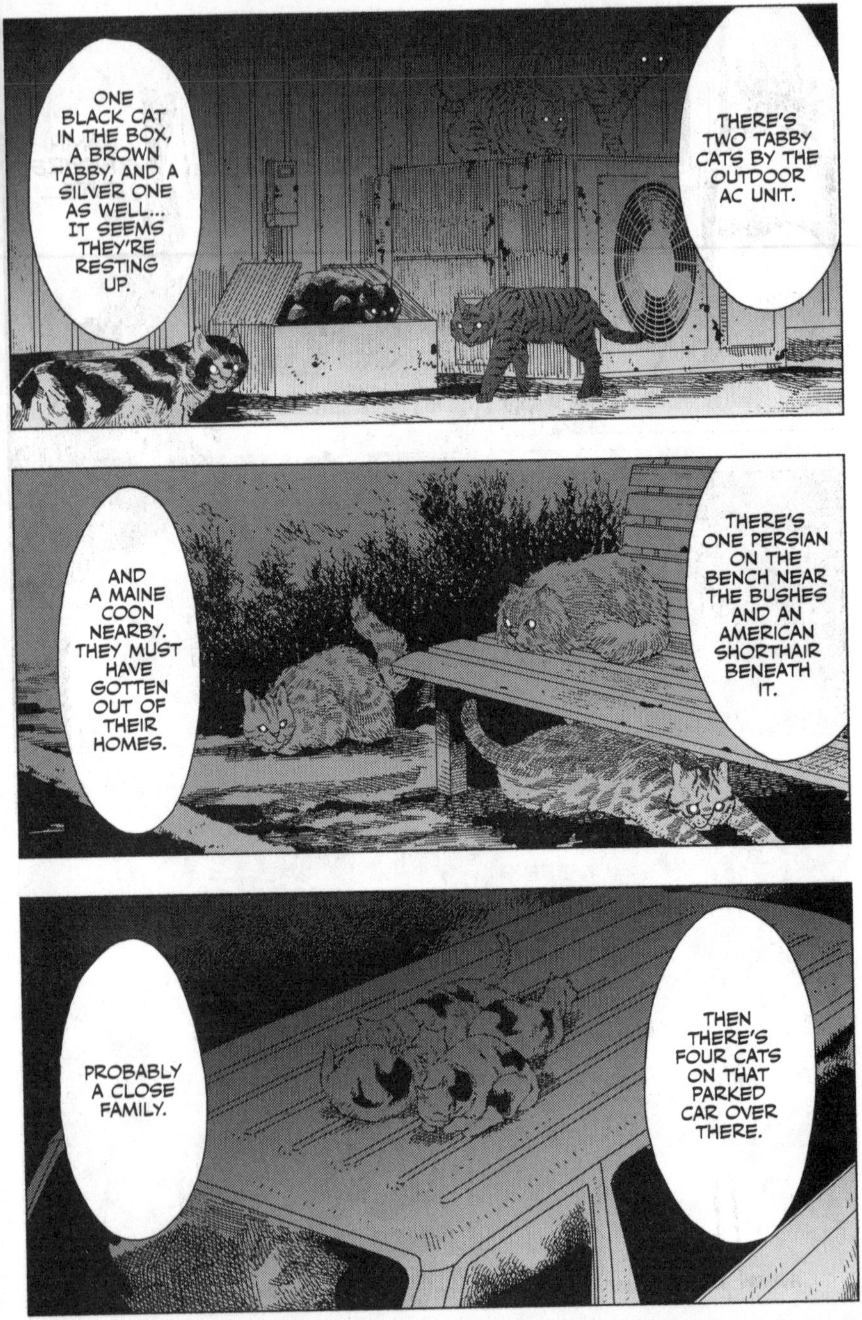
THERE'S TWO TABBY CATS BY THE OUTDOOR AC UNIT.
ONE BLACK CAT IN THE BOX, A BROWN TABBY, AND A SILVER ONE AS WELL... IT SEEMS THEY'RE RESTING UP.
THERE'S ONE PERSIAN ON THE BENCH NEAR THE BUSHES AND AN AMERICAN SHORTHAIR BENEATH IT.
AND A MAINE COON NEARBY. THEY MUST HAVE GOTTEN OUT OF THEIR HOMES.
THEN THERE'S FOUR CATS ON THAT PARKED CAR OVER THERE.
PROBABLY A CLOSE FAMILY.

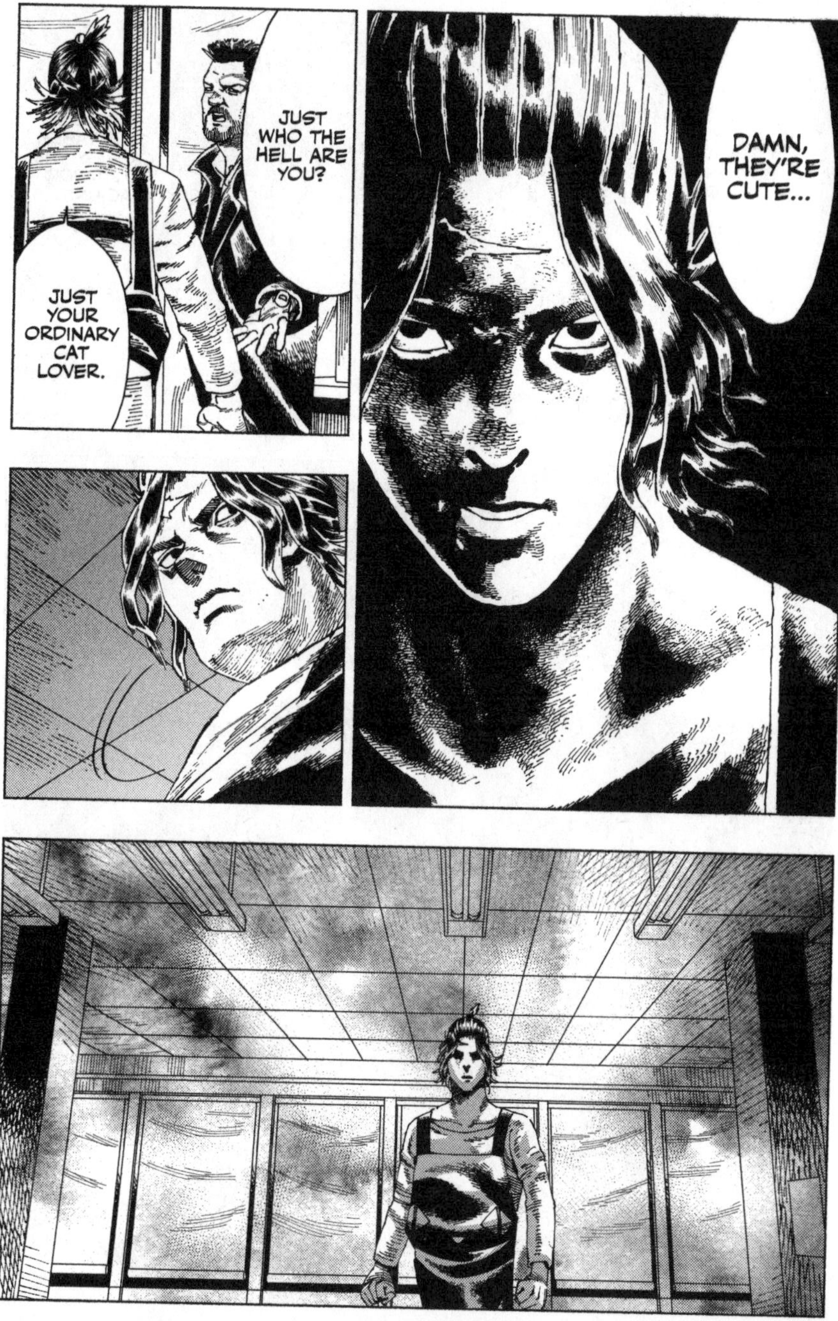
DAMN, THEY'RE CUTE...
JUST WHO THE HELL ARE YOU?
JUST YOUR ORDINARY CAT LOVER.

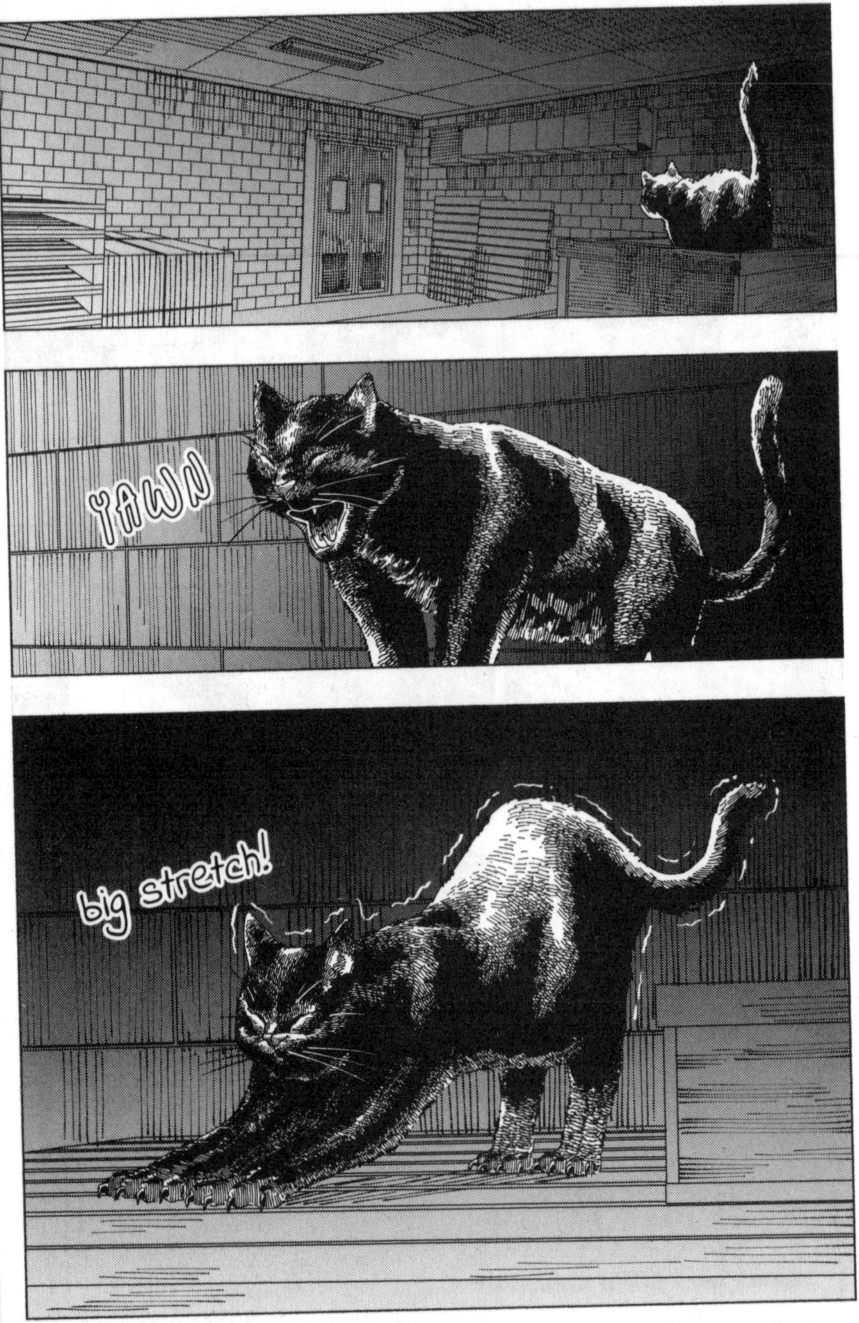
YAWN
big stretch!

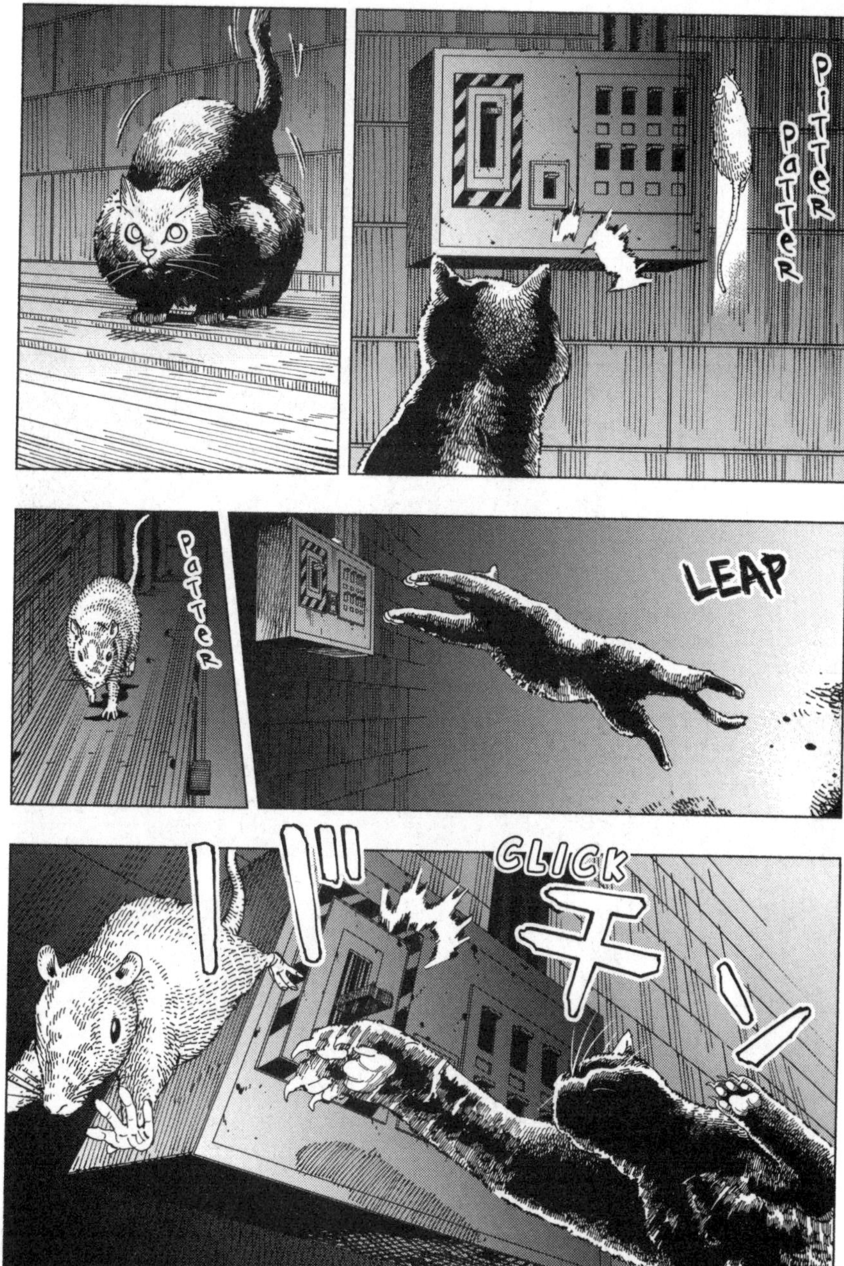
PITTER PATTER
LEAP
PATTER
CLICK

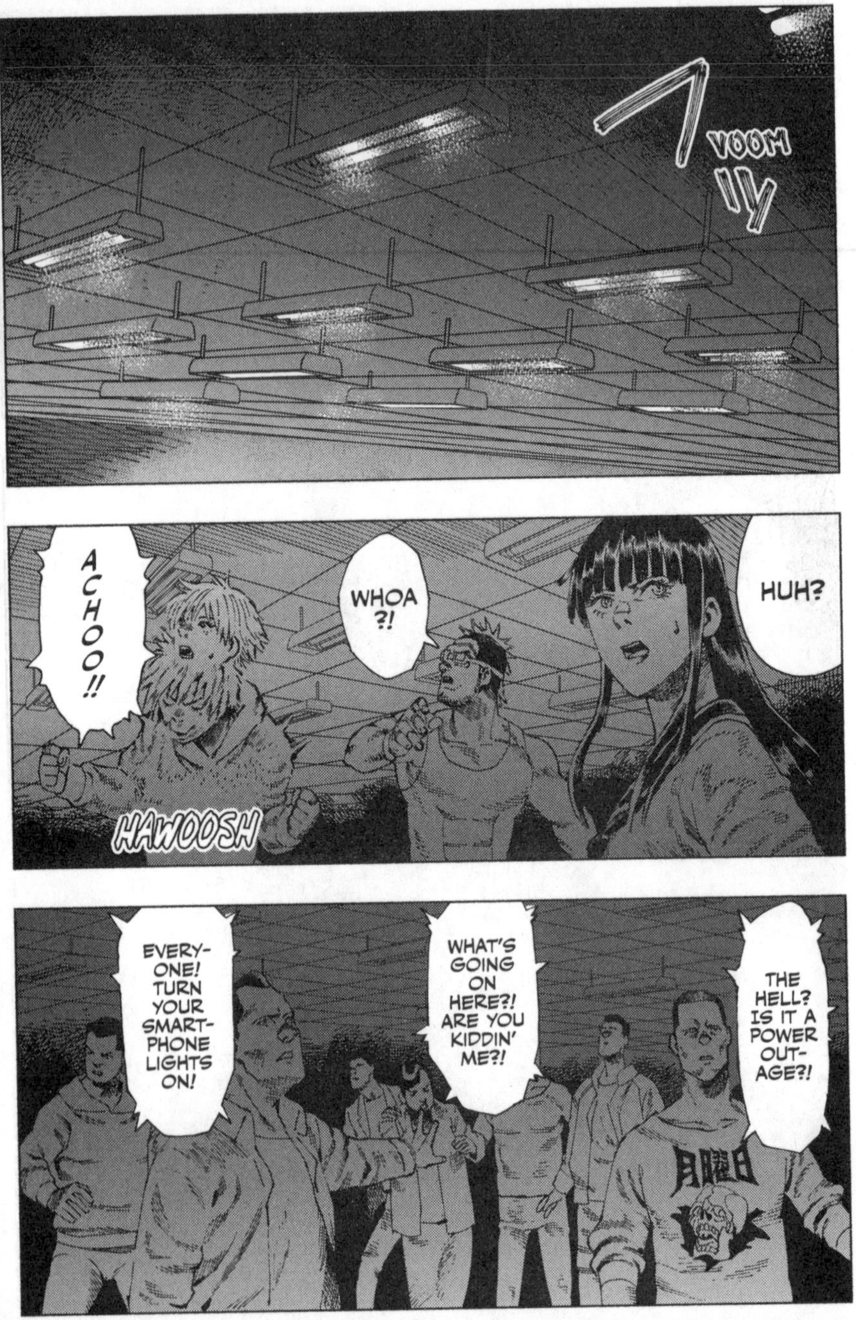
VOOM
HUH?
WHOA?!
ACHOO!!
HAWOOSH
THE HELL? IS IT A POWER OUTAGE?!
WHAT'S GOING ON HERE?! ARE YOU KIDDIN' ME?!
EVERYONE! TURN YOUR SMARTPHONE LIGHTS ON!

GYA!!

WHAT'S GOING ON? IS IT JUST THIS STORE? IT'S TOO DARK OUTSIDE TO TELL.

WHAT ON EARTH...

HUH?

GUUUSH

DON'T SNEAK UP ON ME LIKE THAT!

SHHH...

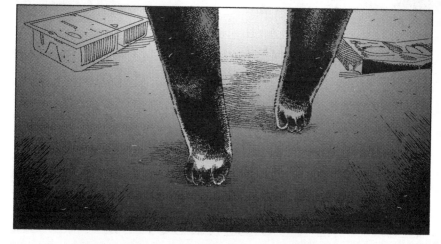

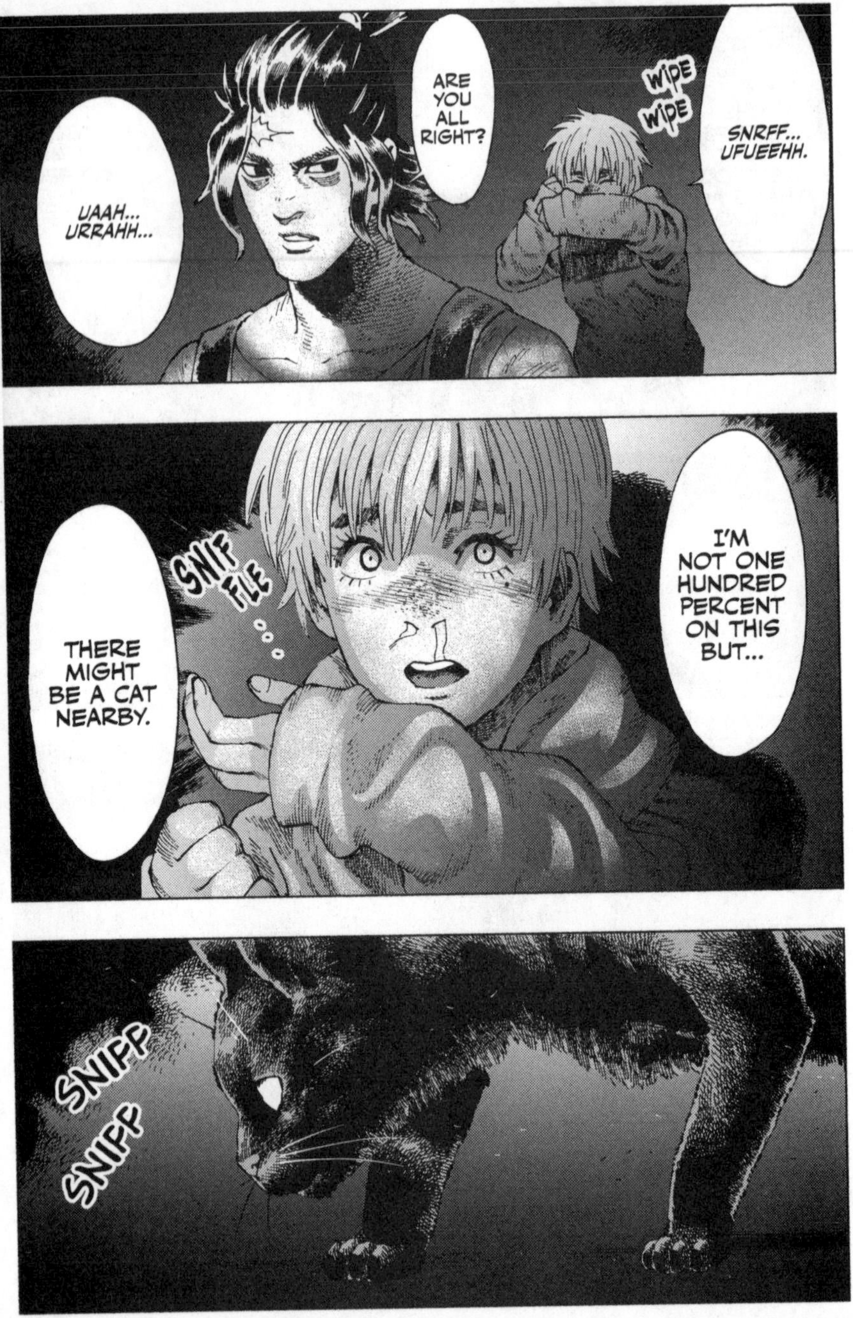
SNRFF... UFUEEHH.
wipe wipe
ARE YOU ALL RIGHT?
UAAH... URRAHH...
I'M NOT ONE HUNDRED PERCENT ON THIS BUT...
SNIF FLE
THERE MIGHT BE A CAT NEARBY.
SNIFF SNIFF

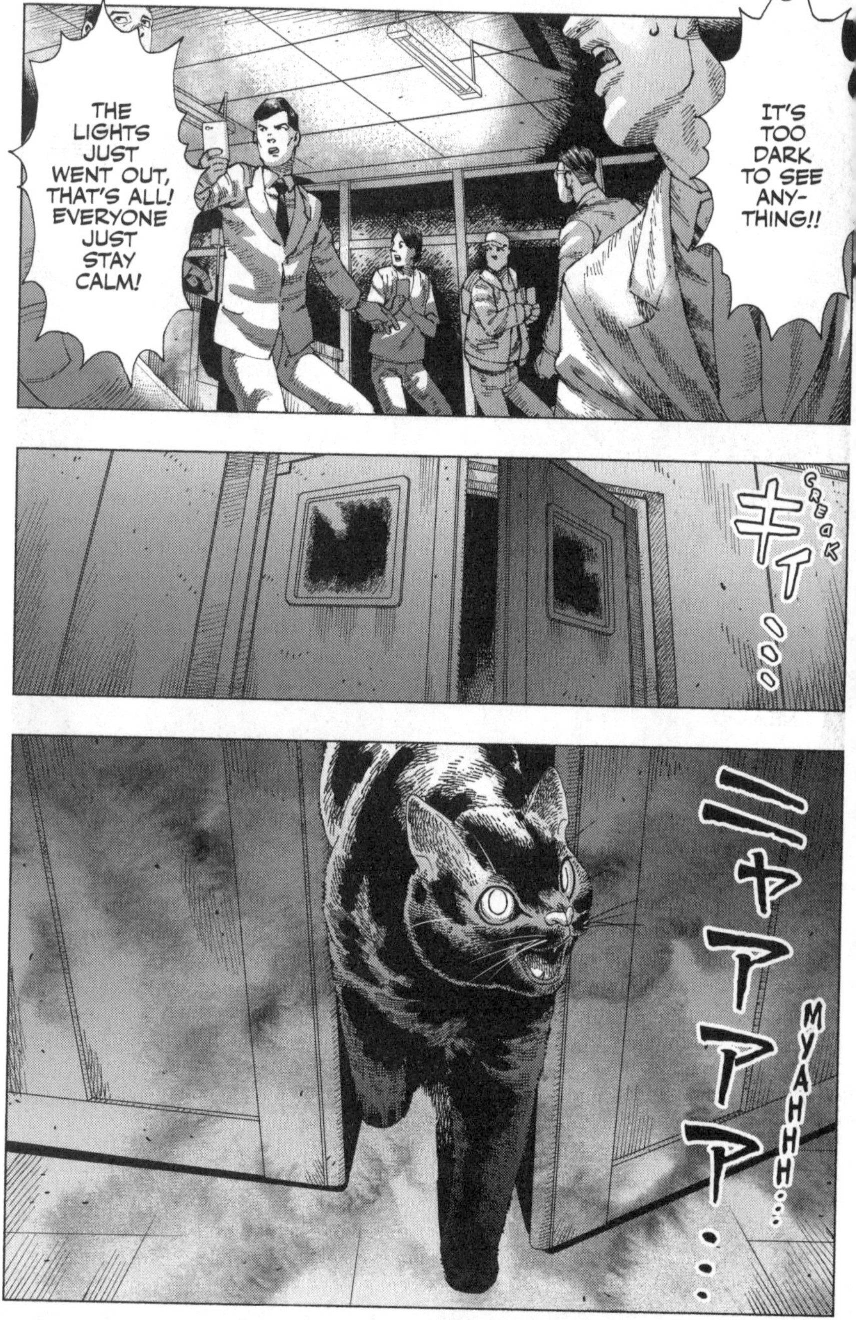
IT'S TOO DARK TO SEE ANYTHING!!
THE LIGHTS JUST WENT OUT, THAT'S ALL! EVERYONE JUST STAY CALM!
キイ…
CREAK
ミャアアア…
MYAHHH…

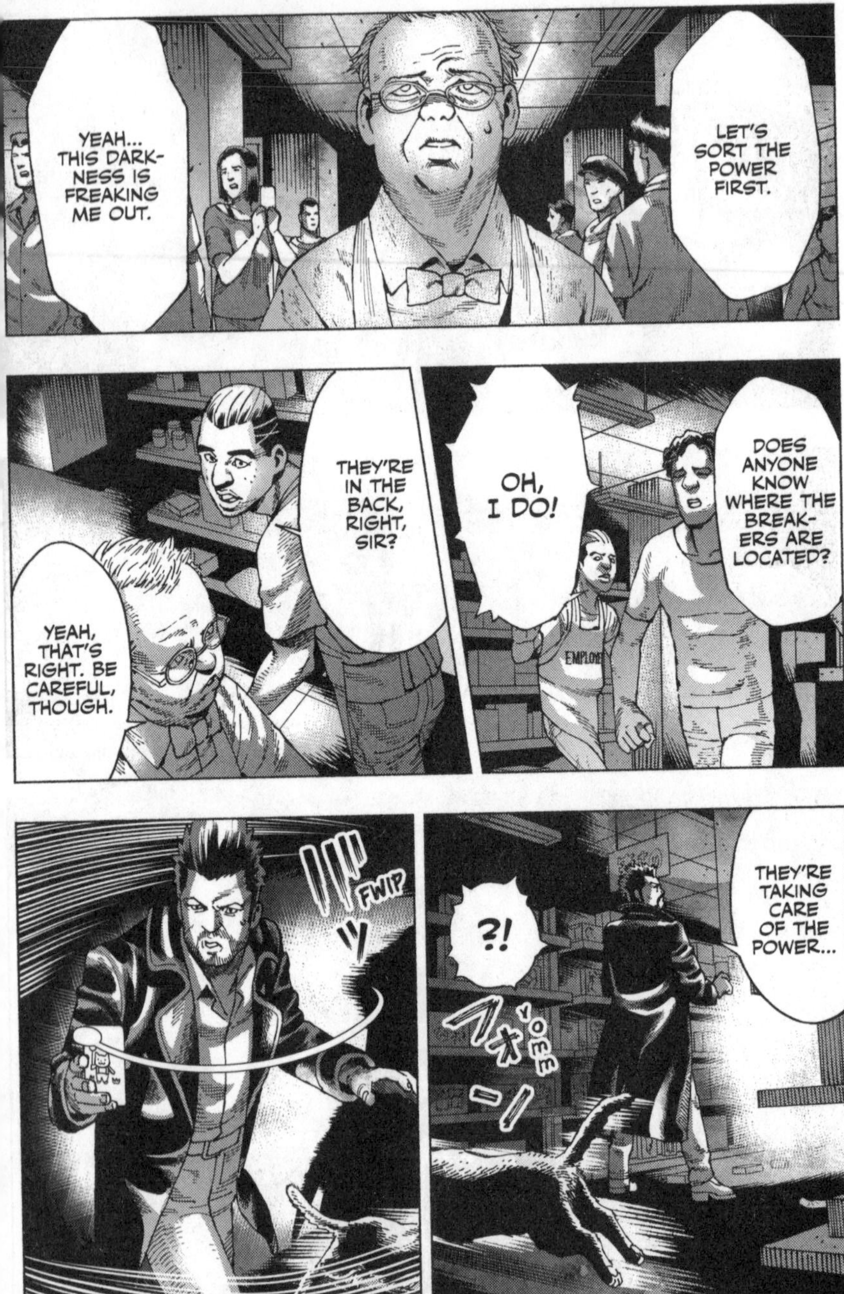
LET'S SORT THE POWER FIRST.
YEAH... THIS DARKNESS IS FREAKING ME OUT.
DOES ANYONE KNOW WHERE THE BREAKERS ARE LOCATED?
OH, I DO!
THEY'RE IN THE BACK, RIGHT, SIR?
YEAH, THAT'S RIGHT. BE CAREFUL, THOUGH.
THEY'RE TAKING CARE OF THE POWER...
?!
YOWW
FWIP

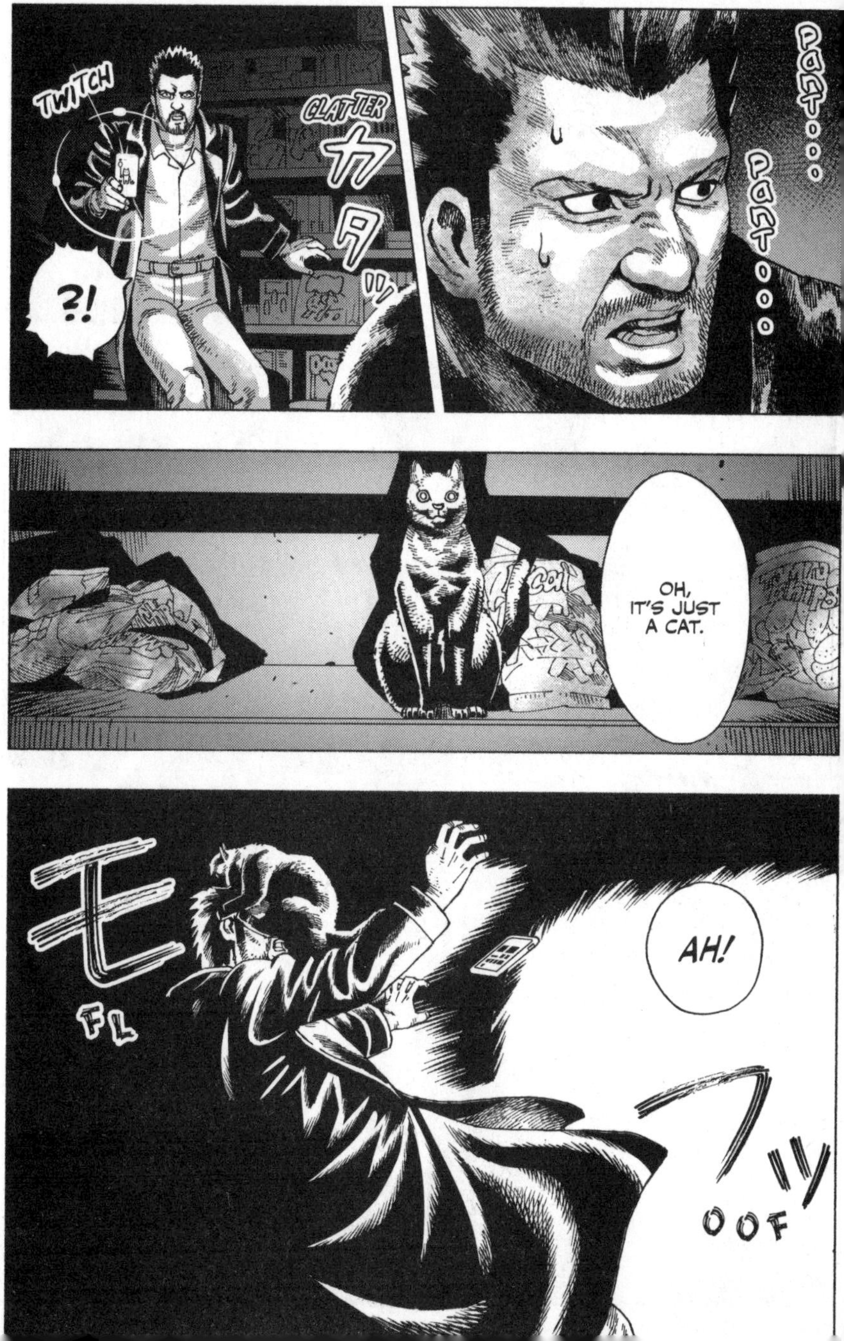
PANT...
PANT...
TWITCH
CLATTER
カタッ
?!
OH, IT'S JUST A CAT.
AH!
FL
OOF

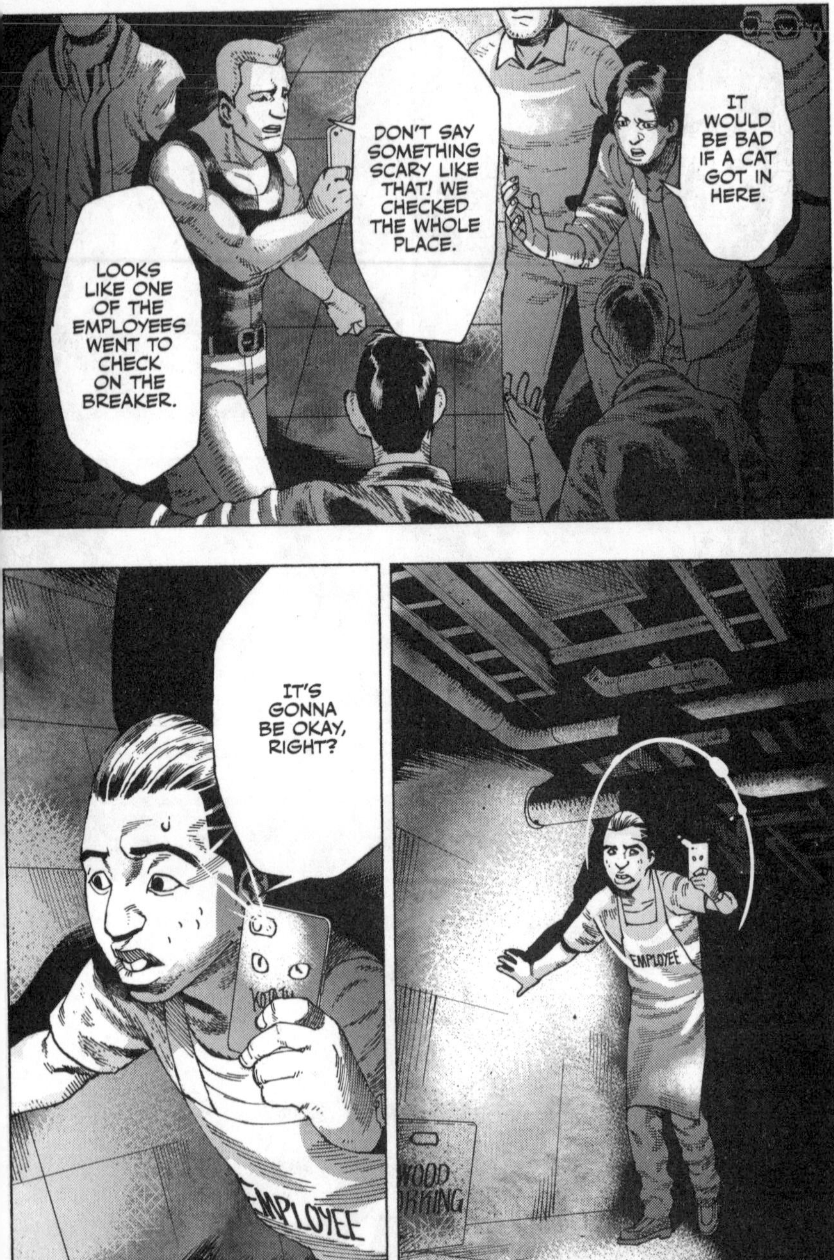
IT WOULD BE BAD IF A CAT GOT IN HERE.
DON'T SAY SOMETHING SCARY LIKE THAT! WE CHECKED THE WHOLE PLACE.
LOOKS LIKE ONE OF THE EMPLOYEES WENT TO CHECK ON THE BREAKER.
EMPLOYEE
IT'S GONNA BE OKAY, RIGHT?
WOOD

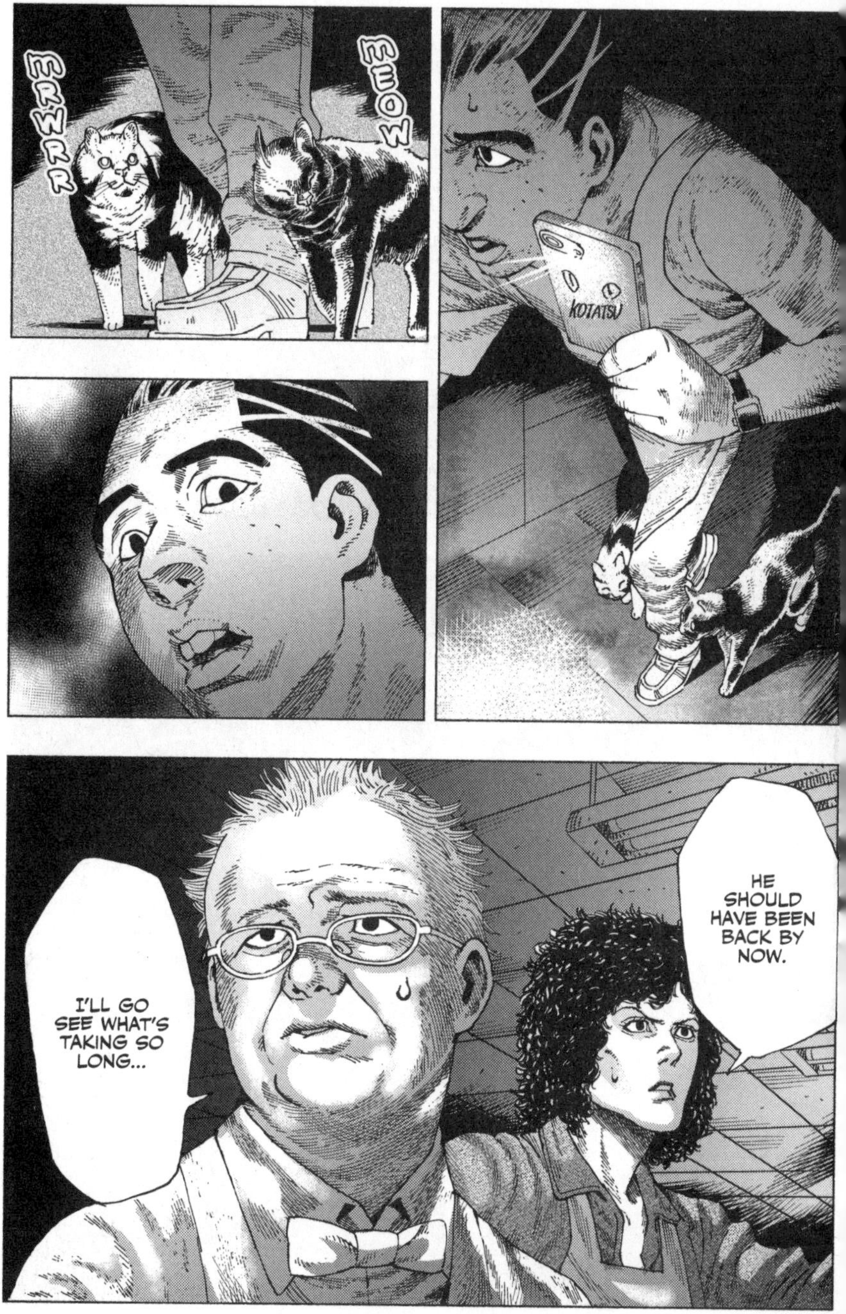
KOTATSU
MEOW
MRWRR
HE SHOULD HAVE BEEN BACK BY NOW.
I'LL GO SEE WHAT'S TAKING SO LONG...

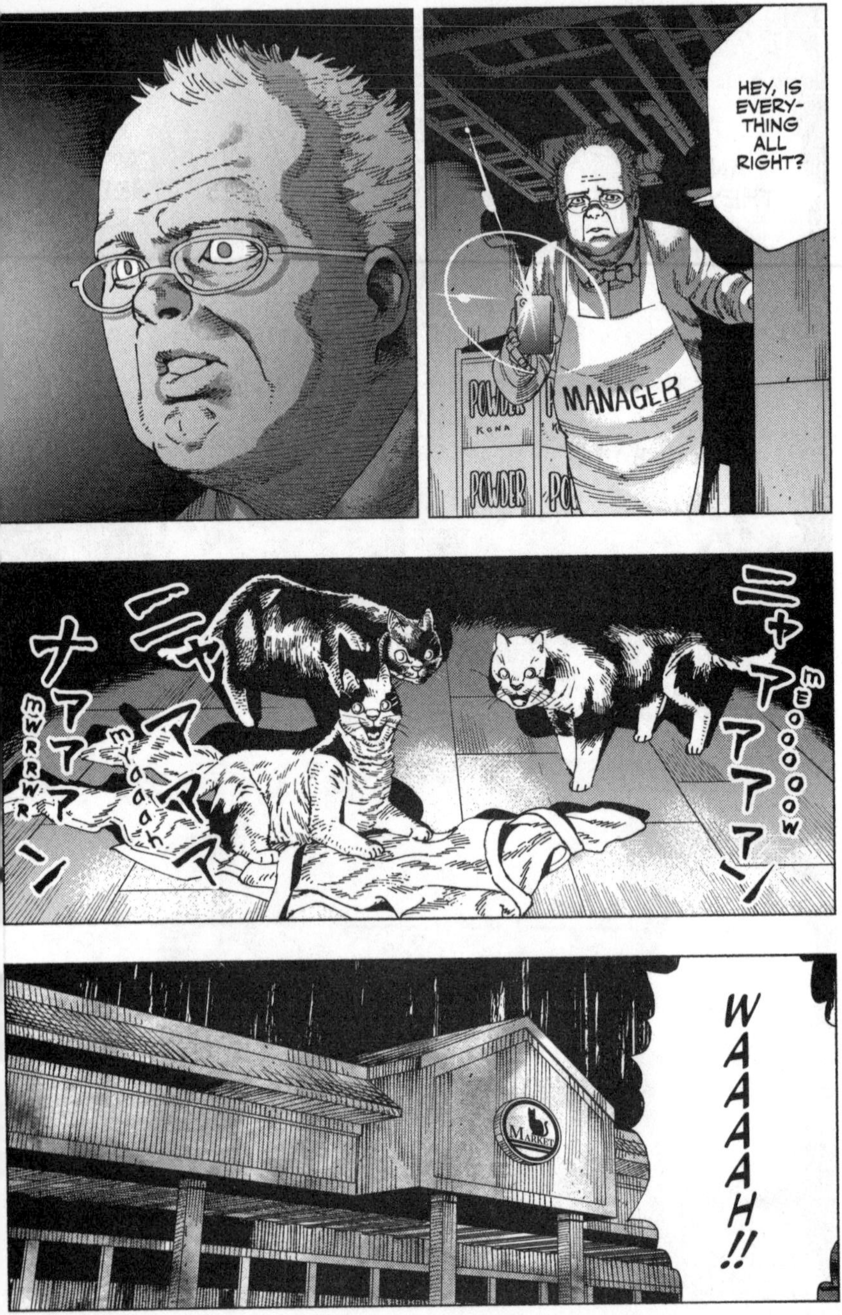
HEY, IS EVERYTHING ALL RIGHT?
MANAGER
POWDER
KONA
POWDER
ニャアアアーン
MEOOOOOOW
ニャアアア
myaaah
ナアアアーン
MWRRRWR
MARKET
WAAAAAH!!

CATS, THERE ARE CAAATS!!
SLAM
AND THEY'RE SO CUUUTE!!
THAT CAN'T BE!
I THOUGHT WE LOCKED THE STORE DOWN!
IT'S THE TRUTH!!
AH!

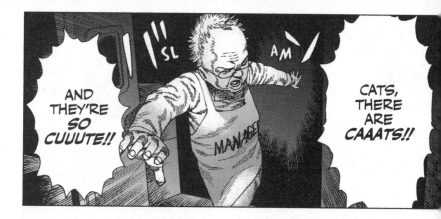

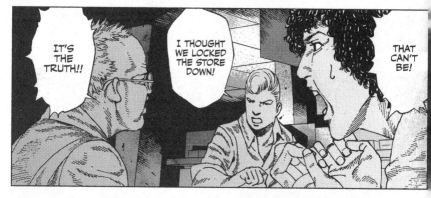

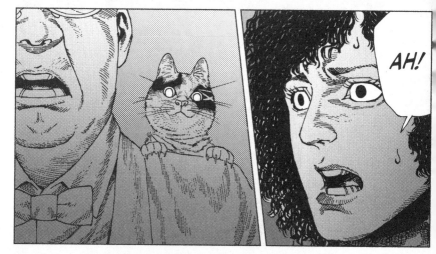

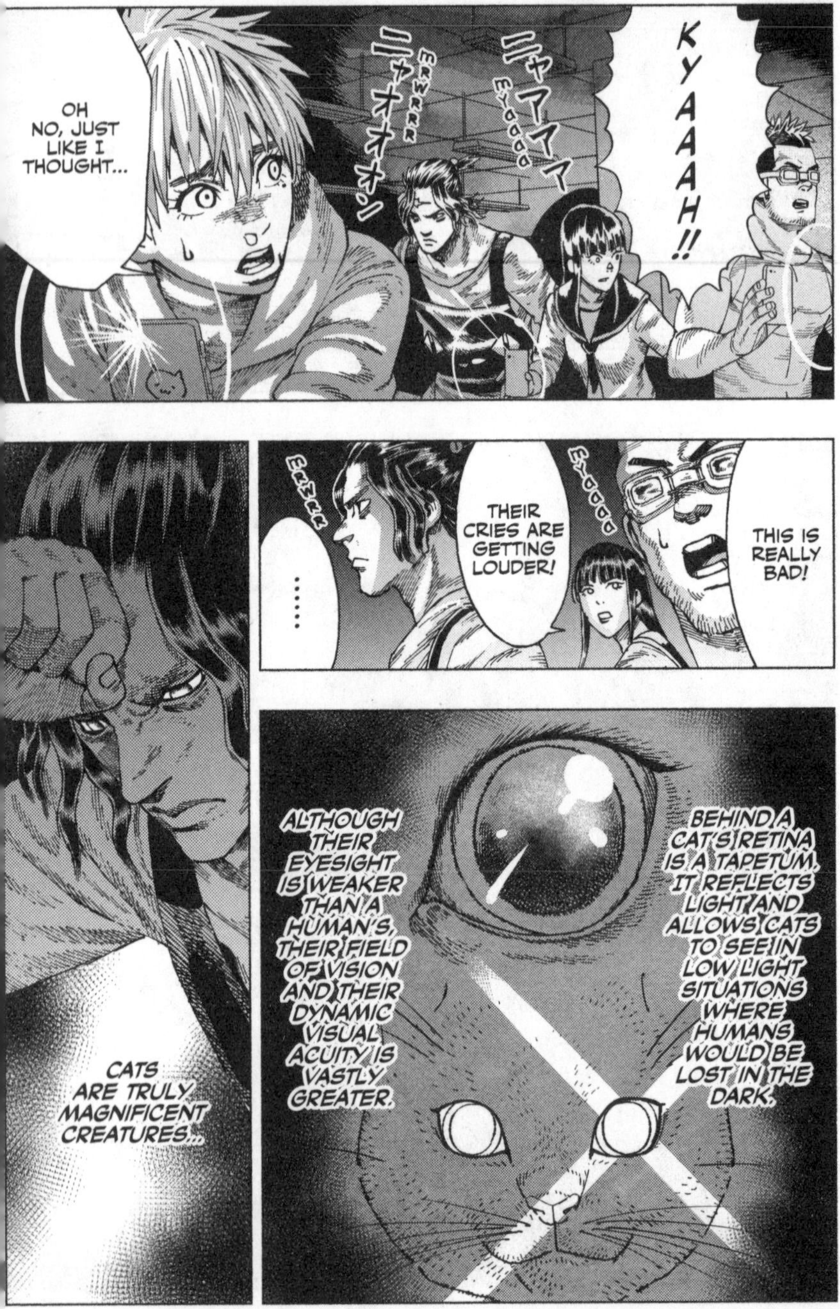

KYAAAAH!!
ニャアアア
myaaaa
ニャオオオーン
mrwrrr
OH NO, JUST LIKE I THOUGHT...
THIS IS REALLY BAD!
myaaaa
THEIR CRIES ARE GETTING LOUDER!
mrwrrr
......
BEHIND A CAT'S RETINA IS A TAPETUM. IT REFLECTS LIGHT AND ALLOWS CATS TO SEE IN LOW LIGHT SITUATIONS WHERE HUMANS WOULD BE LOST IN THE DARK.
ALTHOUGH THEIR EYESIGHT IS WEAKER THAN A HUMAN'S, THEIR FIELD OF VISION AND THEIR DYNAMIC VISUAL ACUITY IS VASTLY GREATER.
CATS ARE TRULY MAGNIFICENT CREATURES...

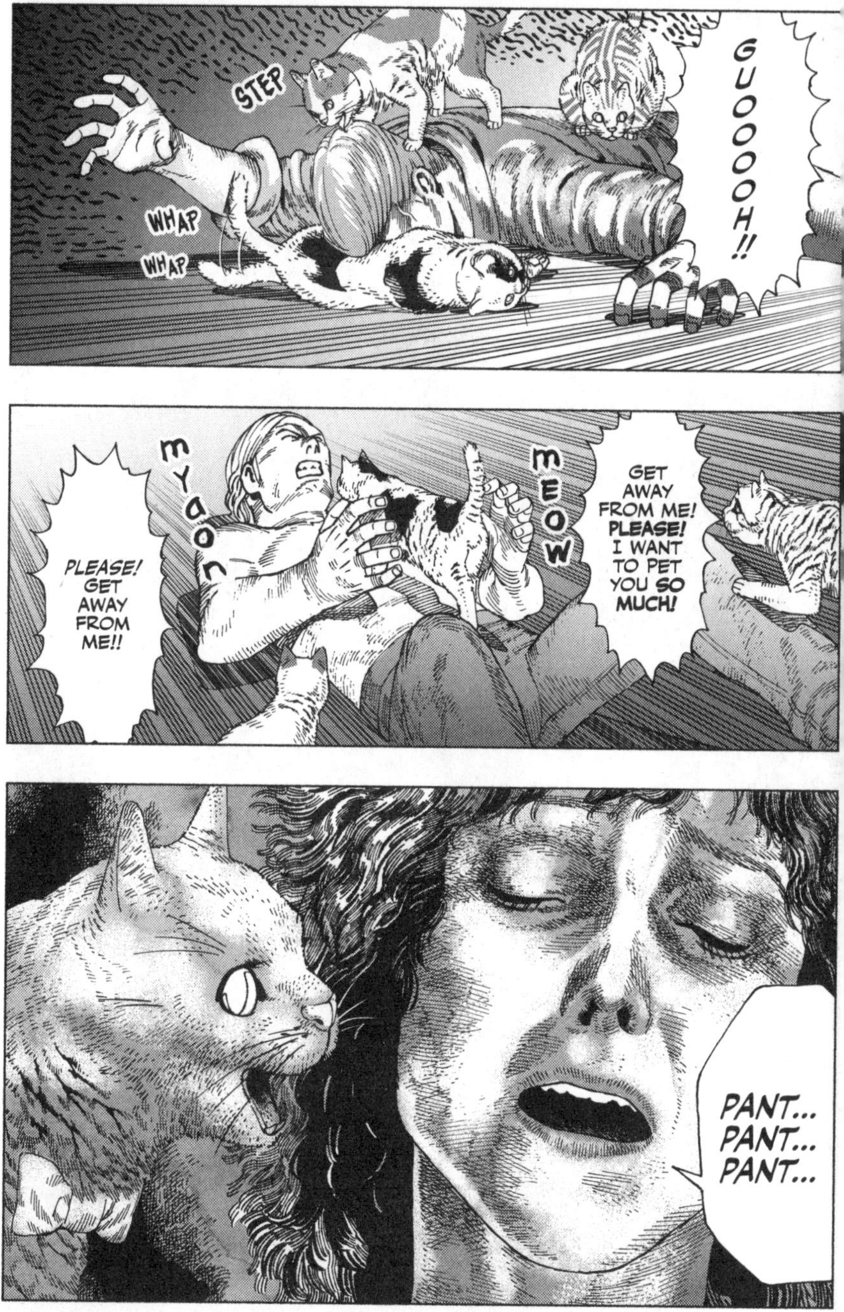
GUOOOOOH!!
STEP
WHAP
WHAP
GET AWAY FROM ME! PLEASE! I WANT TO PET YOU SO MUCH!
MEOW
myaon
PLEASE! GET AWAY FROM ME!!
PANT... PANT... PANT...

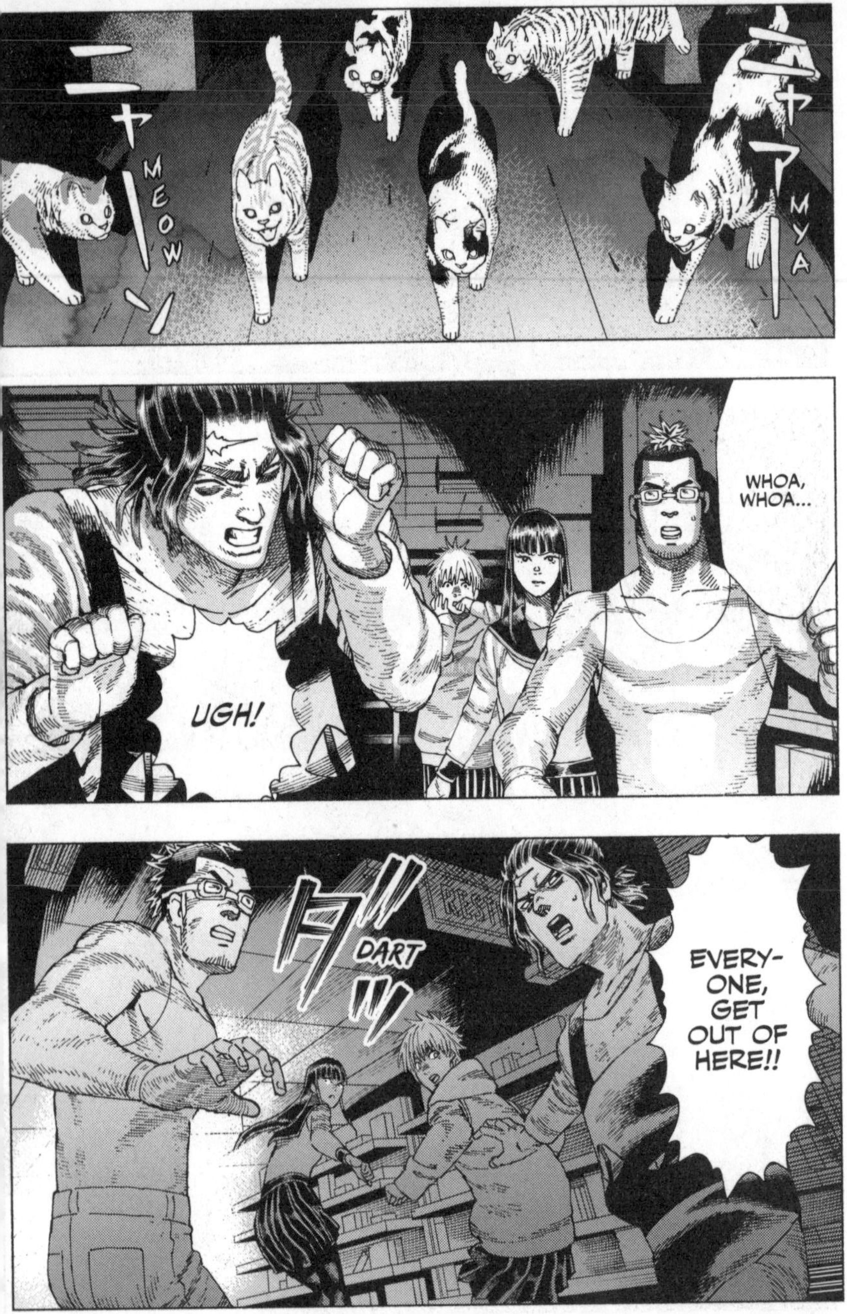
ニャア
MYA
ニャー
MEOW
WHOA, WHOA...
UGH!
EVERY-ONE, GET OUT OF HERE!!
ダッ
DART

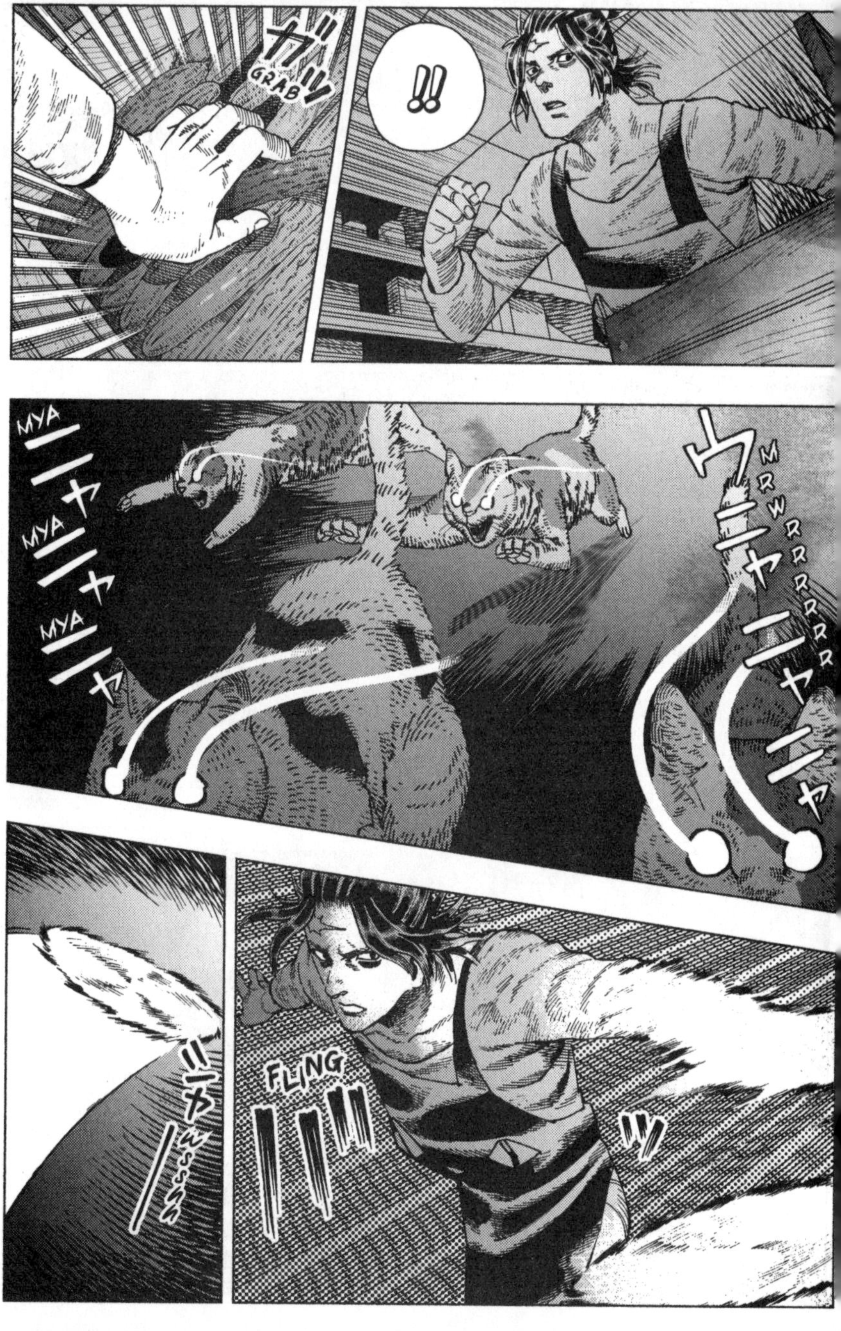
!!
GRAB
MRWRRRRRRRR
MYA
MYA
MYA
FLING
WSSSSS

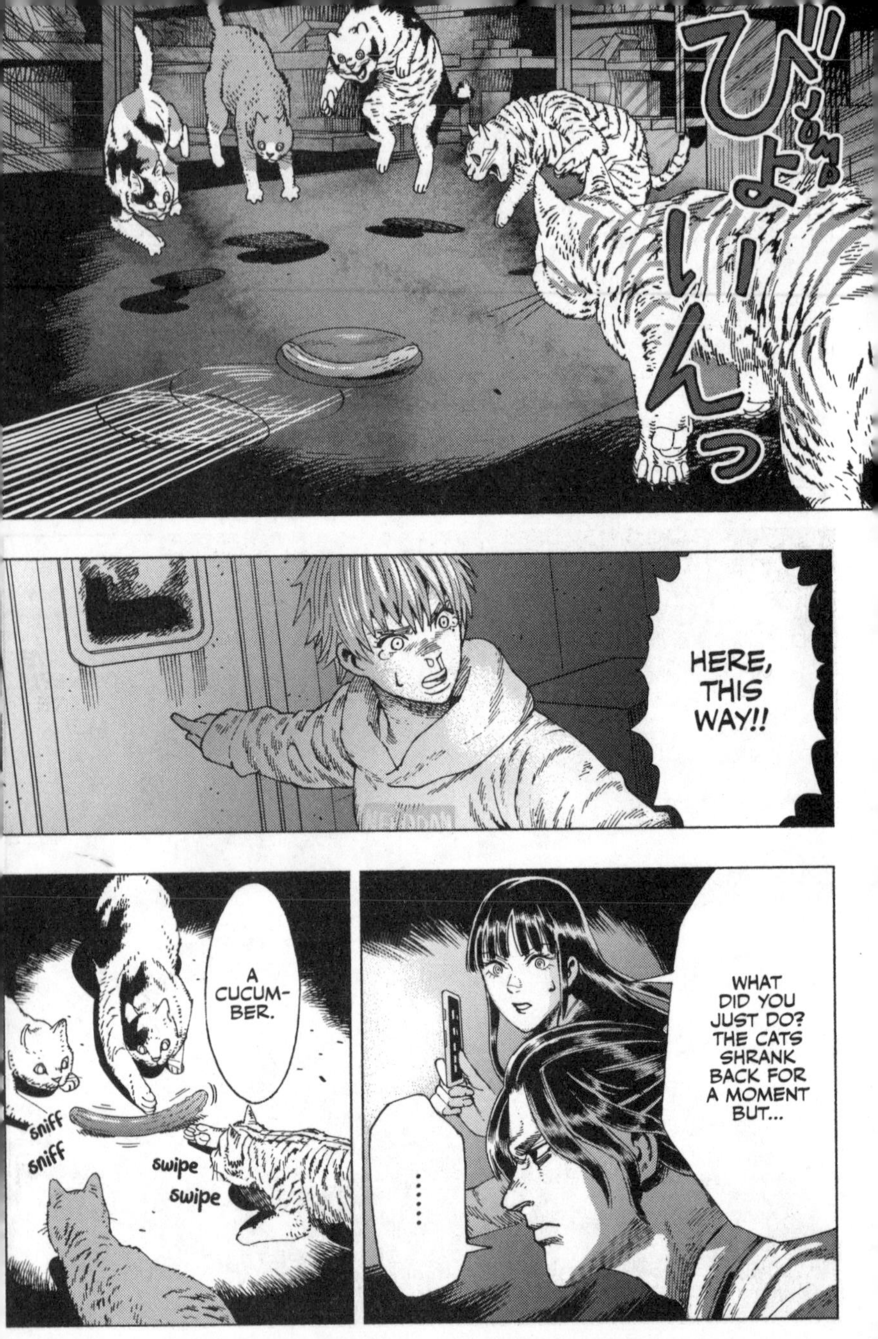
びよーんっ
HERE, THIS WAY!!
WHAT DID YOU JUST DO? THE CATS SHRANK BACK FOR A MOMENT BUT...
......
A CUCUMBER.
sniff sniff
swipe swipe

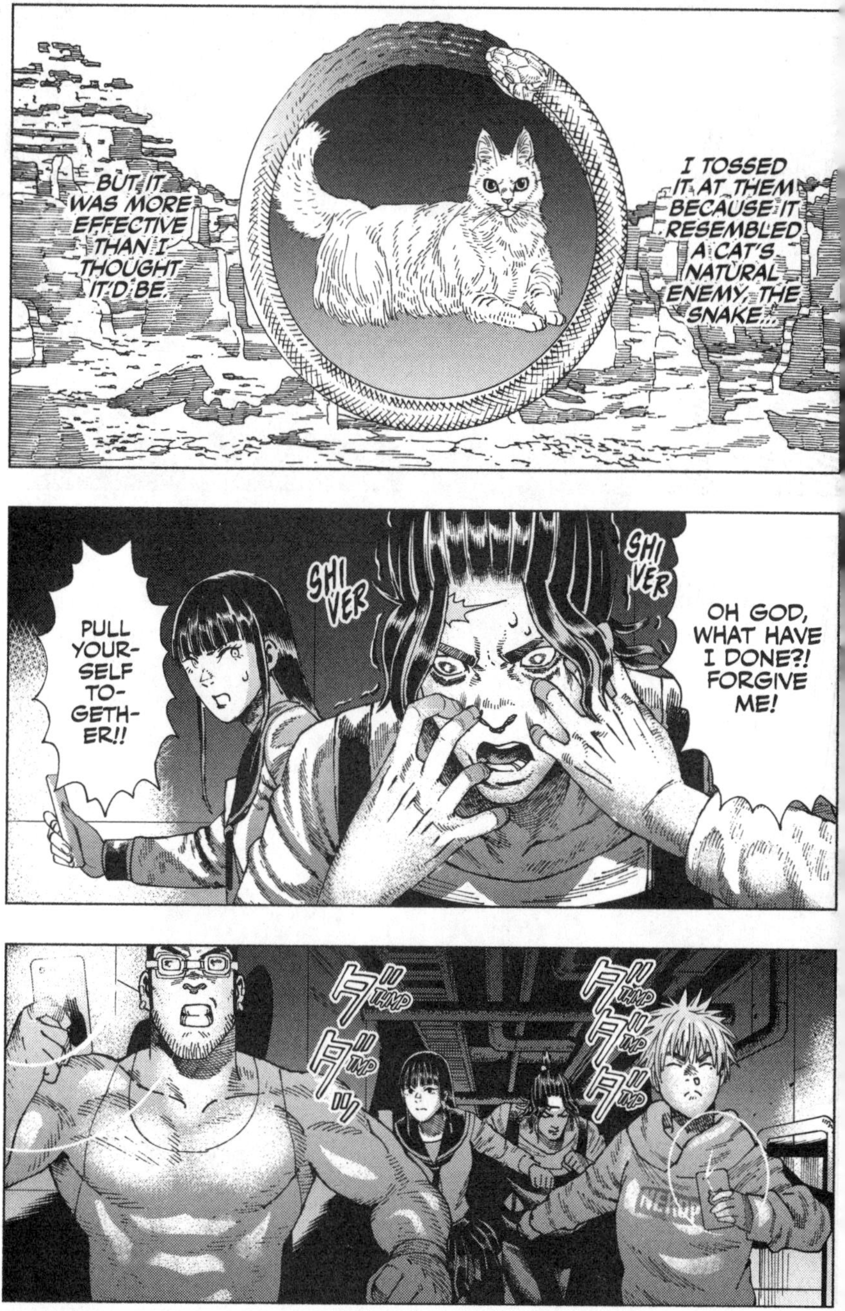
I TOSSED IT AT THEM BECAUSE IT RESEMBLED A CAT'S NATURAL ENEMY, THE SNAKE...
BUT IT WAS MORE EFFECTIVE THAN I THOUGHT IT'D BE.
SHIVER
OH GOD, WHAT HAVE I DONE?! FORGIVE ME!
SHIVER
PULL YOURSELF TOGETHER!!
THMP
THMP
THMP
THMP
THMP

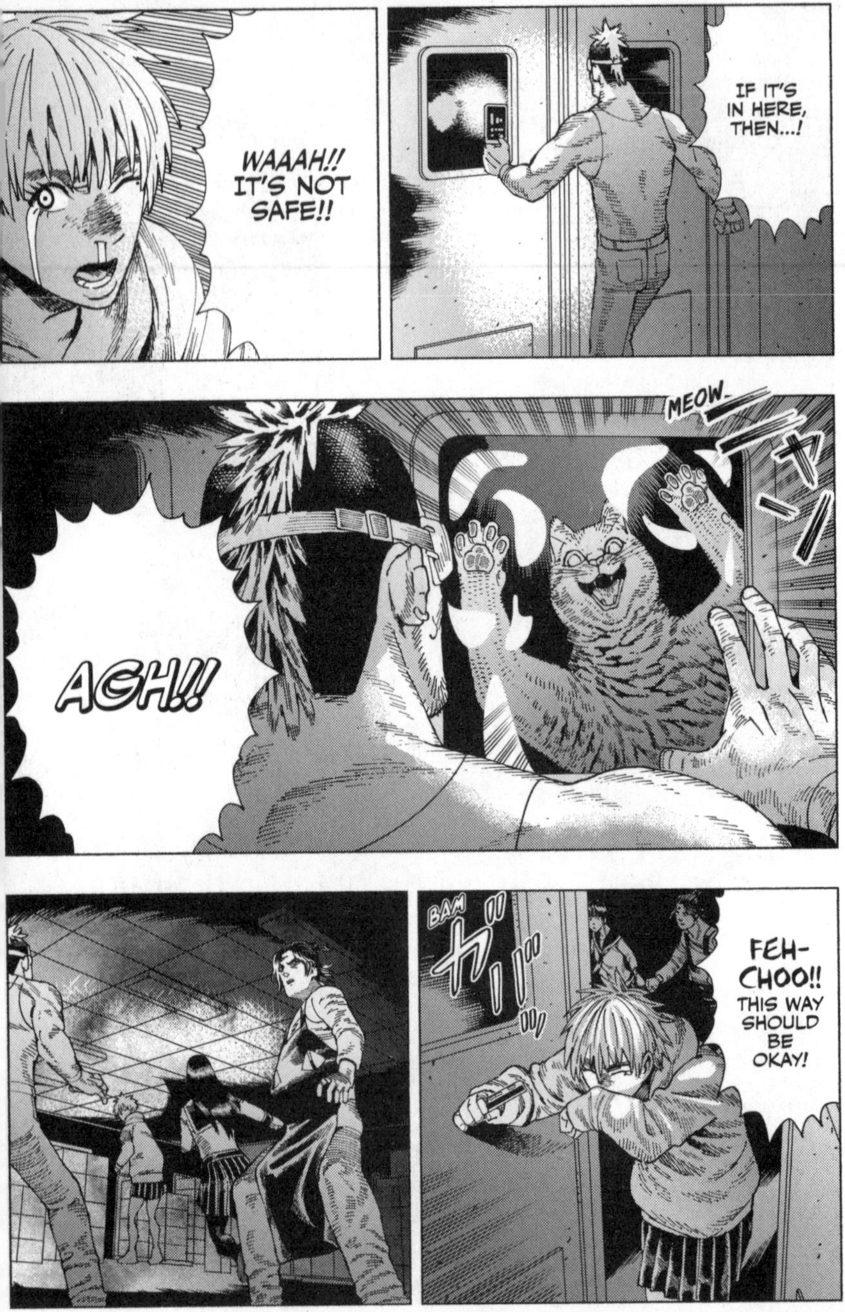
IF IT'S IN HERE, THEN...!
WAAAH!! IT'S NOT SAFE!!
MEOW
AGH!!
BAM
FEH-CHOO!! THIS WAY SHOULD BE OKAY!

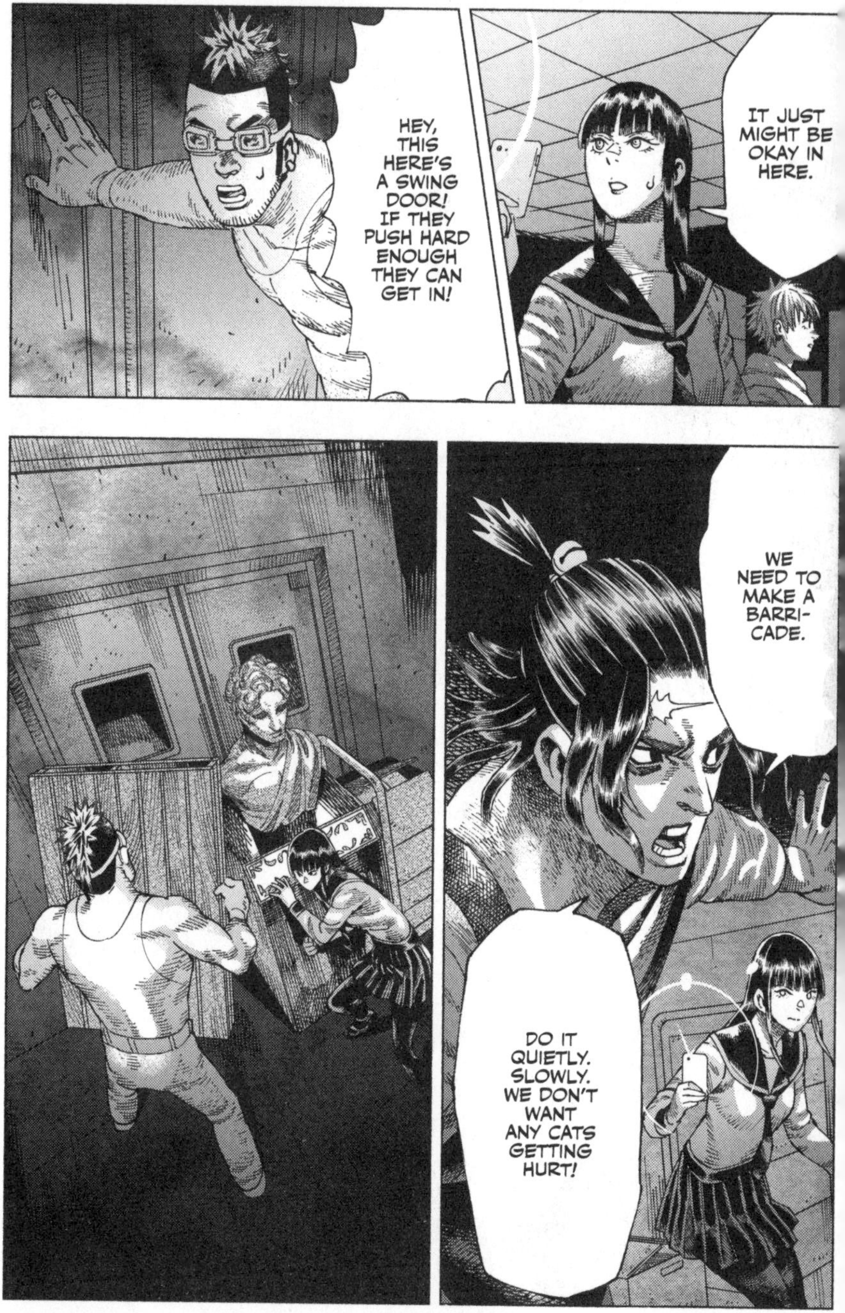
IT JUST MIGHT BE OKAY IN HERE.
HEY, THIS HERE'S A SWING DOOR! IF THEY PUSH HARD ENOUGH THEY CAN GET IN!
WE NEED TO MAKE A BARRI-CADE.
DO IT QUIETLY. SLOWLY. WE DON'T WANT ANY CATS GETTING HURT!

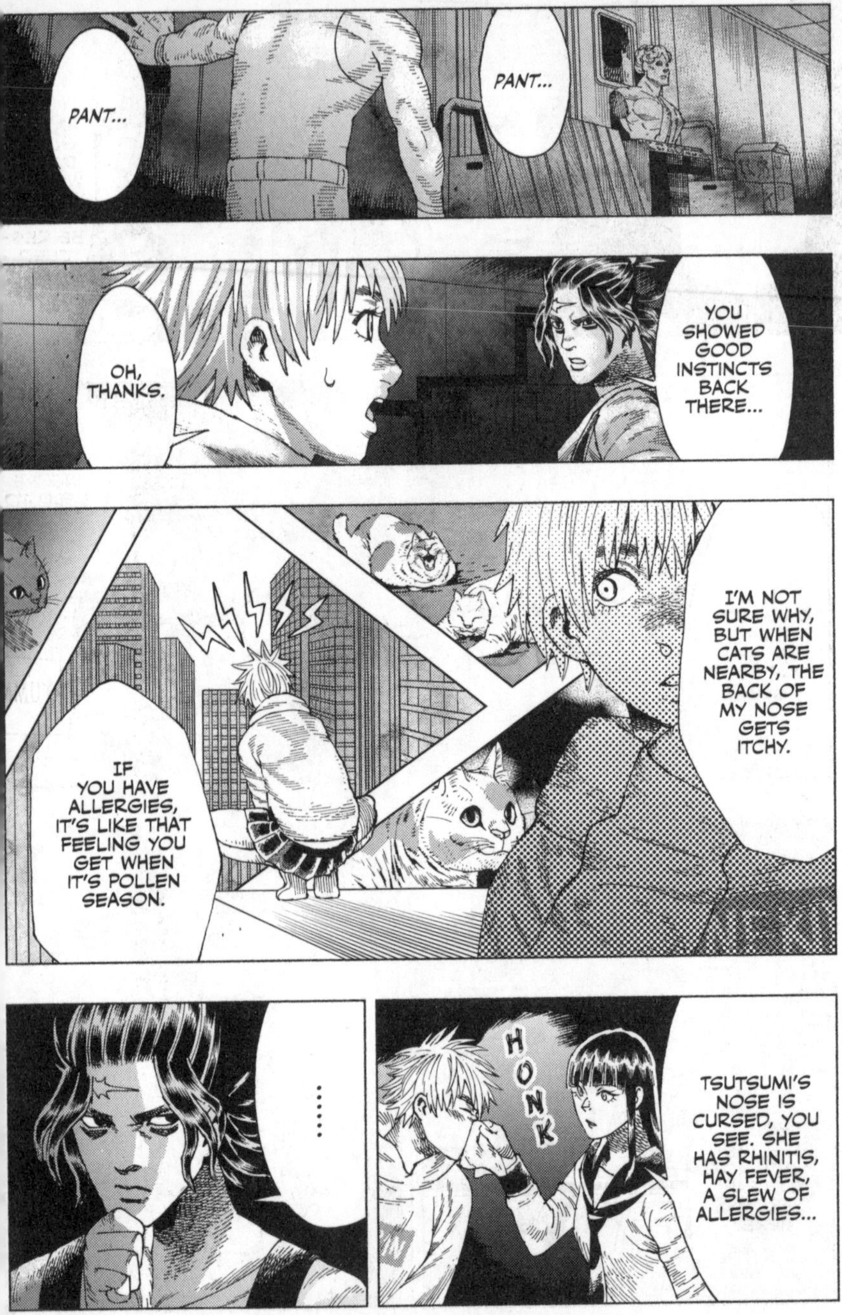
PANT...
PANT...
YOU SHOWED GOOD INSTINCTS BACK THERE...
OH, THANKS.
I'M NOT SURE WHY, BUT WHEN CATS ARE NEARBY, THE BACK OF MY NOSE GETS ITCHY.
IF YOU HAVE ALLERGIES, IT'S LIKE THAT FEELING YOU GET WHEN IT'S POLLEN SEASON.
HONK
TSUTSUMI'S NOSE IS CURSED, YOU SEE. SHE HAS RHINITIS, HAY FEVER, A SLEW OF ALLERGIES...
......

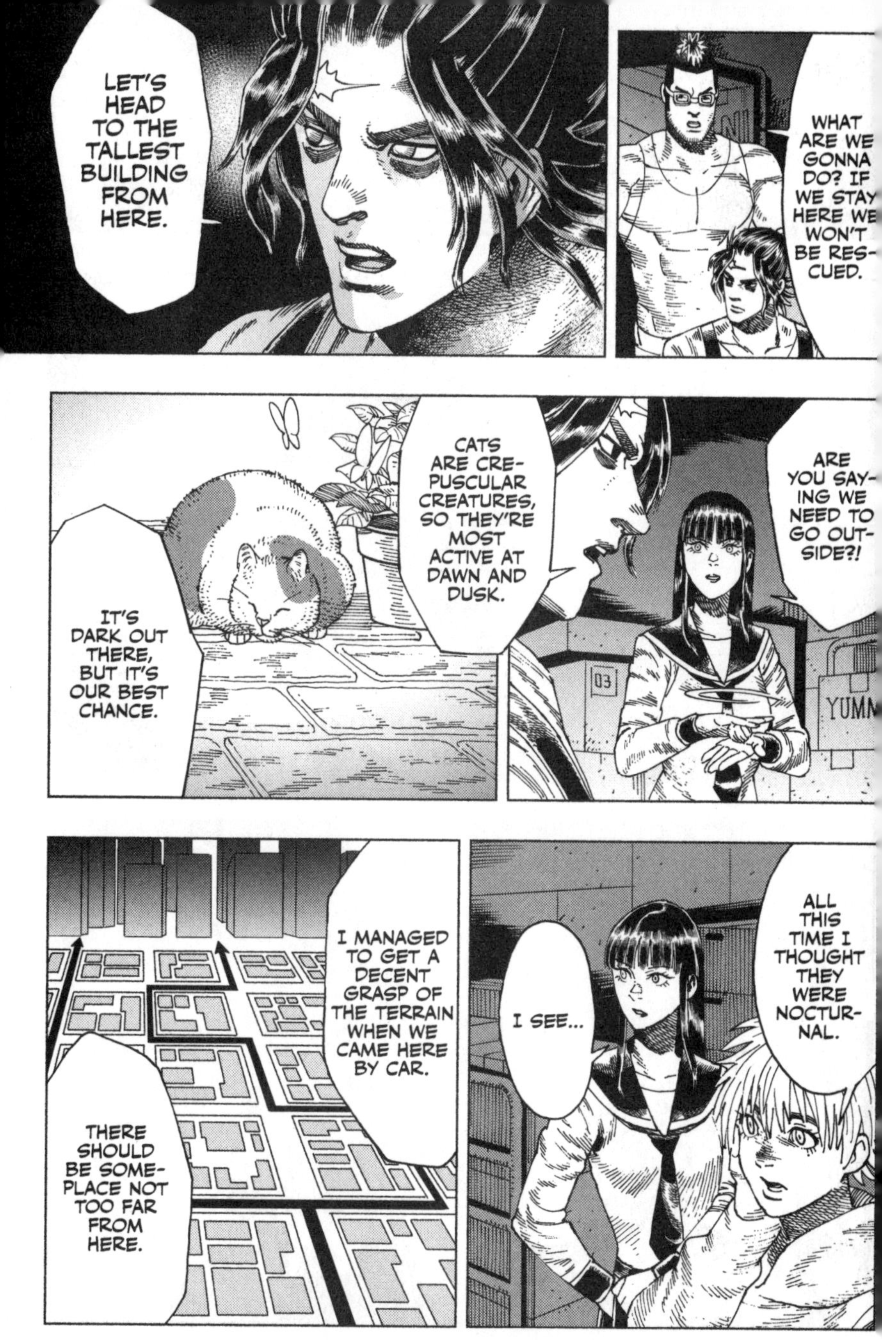
WHAT ARE WE GONNA DO? IF WE STAY HERE WE WON'T BE RESCUED.
LET'S HEAD TO THE TALLEST BUILDING FROM HERE.
ARE YOU SAYING WE NEED TO GO OUTSIDE?!
CATS ARE CREPUSCULAR CREATURES, SO THEY'RE MOST ACTIVE AT DAWN AND DUSK.
03
IT'S DARK OUT THERE, BUT IT'S OUR BEST CHANCE.
ALL THIS TIME I THOUGHT THEY WERE NOCTURNAL.
I SEE...
I MANAGED TO GET A DECENT GRASP OF THE TERRAIN WHEN WE CAME HERE BY CAR.
THERE SHOULD BE SOMEPLACE NOT TOO FAR FROM HERE.

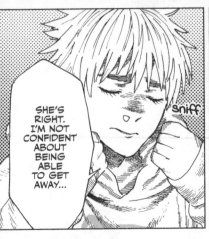

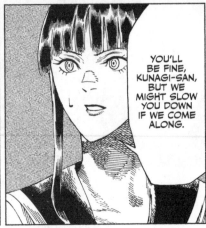

YOU'LL BE FINE, KUNAGI-SAN, BUT WE MIGHT SLOW YOU DOWN IF WE COME ALONG.
SHE'S RIGHT. I'M NOT CONFIDENT ABOUT BEING ABLE TO GET AWAY...
sniff
IF ANY-THING, IT'S THE OPPOSITE.
YOU'RE THE KEY TO THIS PLAN.
To be continued...

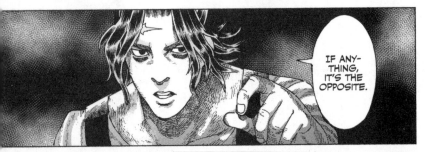

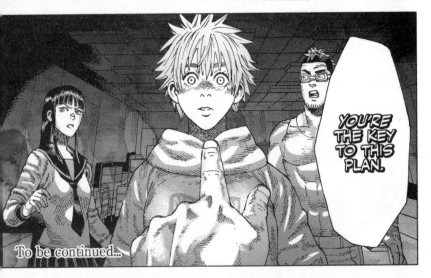

Persian

A cat with an abundance of long hair and a very distinct face. Has been active as a show cat for quite some time. It's believed to have originated in Iran, but its precise origins are unknown.

SEVEN SEAS ENTERTAINMENT PRESENTS

NIGHT OF THE LIVING CAT

story by **HAWKMAN** art by **MECHA-ROOTS** **VOLUME ONE**

TRANSLATION
Nan Rymer

ADAPTATION
Asha Bardon

LETTERING
Jaewon Ha

COVER DESIGN
Nicky Lim

PROOFREADER
Leighanna DeRouen
Krista Grandy

SENIOR COPY EDITOR
Dawn Davis

EDITOR
Abby Lehrke

PRODUCTION DESIGNER
Christa Miesner

PRODUCTION MANAGER
Lissa Pattillo

PREPRESS TECHNICIAN
Jules Valera

PRINT MANAGER
Rhiannon Rasmussen-Silverstein

EDITOR-IN-CHIEF
Julie Davis

ASSOCIATE PUBLISHER
Adam Arnold

PUBLISHER
Jason DeAngelis

Seven Seas press and purchase enquiries can be sent to Marketing Manager Lianne Sentar at press@gomanga.com. Information regarding the distribution and purchase of digital editions is available from Digital Manager CK Russell at digital@gomanga.com.

ISBN: 978-1-63858-581-7
Printed in Canada
First Printing: September 2022
10 9 8 7 6 5 4 3 2 1

READING DIRECTIONS

This book reads from ***right to left***, Japanese style. If this is your first time reading manga, you start reading from the top right panel on each page and take it from there. If you get lost, just follow the numbered diagram here. It may seem backwards at first, but you'll get the hang of it! Have fun!!

1
2
3
4
5
6
7
8
9

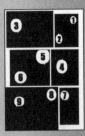

Follow us online: www.SevenSeasEntertainment.com